Developments in Central and East European Politics 2

Developments in Central and East European Politics 2

Edited by

Stephen White
Judy Batt
Paul G. Lewis

First published 1998 by
MACMILLAN PRESS LTD
Houndmills, Basingstoke, Hampshire RG21 6XS
and London
Companies and representatives
throughout the world

ISBN 0-333-72671-5 hardcover
ISBN 0-333-72672-3 paperback

A catalogue record for this book is available
from the British Library.

This book is printed on paper suitable for recycling and
made from fully managed and sustained forest sources.

10   9   8   7   6   5   4   3   2   1
07 06 05 04 03 02 01 00 99 98

Copy-edited and typeset by Povey–Edmondson
Tavistock and Rochdale, England

Printed and bound in Great Britain by
Creative Print & Design (Wales), Ebbw Vale

This book is a direct replacement for *Developments in East European
Politics*, published 1993, reprinted 3 times.

Contents

v

List of Tables and Figures

Figures

Notes on the Contributors

Judy Batt is Senior Lecturer in Central and East European Politics at the Centre for Russian and East European Studies, University of Birmingham. In 1992–3 she worked on secondment to the British Foreign and Commonwealth Office. Her main publications include *Economic Reform and Political Change in Eastern Europe* (1988) and *East Central Europe from Reform to Transition* (1991).

Sarah Birch completed her PhD in Government in 1997 at the University of Essex, where she is currently Lecturer in the Politics of Ukraine. She published articles on Ukrainian electoral behaviour and the effect of electoral laws on the political process in *Europe-Asia Studies, Electoral Studies, Political Studies* and other journals.

George Blazyca is Professor of Economics at the University of Paisley, Scotland. He is a specialist on Polish economic development, and a founder member of the Paisley Centre for Contemporary European Studies. His publications include *Poland into the 1990s* (co-edited, 1991) and *Monitoring Economic Transition: The Polish Case* (co-edited, 1995).

Chris Corrin is Senior Lecturer in Politics at the University of Glasgow. Her work centres on women's political participation and feminist resistance across 'Europe'. Recent publications include *Superwomen and the Double Burden: Women's Experience of Change in Central and Eastern Europe* (edited, 1992); *Magyar Women: Hungarian Women's Lives 1960s–1990s* (1994) and *Women in a Violent World: Feminist Analyses and Resistance Across 'Europe'* (edited, 1996).

Terry Cox is Reader in Sociology in the Department of Government at the University of Strathclyde in Glasgow. His interests include both Russia and East Central Europe and his publications include *Peasants, Class and Capitalism* (1986), *Hungary: The Politics of Transition* (co-edited, 1995), *From Perestroika to Privatisation* (1996), and *Hungary 1956 – Forty Years On* (edited, 1997).

Tom Gallagher is Professor of Ethnic Peace and Conflict at Bradford University, England. He specialises in the politics and history of ethnicity in South-Eastern Europe and its impact on democratisation processes in the 1990s. He has published widely in journal and edited volumes on these subjects. An edited and updated translation of his most recent book, *Romania After Ceausescu: The Politics of Intolerance*, has recently been published in Romania.

Adrian Hyde-Price is Senior Lecturer at the Institute for German Studies, University of Birmingham. A specialist on security and international relations in Central and Eastern Europe, his main publications include *The International Politics of East Central Europe* (1996) and *European Security Beyond the Cold War: Four Scenarios for the Year 2010* (1991).

Krzysztof Jasiewicz is Professor of Sociology at Washington and Lee University in Lexington, Virginia, and a Research Fellow at the Institute of Political Studies of the Polish Academy of Sciences, Warsaw, where from 1991 to 1993 he was Director of Electoral Studies. He was the co-author of a series of political attitude surveys known as the Poles of '80, '81, '84, '88 and '90, and has more recently contributed to the *Journal of Democracy* and the *European Journal of Political Research* as well as to Ray Taras (ed.) *Postcommunist Presidents* (1997).

Paul G. Lewis is Reader in Central and East European Politics at the Open University. He has published numerous items on aspects of Central European politics including, most recently, books on *Central Europe Since 1945* (1994), *Party Structure and Organization in East-Central Europe* (co-edited, 1996) and *Stabilizing Fragile Democracies: Comparing New Party Systems in Southern and Eastern Europe* (co-edited, 1996). He is continuing research into the development of political parties in Central and Eastern Europe.

David M. Olson is Professor of Political Science at the University of North Carolina at Greensboro, where he is also joint director of the Parliamentary Documents Center for Central Europe. His recent publications include *Legislatures in the Policy Process: The Dilemma of Economic Policy* (co-edited, 1991), *Democratic Legislative Institutions: A Comparative View* (1994) and *The New Parliaments of Central and Eastern Europe* (co-edited, 1996).

Richard Rose is Director of the Centre for the Study of Public Policy at the University of Strathclyde, Glasgow, and international adviser to the Paul Lazarsfeld Society, Vienna, with which he has been conducting surveys of more than fifteen postcommunist countries since 1991. Internationally known for his writings on quantitative aspects of comparative politics, his recent writings include *What is Europe?* (1996), *How Russia Votes* (with others, 1997) and a forthcoming study with William Mishler and Christian

Haerpfer, *Democracy and Its Alternatives: Understanding Postcommunist Societies.*

Ray Taras is Professor of Politics at Tulane University in New Orleans, visiting scholar at Harvard's Russian Research Center, and a former national fellow at the Hoover Institution, Stanford University. He studied at the University of Montreal in Canada, Sussex and Essex Universities in England, and the University of Warsaw. His published work includes *Consolidating Democracy in Poland* (1995), *New States, New Politics: Building the Post-Soviet Nations* (co-edited, 1997), *Postcommunist Presidents* (edited, 1997) and *Understanding Ethnic Conflict: The International Dimension* (1998).

Stephen White is Professor of Politics at the University of Glasgow, and a Senior Research Associate of its Institute of Russian and East European Studies. President of the British Association for Slavonic and East European Studies from 1994 to 1997, his recent publications include *Russia Goes Dry* (1996), *How Russia Votes* (with others, 1997) and a comparative survey-based study based on the Czech Republic, Hungary, Russia, Slovakia and Ukraine entitled *Values and Political Change in Postcommunist Europe* (with others, 1998).

Gordon Wightman is Lecturer in the School of Politics and Communication Studies at the University of Liverpool. He is the editor of *Party Formation in East-Central Europe* (1995) and has published on Czech and Slovak politics in a variety of other journals and collections, including *Party Politics*, the *Journal of Communist Studies and Transition Politics, Parliamentary Affairs*, and *Electoral Studies.*

Kataryna Wolczuk is Lecturer in Ukrainian Studies at the Centre for Russian and East European Studies, University of Birmingham. Her research focuses on the constitutional process, consolidation of the institutional framework and democratisation in post-Soviet Ukraine, and she has published on recent political developments in the region.

Preface

It used to be easy to define 'Eastern Europe'. Broadly speaking, it was a group of states on the far side of what was for many years an Iron Curtain. Most of them bordered on the Soviet Union, and most of them were bound to the Soviet Union by economic and military alliances as well as by a close interconnection at the level of their communist party leaderships. Their fate, it appeared, had been largely determined at the end of World War II, when Europe had been divided – however provisionally – into rival spheres of influence. Yugoslavia had successfully separated itself from the Soviet alliance in the late 1940s, and from the 1960s Albania and Romania were increasingly independent. All of the states in the region none the less remained under communist leadership, state ownership was dominant, and public life was framed by the requirements of Marxism-Leninism.

The dramatic changes of the late 1980s and early 1990s shattered these earlier patterns, and brought an end to the division of Europe and – at least in its original form – to communist rule itself. The changes that began in 1989 took a variety of forms, and governments changed more quickly than forms of ownership, still less the habits and practices that had developed over the forty years of communist rule, and in many cases over a much longer period. By the late 1990s, none the less, the Central and East European states were facing a largely similar set of challenges. Could they develop forms of rule, including party systems and structures of participation, that would replace the authoritarianism of the communist years? Could they find a balance between effective leadership, often through a presidency, and accountability, typically to an elected parliament? Could they reverse the economic decline of the late communist years, and could they best do so through 'shock therapy' or by a more gradual process? And could they carry out programmes of change with popular support, notwithstanding the sacrifices that were involved and the increasingly difficult position of the elderly, handicapped, the unemployed and the marginal?

These are just some of the issues that are addressed in this collection, which (like its predecessor in 1993) brings together a group of leading specialists from the European countries and from North

America. We begin with a chapter that explores the dimensions of a changing half-continent, and then in three further chapters we consider patterns of change in parts of the region that share important similarities: East-Central Europe, the Balkans, and the former Soviet republics. We turn, in the third part of the book, to the framework of contemporary politics: constitutions, leaderships, parliaments, political parties and electoral behaviour. The fourth part of the book explores the policy process in more detail, and the form it has taken in the economy, in social relations, and in gender relations. Our fifth and final part looks at the international politics of the region, and at its relations with a wider world; the final chapter reflects more broadly on the prospects for democratic rule.

Developments in Central and East European Politics is intended as a guide to the common patterns as well as the individual variety of a group of states that were formerly modelled on the Soviet Union but which are now a distinctive and varied presence within a continent that has been redefining its own boundaries and values. We hope not only our students, but also our colleagues and readers in other walks of life, will find something of value in the result.

Stephen White
Judy Batt
Paul G. Lewis

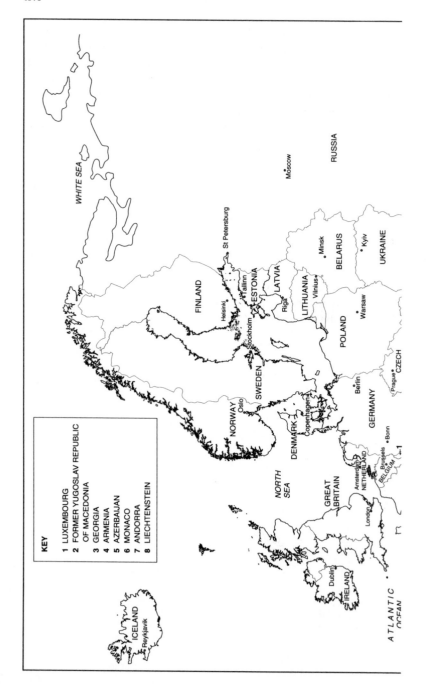

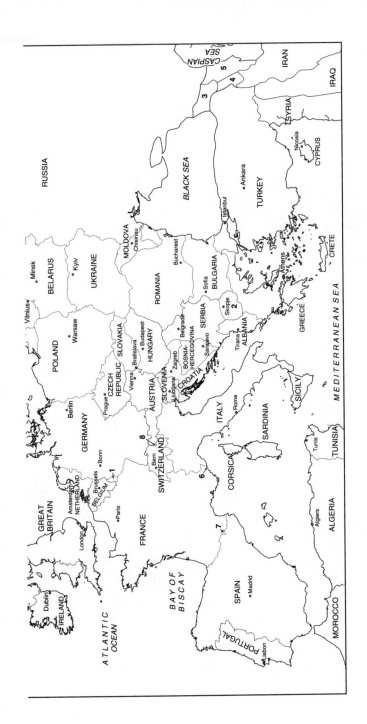

Russia and the former Soviet republics

1

Introduction: Defining Central and Eastern Europe

JUDY BATT

> It is astonishing to discover how, after decades of falsified history and ideological manipulation, nothing has been forgotten. Nations are now remembering their ancient achievements and their ancient suffering, their ancient statehood and their former borders, their traditional animosities and affinities – in short, they are suddenly recalling a history that, until recently, had been carefully concealed or misrepresented. (Havel, 1993, p. 9)

Central and Eastern Europe seems easier to define by what it is not, than by what it is. It is an area without clear geographical borders, stretching from the Baltic Sea southwards to the Adriatic and south-eastward to the Black Sea. In the north, it comprises part of the Great European Plain which extends to the west across north Germany into the Low Countries and to the east deep into Russia. In the centre is the upland plateau of Bohemia-Moravia, and the Danube Basin spreading out between the Alps and the Carpathian Mountains. Further south still is the mountainous, often remote and inaccessible region of the Balkans, and to the south-east the land stretches away into the steppes of Ukraine. These are sometimes called the 'Lands in Between': in between Russia and Germany, Europe and Asia, East and West. This is frontier country, part of Europe, but on the edge of it and not fully integrated with it.

Peoples and Borders, Nations and States

This indeterminate location has had a fundamental impact on the shaping of political identities in the region. The lack of natural

1

borders exposed the region to successive waves of migration over the centuries, while inaccessibility and economic stagnation helped preserve distinctive local cultures, languages and dialects. An enormous variety of peoples has come to settle in the region, not for the most part in consolidated and clearly defined territories, but mixed up together in a complex ethnic patchwork. The region has been chronically vulnerable to invasion and conquest by larger and stronger powers based to the west, east and south. In the sixteenth and seventeenth centuries, when Western Europe was entering what historians now call the 'early modern' period, the Ottoman Empire extended its control into the Balkans and Hungary, cutting these countries off from the cultural influences of the Renaissance and Reformation which so profoundly stamped the West. The Russian Empire in the seventeenth and eighteenth centuries expanded its might southwards to the Black Sea and captured the Baltic region from the Swedes. By the late eighteenth century, East-Central Europe was completely parcelled out between rival Great Powers: Russia, Prussia, Habsburg Austria and the Ottoman Empire.

The establishment of the various empires promoted further migrations of the peoples of the region, as some groups fled before one imperial army to seek protection under another, others moved in to fill their place, and new ruling groups were brought in from far-away imperial capitals to run the local administration. Along with ethnic diversity and intermingling, imperial rule promoted and entrenched complex patterns of ethnic stratification: typically, the landowning nobility was of a different ethnic group from the peasants who worked their estates, and different again from the commercial and professional classes in the towns. Thus for example, in Hungary, Magyar nobles lorded it over Slovak or Romanian peasants; in Galicia, Polish nobles did the same over Ukrainian and Ruthenian peasants; in the Baltic, it was Germans and Swedes over Estonians and Latvians. Servicing the bureaucratic and military needs of empire brought fresh influxes of Germans to the towns of the Habsburg empire, to join long-settled communities of German craftsmen. Russians came to govern the cities of Ukraine, Moldavia and that part of Poland which fell under Russian control at the end of the eighteenth century. 'Phanariot' Greeks came from Constantinople to play that role on behalf of the Ottoman empire in the Balkans. Throughout the region, Jews constituted a significant proportion of the urban population, in trade and commerce, petty crafts and the professions. Ethnic stratification was exploited by imperial rule, which favoured some ethnic groups over others, such as the Germans in imperial Russia's Baltic provinces, or Slavic converts to Islam in Bosnia while it was under Ottoman control, drawing them into the structure of local imperial rule, and fending off challenges to the centre by a strategy of 'divide and rule'.

TABLE 1.1 *Peoples of Central and Eastern Europe under imperial rule in the late nineteenth and early twentieth centuries*

UNDER THE HABSBURG DUAL MONARCHY (AUSTRIA-HUNGARY AFTER 1867):
Under Austria:
Austrian Germans
Czechs
Poles
Ukrainians/Ruthenians
Slovenes
Jews
Serbs, Croats and Muslims in Bosnia-Herzegovina (after 1878)

Under Hungary:
Hungarians
Jews
Romanians
Slovaks
German 'Saxons'
German 'Schwabs'
Croats
Serbs (in the southern Military Borderlands)

UNDER THE TSARIST RUSSIAN EMPIRE:
Russians
Ukrainians
Belorussians
Jews
Poles
Estonians
Latvians
Lithuanians
Baltic Germans
Moldovans (Romanian speakers in Bessarabia)
Gagauzi

UNDER THE OTTOMAN EMPIRE:
Romanians
Bulgarians
Serbs
Serbs, Croats and Muslims in Bosnia-Herzegovina (to 1878)
Macedonians
Albanians

The experience of centuries of living in multinational dynastic empires meant, in the words of the Hungarian historian Istvan Bibo (1991, p. 39):

> the nations living in this region lacked what was naturally, clearly precisely and concretely present in both the everyday life and community consciousness in Western Europe: a *reality in their own national and state framework*. . . In Eastern Europe, by contrast, a national framework was something that had to be *created, repaired, fought for and constantly protected*, not only against the power factors existing in the dynastic state, but also from the *indifference exhibited by a certain portion of the country's own inhabitants*, as well as from the wavering state of national consciousness.

In the course of the nineteenth century, the challenge of cultural, political and economic modernisation posed by the example of more developed and dynamic nation-states in Western Europe began to make itself felt among the peoples of the dynastic empires of the East. The ideas of individual liberty, human rights and national self-determination proclaimed by the French Revolution had an enormous impact on the elites throughout the region. The ideal of the 'nation-state', a political order in which the state was held to be accountable to the 'People', provided would-be reformers and modernisers in Central and Eastern Europe with the intellectual armoury to attack autocracy, feudal privilege, ossified conservative traditions and social injustice in the name of the universalist liberal ideals of individual freedom, equal rights, the rule of law, and constitutional government.

But problems arose with the redefinition of the state as representative of the 'nation'. In the French context, the 'nation' had been conceived of as a free association of individual citizens with equal rights, and this had been taken to include all permanent inhabitants of the existing state's well-established historical territory. Transformation of the Central and East European Empires along the same lines had been blocked not only by the entrenched conservatism of the old regimes but by the lack of consensus on the very notion of 'The People' in whose name the state was to be reconstituted. By the early nineteenth century, under the influence of the German Romantic thinker, Johann Gottfried von Herder, a native of the Baltic province of East Prussia, the idea of the 'nation' had begun to shift from the state-centred political definition emerging from the French tradition towards a definition in terms of cultural and linguistic attributes constituting an ethnic community which existed before the state. The transformation of the dynastic empires of Central and Eastern Europe into modern nation-states immediately ran up against the problem that the existing territorial borders embraced more than one 'nation' claiming the right of 'national self-determination', and different definitions of the 'nation' were adopted to suit the purposes of the different ethnic communities.

The French political definition retained its attraction for the Poles, Hungarians, Croats and Serbs, who employed it to press their claim to 'self-determination' in the sense of recovering the lost independence of their states which had been conquered and absorbed into the empires. But within each of these 'historic' state territories, there existed other ethnic communities, such as Ukrainians and Slovaks, which adopted the Herderian cultural-linguistic definition to press their own claim to national self-determination, and whose claim to a territory in which to practise national self-government challenged the existing borders of the states in which they lived. Given the territorial intermingling of peoples throughout the region, most claims to 'national self-determination' opportunistically combined both 'historic' or state-centred definitions with ethnic-cultural ones: thus the Poles and Hungarians referred to French-style liberal universalist values to both attack imperialist rule and promise equal rights to all inhabitants of their reclaimed historic state territories, while at the same time taking for granted that the 'nation-state' would embody the cultural values of their own, dominant ethnic nation. Similarly, the Czechs sought 'self-determination' for their own ethnic nation within the Crownlands of Bohemia and Moravia, where they barely outnumbered the Germans who had also lived there for centuries; and the Serbs, who claimed as their national birthright not only the territory of medieval Serbia at its greatest extent, but also all lands where subsequently Serbs had settled, such as Bosnia and the southern Military Borderlands established by the Habsburgs in Croatia and Hungary.

The collapse of imperial control over Central and Eastern Europe, which culminated at the end of World War I, seemed to open the way to free self-determination for the peoples of the region, allowing them finally to acquire their own sovereign nation-states, and so to reach political modernity on the pattern already laid down by their neighbours to the west, France, Germany and Italy. The collapse of the

Russian Empire into the chaos of revolution and civil war in 1917 allowed the Estonians, Latvians and Lithuanians to break free and form their own states; and the simultaneous break-down of the Habsburg Empire and the defeat of Germany paved the way for the establishment of a reunited, independent Poland. The Czechs and Slovaks formed a new common state of Czechoslovakia, while the south Slavs of Austria-Hungary united with Serbia in the Kingdom of Serbs,Croats and Slovenes, later to be called Yugoslavia. Romania, which like Serbia had wrested independence from the Ottomans in the late nineteenth century, acquired vast new territories where Romanian speakers formed majorities in Transylvania, formerly under Hungarian control, and Bessarabia, formerly under Russian control. But other nations were less successful, notably, the Ukrainians, whose faction-riven independent republic was short-lived and quickly reabsorbed into the new Soviet state; and the Hungarians, who gained independence from Austria only to lose two-thirds of the territory and half of the population of their historic Kingdom to Romania, Czechoslovakia and Yugoslavia.

From the time of the French Revolution, becoming 'modern' meant for the nation-state builders of Central Europe first of all establishing a centralised state apparatus within clear territorial borders, rooted in an integrated 'body politic' of equal citizens with uniform status and rights. But the heritage of history and the endemic problem of geopolitical vulnerability did not melt away overnight. The new independent states formed after the collapse of the empires faced enormous problems.

First of all, the 'body politic' of citizens was by no means well-integrated and consciously oriented towards the new states which purported to represent them. The question of political identity was an extraordinarily complex one for many individuals, as, for example, the inter-war Central European writer Odon von Horvath:

> If you ask me what is my native country, I answer: I was born in Fiume, I grew up in Belgrade, Budapest, Pressburg, Vienna and Munich, and I have a Hungarian passport; but I have no fatherland. I am a very typical mix of old Austria-Hungary: at once Magyar, Croatian, German and Czech; my country is Hungary, my mother tongue is German. (quoted in Rupnik, 1990, p. 250)

The nationalism which had fired the struggle for political freedom and socio-economic modernisation in Central and Eastern Europe was to prove not only a mobilising, but also a differentiating and polarising force, a source of conflict within and between states and peoples as often as a source of political integration and consolidation. Those new 'nation-states' which became established on the territory of the defunct empires after World War I were correspondingly wracked by conflict. On one side stood the 'nationalising' political elites, bent on establishing centralised political and administrative structures on the French republican model, ostensibly in the name of modernisation, efficiency and civic equality; and, on the other, stood the national minorities, usually included in the new state against their will, for whom the centralised nation-state represented just another form of bureaucratic pressure for assimilation and subjection to the untrammelled 'tyranny of the majority'.

The internal weaknesses of the new 'nation-states' were exacerbated by the external threats posed in the inter-war period by Germany and Soviet Russia, both with ambitions to recover 'lost' territories in the region. Most of the new states were small in size as well as deficient in military organisation and capacities, which raised the question of whether sovereign statehood could really be a viable, meaningful objective at all for the small nations of this region – as Prince Charles Schwarzenberg had suggested back in 1891, when he asked a radical Czech nationalist: 'If you and yours hate this state . . . what will you do with your country, which is too small to stand alone? Will you give it to Germany or to Russia, for you have no other choice if you abandon the Austrian Union' (quoted in Blanning, 1994, p. 206). Once imperial 'protection' had been rejected, regional cooperation was vital for mutual support and defence against these external threats, but this was precluded by the numerous conflicts between the new states over borders and the rights of ethnic kinsfolk living in neighbouring states as national minorities. The experience of the twentieth century seemed to bear out Prince Schwarzenberg's pessimism, as independent states in Central and Eastern Europe fell victim first to Nazi then Soviet domination.

Communism, Nationalism and Democratisation

Communist ideology had an ambivalent relationship to nationalism. On the one hand, it interpreted nationalism as a form of 'false consciousness', expressing the interests of the property-owning bourgeoisie. Capitalism as an economic system was, in communist theory, inextricably bound up with the emergence of the idea and practice of the nation-state, and the associated liberal concepts of individual rights. These served the interests of the bourgeoisie, legitimating their rise to power and their displacement of the old aristocratic ruling classes of the pre-modern, feudal era. Nationalism as an ideology served to divide the workers of the world from each other, and to obscure their common interest in the world socialist revolution. The equality in political rights promised by liberal nationalism was a fraud. It served to camouflage the real inequalities in life-chances between those who owned property – the bourgeoisie – and those who had nothing to sell but their labour – the proletariat. The proletariat were doomed to increasing impoverishment under the ruthlessly competitive capitalist order, and yet formed the bulk of the mass national armies deployed in wars which served only the interests of the various national bourgeoisies and their states. The clear implication was that nationalism would disappear with the advent of socialism. Communism would be the final state where all men could realise their true essence as equal members of a universal human society.

However, when communists came to power, first in Russia after the 1917 revolution, and subsequently in Eastern Europe, after its 'liberation' by Soviet forces at the end of World War II, they recognised at once that nationalism was a force to be reckoned with. It was clearly not only a matter of eliminating the 'bourgeoisie' in each state in the region – a job which Hitler had started, but the communists effectively finished off. The 'proletariat' too appeared inconveniently attached to their various national identities, and support for communist ideology was nowhere sufficiently strong to enable the communists simply to disregard this. Instead, they developed a twofold, economic and political strategy which they expected eventually to 'solve' the national question in the region.

Firstly, they would set about 'building socialism', which meant launching programmes of state-sponsored economic modernisation – rapid industrialisation of these still largely rural societies, coupled with a radical reorganisation of agriculture to promote large-scale, quasi-industrial forms of production on state and collective farms, replacing the small-scale private peasant farms which had been characteristic of the region. This was to bring about massive social change and upheaval, which they believed would prepare the ground for a fundamental change in social values. The mass movement of population to the cities would weaken traditional ties, and especially the hold of religion, a crucial component of most traditional national identities. People would be mixed up together, their style of life and economic circumstances made equal and uniform, and society would become a homogeneous mass of 'new socialist men' in which national differences would melt away.

Communists believed that socio-economic modernisation under state-socialist auspices would 'naturally' tend to produce the desired result, because they saw national identity as basically a problem of socio-economic underdevelopment. However, they were by no means unprepared to help history on its way by active political intervention to accelerate the process. The political aspects of communist national policy involved both coercion and calculated concessions. Coercion was employed against all manifestations of 'bourgeois nationalism' and against the churches. Arrests and constant harassment of intellectuals and priests, strict censorship of the media, tight control of education at all levels and especially in the humanities and social sciences, the restriction of all contacts with the West – all combined in a historically unprecedented, comprehensive system of suppression. At the same time, however, communist rule used and abused national sentiment in a variety of ways. Perhaps the most innocuous form was the promotion of 'popular culture' – the folklore, costumes, songs, dances and artifacts of the peoples of the region. This was contrasted with the 'unhealthy', retrograde nationalism of the 'bourgeoisie', and, cleansed of all dangerous political content, a new culture, 'national in form, but socialist in content', was expected to satisfy the emotional needs of the People. This new culture would draw upon the collectivist, communal strands of Central and East European nationalism, which coincided with communist ideology and, it was hoped, would serve to enhance the attractiveness of socialism among the masses.

Where communists came to power in the multinational states, as in the former Russian Empire, Yugoslavia and Czechoslovakia, a more elaborate national policy had to be pursued. In all three cases, the first task of the communist rulers was to put back together again states which had shattered into national fragments in the course of war. While during World War I, Lenin had supported the 'right to national self-determination', once the communists came to power he fully recognised the incompatibility of this slogan with the interests of communist power. Taken to its logical conclusion, 'national self-determination' would have reduced the territory controlled by communists to that of medieval Muscovy, a medium-sized, landlocked power on the very edge of Europe. But 'history' required the spread of communism throughout the world, not surrender to 'bourgeois' nationalism, and this argument justified the forcible reconquest by the Red Army of as much of the lost imperial territory as possible. In order to pacify the reconquered peoples – the Ukrainians, Georgians, Armenians and Central Asians – Lenin offered them a federal form of state, which would give formal institutional recognition to the major national groups, and to that extent would be an improvement on what had gone before. Soviet federalism was thus 'a compromise device for reaping the benefits of empire without the opprobrium associated with Tsarism' (Pearson, 1991, p. 24).

The communists of Yugoslavia and Czechoslovakia followed the Soviet example. In both cases, the state formed after World War I had been wracked by conflict between its national components, in large part because their new rulers implemented centralised and unitary constitutions which rode roughshod over the aspirations of the smaller and weaker national partners for self-government along federal lines. Hitler had been able to exploit these internal conflicts to bring about the dismemberment of these states and their subordination to the Reich. In particular, the Croats of Yugoslavia and the Slovaks of Czechoslovakia had acquired separate national states under Nazi protection. With the defeat of Nazi Germany, the former states were reconstituted as Soviet-style federations under communist control.

Socialist federalism was designed to assuage national feelings without threatening communist power. The federal state structure was therefore combined with the communists' monopoly of power, exercised through the 'leading role' of a highly centralised and disciplined Communist Party, fully in charge of recruitment and promotion to all posts in the state, and setting policies from the centre to be implemented uniformly throughout the federal state. It was to be 'federal in form, but socialist in content'. But socialist federalism proved unsuccessful as a means of 'solving' the national question. Paradoxically, the republics were ultimately to provide the political framework for the dismemberment of the federal states.

Communist nationality policy failed in both its economic and its political dimensions. Firstly, the economic component of the policy had rested on the assumption that economic development would transform society in such a way as to erode the vitality of national consciousness. But over the course of the twentieth century, the economic determinism of this assumption has been repeatedly exposed as fallacious. Economic development in many third world countries, for example, has in fact been accompanied by rising, not diminishing national consciousness. Examples of the same trend came to abound in communist Europe. Modernisation produced new and more numerous educated elites who were less and less ready to accept the simplistic platitudes of their communist leaders, and more confident of their capacity – and their right – to use their initiative and even to govern themselves. This aspiration inevitably became articulated in a national form. As each of the non-dominant national groups acquired intelligentsias and political elites of their own, they became less dependent on cadres from the dominant 'elder brother' nation which had formed the core of the original party apparatus, and more resentful of the latter's (implicitly or explicitly) proclaimed 'leading role', which began to look to them like a version of the imperialist 'civilising mission'.

Moreover, the migration and mingling of uprooted peoples, which was so characteristic of Soviet industrialisation and urbanisation in particular, in fact increased the awareness of national differences, often leading to friction and even open hostility, rather than the merging and fading of the sense of national identity. This was the case for example in the Baltic Republics, reannexed by the Soviet Union in World War II, where industrial investment in the Soviet period drew in large numbers of Russian, Ukrainian and other peoples as the new labour force. These hapless people were seen by the indigenous Estonians and Latvians as accomplices to the illegal Soviet occupation of their countries, and tools of the Soviet state's deliberate campaign to 'swamp' their republics. Estonians and Latvians feared they would be turned into a minority in their own homelands, thus completing their national dispossession. The immigrants (or 'colonists' as many Balts refer to them) were also believed to be more favourably treated than the indigenous people, especially in jobs and in the acutely sensitive area of housing allocation.

The policy of centrally planned modernisation, favouring investment in the less developed republics of the federal states in order to bring about socio-economic equalisation and uniformity across the whole, in fact provoked resentment on the part of the more advanced republics in all three of the communist federations, which saw their own development throttled back. This was clear by the early 1980s in both the Soviet and Yugoslav federations, which began at that time to exhibit all the signs of major economic crisis, intensifying the competition for resources. In the Czechoslovak case, the policy of 'positive discrimination' in economic policy in favour of the less developed

Slovak republic worked quite successfully to achieve broad equalisation by the early 1980s. But the Czechs began to ask why resource transfers continued to be made to Slovakia thereafter. Moreover, it was also the case that Soviet-style modernisation in Slovakia produced a very different type of economy and society from those of the Czech Republic, whose industrial development had evolved more organically over the previous century. This was later to emerge as a factor producing very divergent interests and perceptions among Czechs and Slovaks in the matter of economic reform and postcommunist economic transformation, and fuelled the nationalist tension which led to the break-up of the state (see Batt, 1993).

In sum, we can say that the economic component of communist nationality policy failed because national identity did not become less relevant as economic development proceeded, and further, because the communist economic system itself failed to deliver what it had promised – a society of universal welfare, security, and material abundance. By the 1980s, communist economies were visibly lagging behind the capitalist West, and, in some cases, like Poland, Hungary and Yugoslavia, the states were virtually bankrupt, having run up huge foreign debts to Western banks and Western governments which their inefficient, uncompetitive economies were simply unable to support. Everywhere, communist governments were confronted with intractable economic problems that could only be resolved by radical systemic reforms, including more or less drastic financial austerity and structural adjustment, which would undermine their capacity to continue to govern in the old way.

These circumstances were compounded by the peculiar, and in some respects unexpected impact of the political component of communist nationality policy. It was indeed predictable that the massive use of force, the essentially coercive basis of communist rule, would eventually prove counterproductive. The terror of the Stalin period in the Soviet Union, the famine, purges and mass deportations of peoples, had affected all, but the non-Russians had experienced these in different ways from the Russians, and in some respects had indeed been deliberately singled out for repression. The legacy of this was to poison national relations in a peculiarly intractable way. In Central and Eastern Europe, communism had come from outside with the Soviet defeat of Nazi Germany in the region. The communist states were thus inextricably linked in the minds of these peoples with Soviet imperialism, and seen not as the expression but the betrayal of the nation's identity and interests. Political dissent was never effectively stamped out in Central Europe, and became increasingly widespread whenever a weakened communist regime sought to appease its people by 'liberal' reforms and a more relaxed form of rule. It was only natural here that the language of dissent should become infused with the national idiom, and that people's understanding of their situation should be framed by their long historical experience of thwarted 'national self-determination'. The preservation of national identity, whether through the 'high' culture of literature and historical studies, or through the reappropriation of popular culture, or through a renewed interest in religion, became a widespread preoccupation and the main means of expressing resistance to the alien, communist state. The echoes of the nineteenth-century struggles reverberated through this rocky twentieth-century terrain.

The communist political elites, recognising the loss of the credibility of communist ideology on its own terms, responded to the situation by renewed efforts to legitimate their rule in a national idiom. In the last years of communist rule, a bizarre process of rehabilitating long-dead 'national heroes', appropriating traditional symbols and historical anniversaries went on, in which the communists attempted to portray these as valid precursors of communist rule, as confirmation of the 'historical necessity' of communism as the culmination of national achievements (see Zaslavsky, 1992). Far from suppressing nationalism, communist rulers increasingly resorted to its most unattractive, chauvinist, collectivist and intolerant forms in the effort to salvage their popular credibility.

Furthermore, in the federal states, local communist elites began to develop and use their institutional bases in the federal-republican state structures as a means of challenging the central authority of the federation. One of the paradoxical developments in the Soviet and Yugoslav socialist federations had been the creation or consolidation of national identities which had only been weakly formed, or had barely existed at all before, around the federal-republican structures. For example, the Soviet era effectively created separate nations in Central Asia and Moldova; while communist Yugoslavia promoted the development of Macedonian and Bosnian Muslim national political identities, centred on their respective republics. The demand for greater autonomy for the republics was discovered to be the most effective way for communist elites to shore up their power, and one which could even win them the support of the previously 'dissident', anti-communist local nationalist intelligentsia. This led to the formation of powerful nationalist political coalitions at the republican level, which the communists seemed at first to believe they could control. But they were swept along by the nationalist momentum, losing ground to the more radical nationalists and opportunists within their own ranks. Eventually, nationalists entrenched in the republican state structures swept aside communist rule and with it the federal states themselves.

Thus the collapse of communism throughout Central and Eastern Europe in 1989–91 showed that the appetite of the peoples of the region for 'self-determination' was undiminished. The Soviet Union disintegrated, which seemed (after the event) to be simply a long-delayed reckoning with the imperialist heritage of its Romanov predecessor; but so also did Yugoslavia and Czechoslovakia, states which were not based on imperial conquest, but were held to express the aspirations for 'self-determination' of their component peoples against Habsburg and Ottoman domination. As a result, there are now more nation-states than ever in Central and Eastern Europe, and the problem of national minorities in these new states has revived. This latest phase of state-formation in Central and Eastern Europe has, ironically, coincided with the emergence in the West of increased uncertainty about the very idea of the sovereign nation-state, its viability and future in light of the erosion of state powers by economic globalisation, and in light of the unfolding European project of supranational political integration. Thus the 'return to Europe' today paradoxically seems to require the states of Central and Eastern Europe at one and the same time to establish and consolidate their independence and to adjust to the pan-European and global trends which seem to transcend sovereignty. Not only has the path to 'modernity' beaten by Western Europe proved a tortuous one for Central and Eastern Europe, but the signposts now seem to be changing.

About This Book

In this book, we aim to cover the full complexity of the tasks of postcommunist transformation in sixteen states with very diverse national histories, social, cultural and economic conditions, but sharing the experience of intense national struggles for survival and emancipation, and the aspiration to join the mainstream of modern Europe as independent, democratic and economically prosperous states. In Part One, we provide overviews of recent political developments in the region. For the purposes of simplicity, we have grouped the states into three: East-Central Europe, the Balkans, and the post-Soviet states. As with all such compressions, there are anomalies.

East-Central Europe includes Poland, Hungary, the Czech Republic and Slovakia. The Poles, Czechs and Slovaks all speak closely related, Western Slavic languages, while the Hungarians are very much out on a limb linguistically, their language not part of the Indo-European group (see Table 1.2). All four peoples have historically been part of Western Christendom (see Table 1.3) and share in the formative political experience of living under Habsburg rule, the most Western-oriented, open and liberal of the European dynastic empires in the nineteenth century. Here, the influence of the Renaissance, Reformation and Counter-Reformation, French revolutionary liberalism and German romanticism – defining elements of the mainstream culture of modern Europe – all filtered through, albeit more weakly in some parts than others. A more ambivalent inheritance is that of Habsburg administrative bureaucratism, a tradition which mixed fabled 'Germanic' efficiency with arrogant rigidity, arcane complexity and often an arbitrary sloppiness, well captured by the nightmarish visions of Franz Kafka. The East Central European countries have been singled out as the 'front-runners' in postcommunist transformation, which is often explained loosely by their more advantageous cultural and institutional heritage. But much of Poland does not share in that heritage, having been under Russian and Prussian rule as well as Austrian from the late eighteenth century. Nevertheless, the peoples of Poland, the former Czechoslovakia and Hungary in the communist period at various times made clear their readiness to seize what opportunities were offered to press for democratic reforms, and these experiences gave them a head start when communism broke down. In all three – now four – countries, the postcommunist transformation proceeded relatively fast and the prospect of early membership in NATO and the European Union was held out to them. But the transformation has not been without its problems, especially in Slovakia, a new state whose political life has been turbulent and whose progress to democracy has been called into doubt. Thus, for the time being, Slovakia alone among the East-Central Europeans has been excluded from the first wave of NATO and EU enlargement, while two other newly independent states, Slovenia and Estonia, have fared better and have been invited to begin negotiations for EU entry (but not, so far, NATO membership).

TABLE 1.2   *Religious traditions in Central and Eastern Europe*

MAINLY CATHOLIC:
Poles
Slovaks
Lithuanians
Slovenes
German 'Schwabs' in Hungary and Romania (Eastern Banat)
Croats

MAJORITY CATHOLIC WITH SIGNIFICANT PROTESTANT
MINORITY:
Czechs
Slovaks
Hungarians

MAINLY PROTESTANT:
Latvians
Estonians
German 'Saxons' in Romania (Transylvania)

MAJORITY ORTHODOX WITH SIGNIFICANT UNIATE (GREEK or
EASTERN RITE CATHOLICS) MINORITY:
Ukrainians
Ruthenes
Romanians

MAINLY ORTHODOX:
Russians
Bulgarians
Serbs
Montenegrins
Macedonians
Moldovans
Gagauzi

MUSLIMS:
Bosnian Muslims
Turks in Bulgaria
Sandzhak Muslims in Serbia

MAINLY MUSLIM WITH CATHOLIC AND ORTHODOX
MINORITIES:
Albanians

JEWISH:
Mainly urban dwellers throughout Central and Eastern Europe; much reduced
by assimilation in the nineteenth century and the Holocaust in World War II.

TABLE 1.3   *Major languages spoken in Central and Eastern Europe*

INDO-EUROPEAN GROUP:

Slavonic
West: Polish, Czech, Slovak
East: Russian, Ukrainian, Byelorussian
South: Serbo-Croat, Slovene, Bulgarian, Macedonian

Germanic
German, Yiddish

Baltic
Lithuanian, Latvian

Italic (Latin-based)
Romanian (including Moldovan dialect)

Albanian

NON-INDO-EUROPEAN GROUPS:

Uralic
Finnic: Estonian
Ugric: Hungarian

Altaic
Turkish
Gagauz

Our second group, the *Balkan states,* includes Slovenia along with
other former Yugoslav republics, Albania, Romania and Bulgaria.
The languages of the peoples of the former Yugoslavia and the
Bulgarians belong to the South Slavic group, while Romanian is
Latin-based. Slovenia, like Croatia, is mainly Catholic, and both
share in the Austro-Hungarian heritage, unlike the Serbs and other
South Slavs and the Romanians, who were under Ottoman rule and
are mainly Orthodox Christians, with some Muslims. This group
shares, to a greater or lesser extent, in distinctive political traditions
which are often attributed to the legacy of Ottoman rule – tendencies
towards personalised power, corruption, and the abuse of the state to
serve nepotistic, clan and family interests. While the Bulgarians have
their own state, for most of this century the other South Slavs lived

together in Yugoslavia and thus became deeply entangled in its complex and intractable ethnic conflicts, and in its exceptional experience as a communist state independent of Moscow's control with a uniquely decentralised and open political and economic model. The levels of economic development and social modernisation have also been distinctly lower in the Balkans than in East-Central Europe. However, Vojvodina in northern Serbia and Transylvania and the Banat in north-western Romania are both relatively prosperous provinces, where the Habsburg heritage makes itself felt, occasionally challenging rule from Belgrade and Bucharest.

The third group, the *Post-Soviet states*, embraces countries which have all been marked by centuries of close encounters with Russian imperialism, whether of the Tsarist or Soviet communist kind. All became sovereign independent states upon the collapse of the Soviet Union in 1991, and all contain sizeable Russian and Russian-speaking minorities, and continue to identify Russia as the main threat to their existence. But their ethnic identities are very diverse, as are the routes these peoples took to independence. The Baltic Republics include Estonians, speaking a language quite close to Finnish and distantly related to Hungarian, while Latvian and Lithuanian are both Indo-European languages of the Baltic group. The Estonians and Latvians are Protestant, while the Lithuanians are as fervently Catholic as their Polish neighbours. All three Baltic nations had two decades of independent statehood in the inter-war period, and thus do not define themselves as 'new' states, but as states which have recovered their independence. This previous experience of statehood brings certain advantages, and helps to explain the relatively rapid consolidation of their independent existence and faster progress in political and economic transformation than in Ukraine and Moldova.

The prospect of joining the East-Central Europeans in an expanded European Union is thus closer for all three Baltic republics. Both Ukraine and Moldova have faced enormous difficulties, not only with Russia's attempt to regain influence over them, but also with their own internal constitutions and identities. Ukraine had never existed as a modern state, and many Ukrainians became russified over the centuries, a process helped along by the closeness of the two languages and the shared Orthodox religion. The most militant Ukrainian national separatists sprang from Western Ukraine, which until World War I was under Austrian control, and thereafter until World War II was part of Poland. Ukrainians in the East were more ambivalent about separation from Russia, as were the Russian minority. Defining the 'Ukrainian nation' has been a fraught process, absorbing much energy which more consolidated states have been able to devote to building democracy and transforming the economy. Moldova is perhaps the most tenuous of all new states, having faced not only Russian-backed secessionist challenges from Russian-speakers in the eastern Transdniestrian region and Turkic-speaking Gagauzi in the south, but also, for a time, pressures from Romania and from Romanian nationalists within the country, who argued that Moldova, with its majority Romanian-speaking population, should rightfully return to its inter-war place as part of Romania. However, a distinct Moldovan identity, nurtured in the Soviet period, seems to have won the day. Moldova seems set to continue to develop as a separate state, but it has yet to restore control over the breakaway Transdniestria, and remains heavily dependent on Russian goodwill for a solution.

The remaining parts of the book focus thematically on the post-communist transformation, whose complexity lies in the simultaneous combination of a number of tasks, each of which alone presents an enormous challenge. We already have experience of transitions to democracy in southern Europe and Latin America, but in all of these cases, the transition was from authoritarian rule, not totalitarian communism. Postcommunist states have to establish democracy while at the same time unscrambling the economic legacies of Soviet-style central planning. While the former dictatorships of southern Europe and Latin America certainly saw the state heavily involved in the economy, nevertheless, these were recognisably market economies with substantial private sectors. In postcommunist Europe, the market and private property have to be created anew. The role of the state, the structures and institutions of the state and its relationship to the economy and society have to be radically redefined. In the midst of these processes, the nations of the region have reawakened, redefining the political communities which the new democratic states should represent, the borders within which they exercise their jurisdiction, and their external relations with each other, with Europe and with the wider world.

PART ONE

Patterns of Politics

2

East-Central Europe: The Czech Republic, Slovakia, Hungary and Poland

PAUL G. LEWIS

The countries of East-Central Europe – Poland, Hungary and Czechoslovakia – led the way out of communist dictatorship in 1989 and have since remained at the forefront of postcommunist change. While issues surrounding the transition to democracy lay at the forefront of attention in the years immediately following the decisive rupture, current discussion of the patterns of politics that now emerge in those countries tends to focus on the issue of democratic consolidation. The end of monopolistic Communist Party rule has been signalled by the holding of competitive elections on more than one occasion (Hungary 1990 and 1994, Poland 1991, 1993 and 1997, Slovakia 1994 and the Czech Republic 1996 – the latter following elections in Czechoslovakia during 1990 and 1992), most of which resulted in a change of government and ruling parties. Despite significant conflicts and major uncertainties in some areas, the broad framework of a constitutional order has been established with extensive civic freedoms, a reasonably well-functioning legal system and a largely free press. The break-up of Czechoslovakia was also carried out peacefully and with due dispatch, although it is universally held that the trajectory of democratisation has been maintained more effectively in the Czech Republic than in Slovakia. In broad terms the process of democratic transition appears to have been completed in the countries of East-Central Europe to an extent that cannot be said of postcommunist countries to the south and east. It is in this context, therefore, that the process of democratic consolidation takes pride of place on the political agenda.

TABLE 2.1 *Basic data: East Central Europe, 1996*

	Population (million)	Area (sq. km)	GDP growth (%)	Inflation rate (%)	Av. Monthly income (US$)	Unemployment (%)
Czech Republic	10.331	78,864	4.5	8.8	374	3.5
Hungary	10.277	93,030	1.0	20.0	360	10.5
Poland	38.600	312,683	6.0	18.5	318	13.2
Slovakia	5.325	49,036	7.0	5.2	273	12.3

Views differ on the degree of democratic consolidation so far achieved in East-Central Europe. From one point of view it has already been concluded that the formal criteria of democratic consolidation have all been met in Poland (Taras, 1995, p. 254). In a broader comparative study Juan J. Linz and Alfred Stepan (1996a, p. 255) express another opinion. The major role played in the Polish transition by the idea of an ethical civil society, the strongly pacted character of the change and the country's semi-presidential postcommunist system all, in their view, produce a 'legacy of ambivalence toward political society which must be transcended before Poland can consolidate democracy'. Although they think it too early to judge conclusively, they are of the opinion that Hungary has major advantages over other postcommunist countries in terms of progress towards consolidation, while the Czech Republic – as distinct from Slovakia – also had its prospects of consolidation significantly enhanced by the break-up of the federal republic. But, although it is now widely referred to in the context of East-Central Europe, what the concept of democratic consolidation actually involves is not wholly clear.

It is not, to be sure, very difficult to define what seems to be at issue. Linz and Stepan (1996b, p. 17), for example, suggest that, in addition to the existence of a functioning state, five other interconnected and mutually reinforcing conditions 'must be present, or be crafted', for a democracy to be consolidated. These conditions are: the development of a free and lively civil society, a relatively autonomous political society, the subjection of all major political actors to the rule of law, the availability of a usable state bureaucracy by the democratic government, and the institutionalisation of an economic society. The precise meaning of some of these terms may be left to one side for the moment, although their general implications are at least quite clear. The main problem really inheres in how these criteria may be applied. To what extent does a civil society have to be 'free and lively' to sustain democratic consolidation – and is it, anyway, always the case that the influence of civil society flows in a democratic direction? How 'relatively autonomous' does a political society (that is, the public arena of political contestation) have to be to assure consolidation? What are the defining characteristics of an effective bureaucracy that is relatively uncorrupt? – for this is what largely is at issue here. These are clearly highly complex questions which require extensive investigation if they are to be answered satisfactorily, although most informed observers would most likely come up quite easily with an equivalent judgement on whether democracies are reasonably well consolidated on more intuitive grounds.

Democracies, further, become consolidated when they have become 'the only game in town', a neat encapsulation of the situation which, Linz and Stepan (1996a, p. 5) spell out, has considerably more complex associations in behavioural, attitudinal and constitutional terms. There remains though, as the authors point out, an ever-present danger of the 'electoralist fallacy', when the *necessary* condition of free elections is seen as a *sufficient* condition of democracy. Amidst the flux of postcommunist political change and the rapidly advancing tide of apparent democratisation it has, indeed, probably been too easy to mistake the dense sequence of well-organised electoral contests for a deeper-rooted process of democratic development and stable consolidation. While the formal rules of democratic practice are well observed, in the sense that reasonably well-organised elections determine key processes of leadership change, other patterns of political life (generally less open, significantly enough, to the international gaze) may run on quite different lines. Games played 'inside' the democratic institutions can be quite different from those dictated by their formal rules (O'Donnell, 1996, p. 41). Elements of 'particularism' – the subversion of public activities by private interests in ways that act as major qualifying limitations on democratic practice – are by no means lacking in the countries of postcommunist East-Central Europe as in many other parts of the supposedly democratic world, and their practice of 'actually existing democracy' may well leave something to be desired.

Yet there are clear signs that countries like Hungary, Poland and the Czech Republic have already established a reasonably stable form of democratic order, albeit one some way from the accepted model of pluralist democracy (or polyarchy) and characterised by continuing elitism, rather weak party systems, poorly developed civil societies and often having dubious links with the freewheeling practices of a rapidly developing free-market capitalism. As in the case of Italy and Japan, though, such democratic peculiarities and apparently aberrant links with diverse social and individual interests may well contribute to the stabilisation of recently democratised systems and their apparent consolidation as reasonably viable forms of a more open political order. In general terms, then, the states of postcommunist East-Central Europe do appear to have developed some form of democratic consolidation, if of an imperfect variety. This chapter will seek to establish how this condition has been achieved and what kind of democracy has actually been established.

The End of Communist Rule

There can be little doubt about the origins of the process. It was clearly the case that Gorbachev's reformulation of Soviet European policy allowed the countries of East-Central Europe to lead the way to postcommunist democratisation. The beginning of the 1980s was hardly promising in this respect, with the imposition of military rule in Poland, the looming failure of Janos Kadar's New Economic Policy of limited reform in Hungary, and the resolute continuation of the policy of 'normalisation' imposed after Czechoslovakia's brief period of reformist experimentation in 1968. Nor did the accession of Mikhail Gorbachev to the Soviet leadership in 1985 seem to carry much promise of significant political change at the time. Gorbachev's attention was initially directed to a number of issues, but the political transformation of East-Central Europe was certainly not at the top of his original agenda. But it gradually became clear that Gorbachev's view of what was possible was radically different from that of his predecessors in the Soviet leadership and a new regional policy eventually emerged (see Lewis, 1994, pp. 229–34). By 1988 an awareness of this was beginning to have a significant effect on decision-making processes in Hungary and Poland. In May 1988 Kadar was finally removed from the Hungarian leadership and the Politburo purged of his supporters. After a further wave of strikes in Poland during the summer of 1988, the party leadership judged the time to be right to bring Solidarity representatives into discussions to lead to some form of power-sharing (or, more appropriately, responsibility-sharing) for measures that might help alleviate the long-lasting economic and social crisis.

But this was not all that was happening. The opposition and forces of civil society took heart from such initiatives and began to strengthen their activities, particularly in Hungary where dissidents and opposition activities developed more organised forms of association which pointed the way to the emergence of independent parties. In Poland a form of military rule had been imposed for a period in the early 1980s, but the independent trade union Solidarity had never been fully crushed or dismembered, while its influential intellectual and religious supporters also remained unsilenced. Equally important changes were taking place within the communist establishment. Both Hungarian and Polish 'communist' parties (actually, the Hungarian Socialist Workers' Party and the Polish United Workers' Party) had overseen periods of considerable repression but, in comparison with ruling parties elsewhere in the Soviet bloc, had more frequently operated with conciliatory forms of political rule which took account of the characteristics of their respective societies and national cultures. The Polish party, for example, had come to terms with the Catholic Church and an independent-minded peasantry which was allowed to retain its private holdings. Having crushed the 1956 revolution and spent some years persecuting its most active participants, Kadar in 1961 adopted a far more open policy and paid considerable attention to securing economic growth and organising the economy on more reformist lines.

Under the conditions of the late 1980s the resumption of the liberal tendency carried more radical implications. In Poland the opening of talks with Solidarity got off to a slow start but began to promise more concrete results when hardliners in the party leadership were confronted at the end of 1988 and major resistance to more radical change overcome. As a result of round-table talks, Solidarity was relegalised in April 1989 and elections offering a qualified – but in Soviet-bloc terms unprecedented – degree of political choice were held in June. Although designed to prop up rather than supplant communist rule this is not what the elections achieved, partly because of misjudgement and faulty planning by the communist leadership. Solidarity-sponsored candidates won the 35 per cent of the seats in the lower legislative chamber they had been permitted to contest and all but one of the 100 seats in the upper house, and they also won the support of the previously subservient auxiliary parties which had formed part of the political establishment throughout the period of communist rule. In September the premiership was assumed by Solidarity representative Tadeusz Mazowiecki, who proceeded to organise a carefully balanced party/Solidarity-influenced government. Its communist elements were, however, rapidly attenuated as the rest of Central-Eastern Europe also took the decommunising path.

The pace of change also quickened in Hungary after Kadar's ouster in 1988. Matters came to a head at around the same time as in Poland, when in February 1989 the party's Central Committee confronted the most fundamental and sensitive event in Hungarian communist history and decided that 1956 had seen a popular uprising and not a counter-revolution. This judgement shook the foundations of communist authority and was immediately followed by an announcement that Hungary should prepare for its transformation into a multi-party democracy. Round-table talks on the Polish model were held, and fully competitive elections, resulting in the removal of even the reformed Hungarian Socialist Party from power, were held in March 1990.

The background to the equally momentous developments in Czechoslovakia at the end of 1989 was quite different. Czechoslovakia's experiment with communist reformism, in the form of Alexander Dubcek's attempt to create 'socialism with a human face', came to an abrupt end with the invasion of the Soviet army, backed up by other Warsaw Pact forces, in August 1968. Orthodox communist rule was restored and all possibility of any significant political and economic reform banished within a framework of the rather surrealistically termed 'normalisation' policy. All that could be said to have been gained from the reformist initiatives of the pre-invasion period – and whose consequences in some ways look more significant in the 1990s than they did at the time – was the continuation of plans to federalise the state and governmental structure, legislation being passed in October 1968 and federalisation coming into force in the new year. Gloomy though the post-invasion period was for most of the population, it was nevertheless made more tolerable by steady levels of economic growth and a reasonably comfortable standard of living. Political quiescence and outward conformity were rigorously maintained by an extensive party organisation and the security forces it controlled. Some dissident groups were established in the 1970s but even one of the most prominent, Charter 77, had no more than 2,500 signatories in 1987 after ten years of existence. Currents of opposition began to strengthen in 1988, but it was not until November 1989 that demonstrations began to shake the communist establishment.

By this stage Poland and Hungary were well into the phase of postcommunist change, and the Berlin Wall was already being demolished in neighbouring East Germany. A domino effect was clearly visible throughout Central and Eastern Europe which meant that established communist regimes were falling with increasing rapidity. So when this happened in Czechoslovakia the pace of change was remarkably fast, and the party leadership installed under Milos Jakes resigned on November 24, just five days after Civic Forum was organised as a comprehensive platform of opposition to communist rule.

Despite its late start in the democratisation process Czechoslovakia, too, held competitive multi-party elections in June 1990, almost exactly a year after the more ambiguous, partially free elections held in Poland. At the time these had been seen as a daring, and rather hazardous political innovation, even under the new conditions of world and regional affairs established by Gorbachev. One year later, Poland's curiously constituted 'contract' parliament, emerging from the formal agreement reached between party leadership and opposition, now appeared to be something of an anachronism in an emphatically postcommunist East-Central Europe. The political system that had been imposed throughout the region something over forty years previously – and, indeed, forcibly reimposed at various times – had rapidly passed from the scene. But the disappearance of Soviet-backed communist leaders from the region (as well as the imminent dissolution of both Comecon and the Warsaw Pact) was not all that was involved in the end of communist rule. Communism had also seen the development of highly distinctive, Soviet-style economic processes and these, too, were set to disappear or were already doing so as Central Europe now underwent a different form of 'normalisation' in joining the mainstream of global capitalist development. This would have further effects of a social and political, as well as directly economic, character in influencing the course of postcommunist development.

The Postcommunist System

The obvious tensions and conflict involved in the multi-faceted process of postcommunist change led most contributors to the first edition of this book to adopt a somewhat hesitant view of the situation in the early 1990s and its prospects of early stabilisation.

It was, of course, a view shared with many other observers at the time. Poland, for example, was seen to be in a 'difficult and dangerous situation in the early 1990s' (Mason, 1993, p. 50). The analysis of Hungary identified a 'potentially dangerous cocktail of increasing unemployment, decreasing social welfare and growing political acceptance of the vocabulary of extreme nationalism' (Swain, 1993, p. 82), while 'Czechoslovakia's disappearance . . . removes what had appeared to be an island of stability in the region' (Wightman, 1993, p. 65). Yet, with the obvious exception of the 'velvet divorce' of the already federalised Czech and Slovak Republics, the territorial integrity of the postcommunist states has been maintained and no significant challenge made either to their foundations or to the basic principles of their operation; elections have been held on time and their outcomes generally accepted; major economic problems have indeed been encountered but broadly weathered, their major social consequences either coped with or largely tolerated. In short, a reasonably effective postcommunist system has been established and proved capable of survival.

The major question-mark over this judgement must, of course, be the disappearance of Czechoslovakia as a single entity. But this was in most ways a highly unusual form of state division, with no overt ethnic conflict or civil violence, and clear signs that the great majority of the population did not desire such a decisive outcome. In contrast to otherwise comparable cases in Yugoslavia, Russia and the Caucasus, the source of the conflict was not primarily ethnic but political in character. While post-1968 Czechoslovakia was indeed federalised, uniform communist parties subject to strict Soviet control ruled in both parts of the country and the division was in that sense more administrative than political. When, in 1990 and 1992, authentic political choices could be expressed and parliamentary divisions began to count, the situation became considerably more unstable. The first election was one of a largely acclamatory nature, endorsing the break with communism and confirming the popularity of the opposition groupings that had formed towards the end of 1989: Civic Forum in the Czech lands and Public Against Violence in Slovakia. But some differences in voting were already evident in 1990 in terms of stronger Catholic sentiment in Slovakia as well as the relatively strong showing of the separatist Slovak National Party with 11 per cent of the vote for the chambers of the Federal Assembly and 13.9 per cent in the Slovak republican parliament.

Clear differences soon emerged also over the complex constitutional question, with Czechs generally fearing a line of change that might threaten the pursuit of a coherent economic policy and Slovaks increasingly attracted by the idea of a sovereignty that – with the Nazi-backed wartime state not counting in this respect – had so far eluded them. Economic differences were also significant, as the free-market stance of the dominant Civic Democratic Party in the Czech republic was increasingly at odds with the more collectivist and protectionist policies favoured in Slovakia (where unemployment was already far higher than in the other part of the country). Such divisions gained stronger expression in the 1992 elections and took on more personal form with the growing dominance of Vaclav Klaus in the Czech lands and that of Vladimir Meciar in Slovakia. Division of the state thus emerged as the most viable solution to the political stalemate that emerged – in a situation, moreover, where important decisions could not be delayed and a complex constitutional wrangle could hardly be countenanced.

But, again, just as important as the division itself was the fact that it had come about through parliamentary means and that the parliamentary arena, in Czechoslovakia as elsewhere, remained the primary locus of political conflict. That is not to say that important changes in parliamentary form, process and composition did not occur. Most obviously, the dissolution of Czechoslovakia meant that new parliamentary bodies came into existence at the beginning of 1993 in the new Czech and Slovak Republics. This was a simple process in that the Federal Assembly was abolished while the National Councils elected by the two parts of the country now became their legislative bodies. In the Czech Republic this left Klaus's Civic Democratic Party (in coalition with the Christian Democratic Party) in government with 76 of the Council's 200 seats. Seven other parties had parliamentary representation, the largest being the Left Bloc (in which the Communist Party played a dominant part).

In the Slovak Council, Meciar's Movement for a Democratic Slovakia (with 74 out of the 150 seats) was dominant and formed a government in informal coalition with the much smaller Slovak National Party. Following on from the turbulent personality politics that had surrounded Meciar in the previous years, though, the coalition broke down after a couple of months (Wightman, 1995b, pp. 67–76). Governments in Slovakia turned out to be relatively unstable affairs. In 1994 further elections were held after Meciar's government had been replaced, in March of that year, by a broad right/centre-left coalition. The need for further electoral consultation was acknowledged by both sides, although elections in the autumn – while giving Meciar's MDS, in coalition with the Peasant Party, a clear plurality (35 per cent of all votes) – failed to provide a solution to the more general problems of representation (see Table 2.2) and it was only with difficulty that Meciar formed a further government (with two other parties) five weeks later.

In contrast to the Slovak situation the parliament of the new Czech Republic lasted the full four years, and elections were not held until the end of May 1996. Vaclav Klaus was again victorious, but this time with the slimmest of majorities (see Table 2.3). The Social Democrats, although failing to overtake Klaus's Democratic Party, in practical terms achieved a real electoral success and followed the electoral example of the Polish Social Democracy and Hungarian Socialists in restoring the electoral fortunes of the left. The difference in the Czech case was that they did not achieve quite enough actually to form a government while, on the other hand, they had somewhat different (some would say more authentic) credentials in resting on a more autonomous social democratic basis and not evolving from the Soviet-sponsored party establishment of the communist period. Klaus thus formed a minority government with the Civic Democratic Alliance and the Christian Democratic Union with the broad agreement of the Social Democrats.

In Hungary the basic shape of the parliamentary system was established at a relatively early stage. A reasonably coherent party system was formed and the legislature elected in 1990 lasted its full

TABLE 2.2 *Slovak parliamentary elections, 30 September/1 October 1994*

	Votes (%)	Seats (no.)
Movement for a Democratic Slovakia/Peasant Party of Slovakia	35.0	61
Common Choice	10.4	18
Hungarian Coalition	10.2	17
Christian Democratic Movement	10.1	17
Democratic Union	8.8	15
Workers' Association of Slovakia	7.3	13
Slovak National Party	5.4	9

TABLE 2.3   *Czech parliamentary elections, 31 May/1 June 1996*

	Votes (%)	Seats (no.)
Civic Democratic Party	29.6	68
Christian Democratic Union – Czechoslovak People's Party	8.1	18
Civic Democratic Alliance	6.4	13
Czech Social Democratic Party	26.4	61
Communist Party of Bohemia and Moravia	10.3	22
Association for the Republic – Republican Party of Czechoslovakia	8.0	18

four-year term. That is not to say that problems of political development were totally absent or that stable democratic procedures were established from the outset. A compact group of six parties entered the newly elected parliament in 1990 and one of the main, recently organised opposition groupings – the Hungarian Democratic Forum – formed a government with two smaller right-wing parties. Although the coalition held together, disputes and parliamentary conflicts were, of course, not absent. More significantly, as in Czechoslovakia, the initial pattern of postcommunist party alignment soon began to show signs of erosion, although unlike Czechoslovakia and Poland, party pluralism had been present from the outset and there had been no broad sociopolitical movement like Civic Forum or Solidarity that had emerged to dominate the early stages of transition. The original party system certainly showed signs of dissolution, and the processes of political fragmentation that were only too obvious in Poland were by no means absent from Hungary. By October 1993 as many as 17 different groupings were identified in parliament. But it was not these institutional pressures that dominated the final phase of the first postcommunist parliament and coloured the unfolding electoral campaign. It was more questions of economic policy and the social impact of the market transformation that shaped the popular mood and brought about a spectacular change in the fortunes of the Hungarian Socialist Party (see Table 2.4).

In 1994 the Socialists, who had only won 10.9 per cent of the votes in 1990, actually gained an absolute majority and were in a position to dominate parliament in a way that had not been possible for opposition forces even in the early postcommunist period. In the view of

TABLE 2.4   *Hungarian parliamentary elections (second round), 29 May 1994*

	Votes (%)	Seats (no.)
Hungarian Socialist Party	45.3	209
Alliance of Free Democrats	28.5	70
Hungarian Democratic Forum	14.9	37
Independent Smallholders' Party	8.8	26
Christian Democratic People's Party	7.0	22
Alliance of Young Democrats (FIDESZ)	7.0	20

careful analysts, in Hungary – even more than in Poland, where many have proposed a quite similar argument – electors had protested quite directly 'against the deterioration of the economic situation of their country and against the pro-market economic reforms' (Markowski and Toka, 1993, p. 96). Others, indeed, saw the electoral failure of the already reformed HSP in 1990 as the outcome of a 'small and brief crisis period which was caused by external effects' (ibid.). But whatever the circumstances the Socialists were reluctant to govern alone – for wholly understandable political and historical reasons – and were happy to form a governmental coalition with the Alliance of Free Democrats under the overall leadership of Socialist Gyula Horn as prime minister.

Something of a similar parliamentary outcome occurred in Poland in 1993 following the second round of fully competitive multi-party elections. The context, however, was quite different. The first free election of October 1991 was a fully proportional one with no threshold applied for parliamentary entry. The body that emerged was, therefore, a highly diverse and fragmented one. Some 24 electoral committees succeeding in getting one of more of their candidates into parliament, in which the slightly smaller number of 18 parliamentary clubs were formed. Even worse, at least in terms of political stability and the likelihood of forming a stable government, was the fact that the Democratic Union (the main party to emerge from the broad Solidarity movement) had the largest number of deputies at 62 while the postcommunist electoral coalition (the Democratic Left Alliance) had only a few less at 60. The previously unified Solidarity movement had become fatally split and its leaders engaged in bitter squabbles. The meagre victory of the DU, however, was also due to the fact that it was led by former prime minister

Mazowiecki, who had also recently failed to be elected president but had implemented and continued to support the liberal economic policy which had caused so much pain to the population, this being the programme which the bulk of the electorate had effectively rejected. The DLA, on the other hand, dominated by newly transformed 'Social Democrats', remained very much a marginal political force still disliked and feared by the majority of the population.

Neither of the main parties was, therefore, in a position to lead a government coalition, while the processes both of government formation and of subsequent political survival were very difficult and gave a strong impression of fragmentation, instability and political ineffectiveness. After several other tries, a Solidarity-led government did eventually emerge in July 1992 (with Hanna Suchocka as prime minister) and in fact proved to be reasonably effective. It was, however, brought down by a vote of no confidence in May 1993 (effectively by the abstention of formal members of the coalition) and new elections were called. When held in October they showed the trend that became more apparent in Hungary the following year and later (though in somewhat different form) in the Czech Republic. A similar reaction against the consequences of postcommunist economic transformation had been seen in Lithuania, but Poland was the first country in East-Central Europe to vote postcommunists into power. The DLA – effectively, its dominant party component, the Social Democracy of the Polish Republic – won 20 per cent of the vote and 171 parliamentary seats. It formed a coalition with the equally successful Peasant Party (itself deriving from a party in alliance with the former Workers' Party), the two parties controlling 303 of the Polish parliament's 460 seats. The Peasant Party leader, Waldemar Pawlak, then became prime minister. While the coalition was maintained, leadership of the government later passed back to the SdRP.

The process was by no means a smooth one and premier Oleksy was forced to resign in January 1996 after his close relationship with a member of the former Soviet security services was revealed, after which Wlodzimierz Cimoszewicz became prime minister. The coalition nevertheless survived, and the 1993 parliament served its full four-year term of office. By 1997, however, many representatives and sympathisers of the Solidarity movement had learnt the lesson of the years of internal conflict that had begun with the bitterly fought 'war at the top' in 1990. When the postcommunist candidate, Aleksander Kwasniewski, also wrested the presidency from Lech Walesa in 1995 Solidarity and other right-wing groups finally made a more concerted attempt to bury the hatchet and proceeded to form a broad political grouping called Solidarity Electoral Action. For some months its popularity ratings shadowed those of the DLA, and it was the source of some surprise when Solidarity Action scored a clear victory in the 1997 election (see Table 2.5).

The countries of East-Central Europe thus showed considerable diversity – not only amongst themselves but also over time. Czechoslovakia, firstly, split into its constituent parts which developed in rather different ways, with the Czech Republic showing more stability of government tenure and greater coherence in terms of policy direction. Hungary developed an apparently stable party system at an early stage and maintained a relatively similar configuration following the 1994 election, albeit one that was differently composed. Poland's highly fragmented parliament of 1991 was replaced by one more akin to those of its neighbours, and similar indeed to that of Hungary in terms of the dominance of reformed Social Democrats, although that picture again changed in 1997. Some changes and contrasts in the region were attributable to the nature of the newly constituted democratic electorate and its shifting inclinations. Institutional features also played a role; the new political parties were generally rather weak, with relatively few members and a poorly developed organisational structure. The postcommunist Social Democrats were different in this respect, and this was certainly one – though by no means the only – factor in their resurgence in Poland and Hungary during 1993 and 1994. The application of different political mechanisms also played their part, and the introduction of a 5 per cent threshold in terms of votes cast for entry to parliament was certainly significant in the drastic reduction of the number of parties represented in the Polish parliament after the elections of 1993 and 1997.

TABLE 2.5   *Polish parliamentary elections, 21 September 1997*

	Votes (%)	Seats (no.)
Solidarity Electoral Action	33.8	201
Democratic Left Alliance	27.1	164
Freedom Union	13.4	60
Polish Peasant Party	7.3	27
Movement for the Reconstruction of Poland	5.6	6

Other factors were also significant and various features of the emerging postcommunist system exerted their influence on the different political outcomes. The role and personal behaviour of the different presidents was certainly important, and the outlook and style of Vaclav Havel and Lech Walesa certainly became well known on the international stage. Less well known perhaps (but not always less important) were the actions of Arpad Goncz in Hungary and Michal Kovac in the new Slovak Republic. While the presidents enjoyed a varied range of formal powers, they all exercised some influence on government policy and the political development of their respective countries. This was particularly true of Kovac in Slovakia, where he effectively emerged as a one-man opposition to the personalised rule of Meciar as leader of the Movement for a Democratic Slovakia. Although a founding member of the MDS, he turned against Meciar during Slovakia's first year of independence during 1993 in the interests of national stability and brought about the downfall of the Meciar government in March 1994. After the autumn elections later that year Kovac nevertheless had little choice but to reappoint Meciar to the premiership, although his relations with the new government remained strained, to say the least (Fisher, 1996, pp. 32–3). The role of the president thus had major political significance under the particular conditions that pertained in postcommunist Slovakia, although presidents were by no means without influence in the other countries of East-Central Europe.

Contemporary Issues

The political systems of postcommunist East-Central Europe thus generally appeared to be reasonably well consolidated some eight or so years into their new existence. This was most clearly the case in terms of their performance in electoral terms and their record of 'playing by the rules of the democratic game' in this basic sense. As suggested at the outset, however, the concept of consolidation itself is not an uncontentious one and some fundamental issues continue to arise in evaluating the nature and process of democratisation. One of these emerged with particular prominence in the case of Slovakia after democratisation threw up significant challenges in terms of the split-up of the Czechoslovak state. There can be little doubt that much of the problem in Slovakia concerned the personal nature of the rule of

Vladimir Meciar. Across the range of postcommunist states the *personalisation of rule* appeared as a common phenomenon, and was one which had extensive roots in the region – both during the communist years and in the inter-war period. In contemporary East-Central Europe such personalisation has been most pronounced in Slovakia, and it is not a tendency that has appeared with great prominence elsewhere (that is not to say that major personalities did not impinge quite significantly on political processes elsewhere – Walesa's performance in the Polish presidency is an obvious example).

Meciar's performance in office has, however, been an unusual one in the context of East-Central Europe. Apart from attacking political opponents he has consistently hit out also at the media, President Kovac and external agencies – attempting both to counter their criticism and to undermine their position, frequently invoking the need to defend rather broadly conceived Slovak interests. The pattern of generalised aggression has been accompanied by tactical practices of clientelism, of 'packing key positions with people loyal to Meciar and dividing up the spoils of power', making particular use of a range of industrial resources and public institutions – and not least those based on the police organisation (Kettle, 1996a, p. 16). Conflicts about distribution of the assets in the course of privatisation also disrupted the alliance formed to maintain the parliamentary dominance of Meciar's MDS after the 1994 elections (the Slovak National Party and the Association of Workers of Slovakia being the junior partners). But such altercations only served to demonstrate that it was Meciar who had the upper hand in such manoeuvres and that his position in parliament, although not based on an overall majority, was one of political dominance. His position was also sustained by the experience of repeated electoral success. Ousted from power both in 1991 and 1994 he nevertheless bounced back on the basis of his undoubted attractiveness to a major portion of the Slovak electorate.

But although winning elections in ways that broadly adhered to the rule of the democratic game, Meciar's adherence to broader principles of *civic freedom and human rights* was also tenuous. His views on the Hungarian and Roma minorities have provoked much conflict, on both the national and international level. His treatment of minorities has emerged as a major sticking point for European and transnational organisations. But Slovakia was by no means alone in this. The widely admired democracy of the new Czech Republic also saw a significant number of racist attacks, the clubbing to death of a Romany in May 1995 being the 28th such murder within six years. While the assailant was sentenced to twelve years' imprisonment, the judge nevertheless ruled that the attack was not racially motivated because no racist slogans had been shouted (Kettle, 1996b, p. 18). It was not only Slovak democracy that showed a weak appreciation of the needs of a legally established civil society. Signs of such attitudes appears throughout East-Central Europe – while they were, of course, far from being absent from the west of the continent either. The anti-semitic views of Istvan Csurka in Hungary helped split the Demo-cratic Forum in 1992, while the analogous views and activities of diverse Polish skinheads and nationalist groups made a similar impact on political life in that country – the furore over the construction of a supermarket in the environs of the Auschwitz death camp in early 1996 and the skinhead march through the camp itself being a major case in point.

Sentiments of *nationalism*, therefore, continue to play a part in the politics of East-Central Europe, although the extent of its role and impact on the contemporary politics of the region (not least with the exception of Slovakia) should not be exaggerated. The salience of questions of national independence throughout the region and rela-tively recent experiences both of German and Soviet domination mean that it is a factor that can never be fully discounted. But in view of the radical social transformation that the region has experi-enced and the turbulence that has affected so many people's lives, the political expression of nationalist sentiments and the growth of a radical right – a common response to insecurity and loss of estab-lished identity throughout twentieth-century Europe – has been relatively muted. In both Poland and Hungary ultra-nationalism and right-wing extremism have achieved only a very minor presence in mainstream political life, although they have been significant in Slovakia and the Czech Republic, where the racist Republican Party captured 8 per cent of the vote in 1996 (Szayna, 1997, pp. 124–6). Nationalism of a less extreme form nevertheless played a part in the victory of Solidarity Electoral Action during the 1997 Polish elec-tions, and the nationalist tendency merged with currents of anti-communism and traditional Catholic sentiments to produce a surpris-ingly strong right-wing reaction against the four-year rule of the reborn Social Democrats.

A further issue in the problematic consolidation of Central Eur-opean democracy that the Polish change highlights is therefore the meaning and implication of the return to power of diverse *postcommunist forces*. Both Hungary and Poland saw the political resurgence of parties which – however thoroughly reformed and recast in the form of a modern social democracy – had origins which clearly lay deeply entrenched in the personnel and structures of dictatorial communist rule. But this was by no means a 'velvet restoration' of the former system. The Polish Social Democracy and the Hungarian Socialists were quite different from the essentially unreconstructed Communist Party of Bohemia and Moravia and the ambiguous (though largely traditional) Communist Party of the Russian Federation. There was, as the rise of the Czech Social Democrats clearly showed, a broad surge of support in East-Central Europe for a democratic socialism broadly similar to that seen in the West. But a communist style of rule and the use of political methods more closely identifiable with those of the former dictatorship could more easily be seen in Meciar's brand of populist nationalism than in most of the formally constituted socialist organisations. The precise reasons for the return to power of left-wing forces (to use a general term for what is undoubtedly a diverse political movement) remain the source of some contention, though, and their democratic credentials were never convincing to a large part of the Polish electorate.

Some, for example, present the common view that enhanced support for the left reflected disillusion on the part of the electorate following the early euphoria of the initial democratisation phase and the continuing resilience of socialist values (Mahr and Nagle, 1995, pp. 393–409). Related analyses also suggest that it has been economic factors rather than party political strategies that best explain the relative success of the communist successor parties in East-Central Europe, and that much of their coming attraction will depend on the future success of market transition (Evans and Whitefield, 1995, pp. 574–5). Others, however, have argued that environmental factors do not provide a sufficient explanation for the evolution of the ex-communist parties and their relative degree of political succcess, and that more important have been the particular dynamics of the transition period (Ishiyama, 1995, p. 163). In other accounts there is a yet clearer emphasis on the organisational strength of postcommunist parties and their possession of specific leadership skills (Lewis, 1996, pp. 17–18; Waller, 1995, pp. 487–8). Further views point to the operation of different sets of factors in Poland and Hungary, with the latter following a general pattern of opposition to deteriorating living standards and the programme of market-oriented reforms, and Poles reacting rather against the political role of the Church and continuing authoritarian trends in public life (Markowski and Toka, 1993).

Others direct attention less to the precise electoral basis of the resurgence of left-wing and postcommunist forces in East-Central Europe than to its overall political significance in a situation marked by the spread of privatisation and the turbulence of marketisation processes. Pointing to the steps taken by strategically placed *appa-ratchiks* and administrators in Hungary and Poland to transform their powers of control over state assets into private property well before the collapse of the communist system, they argue that the return to power of postcommunists just sets a political seal to the processes whereby the former *nomenklatura* has transformed but essentially perpetuated its power under new conditions. There is certainly some evidence to support this view. Analysis of the careers of several hundred top members of the Polish *nomenklatura* from 1988 to 1993 showed that over half had emerged as top private-sector executives, while such tendencies were thought to be even stronger in Hungary (Frydman *et al.*, 1996, p. 5). Perceptions that major portions of the former communist elite have perpetuated their power in the new democracies underlie the continuing strength of sentiments of anti-communism and demands for the passage of legislation to provide for *lustration* – in other words, the banning of former power-holders and police informants from contemporary positions of authority. While early lustration measures in Czechoslovakia produced considerable controversy and provoked Western charges that civil rights were being infringed, the issue refuses to go away and screening laws were introduced in both Hungary and Poland under the postcommunist governments (Druker, 1997, pp. 8–9).

A number of characteristics of political life in contemporary East-Central Europe also point to the existence of significant elements of the *particularism* identified by democratisation theorists as a proble-matic factor in the consolidation of new democracies (O'Donnell, 1996, pp. 40–5). The role of personality in the exercise of key leadership roles has always been an important feature in various forms of political system, but particularism is a more basic threat to the development or survival of democratic practices to the extent that it involves the dominance of individuals and private interests over institutions and formal procedures (especially if both are yet to be fully institutionalised). Such tendencies are by no means dominant in East-Central Europe, but they are certainly prominent in Slovakia. The resurgence of postcommunist forces, similarly, does not raise any particular questions about the democratisation process in that the new social democrats (or democratic socialists) have won power by electoral means (although doubts have risen on the margins of the process – for example, Polish president Kwasniewski's failure to declare his wife's commercial interests or his forgetful claim to an educational qualification he did not quite achieve). More serious doubts arise about the financial links of the reformed politicians with the newly privatised sector. The supposed bankruptcy of the Polish Social Democracy in the face of rising claims concerning the disputed assets of the former Workers' Party is again a case in point. Related *affaires* and scandals are also emerging in Hungary, although these by no means exclusively concern the Socialist Party (Lewis, 1998). But all this may be relatively small beer compared to the forms of personalism and levels of corruption seen in apparently established democracies such as Italy and Japan. If the world of consolidated democracies can embrace such disparate behaviour, there are probably few grounds as yet to question the credentials of the new democracies of East-Central Europe in this respect.

3

The Balkans: Bulgaria, Romania, Albania and the Former Yugoslavia

TOM GALLAGHER

Bulgaria, Romania, Albania and all or most of the former Yugoslavia comprise an area of south-eastern Europe known as the Balkans. It is one where the implantation of democracy has faced long-term obstacles much greater than those encountered by the countries of Central and Eastern Europe. Foreign invasions and occupations stunted the development of indigenous institutions (other than the Orthodox Church) and hampered the development of Western concepts of individual freedom. The long Ottoman subjugation and the resultant wars between the Ottoman empire and rival powers caused many population shifts, both voluntary and involuntary. The complex distribution of languages, religions, and nationalities meant that the Balkans was an ethnographic mosaic which made orderly government difficult to sustain, whatever type of political system was in place.

The first engagement with democracy proved to be a brief and inglorious one after existing Balkan states increased their territory or else were founded in the years before or after World War I following the retreat of imperial powers from the region. Weak states found it difficult to integrate populations divided not only by ethnicity, but by sharp social and economic inequalities. No indigenous, commercially-orientated middle class committed to open political institutions and the rule of law emerged to act as a bulwark for democratic government. The economic fragility of states reliant on the export of a limited range of primary products, and at the mercy of global terms of trade they were unable to influence, was clear even before the onset of

TABLE 3.1   *Basic data: the Balkans, 1996*

	Population (million)	Area (sq. km)	GDP growth (%)	Inflation rate (%)	Av. monthly income (US$)
Albania	3,429	28,750	8.5	17.4	60
Bulgaria	8,487	110,994	−9.0	311.0	50−60
Croatia	4,800	56,538	4.1	3.0−4.0	397
Macedonia	2,075	25,713	1.5	3.0	222
Romania	22,680	237,500	4.5	57.0	145
Serbia	11,101	102,350	5.0	100.0	123
Slovenia	1,990	20,251	3.5	8.0	626

the Great Depression of the 1930s. If they had not been swept away already, disorderly and often corrupt semi-democracies were soon replaced across the region by royal, military or civilian dictatorships.

But the pre-war failure of democracy occurred not just because of unpropitious circumstances, inadequate leadership, or socioeconomic dislocation. There were deeper factors at work which still had a powerful resonance in much of the region sixty years later. Traditions of individual freedom were weak. The word freedom meant freedom from foreign control not the right of the individual to dissent from the government or majority opinion. Many citizens were unaware of their rights or afraid to exercise them. This was not merely because the weakness of democratic institutions gave them few opportunities to act as citizens.

Collective values were paramount which downgraded the status of the individual as a free subject and made him or her subject to group authority. The Orthodox Church (where a tradition of resistance to despotic rule was weak) and the state itself promoted a patriarchal authority which emphasised group values and demeaned individual ones. Combined with the legacy of centuries of oppressive foreign rule, it is not surprising that low political expectations and a submissive mentality before the state were common features in south-eastern Europe before the onset of communist rule in the 1940s.

Balkan Communism

At first sight, the overwhelmingly agrarian and traditional societies of the Balkans were stony ground for political and economic systems inspired by Marxism-Leninism; the industrial proletariat and bourgeoisie, classes supposed to act as the seedbeds of socialism, were hardly in existence. But it suited the new ruling class to start from scratch and be the architect of a new industrial order. The communists did not have to contend with strong social-democratic traditions as in Central and Eastern Europe and it would be much easier to transform society in the image of the Soviet model. The absence of ingrained traditions of resistance to despotism was also beneficial. It enabled communists to acquire control despite a numerical weakness everywhere except in Bulgaria and parts of Yugoslavia. The ruthless way in which the old order was swept aside, and the intensity of the social engineering which followed, stemmed from the need for what had usually been miniscule political sects to establish their total power.

The strength of collectivist values aided Balkan communists in their task. The Orthodox Church, with its tradition of acquiescence to the ruling power, was far less of a headache than Western Christian churches in Poland or later East Germany. Overall, the communist era strengthened aspects of Balkan political culture inimical to democracy-building. In particular, after an interval of internationalism on Soviet terms, it allowed nationalism to be rehabilitated and adopted to suit local communist requirements. The appeal to nationalism made ruthless social engineering policies less intolerable than they might otherwise have been. It enabled the ruling elite to depict the industrialisation drive as the culmination of the struggle for independence. It also provided a cover for the retention of Stalinism and enabled communist hardliners to enjoy a longer tenure of power than in much of Central and Eastern Europe. The manipulation of nationalism also required autonomy from the Soviet Union which, to varying degrees, was won everywhere except in Bulgaria. The idea of the state as the preserve of the majority ethnic group was not long in following, especially in Romania (Gallagher, 1995, pp. 54–70). The revival of pre-1945 inter-state rivalries, and the ill-treatment of minorities, were other dismal features of the rise of hardline national communism which would outlast the communist era.

Yugoslavia under Marshal Tito (1945–80) seemed an exception to these trends. An ambitious and increasingly complex form of federalism was meant to subsume ethnic and regional differences in a common Yugoslav socialist identity. Restrictions on personal freedom were much less apparent than elsewhere and concessions to capitalism were made that were unique in the communist world. But despite the rhetoric of 'worker self-management', Yugoslavia still retained the Soviet command economy as a model and the interests hostile to reform that were associated with it. The cult of personality around Tito was reminiscent of the cults surrounding other Balkan autocrats. Also, conflicts with neighbouring states were relaunched to reinforce internal unity which was soon shown to be fragile after Tito's death in 1980.

The nature of the transition from communism in the Balkans differed from that which occurred elsewhere in the Soviet bloc. An imposed transition from above was attempted by resourceful elements of the communist elite which largely abandoned the Marxist ideology but tried to retain a monopoly of power. Between 1989 and 1992 tentative democracies replaced one-party rule as ex-communist 're-formers' or 'modernisers' replaced Stalinist nationalists. In Yugoslavia, the reverse happened as a process of re-Stalinisation occurred in Serbia, the key republic in the federation, which quickly led to the break-up of the entire state.

The attempt of nimble communists to institute a form of post-communism that fell short of liberal democracy had contrasting outcomes, but it should not be seen as a desperate last-ditch strategy. It had important factors working in its support. Interest groups and the forces of civil society committed to a complete break with the communist past were initially very weak. Major social formations, above all the state bureaucracy, endorsed this survival formula and rallied behind any ruler who seemed capable of defending their privileges in uncertain times. There were no major international pressures to contend with; the Balkans were seen as peripheral to the interests of the Atlantic democracies and Western indifference certainly played a major indirect role in ensuring that the power-struggles in Yugoslavia would quickly dissolve into horrific bloodshed. Soon, examples, not just from the Balkans, would show that ex-communists could win elections by stressing egalitarian themes. Moreover, large segments of the *nomenklatura* could acquire considerable wealth by diverting state resources into their own hands through various bogus efforts at privatisation.

Ex-communist attempts to shape the new political order enjoyed varying degrees of success. In Romania and Serbia, individuals with roots in the communist system largely shaped the transition in accordance with their own limited agenda. In Bulgaria, neither ex-communists nor their centre-right opponents were strong enough to prevail in 1990–1 but, by 1994, the former communists had won an outright parliamentary majority and were soon following anti-reform policies associated with Serbia and Romania. In Albania, the communist establishment fragmented surprisingly quickly in 1991–2 as it was overwhelmed by the scale of popular unrest. The Albanian experience suggests that there is no automatic correlation between the intensity of Stalinism and the subsequent weakness of non-communist forces. As for the successor states of ex-Yugoslavia, they do not merit consideration at this stage because they were not fully independent until 1991–2, but continuities and discontinuities with the past will be noted later.

Across much of the Balkans, former communists took remarkably similar steps to preserve their authority in the context of nascent democratisation. Early elections were announced before any opposition forces could properly organise themselves. Renewed efforts were made to manipulate nationalism. Control of state resources, especially the media, enabled the government to exploit popular fears about ethnic minorities or foreign interference. The innate conservatism of elderly and middle-aged voters who had been subjected to two generations of indoctrination along Marxist collectivist lines was a great advantage. In Serbia and Romania, a plethora of different parties was discreetly organised by those in power to spread confusion among the electorate and make it difficult for their chief centre-right opponents to stand out as a real governing alternative. To be absolutely sure of success, lower-echelon regime officials or enthusiastic supporters directed intimidation and violence against their opponents. This was particularly the case in Romania, where in May 1990 the first of the Balkan elections was held. A party system based on polarised pluralism emerged which would be the harbinger of others in Bulgaria, Albania, and Serbia.

In each of these countries, the opposition refused to recognise the legitimacy of elections which it had lost. Cooperation in drawing up new constitutions or surmounting major political hurdles failed to materialise. No pacts were arranged in which rival political forces combined to work out ground-rules for installing pluralist institutions. But, in at least two states, Bulgaria and newly-founded Macedonia, consensual figures elected as president, the former dissident Zhelu Zhelev and the former communist official, Kiro Gligorov, were able to prevent or minimise confrontation.

Agreement about the management of political competition is essential if nascent democracies are not to be tested beyond endurance by heavily adversarial parties. In Romania, between February 1990 and September 1991 President Iliescu relied upon coalminers to act as a praetorian guard prepared to disperse first his anti-communist foes and then drive his own prime minister from office after the two men had quarrelled over the pace of political reform. In Albania, between 1994 and 1997, secret policemen recruited from President Sali Berisha's home area were used to intimidate and terrorise all those who opposed his increasingly repressive rule, and the opposition leader, Fatos Nano, was jailed for eight years on flimsy embezzlement charges. Serbia's main opposition leader, Vuk Draskovic, was beaten up by police in 1993, while an armed criminal like Zeljko Raznjatovic (Arkan) enjoyed immunity from prosecution and a seat in parliament. Coercive measures taken against prominent opponents were thus a common reflex of illiberal Balkan leaders.

In Yugoslavia, uncontrolled political warfare between aspirants for power would lead to the dissolution of the state in less than five years (1987–91). The Communist Party in Serbia, renamed the Socialist Party of Serbia (SPS) in 1990, attempted to recentralise Yugoslavia around its Serbian core after the removal of a significant number of moderate Serbs from the leadership and the takeover of the autonomous provinces of Kosovo and Vojvodina. The 'Greater Serbia' project provoked a nationalist upsurge in Croatia and Slovenia where declarations of sovereignty, backed by popular majorities in referenda, were made in 1990. Multi-party elections were held in all of the republics at different times, the last taking place in Serbia on 28 September and Macedonia in November–December 1990. Slobodan Milosevic, Serbia's hardline leader, agreed with his fellow ex-communist leaders in Croatia and Slovenia, Ivica Racan and Milan Kucan, that under no circumstances were federal elections to be held. Federal elections might have resulted in a transnational coalition of forces committed to a looser and democratic Yugoslav confederation. Ante Markovic, the popular federal premier of Yugoslavia, actively canvassed such a solution in 1990. Instead, separate elections in the individual republics guaranteed the victory of nationalist parties of differing hues and the slide to war accelerated (Denitch, 1994, pp. 67–8).

The Politics of Elections

Between 1990 and 1991, ex-communists, either retaining some commitment to egalitarian ideas or else publicly breaking with the communist heritage, were elected president everywhere in the Balkans apart from Bulgaria and Bosnia. With the exception (again) of Bulgaria and of Slovenia, the presidency enjoyed considerable influence over other branches of government and, almost without exception, there were attempts to augment presidential power in ways that undermined democracy.

In Albania and Croatia, the principle of a separation of powers was repudiated by two right-wing presidents anxious to disguise previous roles as successful communist officials. In 1994, Sali Berisha sought and failed to obtain popular approval in a referendum for an Albanian constitution that would give him sweeping powers. A year later, Croatia's Franjo Tudjman failed to obtain the two-thirds parliamentary majority that would enhance his power, but this did not stop him setting up a 300-strong Presidential Council which acted as a tame alternative parliament. In both states the independent media found itself under mounting pressure (especially when it criticised the Head of State), the judiciary was prevented from defending citizens' rights, and the secret police was increasingly a law unto itself. Moreover, unreliable public officials were purged on the pretext of making vital savings in public expenditure, or else (as in Romania) officials were obliged to convert themselves into loyalists of the ruling party.

There were compelling reasons why illiberal presidents felt the need to control institutions such as the media, the judiciary, the public administration, and the secret police. The presidents of Albania, Croatia and, not least, Serbia, were building up their own economic power bases in the first half of the 1990s and they were reluctant to allow the process of wealth accumulation either for themselves, or for their political allies, to be subject to scrutiny. In each country, family

TABLE 3.2 *Croatian parliamentary elections, held in two stages, October and November 1995*

	Votes (%)	Seats (no.)
Croatian Democratic Union (HDZ)	45.2	52.5
Joint list bloc (coalition of centrist and regional parties)	18.3	20.0
Croatian Social Liberal Party (HSLS)	11.5	12.5
Others	25.0	15.0

members, close allies, and reliable party hacks were allowed to take charge of important areas of the economy. In Serbia, where sultanistic rule extended furthest, the collapsing economy became a giant government cartel in which the president's wife and her cronies controlled the trade departments that granted (for a suitable payment) import and export licences (Borger, 1996).

Nearly everywhere, privatisation of lucrative areas of the economy, particularly in the retail sector, converted political power and connections into instant wealth. New oligarchies emerged which benefited directly from presidential patronage. In Serbia, the economic spoils were grabbed by ex-*nomenklatura* figures and war profiteers as well as organised criminals; in Croatia, right-wing emigres who had financed Tudjman's rise to power, combined with ex-communists and racketeers to divert much of the country's wealth into their hands; in Albania, supporters drawn from the president's home area in the north were slotted into positions of economic and political power. When a head of state tried to prevent the rise of kleptocracy, he could run into problems, as in the case of Macedonia's Kiro Gligorov who, in 1995, nearly lost his life in a car-bomb explosion widely believed to have been caused by disgruntled mafia elements.

In Romania, President Iliescu refrained from cracking down on the private media or accumulating unearned wealth. He was well aware that Romania remained in the spotlight after the excesses of the Ceausescu dictatorship (1965–89) and that agencies monitoring the country's uneven transition to democracy were closely following his record. But in Croatia, Tudjman was able to ride out international criticism by trading on Croatia's image as a victim of Serbian aggression and by winning the sponsorship of powerful interests in Germany (even though, by the end of the 1991–5 wars in Yugoslavia, systematic abuses of human rights carried out by forces answerable to Tudjman were approaching in scale those that Milosevic had sponsored next door in Serbia).

Given the abuses of power described above, only a small step was required to interfere with the electoral process and this happened with increasing frequency across the Balkans as the 1990s wore on. In Romania, there was strong evidence of systematic electoral manipulation, involving multiple voting, which in 1992 gave the president's party and their nationalist allies a narrow edge (Carey, 1995). In Albania, the Organisation for Security and Cooperation in Europe (OSCE) protested that the 1996 poll had been stolen by the ruling Democratic Party (Schmidt, 1996) and instabilities continued until further elections had been held in 1997. In Croatia, Croats from Herzegovina were allowed to vote in the 1995 elections although they were citizens of a neighbouring state. This assured the ruling Croatian Democratic Union (HDZ) of 10 per cent of seats in advance. Tudjman's opponents captured Zagreb in simultaneous municipal elections, but the president refused to allow the capital to elect a mayor who would oppose state policy, and imposed his own nominee. A diplomat was quoted as saying that the dispute was about patronage and power: 'the ruling party has made a lot of money from the privatisation of state property. Tudjman is not about to turn over the city administration, that can monitor these sales, to his opponents' (Traynor, 1995).

The Culture of Nationalism

The postcommunist leaders of the Balkans have often found nationalism to be an effective means of silencing criticism about their methods of rule. Appeals to national sentiment have been a favoured device far beyond the Balkans, especially where politicians with a poor governing record need the endorsement of voters to remain in office. In the communist era, tactics of nationalist manipulation were refined, especially in countries like Romania and Bulgaria where officials were sometimes selected and promoted on ethnic rather than on meritocratic or even ideological grounds. As the region haltingly embraced pluralism, it proved a durable tactic for a number of reasons.

Political culture remained shaped by nationalist values, especially in states which had languished under foreign rule and whose independence had been shown to be precarious in the 1914–45 period. Communist social engineering created social groups which were receptive to simplistic nationalist appeals. The key one was the new working class drawn from landless peasantry, especially when it was located in failing heavy industries. National communist parties in Serbia and Romania (the Serbian Radical Party of Vojislav Seselj and the Party of Romanian National Unity of Gheorghe Funar) were able to exploit the fears and rural nostalgia of a social formation which is likely to be a problematic factor in the consolidation of democracy even in states which have avoided ethnic polarisation. Finally, there were various ethnic disputes over education provisions or voting rights for minorities, or autonomy demands, which polarised states along ethnic lines and harmed inter-state relations, ones which unscrupulous leaders did not hesitate to exploit for their own ends.

A glance at the politics of the region from 1990 to 1997 shows how nationalism was used and abused in different ways. In Serbia, wars of expansion in neighbouring territories were engineered by Milosevic between 1990 and 1993, years when he believed that the cultivation of radical nationalism could secure his hold on power. Two self-proclaimed Serb states emerged in Croatia and Bosnia in 1991 and 1992 whose goal was to unite with Serbia proper after the expulsion of most non-Serb residents. Greater Serbia was conceived by Milosevic in 1991 as a state that would include Serbia, Montenegro, up to one-third of Croatia, more than half of Bosnia-Herzegovina, and possibly some of the Republic of Macedonia. It was seen as necessary on the grounds that the break-up of Yugoslavia was turning the Serbs of Croatia and Bosnia into minorities likely to face persecution in newly independent states. However, the Serb revolts were prepared, under Milosevic's supervision, well in advance of formal declarations of independence in Croatia and Bosnia. Borislav Jovic, a former President of Yugoslavia and a close ally of Milosevic during the latter's rise to power, made damaging allegations about his ex-chief's role in memoirs published in 1996 (Borger, 1997).

In Croatia, Milosevic's expansionist strategy was imitated by Tudjman. The persecution of Serbs living in the unoccupied parts of Croatia and the expulsion of the Serbs of Krajina in 1995 undermined Croatia's bid to be recognised as an integral part of 'enlightened' Central and Western Europe. Instead, Tudjman's state emerged as one of the most virulent examples of Balkan intolerance. The Croatian leader was a true nationalist believer whereas Milosevic was an arch-manipulator of nationalism who was prepared to abandon the tactic when it ceased to earn political dividends. Tudjman's bid to grab large parts of Bosnia-Herzegovina was thwarted by the USA in 1994 but he encouraged Bosnian Croat hardliners to keep their para-state of Herzeg-Bosnia intact and allowed the mixed city of Mostar to remain in the hands of gangsters who defied the representatives of the EU entrusted with rebuilding the city.

In Romania and Bulgaria, politically well-organised Hungarian and Muslim minorities were harassed to different degrees by the ruling ex-communists in order to appease nationalist lobbies. The spotlight on the 'illegitimate' actions of minorities was meant to deflect criticism about the way that the ruling party had acquired and consolidated power in 1989–90. It was an unsuccessful tactic in

Bulgaria given the shortlived duration of ex-communist rule (1990–1, 1994–7). But it was more effective in Romania where the support of ultra-nationalists kept Iliescu in office until 1996 despite huge policy failures (Gallagher, 1996).

In Macedonia and Slovenia, the post-independence leaderships avoided nationalist extravagance but a sense of national pride was promoted in order to play down internal weaknesses and the difficult process of state-building. The postures struck in inculcating national identity led to serious friction with powerful neighbours Greece and Italy which obstructed the efforts of the former to obtain backing from the EU and the United Nations. Finally, in Albania, Berisha sought international approval for his regime by restraining Albanian nationalists in neighbouring Kosovo and Macedonia where large Albanian communities had grievances against the state authorities. But as his rule became tyrannical, its xenophobic tone increased, culminating in the blocking of broadcasts by the BBC and American stations early in 1997, and it was swept from office in June 1997 with just 25.7 per cent of the vote; the postcommunist Socialist Party won 52.7 per cent and formed a new administration.

Continuing Crises of Legitimacy

Balkan leaderships which linked their fortunes with ambitious nationalist programmes were left vulnerable when these fell far short of success. This was true of the two main states to emerge from Yugoslavia, Serbia and Croatia.

The Greater Serbia project, intended to be swiftly accomplished in 1991–2, instead invited severe economic sanctions. By 1995, when they were lifted by the UN, industrial output had been cut by two-thirds, a country of ten million people had only one million left in formal jobs and another one million were on forced holidays: they remained on the payroll but got little or no pay. A new elite (about 5 per cent of the population) emerged from war profiteers and mafia elements who had benefited from sanctions. Another 20 per cent lived comfortably – police, officials linked to the ruling SPS, and those with relatives abroad (Steele, 1995). But the rest of the population endured miserable conditions, life being especially bleak for Serb refugees from Croatia and Bosnia, the chief Serb victims of Milosevic's failed expansionist drive.

In Croatia, mistakes by Tudjman in the early 1990s partly contributed to the temporary loss of one-third of Croatian territory. Living standards and economic output plummeted, as much the same parasitic elements as in Serbia benefited from dubious privatisations and an economy given over to speculation and the trafficking of illicit goods. Elections held in 1995, shortly after the recovery of most of the lost territory, resulted only in meagre gains for the HDZ despite gross manipulation of the electoral register.

In the Balkan facade democracies, capitalists with a background in the *nomenklatura* were the chief beneficiaries of a flawed and ill-planned lurch towards the semblance of a market economy. Often the new economic oligarchy enjoyed a privileged relationship with the regime which enabled tycoons to evade taxes and to profit from the black economy with the complicity of very senior officials. The catastrophic policy failures of the communist era were thus compounded by short-term and sometimes ruinous actions in the economic sphere by postcommunist elites. In addition, Bulgaria and Romania were particularly hard hit by the loss of key markets and energy supplies arising from the Gulf conflict of 1991 and the crisis in ex-Yugoslavia.

Economic failure had a devastating effect on living and health standards across much of the region, forcing millions of people who had hitherto enjoyed a secure income into outright poverty by the late 1990s. Even those with savings but sometimes only a rudimentary knowledge of how capitalism worked, were at the mercy of savage economic forces. Private bank failures in Romania and Bulgaria robbed hundreds of thousands of their savings. Governments were slow to pass legislation protecting consumers and, as in the case of Albania, were sometimes enmeshed with financial racketeers; in Albania the collapse of pyramid schemes – pseudo-banks based on fraud or organised crime that offer astronomical rates of interest – contributed to a mass uprising in the south of the country early in 1997 that destroyed the authority of the Berisha regime.

In 1996–7 much of the region was shaken by large-scale protests as citizens rose up against governments whose nationalist posturing or promises of social protection had earlier been attractive, but whose record of misrule had deprived them of much of their remaining legitimacy. The scale of the demonstrations, certainly in Bulgaria and Serbia, evoked parallels with the mass protests in East Germany and Czechoslovakia in 1989 and suggested that 'people power' might be enjoying a late flowering in Balkan states where power was draining from failed elites.

In Serbia, a Milosevic regime which had abandoned nationalism to secure the backing of the United States was increasingly fragile as a result of multiple policy failures. Demonstrations over electoral fraud at the end of 1996 spread to industrial workers and much of the middle class which had hitherto remained on the political sidelines. The liberal nationalist opposition was, for the first time, transformed into a credible force which secured important concessions in February 1997. Milosevic relaxed his grip on the state media and allowed the opposition Zajedno alliance to gain control of town halls in the main cities. In Croatia, attempts by the government to acquire a monopoly of the media provoked huge protests in late 1996; Tudjman's regime had become increasingly isolated abroad and there was uncertainty about the future on account of the president's failing health.

Two other Balkan states witnessed a peaceful change of regime against a background of economic crisis and a failure of nerve on the part of ruling ex-communists. In Bulgaria, the Bulgarian Socialist Party (BSP), re-elected with an absolute majority in 1994 after several years of minority cabinets, pursued reckless policies that led to economic collapse. Bread shortages, the collapse of the currency, and the revelation that mafia elements enjoyed close access to government leaders provoked huge demonstrations. In January 1997 the BSP abandoned office and agreed to the main opposition demand of early elections. These were convincingly won in April of that year by the centre-right Union of Democratic Forces.

TABLE 3.3 *Bulgarian parliamentary elections of 19 April 1997*

	Votes (%)	Seats (no.)
Union of Democratic Forces (SDS)	52.2	57.1
Bulgarian Socialist Party (BSP)	22.0	23.7
The Alliance for National Salvation (pro-monarchist) in conjunction with the Movement for Rights and Freedom (ethnic Turkish)	7.6	8.3
The Euro-Left Party	5.6	5.8
Bulgarian Business Bloc	4.7	5.4

In Romania, a sinking economy which had been mismanaged by the ex-communists who had allowed financial speculators to amass huge wealth while living standards plummeted was the background against which a peaceful transfer of power took place in 1996. President Iliescu and the ruling party were defeated in presidential and parliamentary elections. A genuine contest for power, which many thought impossible in Romania's flawed democracy, saw the triumph of the reformist Democratic Convention.

TABLE 3.4   *Romanian parliamentary elections of 3 November 1996 (lower house)*

	Votes (%)	Seats (no.)
Romanian Democratic Convention (CDR) (alliance of the National Peasant and Christian Democratic Party and smaller formations)	30.2	35.8
Party of Romanian Social Democracy (PDSR) (President Iliescu's support group)	21.5	26.7
Social Democratic Union (alliance of Democratic Party and smaller group)	12.9	15.5
Democratic Union of Hungarians in Romania (UDMR)	6.6	7.3
Others	28.8	10.9

Towards A Stable Postcommunist Order?

Simultaneous outbreaks of unrest revived the favoured cliche of the Balkans as a dangerous powderkeg. But there are some indications that the region is moving beyond the grey zone of postcommunism towards more responsible rule.

Ordinary citizens abandoned a stance of apathetic disengagement to politics and were prominent in the street protests. Except in Albania, where the prospect of mass impoverishment licensed mass anarchy, anti-government protests were usually controlled and peaceful. These were not spasmodic explosions of rage of the kind which occur in repressive states after the lid on the political pressure-cooker has been lifted. The response of the authorities was moderate (although in Serbia the state would dearly like to have used coercion), behaviour which denotes a self-limiting state prepared to acknowledge boundaries to its authority. Compromises were reached between government and opposition forces in Bulgaria and Serbia but in Albania only after the country had slid into anarchy.

Inter-ethnic conflict was not a feature of the 1996–7 unrest and beleaguered elites were unable to scatter their opponents by invoking core ethnic loyalties. Indeed the manipulation of nationalism by ex-communists was already failing as an effective control strategy. Its limitations were revealed by Milosevic's retreat from this stance. In Romania, Iliescu's incompetent handling of nationalism hastened his departure from office and the 1996 poll was notable for being free of chauvinist appeals. But unresolved ethnic disputes in Macedonia and Kosovo where restive Albanian communities are pitted against politically dominant South Slavs raise the possibility that ethnic tensions could flare up in either territory.

In Serbia the demand of protesters was for political liberalism and the removal of an amoral leadership which had sacked the country for its own sectional ends. Elsewhere, the motor of change has been the economy. The dismal record of governments which pay lip-service to economic reform while presiding over policy failures and the plundering of the state fuelled protests in Bulgaria and Albania. In Romania, it was economic misrule which caused urban workers to switch to the centre-right opposition in 1996. Ex-communist *apparatchiks* were replaced by a government of the pre-1945 parties, civic leaders, and the Hungarian minority party.

Radical economic reforms launched in Romania during 1997 and proposed for Bulgaria after the April elections were widely seen as the first genuine engagement with capitalism in the Balkans. Popular reactions to austerity measures suggest a willingness to endure further hardships if it leads to the dismantling of economic and political structures inherited from communist times and a relaunch of national institutions along Western lines. But the enormous spread and depth of economic decline in the region during 1990–7 exceeds in magnitude the catastrophe that engulfed the capitalist economies during the Great Depression and there are few examples of infant democracies withstanding unaided the economic and social hardships being faced in the Balkans.

The level of international support for reformist forces entering government after the damaging postcommunist era will probably determine their chances of success. Targeted assistance in the Balkans to help reformist governments improve national infrastructure and mitigate the pain of economic shock therapy will probably be more

beneficial for European security than an emphasis on NATO enlargement or bringing closer the mirage of EU expansion towards the
east.

The region is not a monolith. While it is still weighed down by the
legacies of foreign rule, the strength of collectivist values, and the
damaging effects of Stalinism, the upheavals of the post-1989 era have
resulted in different outcomes. Communist-led transitions aided by
the manipulation of ethnic tension succeeded in Serbia, Croatia, and
Romania but largely failed in Bulgaria and Macedonia. Power-
struggles between ex-communist and non-socialist forces saw the left
repulsed in Albania and Bulgaria where it had been expected that the
communists would retain their grip because of the monolithic character of their rule before 1989. Bulgaria and eventually Romania also
managed to bury traditions of political violence and secure peaceful
substitutions in office. Montenegro, associated with Serbia, showed
signs of restlessness in 1997 as it elected a president keen to build
bridges with the West. Meanwhile, opposition disunity enabled
Milosevic to regain the initiative in Serbia. But the disastrous state
of the economy, the miserable condition of much of the population,
and renewed unrest in Kosovo are likely to prevent this most resilient
of Europe's unrepentant communists from stabilising his rule in the
longer term.

So the Balkans is undeserving of the stereotypical treatment it
obtains in the media and even academic analysis. However, the scale
of its problems – the gulf between state and society, the continuing
role of the politics of ethnicity, and the desperate condition of the
regional economy and social infrastructure – means that there is no
prospect of its fragile engagement with democracy being consolidated
in the forseeable future.

4

In the Shadow of Moscow: Ukraine, Moldova and the Baltic Republics

SARAH BIRCH

The collapse of the Soviet Union in 1991 left in its wake fifteen independent countries that, like their neighbours in Central Europe, have had to face the double challenge of simultaneous economic and political reforms. Yet the former Soviet republics – along with the Yugoslav and Czechoslovak successors – have been confronted with an additional task: the establishment of the institutional infrastructure of independent states. This third project takes logical and temporal priority over the other two: the geographical and civic boundaries of a polity must be defined before any significant reforms can be undertaken in the political and economic domains. But the problems associated with state-building have also interacted in complex ways with democratisation and marketisation. This chapter will analyse the dual trajectories of state-building and reform with reference to five of the newly-independent states on the western fringe of the former Soviet empire: Ukraine, Moldova, and the Baltic republics of Estonia, Latvia, and Lithuania.

In contrast to Belarus, all five countries have managed to establish independent polities in which rulers are chosen by means of competitive election. But all have also encountered significant obstacles to democratisation as a result of difficulties in defining the relationship between the state and the different ethnic groups that inhabit it, as well as the position of the state in the geopolitical configuration of the region. The relative stabilisation of the political systems in all five countries – notwithstanding remaining ambiguity as to the status of

59

TABLE 4.1 *Basic data: the post-Soviet states, 1996*

	Population (millions)	*Area (sq. km)*	*GDP growth (%)*	*Inflation rate (%)*	*Av. monthly income (US$)*	*Unemployment (%)*
Estonia	1.467	45,000	1.8–2.0	14.8	246	4.1
Latvia	2.485	64,610	2.5 (est.)	13.1	179	7.1
Lithuania	3.709	65,200	3.6	13.1	173	6.2
Ukraine	50.853	603,700	−10.0	40.0	80	12.0
Moldova	4.300	33,700	−10.0 (est.)	15.1	42 (1995)	1–2

the self-proclaimed 'Dniester Republic' in Moldova – bears witness to their ability to use the tools of democracy to forge solutions to political problems. The comparison with Belarus is instructive, for it may be, paradoxically, that the clearer definition of ethnic and regional orientation in the five states under consideration here has created an objective need for democratic structures of interest articulation and intermediation which is not the case in their more Russified neighbour. The internal divisions in Ukraine, Moldova, and the Baltics have led to disagreements, but efforts to resolve them have at the same time served to validate political competition and negotiation as mechanisms of conflict resolution.

This is not to imply that these states are all well on their way to democratic consolidation, however, for democratisation does not simply involve popular participation in decision-making and open competition for power; it also requires the establishment of a rule of law. While all five polities have had a degree of success in achieving the first two goals, they have been beset with difficulties in realising the third. The main threat to democracy in the former Soviet republics lies in the ability of people at all levels of the political system to manipulate or circumvent democratically validated decision-making procedures. A facade of orderly elections and economic liberalisation covers a host of irregularities, ranging from administrative incompetence to the worst forms of corruption. Consensus as to the shape institutional structures should take is certainly a prerequisite of successful institutionalisation, but it is not a sufficient condition, and regularisation of political and economic systems is the most urgent task currently facing the region.

Historical Background and the Break-Up of the Soviet Union

The countries on the western fringe of the Soviet Union had long been borderlands between great powers; indeed the very word Ukraine means 'on the edge'. From the middle ages onwards these lands were passed from empire to empire with the ebb and flow of conquest. They had for all or most of the nineteenth century been part of the Russian Empire, with the exception of western Ukraine, which remained part of Austro-Hungary and its successor states until 1939.

One of the characteristic features of the borderlands has been ethnic heterogeneity, accompanied by geographical and occupational differentiation along ethnic lines. Ethnic Estonians, Latvians, Lithuanians, Ukrainians, and Moldovans were and continue to be the dominant ethnic groups in rural, agricultural areas, while Russians, Poles, Jews and Germans long made up the bulk of the urban population. With modernisation and industrialisation starting in the late nineteenth century and accelerating under Soviet rule, urban migration brought the native ethnic groups to the cities. But incorporation into the Soviet Union resulted also in the migration of Russians and other Soviet peoples to the western fringe, partly as a result of Soviet industrialisation and cultural integration polices, and partly due to the attractiveness of the more Westernised borderlands to people from lands further east. Most such immigrants settled in urban areas, preserving the ethnic geography specific to the region.

All five countries gained some form of statehood in the aftermath of World War I, though only the three Baltic republics survived as independent states throughout the inter-war period. Lack of Western support for Ukrainian self-determination allowed the incorporation of eastern Ukraine into the Soviet Union in 1920 and the western part of the country into Poland in 1918, while the Moldovans themselves voted in 1918 to join Romania, with which they have strong cultural and historic ties. The Baltics, Moldova, and western Ukraine were all allocated to the Soviet sphere of influence in 1939 under the Molotov–Ribbentrop pact, were all invaded by Soviet forces in 1939 or 1940, were all taken by the Germans in 1941, and were all definitively annexed by the Soviet Union in 1944. The fate of Moldova and western Ukraine were accepted with relative equanimity by the West, but annexation of the Baltics was never officially recognised by the United States and other Western powers, in view of a formal renunciation of Soviet claims on the region made in 1920. During the post-World War II period, many native residents of the Soviet Union's newly acquired lands emigrated west and many others were deported to the east, resulting in massive losses of life. There was guerrilla resistance to Soviet rule well into the 1950s in the Baltics and western Ukraine, and these were the areas in which incipient nationalist movements were most active in the 1960s.

During the Soviet period, the republics on the western fringe were the most culturally Westernised, the most economically developed (with the exception of heavily agricultural Moldova) and they enjoyed the highest standard of living in the Soviet Union (see Schroeder, 1990). Their liminal position also afforded their inhabitants the greatest amount of contact with countries further west, contact that was further facilitated by historical and cultural ties. Access to Polish broadcasting kept the residents of western Ukraine abreast of the dramatic political changes that occurred in Poland in the 1980s (see Chapter 2), while the residents of northern Estonia (including the capital, Tallinn) could view events from a Western perspective on Finnish television. It is thus no coincidence that the Soviet Union's western republics led the drive for republican autonomy starting in the late 1980s.

Despite these historical and geographical similarities, there is considerable variation across the region in size, ethnic composition, and economic structure. Moldova and the Baltic states are small by European standards. At 4.3 million, Moldova's population is less than some of neighbouring Ukraine's regions, and the Baltic states have among them a population of under eight million. Ukraine, by contrast, has 51 million inhabitants and a territory that stretches over thirteen hundred kilometres from Central Europe to just west of the Caucasus. The five countries also vary considerably in their ethnic composition. In Estonia and Moldova, the titular groups (those which correspond to the name of the country) comprise under two-thirds of the population, while Latvians make up only a bare majority of the population in their republic. In Ukraine and Lithuania, by contrast, the titular groups constitute approximately four-fifths of the total. Yet the ethnic situation in Ukraine is unlike that in the other states, as there is a cultural and linguistic continuum between the two largest ethnic groups – Ukrainian and Russian – making precise delineation difficult, and it is estimated that about half the Ukrainian population speaks Russian as a language of preference (Arel and Khmelko, 1996).

There is also considerable diversity in the cultural heritage of the most prominent groups in each country. Estonians and Latvians are traditionally Lutheran, while Lithuanians and many western Ukrainians are Catholic; by contrast, eastern Ukrainians, Moldovans, and Russians in all countries come from an Orthodox tradition. In linguistic terms, Ukrainians and Russians speak East Slavic languages, to which Lithuanian and Latvian are distantly related. Estonians, on the other hand, speak a language closer to Finnish, while the language spoken by most Moldovans is a dialect of Romanian (though whether or not 'Moldovan' constitutes a separate language is a subject of ongoing political controversy). Finally, the economic structures of the countries in question differ significantly. The Baltics were the most highly developed of all the Soviet republics, whereas Moldova was more agricultural than most, despite rapid industrialisation during the Soviet period. Ukraine's fertile land has made it a natural agricultural region as well, yet due to the intensive development of heavy industry, especially in the east of the country, over a third of the Soviet Union's giant military-industrial complex was located there by 1991.

The break-up of the Soviet Union and the creation of fifteen independent states in its wake were the immediate outcomes of events that unfolded in the European portion of the USSR between 1987 and 1991. Within a couple of years of his rise to power in 1985, Mikhail Gorbachev had introduced two broad policy reforms: *glasnost* (the 'voicing' of what had previously been kept unpublicised) and *perestroika* (economic and political 'restructuring' involving, among other things, devolution of responsibility from the centre in Moscow to lower economic units). The changes that came about as a result of these reforms had two major political consequences: firstly, small groups of people whose beliefs were strongly at odds with official Soviet doctrine were able to organise more easily and to promote their views more freely; secondly, republican and regional leaders found themselves with more leeway to make decisions on policy. The first of these consequences is directly linked to the establishment, starting in 1987, of unofficial organisations to promote civil rights, ethnic identity, and environmental protection.

The level of activism and the willingness of these organisations to challenge the official line varied considerably from republic to republic and from region to region. Many of the most radical groups were located in the Baltics and in western Ukraine. Between 1987 and 1988 these popular movements were largely concerned with their specific issue area, but the semi-competitive all-Union elections of 1989 provided the impetus for them to mobilise politically, demanding democratic rights and greater autonomy for their republics. By 1989, popular 'movements' or 'fronts' in support of reform had been established by writers and intellectuals throughout the western fringe – the Latvian, Estonian, and Moldovan Popular Fronts, 'Sajudis' in Lithuania and 'Rukh' in Ukraine (both meaning 'movement'). These were followed in all but Ukraine by vociferous counter-movements ('Interfronts') established by predominantly Russian-speaking advocates of Soviet unity. In Moldova pro-Soviet sentiment led to the rise of a separatist movement in 1990 on the heavily Ukrainian- and Russian-populated left bank of the Dniester river (which had been an autonomous republic within Soviet Ukraine between 1924 and 1944). At the same time the Christian Turkic Gagauz minority declared autonomy for the southern region where they are concentrated.

Publicity campaigns prior to the all-Union elections in 1989 to the Congress of People's Deputies and the more competitive republican elections of 1990 widened the support bases of the opposition movements at the grass-roots level. In the spring of 1990 the reformulation of Article 6 of the Soviet constitution, which guaranteed the Communist Party a 'leading and guiding' role in the life of the country, paved the way for the introduction of multi-party politics (though parties had begun to organise illegally in the Baltics as early as 1988). Gradually over the course of the period between late 1988 and the final days of the Soviet Union in late 1991 larger and larger sectors of the ruling elite also came to express support for greater republican autonomy, and eventually independence. As early as December 1989 the Lithuanian Communist Party broke ranks with Moscow and established itself as an independent social-democratic party. The communist parties in the other republics began to fragment and split soon thereafter. For some communists, especially in the Baltics, opposition to the centre represented a genuine expression of republican patriotism; for others it was a way of shoring up the gains in power and responsibility they had experienced as a result of *perestroika*, while for still other leaders independence was viewed as more inevitable than desirable, but a boat not to be missed.

Though the general pattern of events was the same across all five republics, there were differences between them as to pace of events and the ways in which their timing interacted with crucial developments at the all-Union level. The most important factor in determining the course taken by the independence movements was arguably

the point at which the communist leadership switched from supporting the Soviet centre to advocating republican autonomy. The timing
of this shift was closely linked to the point at which hard-line
communist first secretaries were replaced by more liberal ones. In
the Baltics this happened relatively early, in June 1988 in Estonia and
October 1988 in Latvia and Lithuania. From this point on, the Baltics
were the leaders in almost all domains: they were the first republics in
which broad-based popular front movements formed, the first in
which the leaderships came out in favour of a break with Moscow,
and the first to hold true multi-party elections. Non-communist
governments were formed in each of the Baltic States following the
republican elections of 1990, and declarations of independence followed in March in Lithuania, and May in Latvia and Estonia (though
an economic blockade by Moscow caused the Lithuanian declaration
to be 'suspended' in May, and the declarations by the other two Baltic
states were issued with provisos for 'transition periods').

Opposition was slower to organise in Ukraine and Moldova, but
when it did it gained momentum fast. Prior to the removal of
conservative party chairmen Shcherbytskyi and Grossu in September
and November 1989 respectively, the Ukrainian and Moldovan
leaderships were conservative by Soviet standards. Democrats in
Moldova, and especially in Ukraine, often looked to liberalisers in
Moscow for support. When Rukh and the Moldovan Popular Front
were first established in late 1988, their missions were the implementation in Ukraine and Moldova of Gorbachev's political reforms;
Moscow was their natural ally, Kyiv and Chisinau (formerly Kishinev)
their opponents. Publicity surrounding the 1989 elections had the
effect of further focusing attention on Moscow as a source of political
innovation. By 1990 the situation had changed. Disillusionment with
Gorbachev's blatant manipulation of the Congress of People's Deputies shifted attention to domestic politics as a potential arena of
contestation. Finally, the electoral cycle contributed to the alteration
of perceptions, as the main object of concern became competition for
seats in the republican legislatures, where Rukh and the Moldovan
Popular Front each won between a quarter and a third of the
mandates in 1990. The simultaneous erosion of the republican communist parties and Moscow-initiated moves to transfer power at all
levels from the party to the state enhanced the political potential of the
legislatures. These developments worked progressively to extend the
oppositions' horizons of expectations. Once achieved, their initial
goals appeared far too modest, and they soon began to press for the

establishment of independent states. As the republican leaderships gradually began to see the benefits of autonomy for their own personal status and power, they also warmed to the idea of severance from Moscow.

The Soviet Union stumbled on for a further year and a half, surviving declarations of legal sovereignty by Moldova and Ukraine in June and July of 1990 respectively. After a half-hearted display of Soviet force in Lithuania and Latvia in early 1991, the Baltics were left in a state of effective legal limbo; Moscow did not recognise their independence, but nor was it in a position to prevent them from running their own affairs. The Baltic and Moldovan leaderships refused to participate in the referendum called by Gorbachev in March 1991 to validate the preservation of the USSR as 'a renewed federation of equal sovereign republics', though at approximately the same time the Baltic republics each held their own independence referendums, which received overwhelming support; 90 per cent of the population of Lithuania, 74 per cent of the population of Latvia, and 78 per cent of the Estonian population voted in favour of independence, indicating that even large numbers of non-Balts in each of the republics supported state autonomy. In Ukraine, which did hold Gorbachev's referendum, 70.5 per cent of voters favoured the 'renewed federation'. But an even larger number (80.2 per cent) also voted 'yes' on a separate question put on the ballot by the Ukrainian parliament: 'Do you agree that Ukraine should be part of a Union of Soviet Sovereign States on the basis of the Declaration of State Sovereignty of Ukraine?' This result put in some doubt Ukraine's loyalty to the Soviet centre.

The project of a 'renewed' Union was aborted in August 1991 after a botched coup by communist hard-liners. When developments in the Russian Federation indicated the possibility of a resurgent imperialism, the Ukrainian parliament declared full independence on 24 August; the republics remaining in the Union soon followed suit, including Moldova, which issued its declaration on 27 August. Gorbachev finally had to admit that the Union of Soviet Socialist Republics was a dead letter; on 25 December 1991 it formally ceased to exist.

The Post-Soviet States

Though the tumultuous events of the late 1980s and early 1990s are what triggered the Soviet Union's demise, the fault lines of its eventual break-up had been implanted in its structure from the start. Soviet economic, regional, and cultural policy had had profound and lasting effects on the ethnic composition and political identity of the states of the western fringe. In Ukraine and Moldova the Soviet Union had established unified and nominally self-determining republics where none had previously existed. In Moldova, Soviet social engineering had gone so far as to create by *fiat* a language and an ethnic group to justify the eponymous polity and defend it against possible claims by Romania, to which it had belonged between the wars. In these two republics (as in Central Asian and the Caucasus) Soviet federalism had an ironic after-life; it had set up the conditions for its own demise by establishing the geopolitical structures upon which new states eventually emerged. In the Baltics, too, the Soviet period was one of national consolidation, but for slightly different reasons. Modernisation fostered the cultural development of the titular ethnic groups, but Soviet immigration policy posed a threat to the ethnic integrity of these republics which led to a perception, especially in Latvia and Estonia, that something had to be done to save the native populations from being eventually outnumbered by newcomers.

It was argued at the beginning of the chapter that before a polity can undertake to decide how to organise its affairs it must determine what 'it' is. Questions of citizenship and borders need to be resolved for consensus on the rules of the game to be possible, for prior to this the concept of 'consensus' has no meaning. Yet it is in the interest of those with strong views on the form that rules ought to take to embed boundaries in the very principles that govern the choice of rules. Thus nationalists in the Baltic republics argued for the legal continuity of the pre- and post-Soviet Baltic states, with the implication that only those inhabitants of the region who were citizens of these states before 1940 or their descendants should be granted citizenship rights in 1991. By defining the majority of the large Russophone populations as 'foreigners', they were seeking to create conditions under which political decisions in Estonia, Latvia, and Lithuania would be made primarily by ethnic Estonians, Latvians, and Lithuanians. Though many Ukrainian nationalists also favoured policies promoting Ukrainian ethnic identity, they had an interest in adhering to a definition of the Ukrainian state in terms of the legal boundaries of the Ukrainian Soviet Socialist Republic, in order to stave off possible irredentist claims on the part of the largely Russian populations of the east and south of the country. Likewise in Moldova, despite the initial popularity of the idea of incorporation into Romania, 90 per cent of voters chose in 1994 to retain their independence within the boundaries established under Soviet rule. By contrast, in regions heavily populated by ethnic minorities – north-east Estonia, the Donbas, Crimea, Transdniestria and the Gagauz region in Moldova being the most notable examples – local populations have appealed to other legal norms and principles to validate their rights to forms of self-determination that would allow them to decide as regions or peoples which polity they would be incorporated into.

In practice, geographical and civic boundary issues have not in all cases been resolved before important institutional choices have been made and party systems formed. This has two main consequences. Firstly, in cases where groups not entirely committed to the polity have been party to decisions on institutions, they have been able to destabilise the process of institution formation by threatening to withdraw from the polity if the choices made do not suit them. This has been the case with some diehard communists in Ukraine, and the blocking tactics of left-wing parties was one of the factors that prevented a new constitution from being adopted before 1996. Secondly, in cases where sectors of the population were initially excluded from decision-making – either by the choice of the titular ethnic group as in Estonia and Latvia, or by their own choice, as in Moldova – constitutional design and party formation have proceeded without them. This has potentially destabilising implications if and when they are subsequently integrated into political structures that have not previously incorporated them. Though relatively inclusive citizenship laws were adopted in Ukraine, Moldova, and Lithuania, Estonia and Latvia opted instead to restore citizenship to those who had possessed it prior to 1940 and grant it to their descendants. More recent immigrants may choose to become naturalised, but this requires in both cases a waiting period and knowledge of the native language. In consequence, approximately a third of the Latvian and Estonian populations are without citizenship and may therefore not vote in national elections (though non-citizens are allowed to vote in local elections in Estonia). As larger and larger sectors of the non-native residents become naturalised, the political systems in the two countries may have to alter to accommodate their demands. This was already evident in the Estonian elections of 1995, when, much to most people's surprise, a party supported mainly by ethnic Russians won 5.9 per cent of the vote and six parliamentary seats.

Unlike Ukraine and Moldova, the Baltic republics had a constitutional blueprint deriving from the period of democracy they enjoyed between the wars. The pre-Soviet legacy did not dictate institutional design, but it had a significant influence on choice of executive structure and electoral system. Estonia and Latvia are alone among the former Soviet republics in having opted for a parliamentary form of government rather than presidential or semi-presidential models, and this choice may be attributed to the fact that the two countries had been successful parliamentary democracies between 1920 and 1934, before authoritarian regimes were established (Norgaard *et al.*, 1994). In Lithuania, parliamentary democracy had given way to authoritarian presidentialism as early as 1926, and there was considerable debate in the immediate post-Soviet period as to the best type of political system. Eventually a compromise semi-presidential system was worked out and ratified by referendum in October 1992. Constitutional change in Ukraine was influenced by developments in Russia, with which most of the country had had long been politically and culturally integrated. Following Boris Yeltsin's success in creating and winning the presidency in Russia, the Ukrainian parliament voted in July 1991 to establish a similar office. On 1 December the parliamentary chairman Leonid Kravchuk, who had (belatedly) come out in favour of Ukrainian independence, won 62 per cent of the vote for president on the coat-tails of a referendum on independence held the same day, which was supported by 90 per cent of those voting. But with the exception of the establishment of the presidency, Ukraine was slow to undertake constitutional reform. The details of the political system were not fully worked out till June 1996, when parliament finally ratified a new semi-presidential constitution. In Moldova constitutional reform was complicated by two factors: separatist movements among the Transdniestrian and Gagauz populations, and efforts by some ethnic Moldovan groups to push for unification with Romania. When the Moldovan constitution was revised in 1994, the country adopted a semi-presidential system.

Of all the major constitutional changes undertaken in the post-Soviet states, judicial reform has been slowest. All five countries have provisions written into their constitutions for independent judiciaries, and in all save Ukraine the courts are relatively free from political interference. But lack of funds and experience has created severe problems for the legal systems in the new states; the Higher Appeals Court in Moldova has for extended periods not been functioning at all because the government cannot afford to run it (US Department of State, 1997). The constitutions of Ukraine, Moldova, Lithuania, and Latvia provide for constitutional courts, and in Estonia the Supreme Court has a Constitutional Review Chamber. Yet there have in some cases been substantial delays in bringing the Constitutional Courts into active operation: neither the Ukrainian nor the Latvian courts was operational until early 1997. In Ukraine especially, the consequence of these delays has been bitter quarrelling between the executive and legislative branches of government over functions and jurisdictions.

The promulgation of post-Soviet constitutions established the institutional frameworks for the five newly-independent states. But state-building must be seen also in the context of the issues that have structured political debate since 1991. These have had important influences on both the pace and the nature of the institutional changes undertaken.

Current Issues

The issues that have dominated political debate in the post-Soviet states can be categorised according to the three tasks facing the newly-independent polities: the development of democratic political procedures, foreign policy, and the introduction of market economies.

Democratisation

Throughout the region, the moment of independence was profound in two senses. The fact of sudden state autonomy reconfigured the decision-making apparatus in which leaders operated, and the structure of political force-lines established at the point of independence had lasting effects on the political cleavages that emerged in the new party systems. During the period leading up to independence, the oppositions in the five republics had mobilised around two issues: anti-communism and anti-imperialism. While the Soviet Union still existed, these two issue dimensions were effectively collapsed into one: republican autonomy was seen as the necessary precondition for political and economic reform. Only if the citizens of the republics could have control over the political and economic policies that affected them could true democratisation and meaningful economic restructuring be achieved. The devolutionary policies of *perestroika* lent ideological weight to this view, while electoral competition channelled the voicing of political difference into distinct positions in favour of or against the status quo. After independence, however, the broad-based consensus in favour of autonomy began to fracture, as differences began to re-emerge between members of the elite whose main desire was to strengthen national autonomy and integrate their states into European political structures, and those whose primary concern was the implementation of market reforms. There was also an inevitable backlash among those who had not favoured independence or were ambivalent towards it, especially ethnic Russians, who mobilised politically within the new systems in favour of closer economic ties with the Russian Federation. The result was a growing differentiation between the two main issue areas, and the creation of a two-dimensional political map that distinguished between, on the one hand, pro-reform and anti-reform positions and, on the other, pro-Europeanist/nationalist and pro-Russianist stances.

In all five cases nationalist reformers initially held the upper hand. In the Baltics the successors to the popular front movements controlled the parliaments elected in 1990; in Ukraine and Moldova the nationalist democratic parties that had emerged from Rukh and the Moldovan Popular Front had preponderant influence over policy formulation in the early post-independence period. But when it became obvious that freedom from the Soviet yoke would not of itself solve the countries' economic problems, those opposed to rapid reforms returned to claim centre stage. The communist successor Lithuanian Democratic Labour Party won an absolute majority of seats in the parliamentary elections of 1992, and former Communist first secretary Algirdas Brazauskas won the presidential election of 1993 with 60 per cent of the vote. In Ukraine the communists gained the largest number of parliamentary seats in the elections of 1994 (see Table 4.2), while presidential elections the same year gave the office to Leonid Kuchma, who had campaigned on a pro-Russian platform and won 52.1 per cent of the vote in the second round. Already by 1992 the Moldovan Popular Front had lost much of its influence, and parliamentary elections in 1994 resulted in a victory for the post-communist Democratic Agrarians (see Table 4.3); communists won the largest share of the vote in both countries in the parliamentary elections that took place in March 1998.

In Estonia, parliamentary elections in 1995 also brought to power a left-leaning government, led by a coalition of parties in favour of slower reforms (see Table 4.4). Only in Latvia has the swing to the left been avoided; the Latvian elections of 1995 gave the greatest number of votes (and seats) to the technocratic Democratic Party 'Saimnieks' – literally the party of 'managers' – who were intent on continuing the economic reforms undertaken by the previous government (see Table 4.5). As the inevitability of reform began to be accepted across the political spectrum, the political centre of gravity in Lithuania and Ukraine swung back to the right. The Lithuanian elections of 1996 gave power to the Homeland Union (Conservatives of Lithuania), the

TABLE 4.2   *The Ukrainian parliamentary elections of 1994*

	Votes (%)	Seats
Communist Party	12.7	86 (25.4%)
Rukh	5.2	20 (5.9%)
Socialist Party	3.1	14 (4.1%)
Agrarian Party	2.7	19 (5.3%)
Republican Party	2.5	8 (2.4%)
Other	7.4	23 (6.8%)
All parties	33.6	170 (50.3%)
Independents	66.4	168 (49.7%)
Total	100	338*

Turnout (first round): 74.8%

Note: * A total of 112 seats in the 450-seat legislature remained to be filled after the initial elections. All but 25 of these were filled in subsequent rounds between July 1994 and April 1996.

TABLE 4.3   *The Moldovan parliamentary elections of 1994*

	Votes (%)	Seats
Democratic Agrarian Party	43.2	56 (53.8%)
Socialist Party/Edinstvo Bloc	22.0	28 (27.0%)
Bloc of Peasants and Intellectuals	9.2	11 (10.6%)
Christian-Democratic Popular Front	7.5	9 (8.6%)
Other	18.1	0
Total	100	104

Turnout: 79.3%

TABLE 4.4 *The Estonian parliamentary elections of 1995*

	Votes (%)	Seats
Coalition Party and Rural Union	32.2	41 (40.6%)
Reform Party	16.2	19 (18.8%)
Centre Party	14.2	16 (15.8%)
Other	37.4	25 (24.8%)
Total	100	101

Turnout: 68.3%

TABLE 4.5 *Latvian parliamentary elections of 1995*

	Votes (%)	Seats
Democratic Party 'Saimnieks'	15.2	18 (18.0%)
People's Movement for Latvia	14.9	16 (16.0%)
Latvia's Way	14.6	17 (17.0%)
For Fatherland and Freedom	11.9	14 (14.0%)
Other	43.4	35 (35.0%)
Total	100	100

Turnout: 71.9%

main successor party to Sajudis (see Table 4.6). Presidential elections in 1997/98 gave the chief executive office to Valdas Adamkus, a 'technocratic' Lithuanian-American, who won the second round of voting with 50.3 per cent over his postcommunist opponent. In Ukraine the left became less and less coherent after 1994 as an increasingly nationalist and reformist president pushed his policies through parliament. In Moldova the presidency was won in 1996 by the former Communist Party general secretary Lucinschi. Like Ukrainian president Kuchma elected in 1994, Lucinschi won in the second round with 54 per cent of the vote on a pro-Russian platform, beating the incumbent, Mircea Snegur (in both cases a former communist who had over the course of his term in office swung to the right), after the latter had gained a plurality in the first round. In both cases also, a left-wing parliamentary speaker came a distant third. The parallels between the two races are striking, and there are signs that Lucinschi, like Kuchma, has gravitated to the right during his term in office.

Across the region, the postcommunist left has been more cohesive than the right, due to the grassroots organisational strengths of the communist successor parties and the fragmentation of the Soviet-era umbrella opposition movements in the wake of independence. Most of the changes in the structures of the emergent party systems have been the result of realignments in the non-communist successor camps. From 1990 onwards, numerous parties germinated, metamorphosed, split, and merged. Proportional electoral laws in Estonia, Latvia, and Moldova have encouraged the development of nation-wide party systems and have limited the number of parties that have gained seats in parliament (four in the Moldovan election of 1994, seven in the Estonian elections of 1995, nine in the Latvian elections of the same year), whereas Ukraine's single-mandate system and Lithuania's semi-proportional law gave representation in both cases to fourteen parties in the most recent elections. The Ukrainian party system has been weakest, partly due to the high degree of regionalism in Ukrainian politics, and partly as a consequence of the single-mandate system which resulted in half the seats in the 1994 elections being won by independents. The Ukrainian Communist Party and

TABLE 4.6   *The Lithuanian parliamentary elections of 1996*

	Votes* (%)	Seats
Homeland Union (Conservatives of Lithuania)	29.8	70 (51.1%)
Christian Democratic Party	9.9	16 (11.7%)
Lithuanian Democratic Labour Party	9.5	12 (8.8%)
Centre Union	8.2	13 (9.5%)
Social Democratic Party	6.6	12 (8.8%)
Other	36.0	10 (7.3%)
Independents	–	4 (2.9%)
Total 137**	100.0	

Turnout (first round): 53%

* Vote percentages for list seats.
** Four seats in the 141-seat parliament remain to be filled.

Rukh are the only parties that have significant representation in all regions, but they do not as yet form the basis for a national party system, as in most cases they do not compete against each other, but against other smaller parties in the regions they dominate. This has led to a highly fluid and unstructured legislature which has had considerable difficulty building consensus. The result has been a slow pace of reform and the relative strengthening of the presidency as an institution.

Though all five systems have manifested a high degree of electoral competition, the proportion of citizens inclined to involve themselves in political decision-making has witnessed a steady decrease since the heady days of 1989–91. Not only has electoral participation dropped markedly since 1990, but falling turnout has also been accompanied by low levels of trust in parties and governments, low estimations of politicians, and disillusionment with politics generally (Crowther and Roper, 1996; Hibbing and Patterson, 1994; Rose, 1995a; Rose and Maley, 1994; Wyman *et al.*, 1995). Moreover, though the institutional framework for democratic decision-making has been established in the post-Soviet republics, parliaments have yet to transform themselves into effective vehicles for representation. Since 1991, elections in the Baltics, Ukraine, and Moldova (with the exception of separatist regions) have all been judged relatively 'free and fair' by international monitoring organisations. Yet electoral volatility has been high, and lack of regularised parliamentary procedures has hindered the passage of reformist legislation (Bach, 1996; Crowther and Roper, 1996; Kask, 1996). All five countries have also experienced considerable difficulties in establishing law-based states. The persistence of clientelistic relations developed during the Soviet period, inadequate legal resources, weak state capacity to implement decisions, the general informalism and personalism of the style of post-Soviet politics, and corruption at high levels of government have contributed to the fragility of rule of law in all five countries.

Foreign Policy

The main foreign policy issues in the region since independence have been, on the one hand, orientation to Russia and the Commonwealth of Independent States (CIS), and, on the other, its position with respect to the institutional architecture of the West, including the Council of Europe, the European Union, and NATO. Ukraine and

the Baltics have been involved in border disputes with their neighbours, though in most cases these have now been resolved. A more
serious problem in all five countries has been the stationing of
Russian troops on their territories. The Baltic republics successfully
negotiated troop withdrawals (completed in August 1993 in Lithuania, and the following August in Estonia and Latvia) and have made
arrangements for limited Russian military access for specific purposes
(manning of the Skrunda radar base in Latvia, passage through
Lithuania to the Russian-owned enclave of Kaliningrad). Disagreements between Russia and Ukraine over the Black Sea Fleet based in
Crimea have caused greater problems, but again negotiation has been
successful in settling the dispute, and an agreement on the division of
the fleet was eventually signed in May 1997. The one area in which a
Russian military presence has remained a problem is in the Transdniestrian region of Moldova, where the Russian Fourteenth Army
sought to defend separatist claims by the local authorities. This
conflict erupted into violence in 1992 soon after Moldova had
declared independence, and though the fighting largely abated as a
result of a cease-fire later the same year, Russia continued to give
military assistance to the separatists, and Moldova has yet to gain
control over the region. Serious negotiations between the central
Moldovan government in Chisinau and the separatist powers in
Tiraspol got under way in the summer of 1997 after a memorandum
of understanding was signed by the two sides in May, but it remains
to be seen whether the talks will settle the matter. Relations between
Moldova and Romanian have also been strained due to pressure from
within both countries for a reunification, and the desire of some
Moldovans to annex the western part of the ancient principality of
Moldavia, lying east of the river Prut in Romania.

Relations between the former Soviet states have been mediated by
two organisations: the Commonwealth of Independent States (CIS)
and the Baltic Assembly. The CIS was established in December 1991
on the grave of the Soviet Union. Ukraine was a founding member,
and though Moldova initially resisted joining, it eventually acceded in
1993. Fearing Russian domination, neither Ukraine nor Moldova has
chosen to integrate fully into CIS structures, which are in any case
frail. The Baltic states were never members of the CIS, but they
formed their own Baltic Assembly as early as 1989 to coordinate
relations between them. This was later supplemented by the Baltic
Free Trade Agreement (1993) and the Baltic Council of Ministers
(1994), the formation of a Baltic Peacekeeping Battalion (1995), and a

number of other agreements. But like the CIS, the Baltic Assembly has remained politically weak, for the Baltic states are more interested in integrating economically and politically with Scandinavia, Finland, Poland, and other countries to the west than they are with each other (Girnius, 1997, p. 21).

By 1995 the five states had all demonstrated sufficient democratic credentials to be admitted to the Council of Europe, but integration into other Western European institutions had been more problematic. All five have hopes of joining the European Union, and all but Ukraine would also like to join NATO in order to secure against possible Russian adventurism. Immediate accession is unlikely in either case, however. Though all three Baltic countries had by the end of 1995 signed the European Agreement granting associate status in the EU, only Estonia has been invited, with the Visegrad countries and Slovenia, to begin negotiations for full accession. Russian opposition to NATO expansion is likely to prevent early admission to this organisation, in view of the strategic sensitivity of the region. Low levels of military preparedness have also made NATO wary of incorporating the post-Soviet forces. However, all have joined NATO's Partnership for Peace, and all but Moldova have participated in peacekeeping missions in former Yugoslavia.

Economic Reform

Before 1991 there was a perception among the republics of the western fringe of the Soviet Union that the more highly developed European portion of the country was being exploited economically to subsidise the poorer regions of the east and south. The logical conclusion was that the western republics would benefit economically from independence, and this perception was one of the main factors that moved many non-titular residents in these republics to support a full break with Moscow in 1991. Yet proponents of the exploitation theory failed to take into consideration two effects of Soviet central planning: the distorted pricing system that afforded them cheap energy supplies from Russia and the east, and the high degree of economic interdependence of the Soviet republics. With independence energy subsidies all but ceased, and trading patterns were severely disrupted. Combined with the problems associated with economic liberalisation and marketisation, these changes brought severe declines in production, plus unemployment, high inflation, and a reduction in living standards. The situation was especially acute in 1992 and 1993, after which it improved somewhat, but for all except a small proportion of the populations in these countries living standards have yet to regain their pre-1991 levels. These problems have been further exacerbated by the inability of the new states to regulate the transition to a market economy due to lack of resources and expertise, lack of institutional infrastructure, difficulty in collecting taxes, and extensive informal economic activity. Finally, crime and corruption have been rampant in all the post-Soviet states. The combined effects of these factors have been rapidly increasing wealth differentials and popular disaffection with the market economy, which has led to electoral support for parties and candidates advocating slower reforms.

As the most highly developed of the post-Soviet states and those that experienced the greatest amount of economic devolution during the *perestroika* period, the Baltics were best positioned to restructure their economies and reorient their trading patterns. Reorientation to Western markets was further facilitated by the concentration in these republics of high technology and light industry, sectors that have been easiest to make profitable under market conditions. Privatisation and economic stabilisation in the Baltic countries have proceeded rapidly by post-Soviet standards, especially in Estonia. Though varying degrees of energy dependency on Russia requires them to maintain trading links with the CIS, the Baltics' attractiveness to foreign investors has allowed them to develop trade with the West as well. Already by 1992 Finland had replaced Russia as Estonia's leading trading partner.

Ukraine and Moldova have experienced far greater difficulties in economic reform and the development of economic links with the West. Their economies are dominated by agriculture and, in Ukraine, by heavy industry, both of which employ outmoded production methods. They are thus less well suited to the export market, and less attractive to foreign investors. These countries have also been slow to undertake serious reform of their economies, and the reform process has been dogged in Ukraine by the sheer size of the country which entails extensive powers for many corrupt local officials, and in Moldova by the concentration of industry and energy production in the separatist Transdniestrian region. The consequence in both cases has been bouts of hyper-inflation in the first two years of independence, continuing declines in production, and widespread poverty.

Conclusion

The post-Soviet states considered in this chapter have made significant progress since 1991 in establishing the edifice of independent market democracies. Yet they have also faced a number of obstacles specific to their Soviet inheritance: uncertainties as to their geopolitical and civic identities, leaders and citizens with little experience of democratic politics, and economic structures in need of serious overhaul. Though the first problem was initially the most intractable, the five states have made significant strides in resolving it. The challenges they currently face are mainly in the political and economic spheres. These challenges are closely intertwined, in that economic reform in a democracy requires popular assent and popular participation. There are two principal problems associated with attempting to bring about market reforms through democratic process in the post-Soviet context. Firstly, representative mechanisms are difficult to implement. In order for representation to be institutionalised, voters and parties alike have to perceive the electoral and legislative processes as being a matter of representation, and the electorate has to be presented with a meaningful choice between parties that have and make known attractive policy positions. Voters must also have access to adequate information about the parties so as to be able to make a decision. Finally, they must have a willingness to vote, and to vote on the basis of perceptions of issue and interest. Lack of accountable representation in post-Soviet polities is partly due to the 'mechanical' inadequacies of the system which have resulted from poor implementation of political institutions through insufficient experience and resources. There is often no clear choice available to voters because parties have weak internal discipline and they are incompetent in conveying their messages. Voters are often not able to make a clear choice for the additional reason that they are bewildered by the large number of unfamiliar parties on offer and they have too many other pressing concerns to have time to inform themselves politically. The low opinion in which legislative organs, parties, and politicians in general are held poses a further disincentive for voters to inform themselves and make a rational choice. These factors have led in some cases to abstention, and have in other cases encouraged voting on the basis of immediate particularistic rewards rather than issues and interests.

The second problem is that corrupt practices infiltrate the political process at various points higher up, undermining the link between rulers and citizenry. Corruption is in many cases related to the economic reform process. The Soviet state was one in which economics and politics were closely wedded. Post-Soviet market reform has generally been conceived as an effort to extricate economics from politics. It might appear that under these circumstances former leaders would be obliged to choose between the quest for economic power and the quest for political power, but in reality many have successfully maintained the link between the two, either gaining political power by means of wealth, or gaining wealth by means of politics (or both). If reforms in the political and the economic spheres are to be successful, this link will have to be broken or it will have to be redesigned. This is the most difficult challenge the post-Soviet republics currently face.

PART TWO

The Contemporary Political System

5

Redefining the State: The Constitutional Process

JUDY BATT AND KATARYNA WOLCZUK

The study of constitutions and constitutionalism had rather fallen out of fashion in political science until quite recently, as the focus of political analysis shifted away from formal institutional frameworks to the social, economic and cultural factors which were held to be more important in explaining how power was 'really' exercised. But in the last decade or so, important developments in political science have led to a 'rediscovery' of the state as an autonomous factor, and to renewed attention to institutions and the 'rules of the game' in shaping the patterns of politics and the outcomes of political struggles. The collapse of communism has given fresh impetus to the study of constitutions and constitutionalism as a form of politics, in the context of new democracies striving to reach agreement on a definition not only of the 'rules of the game' of political life, but also of the state itself: what, and above all who the state is for. As Claus Offe has argued, the postcommunist transition, in contrast to previous 'democratic transitions' in southern Europe and Latin America, reaches beyond the 'normal' political question of 'who gets what', and even beyond the question of what rules are to govern the process, to the deepest questions of the political community and statehood itself:

At the most fundamental level, a 'decision' must be made as to who 'we' are, i.e. a decision on identity, citizenship and the territorial as well as social and cultural boundaries of the state. (Offe, 1991, p. 869)

In Western Europe, constitutionalism evolved gradually within the framework of established states, and has been intimately linked with the growth of democracy: 'the history of modern European constitutionalism is the history of the progressive transfer of sovereignty from princes or kings, under whom state power had been centralised and consolidated, to the people and their representatives' (Kommers and Thompson, 1995, p. 27). The earliest established European democracies, for example France and Great Britain, have been able to take their statehood for granted, having previously established effective control of a given territory. However, in Central and Eastern Europe, the states themselves could not be assumed in the same way. Most of the states in this region today were formed quite recently, many emerging at the end of World War I which saw the collapse of the dynastic empires of Austria-Hungary and Russia. Some only came into existence with the collapse of the communist federal states, the Soviet Union, Czechoslovakia and Yugoslavia in the early 1990s. The very notion of statehood and its territorial, political, cultural and economic parameters have been questioned throughout the region after the collapse of the communist state system. This has brought to the fore a basic point which is often overlooked in longer-established states, namely that before we can define the constitutional 'rules of the game', the political framework according to which society is to be governed, we have to have reached agreement on who belongs to the political community – in other words, who constitutes the *demos* to which the democratic state refers. This means establishing the physical boundaries of the state, and confirming which people have the right to be considered as citizens. All these issues have emerged vividly in the process of constitutional reform in postcommunist states. Especially in the case of newly-formed postcommunist states, a major aspect of the constitutional process is the aim to legitimise or even create a new polity by defining fundamentals: the conception of 'the political community', the meaning of citizenship, and the purposes of the state.

Constitutionalism has historically been closely linked with democracy, and in many respects democracy presupposes constitutionalism. Constitutions are concerned with limiting state power by subjecting it to legal rules which stand above the state itself. These rules organise sovereign power so that individual rights and freedoms are guarded against the arbitrary rule of the state. Constitutionalism developed alongside liberalism and is based on the idea of free individuals – citizens – who establish governments accountable to them for the purposes of defending their rights and freedoms, and furthering their interests. Constitutions define the terms on which state power is to operate by specifying clear rules and procedures. This results in the depersonalisation of political power, and limits the powers of government which are vested in a set of institutions whose roles, responsibilities and functions are clearly specified and most often divided up and balanced against each other according to the principle of the separation of powers.

A constitution is a written document or a set of laws which is like a special type of contract, expressing the consent of the governed and their acceptance of state power as legitimate as long as it is exercised according to the terms specified in it. A constitution usually lists civic and human rights, describes the mechanisms for citizens' participation in public affairs, and defines the institutional framework of the state. Many constitutions include a preamble which defines the political community – the 'body politic' of citizens in whose name the state was created and to whom the state is accountable. Furthermore, constitutions set out the general goals and purposes of the state, and sometimes also include, alongside political rights, social and economic entitlements such as health services, state education, social welfare, and so on. However, democratic constitutions vary greatly, and there is no ready-made template; each is embedded in a particular cultural, social and political context.

But at a certain point, a tension arises in the relationship between constitutionalism and democracy. Constitutions not only organise power, they also place certain issues beyond the reach of everyday political contestation. If we understand democracy as the rule of the people (from the classical Greek word, *demos*), which effectively, in large modern states, means the rule of the majority, then we have to recognise the possibility that democracy, as majority rule, can often come into conflict with the ideal of the constitution as a lasting, superior document which cannot be changed from day to day according to changing popular whim. Democracy assumes the consent of the body of citizenry either directly, by mass plebiscite, or indirectly, through elected representatives, but the existence of a constitution in fact implies the acceptance of some self-limitation in the exercise of the popular will. This is because constitutions exist in order to insulate certain domains such as civic liberties from the reach of a potentially volatile democratic majority. It is usually rather difficult to amend constitutions, and the restrictive procedures involved are a kind of safety valve, guarding society against its own weaknesses. Despite these inherent tensions between democracy and constitutionalism, the latter has become a key feature and guiding principle in the modern, democratic state: 'constitutionalism embraces the idea of the normative penetration of the polity to the effect that its institutions continue and operate irrespective of changing majorities and of the vacillations of politics in general – it is the idea of normative supremacy and continuity' (Preuss, 1995, p. 96).

The ideal of constitutionalism has an enormous appeal to societies attempting to redefine the bases of their political life after the demise of the communist system, which reduced the constitutions to the role of propagating state ideology. The concepts of the separation of powers, checks and balances, human and civic rights and freedoms, and democratic accountability are all hallmarks of what is regarded in Central and Eastern Europe as the 'restoration of normality'. The quest for constitutionalism, seen as the guarantee of greater predictability and stability, has become part and parcel of the aspiration to 'return to Europe'.

The constitutional process in postcommunist Europe did not start from a *tabula rasa*: in fact, all communist states had 'constitutions' in the sense of written documents promising various rights and freedoms and defining the formal structures of the state. But these had little real meaning in so far as the communist parties in fact monopolised power. When communist rule collapsed, the new governments found themselves at first working with these constitutions, for lack of an alternative. In the next section, we explain the problems this has created for the process of establishing constitutionalism. In the following section, we present a case study of Poland to illustrate these problems in more detail. And then we turn to the special case of transforming the former communist federal states, where the struggle for constitutionalism was combined with struggles for national self-determination. Here, the lack of underlying consensus on the basic definition of the political community led to the break-up of these states. In the final section we return to the special problems of establishing democratic constitutionalism in an environment permeated with resurgent nationalism, which has affected almost all postcommunist states, but especially those states which include within the 'body politic' significant national minorities.

From Communist Constitutions to Constitution-Making

The definition of a 'constitutional state' means more than having a written constitution, otherwise the communist states could have been regarded as constitutional states. All of the communist constitutions incorporated a bill of civic rights and liberties in addition to extensive guarantees of social and economic rights. The body of citizens had at their disposal 'representative' institutions such as parliaments, local governments, heads of state, and so forth. And the constitutionally defined procedures and routines were ceremonially and routinely performed. But in practice, the provisions of communist constitutions had very little impact on how communist states actually functioned. Indeed, communist states were very different in nature from states based on constitutional rule. Although they paid lip-service to the idea of popular sovereignty, constitutions were a facade behind which the Communist Party controlled the levers of power. The locus of sovereignty was not in the people, but in the party which claimed to be a 'vanguard' force in the construction of socialism in the best interests of the people. This mission was enshrined in their constitutions as 'the leading role of the party'. Effectively, the party as the supreme political authority was above – rather than subordinated to – the constitution and laws. The party oversaw the exercise of state authority, its institutional arrangements, political interactions and the decision-making process. It had a final say in resolving bureaucratic conflicts between different branches of the state in the execution of policies set by the party. As a result, no 'checks and balances' were built in, which would have thwarted the party's will, or, in the terms of the ruling political ideology, would have held back the overriding goal of 'building socialism'. Instead, constitutions proclaimed the principle of the 'unity of power'.

Parliaments in theory were the highest state bodies, but in practice they acted as a rubber-stamp for the party's decisions. As the party played a supervisory, coordinating and directing role, its structures were largely entwined and merged with those of the state to the extent that communist states could be defined as party-states. The ultimate supremacy of party over state made a mockery of the ideals of constitutionalism, the rule of law and popular legitimacy. The obvious contradiction between the formal provisions of the constitution and the reality of arbitrary rule engendered a pervasive cynicism which fed into the simmering popular dissatisfaction with party rule, and ensured it would never be accepted as legitimate political power. Over time the inherent instability of the political system was further compounded by the evident failure of the centrally administered economy to live up to its own promises of material abundance and social welfare, and thus to live up to the party's claims that its 'leading role' was the ultimate guarantee of government in 'the interests of the people'.

The crumbling of the communist system and the loosening of its grip on society culminated in important changes made to constitutions in the course of 'Round Table' discussions between governments and organised oppositions in 1989. The key result was agreement to hold partially or even genuinely competitive elections. Free elections fundamentally undermined 'the leading role of the party'. Once the people were allowed freely to express their will, the party would, for a change, find itself on the 'receiving end'. The constitutional norm which legitimised the party's 'leading role' was removed, setting it on an equal footing, in legal terms, with all others. From the outset of the transition, a profound change in the mode of exercising political authority was reflected in constitutional reforms, which set the state on the path to constitutionalism and the 'rule of law'. State institutions would begin to function according to democratic principles of accountability, and would be constrained to respect the rights and freedoms of citizens. New constitutions were also designed to prevent in the future the use of the state as an instrument for the implementation of any particular ideology – a clear example of the influence of the communist experience. For example Article 5 of the Moldovan constitution rules that 'no ideology can be recognised as the official state ideology'.

While the enduring ideal of constitutionalism was the driving force for constitutional reform, there was also the more immediate need for the state to continue to function after the demise of the communist parties. The relationships between state institutions were ill-defined and ambiguous, and once the party's 'leading role' was abolished, much confusion and uncertainty permeated the process of government. Thus the shift towards a more clearly defined 'separation of powers' and 'checks and balances' became the order of the day. This became an especially urgent task after the Round Table discussions, which had introduced *ad hoc* institutional innovations such as state presidencies or upper houses of parliament (as in Poland), whose roles were anything but clear.

Thus the most important task that new constitutions had to tackle in the short term was to disentangle the paralysing confusion of functions and clarify the distribution of powers between state institutions. The protection of human rights from government abuse, which had been the primary concern of the oppositional movements represented at the Round Table discussions, turned out by comparison to be a relatively straightforward matter. Containing the institutional power struggle which soon erupted after the demise of communist rule was the key condition not only of improving the efficiency of the new political regimes, but also of establishing their democratic legitimacy.

The construction of a law-governed polity, in which the constitution is enshrined as the supreme authority, is necessarily a long-term process, but it has to start at the top, at the level of the central government. The government itself has to be transparently regulated by legal norms before the rule of law can percolate downwards and gather credibility. Postcommunist constitutions in the first instance served to delineate authority: by providing the rules of the game, politics was to be made more predictable and productive, so that attention and energy could focus on the pressing issues of the day, especially socio-economic reform.

In line with the idea of the 'return to Europe', there has been a tendency to look towards West European institutional devices, which have been successfully 'tried and tested' for their effectiveness in safeguarding civic liberties and preventing the usurpation of power. Yet there is no uniform matrix of governmental design in Europe. While separation of powers, judicial review, checks and balances are general guiding principles, they can take very different forms, such as the Westminster model nurtured by British customs and traditions on the one hand, and the French semi-presidential or German chancellor-based systems on the other. Although constitutionalism as a political doctrine defines the goals, such as the inviolability of human rights, it does not come out with detailed guidelines on how to craft the institutional framework to defend those objectives. However, the plurality of models and the choice to be made was not the only difficulty involved.

The constitutional process took place under the 'old', communist-era rules, partially and inadequately adapted for the changed circumstances. Elster has compared constitution-making in postcommunist states with 'rebuilding the boat in the open sea'. This metaphor captures both dimensions of the process. Firstly, the refuge of the dry dock in which a full-blown refurbishment could take place was not available to the 'pioneers' undertaking this hazardous new task. New constitutions emerged therefore as an amalgam of old and new elements – many old institutions were simply 'given a new coat of paint' while the 'ship of state' was already at sea. Secondly, it was the sailors themselves who had to rebuild the ship: the political actors had to redefine the constitutional rules of the game, while themselves playing that game (Elster, 1993, p. 171).

Most often it was parliaments which were given the task of drafting a constitution, as, having been elected, they had the most obvious claim to legitimate authority. But they were far from the detached, politically neutral Lawgiver envisaged by Rousseau as the framer of the 'social contract'. With ordinary legislatures taking on the extraordinary role of constitutional assemblies, the task of drafting the constitutional rules of the game was assigned to the same bodies which were to be key players in the game itself. This inevitably led to the politicisation of the whole process. The new parliaments (and their internal parties and factions) were far from capable of displaying the detached wisdom and knowledge of the 'public good' and 'general interest' on which ideally constitutions should rest. In the process of reassigning powers between the branches of the state, various partisan interests came into play. Moreover, parliaments were not only working on new constitutions, but tackling at the same time other equally momentous issues of the postcommunist transformation, including fundamental social and economic reforms and international realignment. Political actors thus soon became engaged in multi-issue bargaining, in which trade-offs were often made, which infringed on the coherence and integrity of the final constitutional documents. This *ad hoc* bargaining against the backdrop of the communist-era institutional landscape accounts for the diversity of institutional configurations that can be found in postcommunist states.

A Case Study: Poland

In most cases, drafting new constitutions was a protracted process. In Poland it took as long as eight years to pass a fully revised new constitution. The parliament elected in the only partially competitive elections of the summer of 1989 launched the process of constitution-drafting. However, the lack of democratic legitimacy of that assembly was a stumbling block (65 per cent of the Sejm, the lower house, had been nominated by the Communist Party as part of the Round Table agreement). Then, after the 1991 genuinely free elections, an interim stop-gap 'Little Constitution' was adopted in 1992 which clarified some ambiguities in governmental relations, but also added a few others. It firmly placed Poland in the club of semi-presidential systems, which to a large degree reflected the ambitions of the then president, Lech Walesa. At the same time, a special Constitutional Commission (consisting of members of parliament) was delegated the task of drafting a fully revised new constitution. After four years' work this Commission tabled its final draft in parliament in 1996.

Although Poland has had a long constitutional history, Polish traditions hardly provide a viable model for a modern constitutional democracy. These traditions date back to the end of the eighteenth century, when in 1791 the so-called Constitution of 3rd May was adopted to prevent a slide into anarchy in the face of external threats by introducing a hereditary monarchy. The ill-designed 1921 constitution and the authoritarian 1935 constitution were followed by the Stalinist one of 1952. Thus, in the 1990s the Polish drafters faced the problem of inventing a new model, and the form of government – a presidential or a parliamentary democracy – was the central issue in constitution-making.

However, the protracted nature of the constitution-making process was arguably not without its benefits as constitutional solutions and options could be given more thought and even tested in practice. President Walesa took advantage of every conceivable kind of ambiguity of the Little Constitution (aided by his ingenious legal advisor), stretching its provisions to extend his powers. This led to the 'war of laws' between the anti-communist president and the parliament dominated by ex-communists. After such a trial of strength, Aleksander Kwasniewski as the head of the parliament's Constitutional Commission advocated the trimming of presidential powers. One of these powers was the president's right to veto parliamentary law, which could only be overridden by a qualified two-thirds majority in the Sejm. However, once elected president himself in 1995, Kwasniewski insisted on the reintroduction of the requirement of a qualified majority. Clearly, 'how you see things depends on where you sit'.

The resultant form of government in Poland was the product of an overarching compromise and no clear-cut model was introduced. The juxtaposition of various interests guided final choices, amongst which institutional ones featured prominently as the president, the Sejm and the Senate all vied to expand their respective powers. The case of the Senate illustrates this especially well. The common wisdom was that there was no compelling rationale for a Senate – a second, upper house of parliament – as Poland, a unitary, homogenous state, had no need for the kind of regional representation which a Senate might offer. Yet the Senate already existed as a result of the 1989 Round Table agreement, and had a key role in constitution-making, because it had to consent to the new constitution, together with the Sejm in a joint session of the National Assembly. And so it is hardly surprising that the Senate was preserved in the new constitution: the Senate was hardly likely to legislate itself out of existence.

Furthermore, in Poland, the distinctive and pivotal issue in constitution-making was state-church relations. The Catholic Church, oppressed and yet vibrant under communism, played the vanguard role in bringing down the communist system. The Church itself equated the demise of the 'evil regime' with a return (by default) to a traditional Christian way of life, which, in its view, the Polish state should promote or at least not oppose. The social democratic parties (mainly ex-communists) and liberal centre in turn propagated the secular version of the constitution, giving priority to the rights and freedoms of the individual. The constitutional debate in this way touched upon the issue of national identity at its deepest level. The Church hierarchy and the right-wing nationalistic parties strongly favoured the exclusive notion of national community based on traditions, culture and Catholicism as the fundamental marks of the Polish nation. Thus the liberal-individualist concept of constitutional democracy clashed with the organic notion of nationhood and Christian values as the superior moral order. In the event, the new constitution reflected the ambiguous relationship between the two conceptions of the state, based on different sets of fundamental principles and values (although not that many concessions were made to the right). Eventually, a compromise was mustered between the four main parties in parliament, which then closed ranks behind the draft, while the right-wing opposition (mostly not represented in parliament), with the backing of the Church, proposed its own alternative 'citizen's draft'. They opposed, on the one hand, the liberalism embedded in the official constitution and its allegedly 'anti-national' and 'anti-Christian' character. As the Polish bishops summed it up, 'the constitution does not have a soul'. On the other hand, they questioned the moral right of former communists in the Social Democracy of Poland, now the leading party in parliament, to draft the first postcommunist constitution.

President Kwasniewski argued that the constitution should be ratified in 1996 as in that year no elections were to be held in Poland, so the constitution would not be subject to the horse-trading associated with short-term electoral politics. However, as the constitution was only ready for popular ratification in a referendum in May 1997, four months before the next parliamentary elections were due to be held, the fundamental law became part of the bitter and polarising electoral campaign. The constitutional referendum was supposed to endow the constitution with popular legitimacy, after both houses of the National Assembly in a joint session had promulgated the law by a constitutional majority. The referendum formally ratified the constitution: 53 per cent voted in favour, and 46 per cent against. However, with a turnout of only 43 per cent, the constitution was hardly endowed with an overwhelming popular endorsement. Furthermore the right-wing opposition, with the prospect of winning at last a healthy representation in the new parliament, declared its intention to review and amend the constitution once in power. Although the opposition – united into Solidarity Electoral Action – emerged as the biggest parliamentary faction after the September 1997 elections, its anti-constitutional feelings were tempered by its liberal coalition partner – the Freedom Union (which had voted in favour of the constitution). However, as this restraint depends on a delicate parliamentary balance, the stability of the constitutional order in Poland is far from assured.

The Special Case of Federal States

The transition from communist rule to constitutionalism proved a peculiarly intractable task in the context of the three communist federal states, the Soviet Union, Czechoslovakia and Yugoslavia. All three failed to meet the challenge, and collapsed – in the Yugoslav case, bloodily, but in the other two cases, remarkably peacefully – into a set of new, unitary nation-states, based on the former constituent republics of the federations. Why the transition to constitutionalism proved impossible to manage within the framework of multi-national federations is an intriguing and complex question. Some would argue that the answer is self-evident – these particular federations were never in fact accepted as fully legitimate by the peoples which they united, and were only held together by communist rule, which suppressed the deep-rooted national aspirations for freedom and self-rule. When democratisation began, it was inevitable that nationalism would surface as the most potent challenge to communism, and that these diverse peoples would see the formation of their own national states as the 'natural' and necessary precondition of democratic rule.

It is of course true that the experience of federalism communist-style had profoundly discredited the whole idea of federation as a form of constitutional state expressing in institutional form both national diversity and national equality. The party's unified and centralised hierarchical structure had overridden the formal rights of the constituent republics, and turned them into a facade. The party itself was seen by smaller nations as an instrument for promoting the interests of the largest – Russians, Czechs and Serbs. The federal structures had been unable to counteract the inequalities between larger and smaller, richer and poorer nations. Political oppression in the communist period was experienced by all, but the non-dominant nations argued that they experienced this in a twofold way – both as individuals and as members of national groups specially targeted by the communists' drive against 'bourgeois nationalism'. These bitter historical collective memories simply eroded any possible sense of mutual trust and common interest in a shared political space, the essential base for a genuinely democratic federation.

But the story is a more complex one than this. The so-called 'dominant nations', the Russians, Czechs and Serbs, themselves could also argue they had been peculiarly oppressed by communist rule and disadvantaged by the burden of supporting their smaller and weaker partners. In all three cases of federal collapse, these nations played at least as important as role as their smaller partners. Moreover, communist rule had not been unambiguously anti-national and oppressive towards the smaller nations. In fact, in all three cases, it was only under communist rule that most of the smaller nations finally got symbolic recognition in their own federal republics, complete with all the formal trappings of parliaments, flags, anthems, and education in their native tongue. The centralised redistribution of resources under the communist economic system had promoted social and economic development in line with the party's objective of equalisation of the 'material conditions of life'. The results of this tended, contrary to the communists' expectations, to promote national consciousness and to create national cadres in the republics who were given privileged access to high-status posts in the governmental and administrative structures. In some cases, the communist federal system had even created nations out of ethnic groups which had previously been unaware of, or uncertain as to their political identity – for example, the Macedonians in Yugoslavia were acknowledged as a separate nation from the Serbs when given their own republic; and similar cases can be found in Moldova and the Soviet Central Asian republics.

As a result, the nationalism which emerged with the breakdown of communist rule was not only the product of an oppressed 'dissident' intelligentsia, but was powerfully reinforced by local communist cadres who jumped on the bandwagon, rapidly converting themselves into nationalists. The achievement of independent statehood for the republics was almost everywhere the result of an alliance between these two groups, and correspondingly represented a mixture of motives. For some nationalists, breaking away from the federation was the only way in which political freedom and democratic, constitutional statehood could realistically be achieved. For while small nations might indeed be argued to have compelling interests in forming a political union with others for security and economic advantage, as long as the existing federal state within which they found themselves was associated with the injustices and inefficiencies of communism, this was simply not the right political union for them to remain in. Indeed, a far more attractive one presented itself to their west, in the European Union. The motive of 'returning to Europe' was especially clear in the separatist calculations of the relatively more developed republics, the Baltic states, the Czech Republic and Slovenia.

But for other nationalists, separate statehood was a means to the end of preserving their positions of privilege and power once the communist machine which had created them and held them in post disintegrated. These former communist '*nomenklatura* nationalists' were much less interested in establishing constitutionalism and constraints on state power. To that extent, they saw no interest in renegotiating the communist federation along genuinely democratic and constitutional lines. Instead, they transformed the ideological collectivism of the old regime into a nationalist collectivism, and sought popular support by appealing to national pride, and often the xenophobic nationalist prejudices of the majority people of the republic. The result was the break-up of the federations before constitutionalism was seriously tried. The struggle between the differing conceptions of the purpose of the new national states which emerged became clear in the ensuing debates over their constitutional structure.

Constitutions, Nationalism and State-Building

In new states, constitutions perform wider and arguably more fundamental functions than in established states. At least, that aspect of the constitution which is focused on defining the political community, the basic terms of citizenship, the purposes of the state and its place in the world, tend to take up more time and energy – and to generate more hot air – than in more settled, secure and self-confident states. Nevertheless, the issues of political identity, national identity and 'ownership' of the state have affected the constitutional process in all postcommunist states to some extent, as suggested above in the discussion of the Polish case. The reasons for this can be summed up in the following ways. Firstly, statehood throughout twentieth-century Central and Eastern Europe has been fragile and contested. Borders have been redefined more than once in the course of the World Wars which raged over this territory, uprooting and decimating its variegated populations. The question of who are 'the people' in whose name the state is constituted has remained open to challenge.

But the roots of the problem of statehood in the region can be traced further back to the role played by nationalism in their formation. Nationalism in this part of the world emerged in the nineteenth century as a movement challenging existing dynastic and supranational imperial states (Tsarist Russia, Austria-Hungary under the Habsburgs, the Ottoman Empire) in the name of 'peoples' defined in ethnic, cultural and linguistic terms – in contrast to the 'civic' tradition established in the French Revolution, which defines the nation as an association of free citizens.

When nation-states were established in this cultural and intellectual context, the state was all too readily understood as the property of one ethno-national group, thereby excluding, or relegating to second-class status, the ethno-national minorities which almost everywhere also inhabited the new nation-state's territory. The conflicts this generated weakened the new states internally, and pitted them against their neighbours where these were nation-states claiming to represent the interests not only of their own citizens, but also of members of the same ethno-national group who found themselves (often unwillingly) citizens of another newly-formed state. The instability of this situation was readily exploited in the run-up to World War II by Nazi Germany. After the war, the forcible incorporation of the whole region into the Soviet 'bloc' smothered these tensions without actually doing anything to resolve them. With the collapse of communism, the very depth of the crisis of the state generated by totalitarian rule necessarily led to the reopening of these basic questions.

Most of the new states formed since 1989 have shown their vulnerability to the temptation faced by the earlier generation of nation-states formed in Central Europe after World War I: namely, to assert symbolically and in some cases practically the 'ownership' of the state by the majority ethno-national group. The establishment of constitutionalism in this context has been marked by struggle between the urge to collective national self-assertion and recognition of the need for liberal guarantees of individual rights and freedoms – in other words, by that ubiquitous competition between democracy (as majority rule) and constitutionalism, as pointed out in our introduction, which now reappears in a particular Central and East European form.

We can illustrate these rather abstract points by looking at some of the key issues of contention in constitution-making in new states. One such has been the issue of a 'state language'. One of the earliest signs that Gorbachev's policy of *demokratizatsiya* (democratisation) was taking root in the Soviet republics was the voicing of the demand for 'de-russification'. This led to efforts to strengthen the official role and status of the language of the 'titular nation' – the nation in whose name the Soviet Republic was formally established – and ultimately led to demands to guarantee the primacy, if not the exclusive use, of that language in all official business of the republic, and in its education and cultural systems. Symbolically, this represented a potent challenge to the centre in Moscow, but it also challenged the privileged position of local Russians and Russian-speakers living in the non-Russian republics. These were often regarded by the titular nations as agents of the Moscow centre, 'colonisers' whose rights to live in the republic were implicitly or explicitly questioned. At first, the language issue was welcomed by democrats, including democratically minded Russians, as a healthy sign of popular mobilisation for change and reform. But it also provoked a backlash among Russians and Russian-speaking minorities, especially where their jobs were threatened because they did not have adequate command of the titular nation's language.

While the titular nation justified this measure in terms of rectifying the previous injustices caused by the prevailing use of Russian and the corresponding advantages this gave Russians and Russian-speakers in the non-Russian republics, the latter saw this measure as undemocratic. This conflict was readily exploited by hard-line communist opponents of all aspects of Gorbachev's *perestroika*, and so the language issue became deeply politicised. When the republics became independent, enshrining the national language as the official language of state in the new constitutions was closely bound up with the idea of establishing full independence. The Russian and Russian-speaking minorities left in the newly-formed states had by this time become unfortunately identified with opposition not only to democracy but to the very existence of the new state itself. After independence, they found themselves in a very uncomfortable position, and inevitably turned to the new Russian state for help. This only confirmed the mistrust and suspicion with which they were regarded by the new ruling elites in the new states.

Language has also been an issue in other new states. In Slovakia, the drive to enshrine Slovak as the state language after independence was directed less against Czech than against Hungarian. A sizeable Hungarian minority living along Slovakia's southern border with Hungary had been less than enthusiastic about the break-up of Czechoslovakia, particularly when the increasing stridency of Slovak nationalism and the introduction of language laws signalled that the cultural and educational rights they had previously enjoyed would be whittled away. Since independence, the Hungarians have become the butt of Slovak nationalist extremists, and, despite the recommendations of international human and minority rights monitoring bodies, the Slovaks have still to introduce satisfactory legislation to clarify and guarantee the use of Hungarian in those areas where substantial proportions of Hungarians live.

The language issue is intimately connected with the issue of citizenship in new states. This can be illustrated particularly dramatically in the cases of Estonia and Latvia. Both of these states today claim that they are not in fact 'new' states at all. They existed as independent, sovereign states in the inter-war period, and were only incorporated into the Soviet Union by force in the course of World War II. They were, therefore, under illegal occupation for the whole of the postwar period, and major Western states never formally recognised their incorporation into the Soviet Union. The break-up of the Soviet Union thus opened the way for the restoration of their previous legal status, and although both states have had to revise their pre-war constitutions radically to bring them into line with the changes that have since taken place, nevertheless the basic constitutional principle is the assertion of legal continuity with the pre-war states.

This has had a dramatic effect on the position of those Russians, Russian-speakers and other peoples from the former Soviet Union who migrated into these republics after World War II, by 1991 constituting some 30–40 per cent of the total populations. They are regarded by the new authorities as illegal immigrants. In Estonia, citizenship legislation is based on a law in effect in 1938. Only those inhabitants of present-day Estonia who were citizens of the pre-war republic under this law, or are descendants of those citizens, have automatically acquired full political rights. Note that this is not explicitly ethnic – pre-war Estonia had a small Russian minority who (and whose descendants) have had no problem in gaining citizenship on equal terms with ethnic Estonians. But the rest of the Russian and Russian-speaking population has had to apply for citizenship, a major condition of which is to demonstrate a fair command of Estonian – a difficult language few took the trouble to learn before 1991. Some categories – such as former Soviet military and KGB personnel – have been excluded outright. Although non-citizens have been granted the right to vote in local elections, there are restrictions on non-citizens standing as candidates for election. And the stringent application of the language laws has threatened the careers of many Russian-speakers.

Not all new states have taken this line. In Ukraine, for example, the 'zero option' was chosen, which offered citizenship to all permanent residents of the republic at the time of independence in 1991. The same is true of Slovakia. But in both cases, full citizenship in the broader political sense of equal recognition, respect and status in the republic remains somewhat problematic as long as uncertainty continues to surround the basic question of 'whose state this is'. Both Slovak and Ukrainian nationalists tend to argue as if the state were first of all the state of ethnic Slovaks and Ukrainians. Thus while all may be equal in legal terms, in political life the nationalists suggest that Ukrainians and Slovaks are 'first among equals'. This is implied in the constitutional status of the Ukrainian and Slovak languages.

A key constitutional question for all of these multi-national new states is how to define appropriate rights for national and ethnic minorities. This is not an easy question for any democracy, including the longest-established ones, such as Britain, France and the United States, which have far from unblemished records in this respect. International human rights and minority rights laws and standards tend to be rather minimalist in their definition of the rights of minorities, in part because there is not a great deal of agreement among states, and because the specific conditions and historical origins of minorities vary so greatly between states. Above all, international laws and standards are the product of negotiations among states, which tend to be jealous of their sovereignty and concerned to defend their territorial integrity, which minorities within their own populations are often seen as threatening. So although the new postcommunist states have signed up to United Nations, Council of Europe and other documents on minority rights, these are often seen as inadequate, or as inadequately implemented, by their minority populations.

Some minorities, for example the Hungarians outside Hungary (in Slovakia, Romania, Serbia and Ukraine), and the Russians in some of the post-Soviet republics, have demanded more rights than are provided for in international documents. They argue that they need 'collective rights', not merely individual human rights, because being a member of a minority means being part of a collective culture. What this may imply is the right not only to protection against discrimination, but some form of separate self-government or 'autonomy'. Russians and Russian-speakers concentrated in the Narva region of north-east Estonia attempted to set up a separate region in which the writ of Estonian law, in particular the language law, would not apply. This has since collapsed, but in Moldova, a separate break-away 'Transdniester Republic' was established, and defended itself with armed force (and some support from former Soviet military bases in the region) against all attempts by the Moldovan authorities to restore control. This is now being gradually achieved by negotiation in which the Russian and Ukrainian governments are also playing a part. In another part of Moldova, a second break-away republic was set up by the Gagauz, a minority which was as much opposed to the Moldovan language law as the Russian-speakers were. However, this 'republic' has since come to terms with the Moldovan authorities, and has been granted separate constitutional status as a special region with the right to self-government through its own parliament and elected governor, and the right to use their own Gagauz language and Russian (which most of the educated and professional elite use as much or even more than Gagauz language) as well as Moldovan.

The Hungarian minorities have also demanded 'autonomy', but this has been rejected especially strongly in Slovakia and Romania, which interpret this as a threat to their territorial integrity. This fear arises from historic memories of World War II, when the Hungarian state, in alliance with Nazi Germany, seized back southern Slovakia and northern Transylvania in Romania, both regions with concentrated Hungarian minority populations. But Slovaks and Romanians can also point to the example of the behaviour of Russian minorities in the former Soviet republics to bolster their case that minority 'autonomy' is a right too far, which no state can contemplate. To some extent, they receive sympathy for this view in international circles. However, this sympathy is dependent on their showing more good faith than they have so far in their efforts to make their minority populations feel genuinely 'at home' and equal partners in the states where they have lived for centuries.

The problem of minority rights illustrates some general issues in constitution-making in the context of postcommunist Europe. For instance, while the aspiration to 'return to Europe' may be strong, and may exert a positive influence in favour of the development of liberal constitutionalism, there is no one universally accepted 'European' constitutional model. The French model, which has exerted a powerful attraction throughout the region as the epitome of the modern, democratic nation-state, can often be abused by authoritarians who selectively refer to its strongly centralised traditional form with a dominant presidency and weak parliament; and by nationalists, who point to its emphasis on the rights of individuals and rejection of the idea that diverse groups within the body of citizens might want and need some form of recognition of their different cultural identity, and some special provisions to ensure that they are able to preserve that identity. But the French state itself has reformed and decentralised in the past twenty years, granting more powers to regional governments, in line with a widespread trend in 'postmodern' Europe. It is, moreover, increasingly coming under pressure from its own minority groups, especially of Algerian origin, who are deeply dissatisfied with their status and resent the inbuilt assimilatory tendencies of the French 'model' of universal, undifferentiated citizenship.

While the debate over constitutions and constitutional laws on language and citizenship is often couched in terms of a choice between 'civic' and 'ethnic' models, this can be misleading. All liberal-democratic states in practice embody a mix of 'civic' and 'ethnic' components in the basic assumptions built into their constitutions. The new postcommunist constitutions understandably find it difficult, given their histories and their present sense of uncertainty and insecurity, to strike the right balance. But an equally pressing issue in the postcommunist context is the choice between monolithic and pluralist conceptions of the state. It is again understandable that weak new states with inexperienced leaders (or leaders whose only past experience has been in the communist system) should tend to prefer unitary and centralised state forms. It is even more understandable in the context of new states formed out of recently collapsed federations that there should be resistance to the idea of institutional pluralism. And yet some form of federalism – if not in name, at least in practice – might be argued to be a more appropriate form of state for the purposes of managing ethnically plural societies than the unitary and centralised 'model' which seems to feature so strongly in postcommunist constitutional debate. While one can readily point to ethnic federations in crisis – such as Belgium and Canada – one should not overlook the success of, for example, post-authoritarian Spain, which has stabilised a potentially explosive set of ethnonational tensions, particularly involving the Basques and Catalans, by granting them flexibly defined rights to 'autonomy'.

Again, the point is that there are no ready models to be drawn directly from the European experience. Liberal democratic constitutions have taken an enormous variety of forms. Moreover, the very future of the 'nation-state', the classic form of the liberal state, as a sovereign and internally homogeneous political entity, is today in question. Nation-states in Europe are increasingly being eroded both from above, by political and economic integration, transferring significant 'sovereign' powers to the European Union; and from below, facing rising assertiveness on the part of diverse cultural groups, regional movements and national minorities. Some of the same constitutional challenges faced by the constitution-makers of postcommunist Central and Eastern Europe are ones that now confront the whole of Europe.

6

The Politics of Leadership

RAY TARAS

In the 1990s, the postcommunist states of Eastern Europe have faced the conflicting imperatives of, on the one hand, creating a checks-and-balances system that would limit executive power (which had become immense under communism), and, on the other, ensuring sufficiently strong leadership to govern politically or ethnically divided societies, disaffected social groups reeling from shock therapy, and fragmented party systems. This dilemma can be conceptualised in terms of the perpetual tension between the imperatives of democracy and efficiency.

Communism had been neither democratic nor very efficient, and the institutional pioneers of postcommunism in Eastern Europe expected that democratic capitalism would be both. In practice, built-in biases existed in each country that tilted the emergent system towards one or the other of these imperatives. In this chapter, I examine the character of postcommunist leadership – both how democratic and how efficacious it has been in the region's states. The following chapter focuses in greater detail on representative institutions.

Leadership Confronted with Resurgent Representative Institutions

Ensuring democratic rule and efficient government need not be irreconcilable tasks, as Richard Rose and William Mishler have written: 'The ideal democratic system is representative and has effective leaders. Logically, the two criteria can be mutually reinforcing, in so far as leaders may gain effectiveness by mobilizing popular support, and effective action increases a leader's popular support' 1996b, p. 224). Historically Eastern Europe tended to favour strong leaders. But a backlash against authoritarian regimes, triggered by the experience of communism, created special circumstances in which representative institutions seemed to have become more valued. Has there indeed been a normative shift towards prizing representative forms of government at the cost of valuing strong leadership?

Attitudinal data from the first years of the political transition indicated that the importance of leaders was, on the whole, less esteemed than that of representative institutions. On the basis of survey results from nine states of the region compiled during 1992–3, Rose and Mishler observed: '*Representative democrats* disapprove of the suspension of parliament and reject the appeal of strong leaders; they total 48 per cent of NDB [New Democracies Barometer] respondents, and are the largest group in six of the nine post-communist societies surveyed' (1996b, p. 233). These six were the Czech Republic, Hungary, Poland, Romania, Slovakia, and Ukraine.

Only in Bulgaria, Slovenia, and Belarus did *leadership democrats* – respondents favouring a reform of parliament to allow a strong leader to emerge – comprise a plurality. *Authoritarians* – those calling for the suspension of parliament and the emergence of a strong leader – made up as much as one-quarter of respondents in Belarus and Ukraine but their numbers were insignificant elsewhere. The question is whether this preference for representative processes over strong leadership was registered in the institutional arrangements designed in Eastern European states.

Where the representative democratic tendency comprised a substantial majority of respondents, as in the Czech Republic, Hungary, and, more surprisingly, Romania and Slovakia (Rose and Mishler, 1996b, p. 233), we might expect the balance of power between executive and legislative branches of government to be tilted towards the latter. In this type of system parliament would be more influential than the presidency; and the government (or cabinet, headed by the prime minister), once it had been given a vote of confidence by parliament, would be a more important locus of policy-making than the executive office. If the leadership democratic option was institutionalised in those states where it dominated (mentioned above), a presidential system would be more likely to arise.

But the preferences of electors alone do not determine the shape of a political system. The constitution, drafted by legal experts, seeks to superimpose a given type of relationship between parliament, cabinet, prime minister, and president. The East European constitutions adopted in the 1990s have reflected contingency: on the political traditions of the individual states, as well as the prevailing political circumstances of the day. The pull of the more authoritarian arrangements of the past was mitigated by the attraction of the Western representative system that proved its superiority in the Cold War. Other than France where, since 1958, a powerful presidency was occasionally discernible, Western Europe offered a persuasive case for adopting a parliamentary system of government. For it was a model for political stability and accompanying economic prosperity. The strength of the US presidential system, while often admired, was generally not easily replicated.

Leaders, their personalities, and styles affect the character of a political system, too. Especially crucial in a transition period is the emergence of 'leaders with the personality formation appropriate to democracy' (Lasswell, 1986, p. 196). Returning to Rose and Mishler's terms, a system that resembles representative rather than leadership democracy – a parliamentary rather than presidential one – may still end up with a strong, authoritarian-oriented prime minister. As we see later, Slovakia may be such a case. Equally, Western leaders may serve as role models for East European politicians. For example, the temptation to rule in the style of Margaret Thatcher appealed to Poland's Lech Walesa, while the unexciting, bureaucratic style of German Chancellor Hans Kohl seemed to appeal to Czech prime minister Vaclav Klaus. Leadership styles – political brokers, consensus-builders, imperial presidents, chief executive officers, anti-leaders, charismatics – differ widely and do influence the nature of a political system.

Finally, no matter how committed to representative government a society may be, the very issue of strong or weak leadership will often remain at the top of the political agenda. Individual leaders and the roles they play will always generate controversy: the question is how much. Thus, in the case of postcommunist Russia, David Lane has contended that 'in the early transition period of political change, the sources of political conflicts and the dynamics of social change are to be found not in the mobilization of the non-elites but in contradictions of goals and interests among the elites' (Lane, 1995, p. 46). That one elite prevailed over another is widely held to account for the Czech Republic's economic successes and Bulgaria's reform failures, Czechoslovakia's peaceful break-up and the brutal wars of Yugoslav succession, and the political uncertainties in Albania and Romania until 1996–7, when fair elections brought counter-elites to power. Eastern Europe of the 1990s furnishes cases of strong, effective leadership and also, paradoxically, weak and effective leadership. But we will also find cases where there has been a failure of leadership.

Factors Shaping Executive Power

The executive branch of government in Eastern Europe has been transformed since the fall of communist regimes in 1989. Changes have affected the *process* of choosing political leaders, as well as the *distribution of power* vested in the executive branch. Of particular importance in designing the 'architecture' of power has been the manner of controlling the actions of leaders and, related to this, the relationship between executive and legislative branches of government. For as Robert C. Tucker, a long-time analyst of Soviet politics, hypothesised, 'we can see the possibility of an authoritarian personality serving as leader in the regime of a constitutional democracy, and, conversely, of a democratic personality serving as the leader in an authoritarian system of rule' (Tucker, 1981, p. 68). The 'institutionalised difference between democratic and authoritarian forms of government' is based on: (i) the possibility or prohibition of active public participation in leadership choice; and, (ii) control of or submission to executive prerogatives.

As in such other political spheres as party formation and electoral behaviour (considered in later chapters), the nature of leadership in postcommunist Eastern European countries is idiosyncratic, often owing more to national preferences and traditions than to any cross-national postcommunist 'formula' for ensuring democratisation of executive power. A differing pace of democratising executive power is visible – for example, precocious in the Czech Republic and sluggish in the Balkans.

The experience of communism was a key factor affecting the development of postcommunist executive power. The communist system was quintessentially elitist, with power concentrated in the hands of a small steering group at the head of a massive political organisation. Not surprisingly, in devising new executive structures many of the caretaker governments responsible for political transition sought to avoid communist practice by adopting radical changes: direct election of the chief executive and a premium placed on his or her coalition-building skills in a multi-party setting.

A second influence shaping the emergence of new executive structures has been a country's earlier experience with representative government. The political arrangements of the inter-war period have been particularly important in affecting thinking about new structures. Not in all cases, however, has that experience involved an anti-elitist thrust. Thus advocates of a presidential system in Czechoslovakia or Poland would hold up the examples of dominant inter-war leaders like Tomas Masaryk and Jozef Pilsudski. Postcommunist presidents Vaclav Havel of Czechoslovakia and Lech Walesa of Poland were informed by the experience of their inter-war precursors in contrasting ways. Havel was content to serve in the role of moderator, but Walesa self-consciously strove to become an imperial president.

In the case of Hungary, the authoritarian inter-war leader Admiral Horthy inspired little nostalgia in the 1990s. This may have, if anything, moulded Hungarian political culture into a less leadership-oriented system than elsewhere in the region, reflected in the postcommunist phase as well. Turnout for a referendum in 1990 on the method of electing the country's president was only 14 per cent, suggesting Hungarians' ambivalent attitude to leadership.

Both Bulgaria's and Romania's inter-war experience of illiberal politics and authoritarianism offered a negative learning process for contemporary leaders. Significantly, both countries languished under quasi-communist rule until late 1996. In what used to be Yugoslavia, most South Slav nations took advantage of the collapse of monolithic communism to oppose the restoration of any type of Serb-dominated state. Strong presidencies were established in the former Yugoslav republics of Croatia, Macedonia and Bosnia-Herzegovina. Slovenia's break from Serb rule was sufficiently peaceful and swift that it could afford to forgo a powerful executive.

In addition to the backlash against the communist legacy and the learning experience of inter-war politics, a third factor shaping new executive structures was the self-interest of the architectural team itself. Adam Przeworski has argued that 'The decisive step toward democracy is the devolution of power from a group of people to a set of rules' (Przeworski, 1991, p. 14). But taking this step was hardly a purely technical affair, for 'Each political force opts for the institutional framework that will best further its values, projects, or interests' (ibid., p. 80). In practice, rules were fashioned by political actors whose own resources and interests differed. Especially in the transitional situation, 'the chances of the particular political forces are very different under alternative institutional arrangements' (ibid., p. 40). Those who favoured a strong executive (like Walesa) were frequently precisely the politicians who were the strongest candidates for such office; those who preferred cabinet-type government (like Klaus) were often party leaders who were certain they would do best in a parliamentary system.

In summary, in the transition period political forces battled to tailor institutions to their own needs. Hence the different types of executive structures that emerged in East European states in the 1990s were the products of bidding and bargaining among interested parties – not purely rational outcomes arrived at by disinterested state-builders.

Models of Executive Power

Simple typologies of political executives – whether they are effective (US President) or ceremonial (King of Spain), and individual (German Chancellor) or collective (British Cabinet) – outline the range of alternatives that may exist (Almond and Powell, 1983, p. 106). Institutional arrangements for leadership differ widely, even within a close-knit geopolitical region such as the European Union. Executive power also fluctuates over time, as in the case of the US where a 200-year-old constitution has not prevented changes from taking place to the powers of the president. So it should be no surprise that there are different approaches to executive power in Eastern Europe today.

In postcommunist Eastern Europe there has been a slight preference for direct elections of the president. Even where this system is not in place – Albania, the Czech Republic, Hungary and Slovakia – efforts were made to adopt such a system. Thus the Westminster model of parliamentary democracy has not caught on. On the other hand, the establishment of cabinet government, headed by a prime minister together with a group of ministers responsible for different areas of government, indicates that the US presidential system has also not been accepted.

In many respects, the variation in executive power in East European states can be viewed in terms of preferring the French Third Republic (1870–1940) or its Fifth Republic system (since 1958). In both systems the institutions of the presidency and cabinet government were central. But in the lengthy existence of the Third Republic, and in great measure during the short-lived Fourth Republic (1946–58), the prime minister was ascendant, if at the mercy of rapidly shifting coalitions in the legislature (called Chamber of Deputies to 1946, since then known as the National Assembly). The Fifth Republic created in 1958 by General de Gaulle to suit General de Gaulle transformed France into a strong, but not quite imperial, presidential system. The president was elected for a seven-year term while the National Assembly's was four. The head of state now nominated the prime minister, subject to ratification by the National Assembly. In conjunction with the prime minister, the president selected cabinet ministers. The 'incompatibility' rule of the Fifth Republic further kept the Cabinet and the Assembly off balance: it gave deputies 30 days to resign from parliament if they were to accept a nomination to a cabinet post – a procedure standing in contrast with the British parliamentary system. The purpose of the rule was to prevent deputies from voting down one government after another on the expectation that in this game of musical chairs their number would come up. It also ensured that ministers, divorced from the legislature, would have a tough time building a power base in that body.

In the Fifth Republic either the president or the prime minister can chair the cabinet. The most important power the president has over the legislature is the ability to dissolve it and call for new elections. Further, the constitution grants him emergency powers 'when the institutions of the Republic, the independence of the nation, the integrity of its territory are threatened in a grave and immediate manner'. In such cases the president 'shall take measures required by these circumstances'. In keeping with the powers of the office, French presidents such as de Gaulle, Giscard d'Estaing and Mitterrand have affected aloofness in the office. While de Gaulle especially sought to increase his distance from the rest of the body politic by claiming to be above politics, even socialist president Mitterrand tried to decouple his fortunes from those of his party.

This continental model had obvious attractions to East European states building democracy. To be sure, with the exception of Romania's four-year term, Eastern Europe presidents serve for five years, unlike the French president's seven. Like the French National Assembly, East European parliaments have a four-year mandate (the exception is Slovenia, where it is five). A chief weakness of the Fifth Republic system lies in the possibility that parties of the left and right

would capture different institutions – the presidency and the legislature – thereby creating a constitutional crisis. The Fifth Republic
has weathered uneasy periods of 'cohabitation', such as between a
socialist president and a conservative government from 1986 to 1988,
and a conservative president and socialist prime minister from 1997
on. But cohabitation in the more fragile and volatile conditions of
postcommunist Eastern Europe has not worked as smoothly. Indica-
tive of this is how the election of a democratic president in Bulgaria in
1996 precipitated a wave of anti-socialist demonstrations demanding
the resignation of the socialist government even though it had been
given a mandate to rule to the end of 1998.

In addition to struggles between the ancient regime and the new,
and between competing political parties for representation, the first
years of postcommunism in Eastern Europe featured a struggle
between rival institutional agendas. One was a preference for representative and accountable government, sensitive to short-term shifts
in party fortunes, modelled on a Third Republic-type system. The
other was a desire for strong stable visionary leadership rising above
partisan parliamentary squabbles, along the lines of the Fifth Republic system.

Except in former Yugoslavia (as well as most former Soviet
republics), East European states have adopted parliamentary systems
of government. This choice is explained by several considerations.
First, a presidential system generates a zero-sum game, with the
winning candidate taking all and the losers receiving nothing. Parliamentary systems, by contrast, increase total payoffs, with many
parties and their candidates 'winning' influence. Even clear-cut losers
in this system have a greater incentive to stay in the parliamentary
game with prospects of expanding their representation next time.
Coupled with a climate of continued suspicion about elites, it is
understandable that parliamentarism has emerged as the region's
preferred system of government.

We have outlined the range of choices available to East European
states in designing structures of executive power, and we have pointed
to a preference for Third Republic-type arrangements. Several Balkan
states, like Bulgaria, Romania, and Slovenia, were converted to
parliamentary – more precisely, prime ministerial – government in
the second half of the 1990s. Przeworski has stressed that 'contagion
plays a role. Co-temporarility induces homogeneity: The new democracies learn from the established ones and from one another' (Przeworski, 1991, pp. 98–9). But we should also recognise that 'our cultural

repertoire of political institutions is limited. In spite of minute variations, the institutional models of democracy are very few' (ibid., p. 99).

The Background of East European Leadership

An issue that many in the West would assume would be paramount in
choosing democratic leadership in Eastern Europe is what potential
leaders were doing under the former communist regime. Many
specialists have noted how the majority of postcommunist leaders
had ties to the communist regime. According to André Liebich,

> In virtually all post-communist countries, including those which
> have abandoned old political habits, familiar faces from the com-
> munist past dominate the landscape. . . . Everywhere, individuals
> who have dropped out of the elite since the fall of communism are
> outnumbered by those who have maintained or improved their
> positions, by a ratio of almost nine to one in Russia and over two
> to one in Poland and Hungary. Until age attrition takes its toll, the
> best prospects for success under democracy will belong to those
> who were successful under communism. (Liebich, 1997, p. 68)

The ex-communists who have attained leadership posts in the
young East European democracies bring with them attributes that
post-totalitarian elites share. According to Juan Linz and Alfred
Stepan, 'post-totalitarian leaders tend to be more bureaucratic and
state technocratic than charismatic' (Linz and Stepan, 1996a, p. 47).
Post-totalitarians include men like Ion Iliescu in Romania and
Slobodan Milosevic in Yugoslavia, recruited from and associated
with the former communist organisations in order to consolidate
power. But it is important to differentiate among 1990s leaders who
were 1980s communist officials. Thus, leaders like Alexander Kwasniewski in Poland and Gyula Horn in Hungary came to power *after*
breaking with the communist apparatus and tapped a different base
of political support. While all of these men are ex-communists and all,
to varying degrees, have reflected bureacratic leadership, what dis-
tinguishes 'postcommunists' from post-totalitarians is that they have
embraced the rules of the democratic game.

Dissidents from the old communist regime have not, as a group,
been as successful in taking power as the former communists. It may
seem puzzling that relatively few 'old warriors', hardened by years of

struggle against communism, held power for very long in the 1990s. In part this was because they were too ideological (Vaclav Havel was an exception). Just as often political leadership was entrusted to individuals with negligible apprenticeship in the anti-communist struggle but having the right professional skills – in management, private business, law, economics. Since reform of the economy was the most critical issue affecting postcommunist societies, it was logical that new polities placed high value on such qualifications. Ironically, then, while some communist rulers had been imprisoned in the Stalin period, only a handful of postcommunist presidents and prime ministers had been incarcerated in the communist period: Jozsef Antall of Hungary, Havel, and Walesa.

Regime transition in some ways involved a generational change. Many young professionals in their thirties and forties whose formative years were the halcyon 'goulash communism' period of the 1970s, were catapulted to executive power as foreign, defence, and finance ministers. They were free of an obsession with the horrors of communism and well suited to introduce new agendas. They were largely detached from political storms surrounding release of secret police files naming certain dissidents as past collaborators with the communist state.

Winning popular elections requires different political skills and resources from those needed for winning out over communism. The question 'What did *you* do to overthrow communism?' surprisingly quickly became irrelevant in choosing leaders. Some critics of the new systems have pointed to their flawed character: nowhere was decommunisation carried out with much energy. A contrary view is that there can be no better evidence of the professionalisation of leadership in Eastern Europe than making the communist past irrelevant.

Models of Leadership among the East European States

How have the states of Eastern Europe chosen their leaders, empowered them, and controlled them? Is incumbency a major advantage and re-election all but assured, or is there a high rate of turnover in the elite? Are elections hotly contested, leading to splits in party preferences, or is there a snowball effect where voters bandwagon with the major party? A selective analysis of emergent executive power in the region can help to answer these questions (see also Table 6.1).

TABLE 6.1   *Presidencies in Central and Eastern Europe (as of 1 January 1998)*

	Mode of election	Powers[1]	Incumbent	Affiliation[2]
Albania	By parliament	Weak	Rexhep Mejdani	Postcommunist
Bosnia-Herzegovina[3]	Popular	Strong	Alija Izetbegoivic	Islamic
Bulgaria	Popular	Medium	Petar Stoyanov	Democratic
Croatia	Popular	Strong	Franjo Tudjman	Nationalist
Czech Republic	By parliament	Weak	Vaclav Havel	Democratic
Hungary	By parliament	Weak	Arpad Goncz	Democratic
Macedonia	Popular	Strong	Kiro Gligorov	Democratic
Poland	Popular	Weak	Alexander Kwasniewski	Postcommunist
Slovakia	By parliament	Weak	Michal Kovac	Democratic
Slovenia	Popular	Medium	Milan Kucan	Democratic
Yugoslav Federation	By parliament	Strong	Slobodan Milosevic	Communist

Notes:
[1]   Refers to constitutionally-enumerated powers; the actual influence of the president in the political system is usually greater.
[2]   Refers to the political constituency that the president depends upon for support; in a number of states the president is required not to be a member of a political party.
[3]   The presidency is collective: its members are elected directly, and they then elect a head.

Bulgaria

The office of president was created in Bulgaria in April 1990 after other countries in Eastern Europe had set up the institution. It was given to a communist, Petar Mladenov, who only stayed in office to July 1990, when evidence linking him to communist plans for using force to crush the democratic opposition compelled him to resign. The Grand National Assembly, or Parliament, elected Zhelyu Zhelev as new president. Zhelev had been a critical Marxist in the communist regime and was the author of a celebrated book comparing socialism to fascism. Initially he was a popular leader who embodied a break with the *ancien régime*, but by the time of the country's first direct presidential elections in January 1992, his support had declined. He received 45 per cent of the vote in the first round, forcing him into a runoff. Zhelev obtained just 53 per cent of the vote in the second round, barely defeating Velko Valkanov, a 64-year-old lawyer who, though never a member of the old communist party, received much of its support.

A remarkable phenomenon that occurred in the first years of regime change in a number of postcommunist states was the political appeal of émigré candidates. In the 1992 Bulgarian presidential elections, such an outsider candidate managed to obtain 17 per cent of the vote. A former basketball player and fencer, 52-year-old 'Georges' Ganchev had lived for 25 years in England and the US. He claimed that he was a successful actor in the West; not only that, he had married the daughter of the president of Woolworth's stores. From Armenia to Estonia to Poland, 'making it' in the West attracted votes during the first phase of democratisation. When by the mid-1990s collective wishful thinking that Westernised politicians could bring Western affluence to Eastern Europe ended, leadership choices became more orthodox.

The 1992 presidential elections revealed other sobering characteristics of postcommunist leadership. Few women were rising to high office in the new governments, and Zhelev's narrow margin of victory was attributed in part to lack of voter enthusiasm for his running mate, the poet Blaga Dimitrova. The robust opposition to Zhelev was energised by often-distasteful nationalist, especially anti-Turkish, slogans which had the implicit support of the ex-communists.

Bulgaria's postcommunist constitution limited the powers of the state president to security matters and ceremonial functions. The president could not veto legislation passed by parliament, for example, and governance was effectively in the hands of the Grand National Assembly. Zhelev may have been able to enhance the powers of the office through his ability to broker deals with leaders of the legislature, but he simultaneously suffered from an image of being too pliable. Furthermore, cohabition between a president who had been a Marxist and a democratic movement that made up the government was bound to limit the president's room for manoeuvre.

As with the presidency, transition in the legislative branch was marked by a gradual shift away from communist leadership. The free elections of June 1990 returned a communist majority to the Grand National Assembly. The result could in part be explained by the little time the recently legalised opposition had to organise a campaign. The first prime minister was Andrei Lukanov of the Bulgarian Socialist Party (BSP) – the successor to the Communist Party – but by December 1990 a broader coalition government was set up under

Dimitar Popov, officially not a member of any party but most of whose cabinet was made up of BSP ministers.

In parliamentary elections in October 1991 the Union of Democratic Forces (UDF) – a coalition of opposition parties – won a narrow victory over the BSP (by a margin of 110 seats to 106). A minority government was formed under prime minister Filip Dimitrov, UDF head. His cabinet included a number of ministers who were staunchly anti-communist and, inevitably, it was brought down in the legislature by the BSP. A pivotal role in the making and breaking of cabinets was played by the small Turkish ethnic party, the Movement for Rights and Freedoms led by Ahmed Dogan, which held the balance of power in the National Assembly.

After its lacklustre electoral performances failure the BSP sought to disassociate itself with its communist origins by enacting a generational change. A 32-year-old economist, Zhan Videnov, was selected to head the party, and he led it to an impressive victory in the December 1994 parliamentary elections. The BSP and its allies captured 125 seats to the UDF's 69. Perhaps due to inexperience and perhaps due to lack of commitment to serious reform, over the next two years prime minister Videnov's government presided over a disastrous economic tailspin – even by East European standards – and tolerated widespread corruption in and out of government.

The victory of Petar Stoyanov – a 44-year-old lawyer and self-described product of the Beatles' generation – over the BSP candidate in presidential elections in November 1996 highlighted the popular backlash against the ex-communists. In the runoff against minister of culture Ivan Marazov, Stoyanov captured 61.1 per cent of votes cast to 38.9 per cent for the BSP ticket that also included Irina Bokova, a deputy foreign minister. Stoyanov's popular mandate made it possible for him to extract the resignation of the BSP government a few months later. With a comfortable 125-seat majority in the National Assembly, the BSP could have stayed in power until the end of 1998, but widespread demonstrations forced Videnov to resign as prime minister in December 1996 and the socialist government collapsed two months later.

The April 1997 elections provided the anti-communist bloc with its first absolute majority in parliament since the end of communism. Running as the United Democratic Forces (ODS), it won 137 seats (52 per cent of the popular vote) to the BSP's 58 seats (22 per cent). The Union for National Salvation that included Dogan's Turkish-minority movement took 19 seats (8 per cent) while a newcomer,

Euroleft led by Alexander Tomov, a former socialist deputy prime minister who set up a centrist party for socialist defectors, won 14 seats (6 per cent). The new prime minister was 47-year-old Ivan Kostov, a former finance minister committed to following the International Monetary Fund's blueprint for economic reform. A key ministerial portfolio, foreign minister, went to a woman, Nadezhda Mihailova, who met with her counterpart, US Secretary of State Madeleine Albright, twice, shortly after taking office.

The ODS victory prompted some of its members to push for a constitutional amendment (a two-thirds majority was required) that would enhance the powers of the popular president Stoyanov, seen as a catalyst in breaking the ex-communists' grip on power. But others believed that the ODS should avoid a continuation of the 'war between the institutions' – president and parliament – that the ODS now controlled. And from a royalist faction in the Union for National Salvation came a call for a restoration of the monarchy. King Simeon II took the appeal seriously enough to visit the country after the April 1997 elections.

Czech Republic

Czechoslovakia's 1989 velvet revolution that overthrew the communist regime was engineered by the Civic Forum and its Slovak counterpart, the Public Against Violence – both loose umbrella groups comprising numerous political orientations. Predictably, in 1991 the Civic Forum disintegrated. Its most significant offshoot became the Civic Democratic Party (ODS) of then finance minister Vaclav Klaus, an economist. Two other splinter groups formed the conservative Civic Democratic Alliance and the left-of-centre Civic Movement.

By late 1991 the president of Czechoslovakia, former dissident and playwright Vaclav Havel who had been elected to the office by parliament in December 1989, had been stymied in his bid to gain greater powers for his office. Slovak parties in particular opposed his efforts to centralise power by asking for the right to dissolve the Federal Assembly and call new elections. In January 1992 some Czech parties in the Federal Assembly also joined in to defeat constitutional amendments Havel proposed that would have required both Czech and Slovak parliaments to approve a new federal constitution and Slovakia to hold a referendum on whether it wished to remain federated. At that time polls indicated that a majority of Slovaks would not approve of a break-up of the federation. Slovak prime minister Vladimir Meciar was opposed to such a referendum since he had read the same poll results.

In June 1992 Meciar's Movement for a Democratic Slovakia emerged as the winner of elections to the Slovak regional parliament. Together with Klaus, his winning counterpart in the Czech regional parliament, they began the process of splitting the country into two. Havel realised that the two leaders had left him with a *fait accompli* – the end of a federal state that he had sought to preserve – and by summer resigned as president, admitting that 'it is better to split into two states in a peaceful constitutional manner than to descend into legal chaos'.

Five rounds of voting in the Federal Assembly to find a successor to Havel produced no consensus. It appeared that Klaus, by then Czech prime minister, wished to save Havel for the future office of president of the independent Czech republic. Indeed, in January 1993 when the Czech Republic became a separate state, parliament moved quickly to elect Havel as president and he accepted the office.

The political system of the Czech Republic vests power in parliament and the party that commands it. The enduring popularity of Havel (he was by far the Republic's most popular politician in late 1997 with over 70 per cent approval ratings) may have been produced in large part by the perception that he was not hungry for power. His wish to craft a presidency in his own image had, therefore, built-in limits. But the weakened position of Klaus's government following the June 1996 elections gave the president greater influence. Klaus's ODS and its two junior partners lost their majority in parliament: capturing 44 per cent of the popular vote among them, they gained 99 seats in the 200-member parliament, down from 105 in 1992. The largest gain was recorded by the Social Democratic Party (CSSD), whose support rose from just 6 per cent in 1992 to 26 per cent in 1996. Extreme parties of the left (10 per cent) and right (8 per cent) also improved their positions, making for a stalemated parliament. Havel stepped in to broker a deal by which Klaus became prime minister of a minority government while Milos Zeman, CSSD head and, like Klaus, an economist, became parliamentary chairman. In June 1997 Klaus narrowly survived a vote of no confidence (by a margin of 101–99), and Havel called on the prime minister to restore trust in his government.

Klaus's increasing unpopularity boosted the fortunes of other party leaders within his alliance. One was ODS deputy leader and foreign minister Josef Zieleniec. Another was Josef Lux, head of the ODS's coalition partner, the Christian Democratic Union, a small rural party. Lux began to play the role of kingmaker in the weakened government. A third was Civic Democratic Alliance head Michal Zantovsky, former Czech ambassador to the US, a translator by profession, and President Havel's spokesman after 1989. What the 1996 elections made clear was that leadership in the Czech Republic would no longer be dominated by Klaus and Havel. Indeed in December 1997 Klaus resigned as prime minister over, officially at least, a campaign funding scandal. With perhaps too many would-be successors ensconced in the major parties, Havel turned to a political outsider, Central Bank governor Josef Tosovsky, to form a new government.

Hungary

The country's first free postwar election, held in March and April 1990, was won by the right-of-centre Democratic Forum. Aspiring to become a dominant Christian Democratic party like the Christian Democratic Union in Germany, it received 24 per cent of the popular vote and 43 per cent of parliamentary seats. The Forum anchored a coalition government with two smaller parties – the Independent Smallholders' Party and the Democratic People's Party. The prime minister was Jozsef Antall, a historian, son of an official of the inter-war Horthy regime, and self-styled Hungarian Konrad Adenauer. Having ties with the Hungarian aristocracy, outdoing most of his opponents in his anti-communism, and calling attention to his participation in the 1956 insurrection against the communist regime, Antall's political pedigree was unassailable.

Yet Antall's strong position contributed to problems with coalition partners, with the country's president and, by late 1992, within his own party. Smallholder Party leader Jozsef Torgyan soon abandoned the coalition. A lawyer by profession, Torgyan's popularity extended beyond the countryside and into the urban middle class, where his bluntness and wit (reminiscent of the younger Walesa) were appreciated. He deflected criticism that his doctoral dissertation, praising the Soviet Union for its magnanimity in dealing with Hungary after the war, revealed an opportunistic character.

In May 1990, after bargaining between the Democratic Forum and the opposition Alliance of Free Democrats, Arpad Goncz, a member of the latter party, was elected acting president of parliament. But after a referendum on direct presidential elections was voided (only 14 per cent of voters took part), Goncz was confirmed as president of the Republic in August 1990 and was re-elected to a second term in June 1995. During his first term it appeared that he would challenge the primacy of the prime minister. But since the president was elected by parliament by a two-thirds majority and could only exercise most of his powers with the consent of the prime minister and respective ministries, Goncz's office was weak. The Constitutional Court whittled his powers down further, ruling that the president had to approve the appointment of candidates for state positions put forward by the government except if democracy was in danger. The president could only give guidelines, rather than orders, to the military. He could not veto legislation but could, at most, request parliament to reconsider bills. Still, Goncz's deftness and grace in office had the effect of checking Antall's powers.

The prime minister's problems within his own party were caused by a manifesto published by Democratic Forum vice-chairman Istvan Csurka in 1992. Neo-fascist and anti-Semitic in tone, it was an embarrassment in itself, but Antall's failure categorically to condemn it proved a political blunder. Polls showed that the Party of Young Democrats (FIDESZ), headed by the charismatic Viktor Orban, was taking support away from Antall. The news that Antall was suffering from cancer was the final blow to his party's fortunes. He died in December 1993, before the next elections to the National Assembly took place.

In these, held in May 1994, the Hungarian Socialist Party (re-formed communists) won a majority of the popular vote (54 per cent) and of parliamentary seats (209 of 386). The Alliance of Free Democrats placed a distant second (18 per cent, 70 seats), only then followed by the Democratic Forum (10 per cent, 37 seats). The new prime minister was Gyula Horn, Soviet-educated, a career diplomat under the communist regime, but an ardent advocate of reform in the last years of communist rule. Though he did not need to, Horn broadened the base of his government by inviting the Free Democrats to join. They agreed but there were tradeoffs for the socialists. Free Democrat leader Ivan Peto had to resign in 1997 after a scandal erupted about a $5 million payment he made to a privatisation consultant. Peto was replaced by Gabor Kuncze, interior minister in the Horn government. The major advantage for the Socialists in having the Free Democrats as partner was the harmonious relations established with President Goncz (a Free Democrat). The socialists manoeuvred for an advantageous position in the run-up to the 1998 elections.

Poland

The struggle for power between executive and legislative branches of government was particularly intense in Poland in the first years of the transition. The imperious personality and great ambitions of President Walesa were the primary cause of this struggle, but an ineffectual series of governments and bickering among the many parties in the legislature, the Sejm, contributed to the problem. Walesa himself described this conflict in 1992 as a 'Bermuda triangle' involving himself, the Sejm, and the government. Cynics described Walesa as having founded a dictatorship of the proletariat that the communists were unable to do. The reference was to Walesa's working-class origins – one of few postcommunist leaders (Horn in Hungary is another) from such a social background.

Walesa was elected president in November 1990 after suffering the embarrassment of being forced into a runoff with an unknown émigré, politician, 'Stan' Tyminski. But Eastern Europe's first noncommunist prime minister, Tadeusz Mazowiecki, a Catholic intellectual and journalist, suffered a greater indignity in being eliminated from the runoff by Tyminski, a self-described millionaire with a 'trophy wife' who said he had made a fortune running a cable company in the Peruvian jungle. In spite of his bluster, Walesa proved to be a weak president, failing among other things to obtain Sejm approval for his version of a 'little constitution' (that is, a temporary one) that would have enhanced the powers of the executive branch. His style, involving populist forays into factories and dairy cooperatives, and occasionally ungrammatical language, were criticised for bringing the dignity of his office into question. To be sure, more than any other person – Reagan, Thatcher, and Gorbachev included – the founder of the Solidarity trade union movement was responsible for destroying communism in Eastern Europe and not giving neo-communists a chance to return to power. But Walesa's very assuredness and confrontational style made him vulnerable to defeat at re-election time.

In November 1995 a former physical education minister in the communist regime, Alexander Kwasniewski, replete with an attractive wife, a youthful, slim appearance (he went on a crash diet before the campaign) and French campaign managers, beat Walesa by three percentage points – 51.7 to 48.3 per cent – to become democratic Poland's third president (General Wojciech Jaruzelski was the first, stylishly presiding over the transition from communism). Kwasniewski campaigned against Walesa as a champion of parliament, so the war of institutions ended when, with his backing, a new constitution was approved in May 1997 formalising a parliamentary system for Poland.

Poland had eight prime ministers between 1989 and 1997. These included people from different socio-occupational backgrounds – intellectuals, professionals, businessmen, peasants. One, Waldemar Pawlak, a young farmer with an engineering degree from Warsaw Polytechnic, was named prime minister twice. As head of the Polish Peasant Party, which could count on a sizeable constituency in a country where one-third of the population is still rural, Pawlak served under coalition governments of both anti-communists and former communists. Poland's only woman prime minister was Hanna Suchocka, in 1992–3, who pursued market reforms and was unfortunate to lose a vote of confidence in the Sejm. One prime minister, Jozef Oleksy, an apparatchik in the old communist party, had to resign in 1996 amid allegations that even as prime minister he had been in contact – naively or knowingly – with a Russian agent. His successor was Wlodzimierz Cimoszewicz, a farmer with a doctorate in law and a onetime Fulbright scholar.

In September 1997 parliamentary elections were held which were dominated by two long-time rival blocs – a coalition of Solidarity parties and the reformed communists running as social democrats. After years of splintering, the many small Catholic, conservative groupings joined with the still-functioning Solidarity trade union to loosen the stranglehold of social democrats on power. As elsewhere in the region, an incumbent government – whether socialist or conservative – found winning re-election difficult. The victorious Solidarity alliance (called AWS) was led by Marian Krzaklewski, an academic and later union activist who successfully transformed himself into a national leader. Of his bloc's 201 parliamentary seats, 52 were won by the trade union, 45 by Catholic activists, and the remainder by various conservative groups. Kwasniewski's choice as prime minister fell on Jerzy Buzek, also an academic (a chemical engineering professor) and union activist but a member of the Protestant Evangelical church.

The AWS needed a coalition partner to govern and chose the under-achieving Freedom Union. Although it had won just 13 per cent of the vote, its ranks had produced prime ministers Mazowiecki and Suchocka as well as the economist Leszek Balcerowicz, architect of the country's market reform plan. The youthful, pro-Western Balcerowicz assumed his former posts of deputy prime minister and finance minister in the Solidarity-led government, while his party colleague, long-time intellectual dissident Bronislaw Geremek, became foreign minister. By the late 1990s, shuffling the deck seemed in Poland to produce many familiar names.

Slovakia

As with the Civic Forum in the Czech lands, in Slovakia the anti-communist opposition bloc Public Against Violence split up shortly after the 1989 velvet revolution. One offshoot was the nationalist Movement for a Democratic Slovakia of prime minister Meciar, another the Christian Democratic Movement of Slovakia, at best lukewarm about federalism, headed by Jan Carnogursky. The former Communist Party of Slovakia also metamorphised into a nationalist group calling itself the Party of the Democratic Left.

Controversy swirled around Meciar even before Slovakia became independent in January 1993. Some accused him of having becoming a Slovak nationalist only after he had been removed as prime minister in 1991 by Carnogursky. Meciar indeed depicted himself as the liberator of the Slovaks from the Czechs and as head of 'patriotic forces' in the style of Iliescu in Romania. Others pointed to his autocratic, populist style that was the main objection given by the US (especially through its ambassador in Bratislava) to admitting Slovakia into NATO in summer 1997. The inevitable accusations of Meciar having once been a communist secret police agent (alias 'Doctor') also surfaced.

In January 1993 Meciar pressed parliament to appoint Roman Kovac as independent Slovakia's first president. But the fragmented parliament baulked and instead chose Michal Kovac, a onetime communist expelled from the party in 1970 and last chairman of the Czechoslovak Federal Assembly. As head of the single largest bloc of deputies in the Slovak legislature, Meciar remained prime minister until his running feud with the new president brought about his temporary removal, in March 1994. In October of that year, in Slovakia's first parliamentary elections, Meciar's Movement for a

Democratic Slovakia remained the strongest party, winning 35 per cent of the popular vote and 61 of 150 seats. The next three strongest electoral alliances – the left-wing Common Choice, the Hungarian coalition, and Carnogursky's Christian Democratic Movement – each obtained 10 per cent popular support and 17–18 seats. With the backing of junior coalition partners, the Slovak National Party and the Union of Workers, Meciar returned to his post as prime minister. In June 1997 he appointed Zdenka Kramplova as foreign minister, the highest post attained by a woman in democratic Slovakia to date.

The conflict between president Kovac and prime minister Meciar took many bizarre turns. It included the abduction under mysterious circumstances of the president's son and his eventual safe return. Another was the outcome of a referendum held in May 1997 on support for membership in NATO and on the direct election of the president. Meciar's interior minister, Gustav Krajci, refused to include the question on the method of electing the president on the ballot even though mandated to do so by the Constitutional Court. It was no coincidence that polls indicated that 75 per cent of respondents favoured direct elections, which would have strengthened the position of Kovac. In July 1997 round-table talks were held between Meciar and the various opposition parties, but they produced no result. All this time Kovac reminded Slovaks that, despite the support of the country's neighbours (the Czech Republic, Hungary, and Poland), Slovakia was excluded from NATO because of Meciar's undemocratic leadership.

Conclusion

Writers, electricians, economists, philosophers, geologists and communist bureaucrats have ruled Eastern Europe in the 1990s. While occupationally diverse, they have been predominantly male and somewhat younger than East Europe's previous ruling generation. They have used free market, nationalist, pan-European, socialist, and 'third way' rhetoric to get elected. They have almost never used political violence to stay in power. Most have learned to be expert in the art of coalition-building.

Generally, East European leaders have not stayed in their offices very long. Being re-elected has not been a talent they have developed successfully. The reformed communists of Bulgaria have performed the feat of twice being elected to power and twice being swept from power. Albania's democratic transition may paradoxically have begun when self-styled democrats failed to be re-elected in 1997. Winning a majority of seats in parliament in two successive elections is a rare accomplishment in Western democracies; it has been even rarer in the new Eastern Europe. Even the former communists that have returned to power everywhere in the region (except the Czech Republic) are entrenched in power nowhere.

Failing to be re-elected is a phenomenon less widespread among presidents. The longest-serving executive is Havel, an anti-leader by temperament. Next are Goncz and Kucan, presidents throughout the 1990s who have survived largely due to their conciliatory and low-key approach to politics. Tudjman of Croatia and and Milosevic of Serbia, both strong rulers in the best Balkan tradition, have also been presidents throughout the 1990s, but not because of their mild manners. Havel and Goncz were elected indirectly, Tudjman and Milosevic by popular acclaim. The method of election clearly affects the style of leadership.

There have been some fifty prime ministers in Eastern Europe in the 1990s. The longest-serving have been Klaus in the Czech Republic and Drnovsek in Slovenia, but while Drnovsek was reappointed in 1997, Klaus was forced to resign by the end of that year. Meciar in Slovakia was twice removed as prime minister but sprang back each time. The names of only a handful of the fifty-odd prime ministers remain familiar to East European observers.

East European states have opted for a parliamentary-dominant system where elected legislatures control the actions of the executive branch. A parliamentary system is more closely associated with a liberal philosophy than is presidentialism. Indeed, the few states employing a strong presidency (Croatia, Romania under Iliescu, and Serbia) have come under attack for human rights abuses. This does not indicate a cause-and-effect relationship, only that embracing presidentialism and giving priority to strong leadership over representative factors may signal the existence of deeper political cleavages in society.

The probability of political instability returning to postcommunist Eastern Europe differs from one country to another. Dispersal of power, inherent to a parliamentary system, carries certain risks, just as empowering executives with too many prerogatives does. Holding executives accountable to representative institutions yet freeing them sufficiently to provide strong leadership has been a perpetual problem of government. A decade after the *annus mirabilis* of 1989, East

European states have reached a functional equilibium. Leslie Holmes has cautioned that 'Postcommunism was in its honeymoon period during the early 1990s. There may have been more tolerance then than there will be in the future' (Holmes, 1997, p. 195). But the more recent politics of leadership in the region provide grounds for greater optimism.

7

The Parliaments of New Democracies and the Politics of Representation

DAVID M. OLSON

The new parliaments in the early postcommunist transition of Central and Eastern Europe are at the heart of both policy decisions and the institutionalisation of new democracies. The opportunities for legislatures to be active and influential in their political systems are probably much greater in new than in established democracies, for the external constraints, such as powerful executives and well-organised interest groups and parties, are not yet in place. Yet the capacity of parliaments to act responsibly are probably at their lowest, for the new members have not had the time to learn, nor the institutions time to develop, the complicated internal structures of political parties, procedures and committees. The paradox – the gap between high opportunity and low capacity – is experienced by all institutions of self-governance in new postcommunist democracies.

The democratic legislatures of postcommunist Central and Eastern Europe are at their beginning. They are experiencing the start-up stages, which could last for decades, of a new democratic political system and of its institutions. The new institutions face in the present, and all at once, the same dilemmas and tensions experienced and resolved more slowly and sequentially in older and more established democratic legislatures.

This chapter places the newly democratised parliaments in the context of the political system transformation. The legislatures are both participants in and objects of the broader democratic system transitional processes. Following a review of the profile of the new parliaments, attention will be given to parliaments in a double transition, and to their members, their internal structures and procedures, the circumstances of the subset of countries with bicameral parliaments, and to their working relationships with executives. The problems and circumstances of new legislatures in newly forming democratic political systems will be summarised in the form of a series of institutional paradoxes, which themselves change over time.

Profile of Parliaments

A profile of the newly democratised parliaments of Central and Eastern Europe is presented in Table 7.1. Most of the newly democratised legislatures are unicameral. Of the bicameral ones, only in Romania do both chambers exercise equal and full legislative powers. In the other bicameral systems, one chamber is superior to the other in both formal authority and political importance.

In size, the legislative chambers range from a low of 68 members in the Croatian House of Counties and 81 members in the Czech Senate, to a high of 386 in Hungary and 460 in the Polish Sejm. The smaller ones tend to be the additional chambers in bicameral parliaments. In a few countries, a small number of seats are either appointive, or are reserved for ethnic minorities.

The stipulated term of legislative office is usually four years. Only in Latvia is the term three years. The many changes of parties, policy preferences, and governmental systems have in all instances but Hungary led to shortened terms of about two years for the initial postcommunist parliament. As the new democracies have experienced their second and even third elections, the actual term of office has lengthened.

By contrast, the office of president usually has a term of 5 years. In Central and Eastern Europe, the president was initially selected by the legislature, though in Poland, Romania and Bulgaria, as we have seen in Chapter 6, direct popular election was soon instituted in the 1990–2 period. The constitutional definitions of the status and powers of president and parliament are not at all settled or uniform among the postcommunist states.

The newly democratised parliaments of Central and Eastern Europe, while reflecting their individual historical experiences, tend to resemble a mix of the French National Assembly of the former Fourth Republic with the current German Bundestag. As part of Europe, they borrow from the leading democracies of the western

TABLE 7.1 *Structual profile of Central and East European parliaments*

Region and country	Chamber structure	Election years	Chamber names	Size
Central Europe				
Czech Republic	Unicameral	1990 & 1992	Chamber of Deputies	200
	Bicameral	1996	Chamber of Deputies	200
			Senate	81
Poland	Bicameral	1989,	Sejm	460
		1991, 1993	Senate	100
		& 1997		
Slovak Republic	Unicameral	1990, 1992 & 1994	National Council	150
Hungary	Unicameral	1990 & 1994	National Assembly	386
Balkans				
Albania	Unicameral	1991	People's Assembly	250
		1992, 1996 & 1997	People's Assembly	140
Croatia	Bicameral	1992	House of Representatives	138
		1993 & 1997	House of Counties	68
		1995	House of Representatives	127
Bulgaria	Unicameral	1990	Grand National Assembly	400
		1991, 1994 & 1997	National Assembly	240
Romania	Bicameral	1990	Chamber of Deputies	387
			Senate	119
		1992 & 1996	Chamber of Deputies	341
			Senate	143
Slovenia	Bicameral	1992 & 1996	National Assembly	90
		1992 & 1997	National Council	40
Baltic States				
Estonia	Unicameral	1990	Supreme Council	105
		1992 & 1995	State Assembly	101
Latvia	Unicameral	1990	Supreme Council	201
		1993 & 1995	Saeima	100
		1995	Saeima	100
Lithuania	Unicameral	1990	Supreme Council	141
		1992 & 1996	Seimas	141
Other former Soviet Republics				
Ukraine	Unicameral	1994 & 1995	Verkhovna Rada	450
Moldova	Unicameral	1993 & 1994	Parlamentul	104

Source: Inter-Parliamentary Union 'PARLINE Database', at http://www.ipu.org; Jasiewicz (1993); McGregor (1994); and Parliamentary Documents Center for Central Europe.

portion of their common continent. They copy the Westminster tradition not at all.

Parliaments in the Double Transition: Democracy and Statehood

While the parliaments of Central and Eastern Europe have been at the heart of the postcommunist democratic transformation, they have also been at the core of the changing definitions of statehood and national boundaries. Parliaments in newly created states have participated in, and experienced, a double transition of democracy and state definition.

The immediate transitional event was the removal of the Communist Party from power in 1989–90. Negotiations between the communist leadership and the democratic opposition usually occurred outside the existing communist legislature. As legal changes were required by negotiated decisions, such as new electoral laws to permit party competition, the legislature did what it was told. Parliaments at this beginning stage of political system transition were as compliant as during the communist period, acting as directed by outside political leadership which for the first time, however, included oppositional groups. The major exception to the initial pattern of legislative exclusion and compliance was found in Hungary, in which the parliament itself was a major source of transitional change (Agh, 1996).

The first major task to be faced immediately in the transition was amendment of the constitution, while the second was election of a new parliament. The first was accomplished through the simple elimination by the existing communist parliament of the most obnoxious features of communist constitutions, namely, the designation of the Communist Party as the 'leading force' in government. The second task, the initial democratic elections to parliament, were held within months of the collapse of the Communist Party, under rapidly written new election rules. In this set of initial elections, the first was in Poland in May–June 1989, with the last in spring 1991 in Albania.

In most countries in Central and Eastern Europe, the initial election was much more a regime-change referendum about the removal of communists from power than a selection among competitive political parties. Most of the participating entities in the initial parliamentary election were not political parties, and did not consider themselves as parties. They were, rather, broad and diverse citizen movements and coalitions to purge the discredited old, and by that time powerless, government.

In most countries, the original expectation was that the new democratic parliament would write a new constitution, and would soon disband for new elections within the rules of a new democratic constitution. Though in most cases a new constitution was not adopted, the initial parliament served a short term of about two years, leading to a subsequent round of elections beginning in late 1991. It was during the ensuing term of the first freely elected parliaments that political parties began to form within the anti-communist reform movements. The instability and fragmentation among them led to shortened terms. Parliaments were, during this period immediately following the initial regime change election, the 'central site' of the democratic transition (Agh, 1995). In Central and Eastern Europe, the major political personalities met and interacted with each other in parliament. It was in parliament that the new political groupings were formed to contest subsequent elections (Olson, 1993a).

The collapse of communism has not only opened the question of political system, but has reopened the vexatious dilemma of state-hood. While some countries have remained as whole single entities (Poland, Hungary, Bulgaria, Romania, Albania), others are newly created (including Slovenia, the Czech Republic and the Slovak Republic) or have regained previous independent statehood (the three Baltic states). The new internationally recognised smaller states have elevated their former provincial-level structures of executives, minis-tries and legislatures to the status of sovereign bodies.

In this intergovernmental-level transition, the elevated legislatures may encounter several difficulties. One is a confusion of political status. The leading political figures of a new country could very well hold office at the prior country-wide level, while secondary figures held office at the provincial level and thus when the province becomes an independent state, its legislators may lack the highest leadership experience available within their new countries. A second liability of the newly elevated legislature is the lack of either rules or staff. Third, their staff and buildings are usually less well equipped than were their country-level counterparts, even within communist systems. The legislatures of self-governance in the newly formed countries in this region accordingly face a double hurdle. Not only does the commu-nist inheritance leave them unprepared for competitive democracy, but their previous status as provincial bodies leaves them unprepared for international and country-level responsibilities. Suddenly the whole gamut of nation-state responsibilities in the welfare-industrial era has become theirs.

The paradox of democratic development – the gap between external opportunity and internal capacity – is experienced by all of the newly energised parliaments of postcommunist countries. All confront the incongruities of new and inexperienced members suddenly placed in old buildings with communist-era rules. The dynamics and problems experienced by the newly elevated legislatures of Central and Eastern Europe are not only an intensification of the difficulties faced by all newly democratised legislatures, but are additional ones: they experience the burdens and opportunities of a double transition from communism to democracy and from provincial to national responsibilities.

Elections and Political Parties

Every postcommunist country of Central and Eastern Europe now has some type of multi-party system. The single ruling party, following collapse of communist rule, was rapidly replaced by many parties. In the 1991 Polish election, for example, the two largest parties each gained only 13 per cent of the Sejm seats (Jasiewicz, 1993). The many parties, and the unstable balance among them, has greatly complicated the choices of electoral systems. Romania, the Polish Senate, Hungary, and the Czech and Slovak Republics have retained their initial election systems, while the other countries and chambers have changed from a majority to a proportional representation system, combining features of their former communist elections with borrowings from Western democracies (for a fuller discussion, see Chapter 9).

The inherited communist election system usually included single member districts with a majority vote requirement, including a possible runoff. In addition, voter turnout had to exceed 50 per cent of the eligible voters. These elaborate double majority requirements made no difference in a one-party election, but proved cumbersome in the extreme as soon as there was more than one party or even candidate.

Hungary and Lithuania use the German dual election system, in which about half (45 per cent in Hungary) of their parliaments are elected in single member districts, and the other portion elected from regional multi-member districts. Many of the new democracies with proportional representation impose a 'threshold', a minimum proportion of the vote (usually 4–5 per cent) that a party must obtain to place any of its candidates in parliament. In new and unstable democracies, the many small parties in any one election can accumulate a sizeable share of the vote, up to 25 per cent in Bulgaria and Czechoslovakia, and 30 per cent in Poland, for example. These sizeable proportions of voters have been without direct representation in parliament.

The new democracies have often changed their electoral laws in reaction to the latest election. The election system for the Polish Sejm in 1991 emphasised party splits and independent local candidacies, for example. The next election law introduced a threshold, resulting in a greatly reduced number of parties in the 1993 parliament. In the subsequent elections, however, the Polish Senate results, with a very different election system, closely paralleled the Sejm party results (Gebethner, 1995). Estonia also changed its election law several times (Kask, 1996).

In the series of two and three elections in the 1989–96 period there often have been dramatic reversals of outcomes, in at least two respects. First, the shape of the party system has greatly changed from one election to the next. The usual pattern in the initial elections has been fragmentation of the party system in parliament, while subsequent elections have begun to consolidate the many small parties into few larger ones. Exceptions to this pattern include Hungary and Bulgaria, in which a few parties dominated parliament from the beginning.

Second, the reformed communist parties, now universally calling themselves democratic and socialist, have made spectacular recoveries in Poland (1993) and Hungary (1994), thereby placing themselves in government. Their recovery has been the reverse side of the fragmentation of the reform movements (Mair and Nagle, 1995). An exception to this pattern of electoral recovery of the reformed postcommunist parties was the Party of the Democratic Left in Slovakia, which lost over a third of its vote in the 1994 election from the previous election of 1992. Likewise, the Alliance of the Democratic Left in Poland was reduced from the largest to the second largest party in the 1997 elections.

Government formation is one of the most important consequences of an election, expressed through the party division of parliamentary seats. In Poland, with no majority party in the 1991–3 term, each of three successive governments was an unstable coalition. But in Poland in the 1993–7 term, and in Hungary and the Czech Republic, the relatively few parties were better able to form a stable majority coalition, which continued in office for the full four-year term.

The contrast between the Czech and Slovak Republics illustrates the importance of the party system within parliament. Both, elected June 1992 as provincial bodies, became sovereign parliaments at the beginning of 1993. While the parliamentary parties in the Czech Republic were stable and the coalition government thus remained in office, the Slovakian parties slowly regrouped within parliament, the government changed from one party alliance to another, and new elections were called within the first two years of independence (Malova and Sivakova, 1996; Wolchik, 1997; Olson, 1997b).

Members

With the collapse of communism, the existing leaders were repudiated. Many economic enterprises, labour unions and women's groups, and often the universities, were all subject to *nomenklatura* appointment. Thus, those leadership positions which had been recruitment sources for parliament in the communist system were foreclosed in the new democracies. How this constriction worked in practice varied among the countries, the specific institution, and even also by personality.

Lech Walesa the electrician and Vaclav Havel the dramatist symbolise the types of positions in communist society which could more clearly support anti-communist leaderships. It was especially the independent professions and the creative and expressive arts which supported dissident movements during communist rule and which, after communist collapse, served as the recruitment basis for the new members of the newly democratised parliaments (Wasilewski, 1992). In the initial postcommunist parliaments, the newly elected members were largely drawn from the highly educated ranks of the professions and arts. Prominent musicians and actors were also recruited for their electoral utility, not their legislative capacity – to lend visible prestige to candidate slates in the initial elections.

The new members largely lacked the experience of participating in large-scale decision-making bodies. In several parliaments, anti-communist reform members have observed that the reformed communist party members are the most effective members in the newly democratised parliaments. They had learned skills of negotiation and deliberation as part of a previous regime, which others as either dissidents or drop-outs did not. Compared with the communist-era legislatures, the educational level of the newly democratised parliaments is high. The proportion of administrative managers is down, and the proportion of artists and researchers much higher. The members in communist parliaments to fill the social mirror quotas for women and workers are largely absent in the new parliaments (Siemienska, 1991; Reschova, 1992; Wesolowski and Wasilewski, 1992; Loewenberg, 1994; Patzelt, 1994; Jackiewicz, 1994).

While this occupational and educational profile of parliamentary deputies has continued into subsequent parliaments, the members are largely different persons. That is, there is a relatively low incumbent reelection rate, at about 20–30 per cent in the last several elections (Kask, 1996, p. 199; Bach, 1996, p. 215; Zajc, 1996b). The members of the new democratic legislatures, indeed, have been called a 'transitory political elite'. As almost accidental members, they have not been inclined to 'learn politics' (Agh, 1996, p. 30; Brokl and Mansfeldova, 1995). More than once, it has been observed that a musician member would rather return to his guitar than to parliament. They could no more live 'from' politics than 'for' politics (Weber, 1921).

Internal Organisation and Procedures

Though the policy demands upon the newly activated parliaments of postcommunist legislatures are huge, the capacity of legislatures to respond is conditioned by the rudimentary internal structure and rules of procedure inherited from the communist predecessor bodies at the time of system collapse.

Of the two main means by which legislatures typically organise their members and also their workload, the committee structure inherited from communist parliaments was more adaptable to new circumstances than was the party structure. While many of the communist-era legislatures had some type of committee system to receive and consider legislation, the existence of one controlling party did not allow for disagreement or competition among several parties. Likewise, the rules and procedures of communist parliaments were inadequate to either express or resolve policy disagreement among several parties in contention.

Leadership and Rules

The presiding officer of a legislative body (variously termed Speaker, President, Marshal) and several vice-chairs, constitute a governing committee, in association with other members to represent political parties. Collectively, they are responsible for schedules, formation and membership of the committee system, and management of the whole institution. In the first Hungarian democratic parliament, for example, the heads of all the parliamentary parties, including a representative of the independents, constituted the 'House Committee' together with the Speaker (Agh, 1996, p. 24).

In some cases, the presiding officer is a leader of a major party. That person may become a government minister or run for president, thereby compounding the potentially conflicting demands of parliamentary leadership between loyalty to one specific party and responsibility for the whole institution. Selection of the presiding officer, however, is usually the product of inter-party negotiations over formation of a government coalition and the allocation of posts among its members.

The aftermath of the 1996 parliamentary elections in the Czech Republic illustrates the party and government salience of leadership positions. In the Chamber of Deputies, the Speakership was allocated to the leader of the Social Democrats, the leading party in opposition to the government coalition. That coalition, however, was one seat short of a majority. The Social Democrats approved continuance in office of the coalition in exchange for a share of leadership positions in the committees as well as the post of Speaker.

One of the important functions of the leadership group of a legislature is to decide the schedule of sessions and the agenda of issues on a weekly and even daily basis. In postcommunist legislatures, weekly and daily agendas are decided by plenary debate and vote. While such matters are often lamented as a waste of time, they are also decisions of high political controversy (Kask, 1996, pp. 206–7). As an example, inter-party conflict in Slovakia has resulted in rejection and abrupt changes in the parliamentary schedule (Fisher, 1996).

Political Parties

The frequent debates over agenda reflect the ambiguous status of political parties in new legislatures. They have not become fully accepted by parliamentary members as suitable organisations through which their schedule and agenda can be managed. Nor do they always vote as cohesive units on the floor.

Parliamentary parties are neither exclusive nor stable (Malova and Sivakova, 1996, p. 116; Agh, 1996, p. 21). They are certainly not uniform in structure. It has been possible, for example, in the Estonian legislature for deputies to belong to more than one parliamentary party (Kask, 1996, p. 202). In fragmented legislatures, many of the parties are very small; the Polish Sejm recognises the small groups through the definition of two types of groups – the parliamentary party (Klub) and the smaller circle (Kolo). In Slovakia, the organisational profusion and variety in the 1994 election among seven victorious electoral lists resulted in deputies in the ensuing parliament belonging to an assortment of 16 different political parties and groupings (Zemko, 1995).

Candidate groupings and electoral lists use a variety of terms to designate themselves, such as alliance and movement. The avoidance of the 'party' designation reflects both the communist legacy and the profusion of candidates and their organisational vehicles (Bielasiak, 1997, pp. 24–5).

The term 'party tourist' refers to the practice by which members change party groups within parliament. In the four-year Hungarian parliament (1991–5), for example, 15 per cent of the deputies changed parties at least once (Agh, 1996, p. 25; Szarvas, 1995, p. 203). In the Czech Chamber of Deputies, whole party groups have disappeared. In some instances, new parties are formed, while in others, mobile members affiliate with existing party formations. It is typical in the early years of new legislatures that the number of 'independent' members grows through a term of office; that category itself was a designation of a type of member in communist parliaments.

The rules governing the formation of parliamentary parties are often contentious (Agh, 1996; Somogyvari, 1996, pp. 105–6). What, for instance, is the minimum number of members authorised to form a parliamentary party? Under what conditions may a deputy either leave an existing parliamentary group and enter another, or perhaps form a new one? In the extreme case, illustrated by Slovakia in 1996–7, a member could be expelled from parliament if he resigned from his parliamentary party. A more typical problem concerns the minimum size stipulation, illustrated by the Polish Sejm: the minimum size requirement of five was changed to 15 members. The Hungarian parliament in its second term reacted to its experience of party fluidity in the first, by similarly limiting the ease of party change and by increasing the minimum size of party formation.

There are clear consequences for both the policy activity of parliament and for government control over parliament from the pliable and unclear position of party in parliament. The newly active parliaments provide much more latitude for individual member initiation of legislation than typically occurs in more established legislatures. Likewise, the government is not always supported in floor votes by members of its own parties. Individual deputies, including members of the government parties, also have proposed amendments on the floor on government measures against government opposition (Simon, 1996; Agh, 1996; Karasimeonov, 1996). The fluidity and partial character of party formation in parliament is, however, the essential dynamic in the formation of stable political parties in the wider political system. In the first half-decade of postcommunism, political party formation has been centred in parliament. Parliaments provide by largest number of elective offices at the national level. Even countries with directly elected presidents have parliamentary elections more often than presidential ones. The possibility of early parliamentary elections further increases the necessity, and thus opportunity, for party organisation to form around the capture of power in parliament.

A trend in the number of parties is discernible over a series of three elections. The effective number of political parties in the initial transitional elections averaged 4.1, while in the second election the average rose to over 7 parties. In the ensuing third series of parliamentary elections, the average effective number of parties declined to just under 6. In each series of elections, the resulting number of parties in parliaments was somewhat lower, showing the practical effects of the threshold requirement in election systems as a means of reducing the working number of parties in parliaments from the dispersion of the vote on election day.

Committees

The number of committees in the first half-decade in Central and East European parliaments ranged from ten up to 24 (Norton and Olson, 1996, p. 237). The committee system of the newly democratic parliaments resemble, at least in formal structure, those of the continental European democracies and the US Congress much more than the British Westminster model. They also resemble the continental pattern in that the permanent committees largely parallel the structure of the ministries, and hold a variety of supervisory and budget, as well as legislative, relationships with the ministries. Some committees, however, have more a functional task, such as budget and legal affairs, which encompass a variety of ministries and chamber committees with their more specific policy concerns.

The committees of the new parliaments usually reflect party ratios in the distribution of memberships. Committee seats are allocated to political parties proportionally to their share of seats in the chamber, at least within broad limits. The distribution of chairmanships, however, is more variable among the parties. Committees typically consider proposed bills before floor debate. Even the 'first reading' of bills can be conducted in committees rather than on the floor, as illustrated by the Polish Sejm (Olson *et al.*, 1998). Members of the responsible committee lead debate and the amendment process on the floor of the chamber. In bicameral systems, the committees continue their responsibility for bills within their jurisdiction in reconciliation of different bill versions between the two chambers.

The complexity of public policy in the new democracies often means that any single legislative proposal crosses committee jurisdictions, creating the need for coordination among two or more committees. Multiple committee coordination is achieved in the newly democratised parliaments through several organisational innovations, not often found in established democratic legislatures. One device is the special coordinating subcommittee, formed of the members from several permanent committees. Another means of coordination is the permanent Committee on Law and Legislation (variously named in different legislatures). With formal responsibility to harmonise language of bills with standards of legal draftsmanship, this committee shares jurisdiction on all bills. Its activities can go far beyond its formal responsibility, however, to exercise policy coordination among the committees. As a result, it is often the target of criticism, such as 'super committee' in Hungary or 'mini legislature' in Bulgaria (Agh, 1996, p. 33; Karasimeonov, 1996, p. 52).

Compared with the committees of Western democratic parliaments, the committees in the newly activated parliaments of the new democracies are both freer of external control but less well developed internally to resist external control. The previous discussion of the ambiguities of political parties suggests that one consequence is the relative inability of parties to control their own members on committees; indeed, for deputies who have resigned from their party, or whose parties have dissolved, they can act as party-free members on the committees to which they had originally been assigned.

The Other Chambers

The intersection of democratisation with state dissolution and formation has had varying and inconsistent consequences for the cameral structure of parliaments in Central and Eastern Europe. Of the bicameral legislatures, all, with the exception of Romania, have one active and powerful chamber, while the other chambers are limited in policy scope and in legal authority. The term 'other' chamber more accurately characterises the status of these chambers which more conventionally would be termed 'upper'. They are, however, curtailed and subordinate to the lower but more active and authoritative chamber within their bicameral legislatures.

While the dissolved states were federations and thus also had varieties of multi-cameral parliamentary structures under communism, neither the continuing nor the new states are uniform in their choice between single and bicameral structures in their newly democratised and also elevated legislatures. Of the new states, Slovenia and Croatia continue their pattern of more than one chamber, while Slovakia and the Baltic states continue as unicameral systems, though the Czech Republic has become bicameral. Of the continuing states, Poland and Romania are bicameral, while Hungary and Bulgaria are unicameral.

With the exception of Slovenia, in which the other chamber is corporatist and indirectly selected, all of the other chambers are directly elective, thus introducing an incongruity into the legislative structure between representation and authority. A profile of the 'Other Chambers' is presented in Table 7.2.

The formal constitutional functions of the truncated other chambers are, first, to exercise a suspensive veto over legislation from the more active chamber, and second, to initiate its own legislation. They may also have a range of additional legal powers. In Poland, for example, presidential requests for a referendum must receive the approval of the Senate, but not of the Sejm. In the Czech Republic, the Senate would act as a substitute for the lower chamber in event of dissolution of the latter. The former Czechoslovak Federation displayed an unusual form of bicameralism. The members of the upper house, the House of Nations, voted on critical issues as two separate

TABLE 7.2 *The other chambers in Central Europe*

Attributes	Romania	Poland	Czech Republic	Croatia	Slovenia
Name					
English	Senate	Senate	Senate	House of Counties	National Council
National	Senatul	Senat	Senat	Zupanijski Dom	Drzavni Svet
Composition					
N members	143	100	81	68	40
Term (years)	4	4	6 (staggered)	5	5
Age minimum	35	21	40	none	none
Male/female	141/2	87/13	NA	60/3	39/1
Selection					
Means	Direct	Direct	Direct	Direct	Indirect
Election system	PR	Plurality	Majority	PR	NA
N districts	42	49	81	21	NA
District basis	Counties	Voivodships	Senatorial districts	County	Electoral colleges
N seats/district	2 to 13	2 to 3	1	3	NA
Term coincident	yes	yes	No	no	no
Powers					
Government Confidence	no	no	No	no	no
Legislation	Equal	Suspensive veto	Suspensive veto	Suspensive veto	Suspensive veto
Main house override[*]	NA	50% absolute	50% absolute	50% absolute	50% absolute
Amendments	yes	yes	Yes	no	no
Time limits: days	NA	30/7	30	15	7
Legislative Initiative	yes	yes	No	yes	yes
Referenda	NA	yes	no	advisory	obligatory
Elect President	no	no	Yes	no	no
Question Ministers	yes	yes	Yes	yes	yes
Organisation					
Full/part-time	full	full	full	full	part
Salary	yes	yes	yes	yes	no
N committees	14	12	8	4	6
Joint sessions	yes	yes	yes	no	no
Joint committees	two	one	no	no	no
Constitution					
Articles	58–79	3, 4, 17	33, 45–7, 54	81, 86, 121, 122	91, 96

[*] Requirements vary between constitutional and ordinary bills.

groups, Slovakia and the Czech Lands, each of which had to supply its own majority for the chamber as a whole to be deemed to have adopted a measure (Olson *et al.*, 1993; Olson, 1994). On crucial issues, the formal bicameral appearance became an operative tricameral system.

Members of several of the truncated other bodies serve longer terms of office than do members of the active chamber, with Poland and Romania as exceptions. In Slovenia, the term of office is five years, while the term for the active chamber is four. In the Czech Republic, members serve for overlapping six-year terms, while members of the active body serve a term of four years. The other bodies, equally, are all smaller than the main chamber. The small size in combination with different election systems results in different districts as well, with the exception of Romania. The age requirement is usually higher than for the main chamber, excepting Poland.

The immediate circumstances for the formation of truncated other chambers reside in the exigencies of the sudden collapse of communism, coupled with the dissolution of multi-ethnic federations. In each case, the bicameral structure of parliament was an essential ingredient in both the democratisation and state formation processes of the 1989–92 period. In Poland, the problem in early 1989 while the communists were in control was how to reconcile the communist government's need for Solidarity's cooperation without yielding power. The solution, suggested by a communist negotiator, was free elections to an undefined new Senate. In the formation of the new states of Slovenia and Croatia in 1990, the problem was how to reconcile their own traditions with need for quick approval of a constitution. In the Czech Republic, the need for speed in 1992 to create the new state in place of the disintegrating federation also led to a formal stipulation in the Constitution for a Senate. In none of these new democracies (and three new states) was the need for a second chamber clearly defined or widely accepted. In most countries, an additional chamber was offered by some parties as a symbolic gesture to persuade others to accept the new political system. Romania seems an exception, in that a bicameral structure was assumed as part of its pre-war constitution.

In most instances, there also was, however, a strong desire to create a means by which constructive persons could rise above the immediate considerations of partisan strife and competition to consider fundamental principles and long-run issues. The long terms of office, the staggered terms in the Czech Republic, the different electoral bases in most countries from the active chamber, are all efforts to build a body somewhat removed from the partisan contest. The Polish and Romanian Senates are clear exceptions to this anti-party and even anti-popular tendency. In both, members are elected in partisan contests at the same time as are members of the main chamber, and in both, the same parties hold about the same proportion of seats.

The limited legal authority of the other chambers is potentially at variance with their electoral base. Direct popular election places them in a potentially critical position. They could, if power was precariously balanced in the main chamber among parties or between government and opposition, become the pivot point in their political system. The crucial political relevance to the wider political system was unexpectedly demonstrated in Poland following the 1989 elections. But within a normal and settled democracy, power can also be precarious, as illustrated by the 1996 election in the Czech Republic. The incumbent government coalition lacked a majority of two seats in the main chamber: the pending election to the Senate several months later quickly assumed an importance to the allocation of political power which had not been previously anticipated (Olson, 1996).

Executives, Governments, and Presidents

While most of the new democracies of Central and Eastern Europe have become parliamentary systems on the model of Germany and Scandinavia, some have adopted a dual executive with both a prime minister and a president, on the model of the French Fifth Republic (Shugart, 1996; see also Chapter 6). In most of the new democracies the president is elected by parliament. In Poland, Romania and Bulgaria, as well as in most of the former Soviet republics, however, that office is now filled through direct election with a majority requirement, often leading to a runoff.

In formal authority in relationship to the legislatures, only half of the presidents are authorised by the constitution to veto legislation, or to even send messages to parliament or to propose legislation (McGregor, 1994). Presidents selected by parliament can, nevertheless, exercise independent judgement. The Hungarian president, for example, openly quarrelled with parliament and prime minister over control over a mass media board. The Czech and Slovakian presidents each have about the same grant of limited constitutional authority; the two presidents, in very different political circumstances, have exercised their authority in very different ways.

The most active president–parliament conflict occurred in Poland. During the 1991–3 Sejm, in which a fragmented parliament produced three governments, there was a constant struggle over the president's powers to nominate and reject potential candidates for prime minister. It was during this period that Poland's 'Little Constitution' was adopted (December 1992), defining the president's powers in a five-stage selection of the cabinet. As another example, in late 1994 the president called for the resignation of the defence minister, against the wishes of the prime minister. President Walesa himself referred to the presidential–parliamentary relationship as the 'Bermuda Triangle' of Polish politics (Simon, 1996).

Cabinet formation is itself a sensitive and major issue. In all Central and East European new democracies, every government has been a coalition. Cabinet minister selection and removal usually requires at least the formal approval of both president and parliament. At times, the Polish Sejm has refused to accept the resignation of a minister; at times the Slovakian president has refused to accept the nomination by the prime minister of a cabinet minister. Government formation and the enactment of legislation are only weakly linked to each other. Through shifting party formations and weak party discipline, governments have not been able to rely on guaranteed majority support for their legislation.

One characteristic of the transitional countries is an unstable party system. That feature has been joined to a vaguely defined presidency. The result has been a highly variable exercise of the office in relationship to parliament under circumstances in which neither president nor parliament can predict the other's actions.

Transitional Legislatures in Transitional Democratic Political Systems

The parliaments of the new democracies are successor – and in some cases remnant – institutions of communist-era predecessors. The existing communist legislatures were transformed into democratic parliaments, but at different rates of speed and under different conditions throughout the region. Parliaments have been both subject and actor in the democratic transitions.

The legislatures of the new democracies had unprecedented opportunities to act, but also lacked the preparation, experience, and

resources of normal democratic parliaments. The turmoil and uncertainty of the new democracies led to a rapid sequence of elections,
each of which produced a very different configuration of political
forces in parliament. The length of governments in office was likewise
truncated. Simultaneously, legislatures attempted to define a new
constitution, and to define the existence of new states in some
instances, as well as to adopt the rules for a new economic order.

The Central and East European states and their parliaments varied
greatly from one another. While democratisation was initiated within
the Hungarian parliament, the Romanian parliament reacted to
external events. In Poland, the 'contract' parliament was an integral
part of the political transitional process over a two-year period, while
in Czechoslovakia, the 'reconstructed' parliament served only a half
year; all had the tasks of laying the foundation for the democratic
transition.

The postcommunist parliaments both participated in the regime
transitional process and themselves experienced their own internal
transitions. Typical transitional quandaries faced by the legislatures
in their initial years included: marginality of members, ambiguity of
parliamentary parties, diffuseness of committees, unclarity of rules,
and potential threats from executives. These dilemmas summarise
both the opportunities and limitations faced by the new legislatures in
the initial decade of postcommunism (Olson, 1997a).

Members

Members of the transitional parliaments were often sporadic in their
attendance and participation. In the old parliaments, they had been
elected under old rules and old expectations – meetings twice a year
for two days each, with little independent thought or action either
expected or possible. The new members from the transitional elections
suffered a reciprocal incapacity: though they often wished to be active
and innovative, they lacked relevant experience. They, too, were
preoccupied by the necessities of their private occupations. They have
found the time demands of an active legislature to be far more
onerous than they had anticipated.

Parliamentary Parties

In the initial elections of the 1989–90 period, many members had been
elected on vaguely defined electoral lists or as sponsored by variously

named movements, all of which were in turn loose and hasty coalitions of equally vaguely defined groups. Party groupings within parliament formed and dissolved rapidly, so that the term 'faction' was more accurate than 'party' to characterise relationships among the members. Yet, over the sequence of only a few elections, the party systems are beginning to consolidate.

Committees

Parliamentary committees had defined jurisdictions but unclear rules. Though placed on committees by party leaders, they became independent members as soon as their vaguely defined parliamentary groups disintegrated (as in Poland and Czechoslovakia). That many members were either inexperienced or busy with their own occupations meant that committees, as well as the whole body, functioned with only an active minority of its full membership.

Leadership and Rules

The rules and leadership were in equal flux. The fluidity of party groupings provided no clear basis for the selection of representatives to a central coordination body, so that new leadership groups became self-directed without clear responsibilities to, or control over, the membership. One immediate consequence was long periods of floor debate over procedure and time limits on debates.

Chief Executives

Both prime ministers and presidents depend upon the constellation of party size and alignments in parliaments. The former gain from stable power in parliament, while the latter tend to gain from the opposite condition. The whole selection process of prime minister and cabinet is greatly complicated in systems with externally elected presidents, in part because of the related inability to agree on new constitutions.

Emerging Types of Postcommunist Legislatures

The postcommunist parliaments both participated in the system transitional process and themselves experienced their own internal transitions at different rates and with differential degrees of stabilisation of change. These variations appear to have produced two very broad sets of countries and parliaments, at the midpoint of the initial postcommunist decade. In one set of parliaments, the initial transitional changes seem to have stabilised, while in the other, parliaments and the constitutional order continue in a state of flux and uncertainty.

In the more stabilised parliaments, the major features of new organisation and new procedure seem to have become a continuing part of legislative activity. Parliamentary parties have become the accepted means by which the members organise themselves to manage the collective affairs of the legislature. As both a result and an indicator, a collective coordinating group has become defined and continues over a series of terms. Committees continue over terms, and parties are the main means of committee member selection. The committees have developed means of inter-committee coordination, and they are becoming the main means by which the legislature considers policy questions. This set of relatively stabilised parliaments would include several in Central and Eastern Europe, especially Poland, the Czech Republic, and Hungary, as well as the three Baltic states.

Other parliaments would appear less consistent in their internal structure and procedures. Their parliamentary parties continue to form and recombine and their committees are subject to change in structure, composition, and procedures. Central leadership is both more unilateral and arbitrary by the current majority, and subject to criticism by the current minority, than in the more stabilised parliaments. This category of parliaments would include Romania, Bulgaria and Slovakia.

In the suddenly activated legislatures of the new democracies of postcommunism, the opportunity for constitutional experimentation and legislative innovation will occupy more than a single decade. There has been no one 'founding' election, and no single clarifying 'moment'. We may be witnessing a rolling series of transitions and stabilisation processes, occurring at different times, at different speeds, and with a different content from one postcommunist country to another.

8

Parties and Politics

GORDON WIGHTMAN

Less than a decade after the end of communist rule in Central and Eastern Europe, good progress had been made towards the establishment, or rather re-establishment, of pluralist party systems. Throughout the region, the one-party or hegemonic party system that had been a key feature of communism had vanished and even the formerly dominant parties had come to accept political competition as the norm.

This is not to suggest that there is uniformity across the region. As in so many other aspects of life in Central and Eastern Europe, diversity was the most striking feature of the party systems that took shape in the 1990s and, as time passed, the differences between countries appeared if anything to increase. That was itself nothing new. The states in Central and Eastern Europe had divergent histories, levels of economic development and political experiences, not least during communist rule. The Czech Republic and to a lesser extent Hungary had a long and rich tradition of political parties and parliamentarism dating back to the last quarter of the nineteenth century, whereas most other countries had an acquaintance with party-based politics which was much shorter and at its optimum for a short time in the inter-war period. In terms of economic development, the Czech Lands had been the most industrialised region not only in the Austrian Empire but also of the Soviet bloc (East Germany apart), and even after forty years of communism it remained one of the most economically advanced in the area. A widespread perception that they had nevertheless fallen behind during communist rule, combined with the particular severity of the communist regime for most of those four decades, in part accounted for a more hostile attitude among the Czechs to their communist past and to the Communist Party in the 1990s than was to be found among their more recently industrialised neighbours in Slovakia, Hungary and Poland.

In so far as multi-party systems were revived after World War II they generally proved short-lived, as the imposition of communist rule saw either the eradication of alternative parties to the communists or their emasculation and subordination to the new ruling party. In most countries, the Communist Party was thereafter the single party organisation permitted to operate, and the survival, in Czechoslovakia and Poland, throughout the four decades of communism of a plurality of political parties was yet another example of the lack of uniformity found in the region. In practice this particular brand of 'multi-partyism' meant very little. The existence of other parties, whose policies were in fact determined by the ruling party, whose membership levels were fixed by the ruling party and whose leaders were chosen only with its approval, maintained the facade of a multi-party system. Few were fooled, however, even by the inclusion of representatives from these parties in parliament and occasionally even in government, into believing that these were any less one-party systems in practice than elsewhere in the then Soviet bloc. Nevertheless, however weak and compromised the satellite parties were in reality as a result of their subservience to the communists, they provided one of a number of elements on which a new multi-party system could be, and to some extent was, based in those two countries in the 1990s.

Parties in Postcommunist Central and Eastern Europe

Satellite parties only regained an independent voice once communist rule had been challenged – in Poland, after the semi-competitive elections of June 1989 (see Lewis, 1990), and in Czechoslovakia once the 'Velvet Revolution' had got under way in November of that year. The return to genuine multi-party systems in Central and Eastern Europe after forty years of communist rule thus had to begin more or less from scratch in 1989 and 1990 once the communists' power monopoly was brought to an end. Hungary, it is true, was something of an exception in that respect. In that country, new political movements – Hungarian Democratic Forum, the Alliance of Free Democrats and FIDESZ (the Alliance of Young Democrats) – had begun to form with official sanction even before they were given the opportunity to compete for power in the March 1990 parliamentary elections. Elsewhere, oppositional activity had been forced to take place clandestinely, and the formation of new political parties and movements or attempts to revive historical parties which had been suppressed in the 1940s had to await either the defeat of the ruling party or its acceptance that it could no longer prevent competitive political activity.

New parties and reconstituted historical parties were only two elements in the politics of Central and Eastern Europe in the 1990s. Another was the former ruling parties, or rather the more adaptable factions within them. These were to prove more resilient than might have been expected at the time of the communist collapse and generally, under new names and leaders, found roles to play in the postcommunist world. The fortunes of these successor parties proved as varied as the names they adopted. Even under communism, of course, ruling parties had adopted a variety of titles, ranging from those which identified themselves unequivocally as Communist Parties, for example in Bulgaria, Czechoslovakia and Romania, to those which preferred the alternatives of United Workers' Party, as in Poland, or Socialist Workers' Party, as in Hungary (between 1956 and 1989). In that context, it was hardly surprising that successor parties, too, opted for a variety of alternatives, many familiar from Western European practice, from Social Democracy in the Polish case to Socialist Party in Bulgaria and Hungary and Party of the Democratic Left in Slovakia. Only the Communist Party of Bohemia and Moravia resisted pressure to change and resolutely adhered to its traditional label, regardless of the negative associations that it had for the vast majority of Czechs.

Historical Parties

Historical parties did not, on the whole, prove to be major actors in the postcommunist world. Some pre-communist parties which had vanished following the imposition of one-party rule in the 1940s were able to revive. In Hungary, for example, the Independent Smallholders and the Christian Democratic People's Party re-entered parliament in 1990, although, in the former case, with nowhere near the level of support they had attracted four decades earlier. The Social Democratic Party in the Czech Republic, which had been forcibly amalgamated with the communists in 1948, failed to attract sufficient votes to re-enter parliament until 1992, and it took another four years before it reached second place in terms of electoral popularity and was able to play an influential role in contemporary politics, if not yet in government. By then whatever connections it retained with pre-1948 Czechoslovak social democracy were slight, and the major source of its 1996 success, its leader Milos Zeman, was a newcomer to its ranks in the 1990s.

In many other cases, the break with the past was too long and society too different for pre-communist parties to make a successful renascence. The traditionally more centrist Socialist Party, a major force in pre-war Czechoslovak politics and then a satellite party throughout communist rule, for example, failed to find a secure place on the Czech political scene despite its existing organisational network, membership and wealth. That party's failure in part reflected its record of subservience to the communists, the consequent discredit it incurred, and in part the loss of its traditional clientele (middle-class intellectuals and specific sections of the working class like railway workers, whose loyalty transferred elsewhere in the postcommunist period).

The historical parties which made a mark in the 1990s were often those which appealed to social strata which had not been eradicated under communism. The survival of a rural 'interest', usually linked with clericalism, was one factor that helped several pre-communist parties in the region rediscover a place in postcommunist politics. The Polish Peasant Party was not simply a continuation under another name of the former satellite United Peasant Party. Its formation in May 1990 as the result of an agreement between the latter and representatives of émigré parties allowed it to lay claim to older pre-war traditions. Its viability in the new Poland was made clear when, in late 1993, it formed a coalition government with the Democratic Left Alliance (in which the postcommunist Social Democracy of the Polish Republic was the dominant partner) that was to last four years until the next parliamentary elections in September 1997. Another former satellite party with roots going back to the pre-war period, the People's Party (which appended the designation Christian Democratic Union to its name in the early 1990s), re-established a sound electoral base in the Czech Republic in the first postcommunist elections in 1990 and became a key member of the governing coalition in the Czech Republic two years later. A similar rural/clerical dimension underpinned the revival of the historical Christian Democratic People's Party in Hungary and the formation of the new Christian Democratic Movement in Slovakia.

New Parties

The reappearance of parties with attested historical antecedents like the Polish Peasant Party, the Czech People's Party and Social Democrats, and the Independent Smallholders in Hungary was one distinctive feature of the postcommunist political scene. During the first postcommunist years, however, they played a less distinctive part within the emerging party systems in Central and Eastern Europe than the new political organisations created, for the most part, after the collapse of the communist power monopoly but which, in many instances, originated in the opposition movements of the 1980s (and in some cases earlier).

The most significant, initially at least, were the broad-based political movements, ranging from Civic Forum in the Czech Republic and Public Against Violence in Slovakia to the Union of Democratic Forces in Bulgaria, whose aim was to embrace as many of the communists' opponents as possible. Their strengths as movements seeking to challenge the communists was, however, in a longer timespan a source of weakness. The breadth of opinions represented within their ranks and their initial disparagement of traditional party hierarchy and organisation were hardly conducive to political durability, and even those movements which did not disappear from the scene early suffered from fissiparous tendencies and pressure to transform themselves into conventional political parties.

The need for a more traditional form of party was the issue that led to the early disappearance of one of the best-known attempts to realise the 'non-political' politics that was embodied in these movements, Civic Forum in the Czech Republic. Its first chair, Vaclav Klaus, elected to that post eleven months after the movement was established in November 1989, was vocal in his arguments against attempting to tread along a new and untested path in search of a different kind of political organisation. He argued that the vision of the broadly-based political movement represented by Civic Forum was a 'third way' in politics comparable to the 'third way' in economics associated with the 1968 Prague Spring and still espoused by many former reform communists. Just as he favoured supposedly tried and tested 'standard' liberal economics, Klaus argued against experiments in political organisation and in favour of the tried and tested model of a traditional, hierarchical party which had a clear programme and which was capable of effective action. It was a trend that was to be followed, in varying degrees, elsewhere as other movements saw the advantages of more disciplined organisational principles.

As a mechanism for uniting ideologically diverse groups who shared little other than their opposition to the communists, the concept of the broad political movement was useful, and for that reason survived for some time in a number of countries. Confronted by a still powerful Socialist Party that continued to attract greater electoral support, the Union of Democratic Forces in Bulgaria, for example, maintained an 'umbrella' character well into the 1990s (see Henderson and Robinson, 1997, pp. 350–4), but after its defeat in the 1994 parliamentary elections it too faced what the Bulgarian political scientist Georgi Karasimeonov described as a crucial decision, whether to remain a broad movement or turn itself into a more cohesive political party (Karasimeonov, 1995, p. 585). More commonly, the political movement was succeeded by parties which had evolved from within it as time, internal conflicts and the political demands of the present led to the crystallisation of new forces.

Thus, out of Civic Forum in the Czech Republic came two parties which remained key actors in the late 1990s: Vaclav Klaus's Civic Democratic Party, founded in 1991, and the Civic Democratic Alliance which had originated in dissent in the late 1980s but operated initially under Civic Forum's 'umbrella'. In Slovakia only the Movement for Democratic Slovakia among parliamentary parties could be regarded as a direct survivor of Public Against Violence, although a number of subsequent breakaway parties from the MDS could be said to be indirect descendants. In Poland, too, Solidarity appeared to have given way to a range of political parties linked with individual leaders or groups (for example, the Democratic – and later Freedom – Union and former prime minister, Tadeusz Mazowiecki). The political resurgence of the trade union itself in association with a multitude of smaller groups in the form of Solidarity Electoral Action in the 1997 elections owed more to a common antipathy among participants in that coalition towards postcommunist opponents in the outgoing government than to continuing attachment to the principles of the original movement, although the legacy of that shared history did play some part.

Making sense of the party scene in Central and Eastern Europe in the 1990s was not made easier by the proliferation of new political organisations, some called parties, others preferring alternative labels like forum, union, alliance or association. Nor were the variations in party nomenclature from country to country an aid to understanding (although in that respect postcommunist Europe was hardly different from more established multi-party democracies in the West). There was nevertheless some common ground within the region and across East–West boundaries. Christian Democratic parties – in the Czech and Slovak Republics, and Hungary – suggested parties occupying a similar point on the centre-right of the political spectrum to their West European counterparts and, at least in the Czech and Slovak cases, the names were chosen to make that western link. The Hungarian party, on the other hand, was much older and followed an established tradition.

Many other parties were *sui generis* and their politics less than self-evident. There was no reason to assume that the Alliance of Free Democrats (in Hungary), Freedom Union (in Poland), Democratic Party (in Slovakia) and Civic Democratic Party (in the Czech Republic) should all be placed in a broadly similar position on the political spectrum (to the right of centre), nor was it obvious solely from its name that the Movement for a Democratic Slovakia might be better situated at a different point, somewhere to the left of centre. By contrast, the new names adopted by most of the former ruling parties, whether that was Party of the Democratic Left as in Slovakia, Socialist Party as in Hungary and Bulgaria, or more audaciously Social Democracy as in the Polish case, were usually familiar from Western polities, even if they too varied from state to state.

The Successor Parties

Not all former ruling parties, as was noted earlier in the case of the Czech Communists, opted for change. Unlike the Party of the Democratic Left in Slovakia, the Hungarian Socialist Party and Social Democracy in the Polish Republic, where elites predisposed to adapt to the prevailing pro-market and pro-democratic climate remained *in situ* and traditional Marxist-Leninists defected to create their own organisations 'loyal' to what was clearly a lost cause (especially after the disappearance of the Soviet Union at the end of 1991), the Communist Party of Bohemia and Moravia followed the opposite path. Those who wished it to remain 'faithful' to its past stayed put while more flexible pro-reform members left to create separate democratic socialist organisations (none of them successful in the long term). In Romania, another route was taken when the immediate successor to the Communist Party of Romania adopted a name, the National Salvation Front, which bore little suggestion of links to the former ruling party, and stressed its comparability with anti-communist political movements elsewhere in the region rather than its origins among communist opponents to the ousted and executed Romanian leader, Nicolae Ceausescu.

Any observer of the political scene in Central and East Europe towards the end of the 1990s had to note the remarkable success of many of the former ruling parties not merely in adapting to the circumstances that had confronted them after the collapse of communism a decade before, but in several cases in persuading the population to return them to power. Not all former ruling parties had, of course, been ejected in 1989 and 1990. Some parties (in Bulgaria and Romania, for example) had demonstrated their resilience early on and, while accepting the need for party competition and pluralism, contrived for a few years at least to hang on to power in one form or another (although only intermittently in the Bulgarian case). Others accepted their defeat, went into opposition and bided their time in the hope that their patience would be rewarded.

In some cases, their optimism proved justified. In Poland, for example, the Social Democracy of the Polish Republic found itself once more a partner in government at the end of 1993, albeit after standing in the elections as part of a broader Democratic Left Alliance, and in coalition with the Polish Peasant Party. In Hungary, the Hungarian Socialist Party (the successor in 1989 to the disbanded Hungarian Socialist Workers' Party) was even more convincingly returned to power with a clear parliamentary majority in 1994 only four years after its crushing defeat in the first competitive elections to be held in that country since 1947.

This revival of fortune for the successor parties scarcely meant that the overthrow of communism in 1989 and 1990 had been put into reverse. The region continued to be in flux even in the late 1990s and inter-party struggle produced divergent outcomes in different countries at different times. Some successor parties were returned to power after an interval which, though relatively short, was sufficient to break what Michael Waller has termed the communist power monopoly (Waller, 1993) and to put paid to the four-decades-long experiment in state planning and ownership of the economy. Other parties, which had initially managed to remain in power and ensure some renewal by a changing of the guard and the immediate promotion of more reformist sections of the (former) communist elite, were eventually forced to give way to their opponents. Romania provides one example of a country where there was direct continuity from the Romanian Communist Party via the National Salvation Front to the Party of Social Democracy, which finally lost power only in the autumn of 1996.

The return to power in Poland and Hungary in 1993 and 1994 respectively of parties which had been rejected only a few years earlier scarcely indicated a popular desire for a return to a form of socialism which had clearly been discredited and could hardly be restored, or for a return of old-style hegemonic parties. In both countries, hardship consequent on poor economic performance since the end of communist rule and knowledge that those parties contained well-qualified experts and specialists made the reformed former ruling parties look attractive to voters who wanted change and security, not a return to the old regime. By contrast, in the Czech Republic, the experts and specialists were only too clearly to be found among the ranks of the opposition to the communists within Civic Forum between 1989 and 1991, and largely became the backbone of the right-of-centre parties that formed the government coalition from 1992 onwards.

The Polish and Hungarian successor parties had themselves changed and, like most of the former ruling parties, had discarded discredited leaders, brought forward some whose role in the former party had been less prominent, and incorporated elements of a new generation, often technocrats and experts, who provided some assurance of competence. As Alison Mahr and John Nagle pointed out, in Poland and Hungary the two successor parties had prepared themselves well during the four years they had spent in opposition by 'effectively shedding their negative image, in part by fielding candidates untainted by close association with the old leadership or candidates who represented the reform wings of the communist parties' and by successfully embracing democracy and a market economy on the one hand while presenting themselves as 'the authentic representatives of the postcommunist value culture, which is still heavily socialist', on the other (Mahr and Nagle, 1995, pp. 398–9). In effect, the successor parties in Poland and Hungary had managed to take advantage of popular discontent with the economic policies introduced by non-communist governments in the early 1990s and, Mahr and Nagle suggested, to occupy 'the sociopolitical niche which was expected to be filled by social democratic parties'. Where postcommunist parties had clung to power (as in Bulgaria and Romania) it was, paradoxically enough, economic failure that brought about their eventual replacement by their pro-reform opponents.

In most of the region, then, the successors to the former ruling parties came to be either the main party of government or the leading opposition force, with every prospect in future years of a repeated alternation between the front and back benches, to use a phrase from British political discourse rather than that of Central Europe. The major exceptions in that respect were the successor parties in the Czech Republic and Slovakia. In the former the defeat of the former ruling, but unrepentant, Communist Party was complete. Although it remained a parliamentary party, its electoral support declined with each succeeding parliamentary election. It had no prospect of a return to power (and little, either, of a revival in its fortunes) in part because, unlike its counterparts in neighbouring states, it was un-willing to adapt and, in part, because by the mid-1990s the Czech Social Democratic Party had come to be seen as a viable alternative for the democratic vote on the left. In Slovakia, the former Commu-nist Party, despite its convincing transformation into the social democratised Party of the Democratic Left and a short period in a broad coalition government in 1994 (Wightman, 1995a), was doing little better by the mid-1990s than its hard-line Czech counterpart which had refused even to change its name, let alone dissociate itself from its past at the head of one of the most repressive regimes in the region.

Yet, the fortunes of the former ruling parties were not solely a matter of their own choosing or of their responsiveness to the moment. The attractiveness to the electorate in the Czech Republic of right-of-centre parties advocating radical economic reform, a phenomenon not registered so markedly elsewhere, was only in part a reaction against the particular harshness of the communist regime in Czechoslovakia in the 1970s and 1980s and, in the Czech case, of the Communist Party's inability and unwillingness to distance itself from its past. It also reflected a perception that marketisation and priva-tisation would bring a prosperity of which the country had been deprived under communism and of which it had shown itself capable in the period between the two world wars, and indeed even before the Czechs gained their independence from Austria in 1918. The Czechs, however, were exceptional in that respect. The success of pro-market parties there directly contrasted with their failure in Slovakia, thanks in large part to fear among Slovaks that the same reform that attracted the Czechs would have more deleterious consequences in a country whose economy remained less advanced, where unemployment was over three times that found among the Czechs even before the break-up of Czechoslovakia, and where, by contrast, communism had brought modernisation rather than decline. However, unlike Hungary and Poland, it was not the successor party (the Party of the Democratic Left) which benefited from those fears, but the new Movement for a Democratic Slovakia, in which many former communists were to be found.

It is clear that most countries in Central and Eastern Europe can claim some degree of exceptionalism, but developments among political parties in Slovakia in the second half of the 1990s were more exceptional than most. That was not simply due to the presence in parliament and in the government coalition from the end of 1994 of two extremist parties – the Slovak National Party and the Workers' Association of Slovakia – which were unsympathetic to Western liberal democratic values or to capitalism and which developed links to anti-system parties in the West (the French National Front and Force Ouvrière, respectively). Extremist parties were not unique to Slovakia among postcommunist states. The Czechs, too, elected an anti-system party to parliament in 1992 and 1996 in the form of the right-wing Republican Party. The Hungarian electorate, it is worth noting, by contrast, rejected attempts by Istvan Csurka and his Justice and Life Party to exploit xenophobic nationalism and win seats in the Budapest parliament in the 1994 elections.

Slovakia was different, however, in another way. Whereas elsewhere in the region parties and movements had evolved that could mostly be placed in a normal conservative–liberal–social democratic spectrum, the Slovak political scene in the second half of the 1990s appeared to comprise a dual structure of 'standard' and 'non-standard' parties, a structure in which 'standard' left–centre–right parties were mirrored by 'non-standard' parties on similar parts of the spectrum, but distinguished by their inclination to authoritarianism, populism and confrontational politics (see on this point Meseznikov, 1995, pp. 106–7). The main party of government, the Movement for a Democratic Slovakia, which had broken from the Public Against Violence in spring 1991 and which claimed to be in the political centre, belonged among the latter 'non-standard' parties in that view. In practice it embraced a wide spectrum of opinion, but it had been born as the product of bitter division within the new Slovak political elite and as a vehicle to achieve the political ambitions of its first leader, Vladimir Meciar. Rather than a moderate party in the political centre, it was a populist movement which increasingly acquired a tightly-knit organisational internal structure and followed the authoritarian inclinations of its overbearing chairman.

Sources of Party Strength and Weakness

One weakness of the new parties in Central and Eastern Europe in the 1990s could often be traced back to the manner of their emergence. Bill Lomax's observation, with regard to Hungary, that new parties 'were created from above by small groups of close personal friends', that they were 'not born of wider social movements, nor were they brought into being to represent social interests . . . but were formed primarily in terms of cultural and ideological conceptions' (Lomax, 1996, p. 38) had wide validity across the region.

Parties of that kind were often more prone to internal conflict, splits and defections. Differentiation was clearly necessary in the early years in movements as broad as Civic Forum in the Czech Republic, Public Against Violence in Slovakia, Solidarity in Poland or the Union of Democratic Forces in Bulgaria but, as the first decade of postcommunist rule neared completion, it was by no means clear that the process was always a positive one. Continuing divisions over 'cultural and ideological conceptions' fed into arguments over policy, principle or personality and came to threaten the viability of some of those new parties, including some which appeared to have become permanent features of the political landscape. In Hungary, Hungarian Democratic Forum survived the defection of the militant nationalist, Istvan Csurka, in 1993 but after the 1994 elections its representation in parliament was sharply reduced. In late 1997, the Christian Democratic People's Party also saw its parliamentary group disintegrate.

In the Czech Republic several parties were hit by internal dissent. Within six months of the 1996 parliamentary elections two deputies defected from the Social Democrats, one to the Civic Democratic Party, another to the backbenches. By late 1997, the survival of the small Civic Democratic Alliance was increasingly in question as support waned in opinion polls and disagreements between its more purist founding members and more pragmatic newcomers hardened into a factionalism that threatened to split the party. In Poland, too, considerations of personality, principle and pragmatism influenced party development. Most recently they led to the creation of an electoral force, Solidarity Electoral Action, which in September 1997 succeeded in ousting its postcommunist rivals from power, although there was no guarantee that a formation created largely out of expediency would survive for very long.

Even in the latter half of the 1990s, parties in Central and Eastern Europe rarely represented sectional or group interests. An obvious exception in that respect were those parties mentioned earlier which identified with a rural interest. The urban/rural divide, however, was not the only source of social differentiation that had not been eliminated by communism and remained a relevant factor in party formation during the 1990s. National identity was another. In Bulgaria, Romania and Slovakia, for example, ethnic minorities, whose interests the internationalist communist parties had claimed to represent in the past, only exceptionally joined forces with the majority nation in the postcommunist era and preferred to create their own organisations. In pre-split Czechoslovakia, the Coexistence movement may have begun with the intention of crossing the ethnic divide and appealing to all ethnic groups, but it soon became a party restricted effectively to the Hungarian minority in Slovakia and, partly in response to the more jingoistic voices that had emerged in some Slovak parties, itself became increasingly nationalist in its rhetoric. Action in Bulgaria against the Party of Rights and Freedoms, which had been the party of the Turkish minority, and the attempt to introduce a ban on ethnic parties seemed not only counter to democratising trends in Europe, but doomed to failure as the Turkish vote transferred elsewhere.

Any explanation of the success of the former ruling parties, and of at least some of the former ruling parties, in much of Central and Eastern Europe must take into consideration their readiness to adapt to the new circumstances of the 1990s. Nevertheless they also had a number of advantages over new parties and the recently revived historical parties. Former ruling parties, for example, inherited an organisational structure, financial resources and a sizeable membership which new parties generally lacked at the outset.

These legacies from the past did not remain untouched by the collapse of communism. All former ruling parties, for example, had to disband their workplace branches and, in anticipation of competitive elections, rebuild their organisations to conform with the electoral districts where one level of the political struggle would inevitably be fought. This was not necessarily a great problem for those parties in so far as new constituencies coincided with earlier administrative boundaries and thus with the party's traditional territorial structure. In this respect, communist-era parties had the advantage over new parties of retaining at least the skeleton of their earlier organisational network.

Attempts were made to deprive former ruling parties of the financial resources they had amassed (improperly, it could well be argued) as a result of their power monopoly and fusion with the state. But this could be only a first step towards establishing a level playing-field. In most states (Poland was one notable exception), an attempt was made through state funding to try and ensure that new parties would not be at a disadvantage. State support took different forms in different states, but generally included reimbursement of election costs (at least for successful parties) and subvention of parliamentary groups, as well as the more customary provision of deputies' salaries and expenses (for more information on this topic, see Lewis, 1998). Those, of course, were not the only sources of financial support. New parties often obtained help (and not only financial) from sister parties abroad, and parties often found additional funds through sponsorship, gifts and bank loans (not always without subsequent embarrassment, where sponsors' identitites were queried or loans proved difficult to pay off).

With the collapse of the communist dictatorships, membership was no longer the *sine qua non* for career advancement that it had been in the past and all former ruling parties suffered a dramatic drop in numbers from the extremely high levels of earlier times. The Communist Party of Bohemia and Moravia, for example, saw its numbers fall from around one million in 1989 to just over 317,000 at the end of 1992. In Slovakia, the Party of the Democratic Left (the successor to the Communist Party of Slovakia), which unlike its Czech counterpart had undertaken a complete break with its Marxist-Leninist past, experienced an even steeper decline – from 300,000 in 1989 to 25,000 in late 1994 (Meseznikov, 1997, p. 25). In the Slovak case, the contraction in membership at that point in time coincided with a serious fall in electoral support. The Party of the Democratic Left, standing within a broader coalition called Free Choice, secured just over 10 per cent of the vote in October 1994 – nearly 5 per cent less than in the 1992 parlaimentary elections and less than half the support its leadership expected (Wightman and Szomolányi, 1995, pp. 610–12).

Yet there was no straightforward correlation evident in Central Europe between the size of the membership and a party's electoral popularity. In Hungary, the postcommunist Socialist Party obtained over half the vote in the 1994 elections although its membership stood at around only 40,000 by the mid-1990s (Lomax, 1996, p. 27). In Poland, the Democratic Left Alliance, in which the successor party (the Social Democracy of the Polish Republic) was the dominant force, did much better in the 1993 elections with 20 per cent of the vote than the Polish Peasant Party which attracted just over 15 per cent, despite claims that its membership was three times that of the Social Democrats (in 1995, the Peasant Party claimed to have 180,000 members, according to Lewis and Gortat, 1995, p. 600).

The reliability of membership figures may well be open to doubt but it is worth noting that in the Polish and Czech cases at least, not only former ruling communist parties but also former satellite parties tended to claim membership levels that were much higher than among new parties.The Czech People's Party, for example, claimed to have as many as 80,000 adherents in late 1993. Membership in the two electorally most popular new parties in the Czech Republic in the mid-1990s, the Civic Democratic Party and the Czech Social Democratic Party, by contrast, was much lower than that: 24,000 and 12,000 respectively (Kopecky, 1995, p. 524). In Poland the Freedom Union (formerly called the Democratic Union) had only 18,000 members in 1995 and the somewhat older Confederation for an Independent Poland (which had first surfaced in 1970s) 25,000 (Gebethner, 1996, p. 130).

Interestingly enough, it was the resuscitated historical Independent Smallholders' Party in Hungary that claimed a membership level higher than the other Hungarian parliamentary parties at 50,000–60,000 (Lomax, 1996, p. 32), and thus to that extent resembled the former satellite parties in the Czech Republic and Poland. Hungary was also different inasmuch as both the Alliance of Free Democrats and Hungarian Democratic Forum claimed levels of membership close to the 40,000 recorded by the Socialist Party: the Free Democrats 34,000 and Democratic Forum 37,000, although of those as many as 10,000 were reportedly late with their membership fees (Lomax, 1996, pp. 24–6). Lomax, however, noted that some sources cited a much lower figure in the case of the Free Democrats and it would perhaps be wise to record a note of caution about the reliability of these statistics more generally.

Many observers have explained what they saw as low participation rates in political parties in East-Central Europe since the end of communist rule as a reflection of the degree to which parties were

discredited in general as a result of their identification in the public
mind with the former ruling parties. The Polish political scientist,
Stanislaw Gebethner, for example, has argued that

> under the conditions that prevailed following the failure of the
> former political system of 'real socialism' the great majority of
> Poles deeply distrusted any political party. This was as true of new
> parties as of the old ones. Such anti-party feelings are characteristic
> of all the postcommunist societies of Central and Eastern Europe.
> (Gebethner, 1996, p. 121)

Party membership in the 1990s had certainly declined in comparison
with the communist era. However, as Lewis (1996, pp. 14–15) has
pointed out, while the party membership base in Poland, Hungary
and the Czech Republic was quite small in relation to population (at
between 1 and 4 per cent), and compared unfavourably in that respect
with neighbouring Austria and with more distant Scandinavian
countries where membership levels were high, it was no lower overall
than in the Netherlands and the United Kingdom.

Turnout at election time, moreover, has not positively confirmed
public distrust of political parties and politicians. In most of Central
and Eastern Europe, participation in parliamentary elections since
1989 has generally been above 70 per cent (see Holmes, 1997, pp. 157–
65). The massive 96 per cent turnout in Czechoslovakia in June 1990
was something of an exception for democratic elections in the
postcommunist era and suggested that the electorate was treating
the poll as a kind of plebiscite for democracy, although two years
later (in June 1992) when more clearly identifiable parties had formed
participation still remained as high as 85 per cent. Even after the
break-up of Czechoslovakia, turnout remained near the 75 per cent
level when Slovakia went to the polls in October 1994 and the Czech
Republic in June 1996. The lowest turnout in the Czech Republic was
seen during the first elections to the Czech Senate in November 1996
when it fell to 35 per cent, but in this instance scepticism as regards
the value of a second chamber was the main source of public
indifference rather than a lack of appeal of political parties or their
candidates. The only countries in Central and South-East Europe to
see turnouts lower than 70 per cent were Hungary and Poland,
although even in Hungary over 60 per cent of the electorate took
part in the first rounds of the two-stage elections in March 1990 and
May 1994. Only in Poland, in October 1991 when only 43 per cent

took part in the first truly competitive parliamentary elections, and again in September 1997 when only 48 per cent voted, was there clear evidence of public indifference.

Any explanation of poor levels of recruitment should not be limited to the result of the public's alienation from political parties but should also take into account a lower level of interest among the parties themselves in recruitment. Even the former communist parties no longer required the high membership levels they had pursued when in power as a means of ensuring political control over society and the realisation of their policies. Moreover, as Petr Kopecky (1995, pp. 517–21) has noted, parties in East-Central Europe in the 1990s were no longer likely to see a large membership as important, for three reasons. Firstly, they were not dependent on members for funding, thanks to state subsidy. Secondly, leaders, who in many instances had been the founders of new parties, would not be over-keen on searching for the potential sources of conflict that might appear in the shape of new recruits. Thirdly, they faced serious difficulties in finding motivated people. Membership, moreover, was no longer a key means of political communication in the age of television.

In that respect the former ruling parties, and the satellite parties in the cases of Czechoslovakia and Poland, had rapidly lost their privileged positions in the media. Communist control had relied on the media 'serving as a "transmission-belt" – not from the masses to the party . . . but rather from the party to the people' (O'Neil, 1996, p. 1). In many cases, former communist newspapers remained among the most widely read printed dailies in individual countries but the pressures of the market, the need for foreign investment, desire for editorial independence and a desire by the papers themselves to adapt to the new democratic environment led them to end their direct connections with the successor parties and establish their independence. In some countries, new parties tried to establish newspapers of their own but for the most part these soon collapsed. By and large, parties in the postcommunist world had to rely on finding favourable reporting in newspapers whose editorial sympathies lay broadly in their part of the political spectrum rather than relying on having their own voice.

Throughout the region, concluded one analyst from a comparative study conducted in the mid-1990s (Milton, 1996, pp. 19–21), governments, unlike political parties, continued to expect support rather than criticism from the media. This was particularly true of the broadcasting media where intervention was more frequent than in the press. In some countries there were attempts to secure equal access to current affairs programmes among parliamentary parties; in others this was less clearly the practice. In all, access was generally equal during election campaigns which were subject to precise regulation.

Conclusion

Almost a decade after the end of one-party rule, the political land-scape of the countries of Central and Eastern Europe had changed almost beyond recognition and indeed many of the features of that landscape were quite different from those that had appeared domi-nant in the early years. The disappearance of the broad-based and ill-defined political movements, though not universal across the region, was far from unexpected but it is worth noting that they often gave birth to potentially more effective and durable political parties. Few, however, would have predicted the resurgence of the successors to the ruling parties in Hungary and Poland in the light of the near-total rejection of those parties in the parliamentary elections of 1990 and 1991.

Any analysis of party systems in Central and Eastern Europe in the late 1990s must recognise, with Jack Bielasiak, that 'The movement from party fragmentation to a pluralist party system in ECE is evident, but not complete.' Throughout the region, multi-party systems had clearly emerged but, as he noted, 'it is more appropriate to talk about the pluralisation of the party system than to proclaim the stability of a polyarchical party structure defined by strong parties with roots in the constituency' (Bielasiak, 1997, pp. 40–1). The survival of even apparently strong parties cannot be guaranteed and it remains to be seen how far the success of individual parties during the first postcommunist decade was dependent on the personalities of individual leaders at the time and their individual skills in commu-nicating with the public, and how far their successors will be able to build on their record.

That is, of course, not the only factor likely to affect the develop-ment of political parties in Central and Eastern Europe. It remains to be seen whether close relations with the European Union and NATO, at least for some states, as well as the influence provided by better established democracies in Western Europe and the USA, may bring yet greater consolidation of the party system than has so far been achieved. Whatever the outcome, the evidence to date has confirmed the importance to the future of democracy in these states of the establishment of effective political parties and party systems.

9

Elections and Voting Behaviour

KRZYSZTOF JASIEWICZ

It is conventional wisdom that the Central and East European revolution was won on the streets of Prague and Leipzig, Timisoara and Bucharest, in the shipyards of Gdansk and steel mills of Cracow. This point of view hardly can be disputed, but it is also true that this revolution was won in voting booths across the region. Street demonstrations and strikes usually initiated the change and often delivered the ultimate blow to the old regimes, but with almost no exception competitive elections were the real turning point in the process of political transition. Ever since this breakthrough, the (usually) free and fair elections have been a focal point of Central and East European democratic consolidations. And even in those countries which stumbled on their road to democracy, elections never became irrelevant. For instance, the spectacular 1996–7 street demonstrations in Belgrade, which lasted several months until the final success of protesters, were caused by the government's refusal to recognise opposition victories in local elections.

In the late 1980s all Central and East European communist regimes faced – although most of them failed to recognise it – a crisis of legitimation (Rigby and Feher, 1982; Rychard, 1992). Since their rise to power after World War II, the communists of Central and Eastern Europe legitimised their rule through two mechanisms. The first may be called 'legitimisation through utopia': a promise to create an ideal system of social, political, and economic institutions, guaranteeing all citizens equal rights and equal access to the benefits of a welfare state; a system that would eventually generate an affluent society, free of exploitation and conflict. The second was a legitimisation through 'the Soviet tanks factor': the adoption of the Brezhnev doctrine (well

166

before the term was invented) to convince the potentially rebellious populations that the Soviet Union would not tolerate other than communist regimes in the region, and that the only alternative to a national communist government and limited sovereignty would be a direct Soviet occupation. The technically democratic procedures, such as elections, sessions of parliaments, and nomination of cabinets, served only as a rubber-stamp for the legitimisation achieved through the above-mentioned mechanisms. None the less, these rubber stamps were perceived by the communists as very important devices. Very seldom would they implement any decisions without subjecting them to a process of such a formal legalisation; very often they would prosecute oppositionists for alleged violations of law and 'constitutional order'.

By the late 1980s both mechanism of legitimisation had exhausted their potential. The promise of a better, more just political system and society was never fulfilled, and even the communist leaders occasionally had to admit this. But above all, the countries of Central and Eastern Europe experienced economic crises, or, at the very best, stagnation. The gap between their 'economies of shortage' (Kornai, 1980) and the affluent market economies of Western Europe and North America became wider then ever. The people responded with disbelief to the official statistics on economic growth, which were themselves much less impressive than in the 1950s or 1960s. In recognition of these facts the communist leaderships in Hungary and Poland launched programmes of economic reforms, but the ultimate failure of these programmes contributed to the further delegitimisation of the system.

The election of Mikhail Gorbachev as the Soviet leader originally did not place in question the validity of the Brezhnev doctrine. But in 1987 and 1988 he and his aides began to encourage the communist leaders of Central and Eastern Europe to experiment with their economic and political institutions – within, it should be remembered, the framework of a 'socialist state'. These friendly suggestions received a very mixed response from those to whom they were directed. Only the reformist factions of the Polish and Hungarian communist parties understood them as a backing against their own hardliners and pursued cautious policies of liberalisation. None the less, the hardline leaders of Czechoslovakia or the GDR could not any longer present their conservative positions as congruent with the Soviet line. The window of opportunity for the opposition and dissatisfied populations had been opened. Still, it was not until the formation of a Solidarity-based government in Poland and the over-throw of the Berlin Wall in 1989 that the Brezhnev doctrine could be pronounced dead.

Electoral Legitimisation and Regime Transistion

The communist reformers of Poland and Hungary were the first to recognise an urgent need for a renewed legitimisation of their rule. They did not plan to transfer power to the opposition. Rather, they were hoping to co-opt moderate opposition groupings to the system and share with them responsibility for the implementation of further economic reforms, which would carry necessary austerity measures, in all likelihood extremely unpopular among the populace. Despite the different strength of opposition forces in Hungary and Poland (in Poland strong, since 1980 united in the political movement of Solidarity, in Hungary weak and isolated) the communists of both countries applied very similar strategies. They opened up a process of negotiations, legitimising the opposition but also forcing it to recog-nise as legitimate the institutions of the system. Among the major items on the negotiation table were the terms for new general elections – elections that would broaden the legitimisation base of the renewed institutions of political representation. The Hungarian and Polish communist reformers were undoubtedly hoping to win these elections. With such an outcome, they would have regained unquestioned legitimacy, in exchange for granting the leaders of opposition a limited access to power (which would also mean joint accountability). Neither in Poland nor in Hungary were the communists able to achieve their goals.

In Poland the Jaruzelski/Rakowski government was forced to open negotiations with Solidarity after a series of industrial strikes, which took place in the spring and summer of 1988. They perceived this decision as the only way to overcome a stalemate, or a 'catastrophic balance' of power (Arriagada, 1992, p. 180). Similar perceptions dominated among the leaders of Solidarity. The formal negotiations began in January 1989 in a palace in Warsaw, with the members of the opposition and the government seated not face-to-face across a long, rectangular table, but around a round one. The symbolism of this spatial arrangement was obvious: 'we meet here not to bargain and struggle against each other, but to jointly work for the benefit of Poland'. The outcome of this effort was the so-called Roundtable

Accord (April 1989). According to this contract, 65 per cent of the 460 seats in the forthcoming elections to the Sejm were allocated in advance to the communists (Polish United Workers' Party) and their allies (United Peasant Party, Democratic Party, and pro-communist Catholic groupings). The remaining 35 per cent were subject to an open contest. In addition, the upper chamber of parliament, the Senate, was re-established, with 100 seats to be filled in a free, unrestricted election – the first such election in Central and Eastern Europe for more than 40 years. In the elections, held on 4 June and 18 June 1989, Solidarity won all but one of the seats it contested. The communists acquired their allocated seats in the Sejm, but none in the Senate. Moreover, their leaders were humiliated by the failure to obtain 50 per cent of the votes necessary for election from the uncontested national list. Jaruzelski was elected president by the National Assembly (the Sejm and Senate in a joint session), but the communists failed to form a coalition government, after the desertion of Peasant and Democratic parties to the Solidarity camp. Eventually, Tadeusz Mazowiecki, a long-time advisor to Lech Walesa, formed a Solidarity-dominated coalition government.

Less than a year after this historic achievement many Poles felt that they were 'penalised for taking the lead'. The revolutions swept the communists from power across Central and Eastern Europe, but in Poland still there was a communist president and 'only 35 per cent democratic' Sejm. Under pressure from below, Jaruzelski tactfully resigned, and – following a constitutional amendment – a popular election to the presidency was held in November/December 1990. Solidarity, thus far remarkably united, split into two factions: one supporting Lech Walesa, the other Mazowiecki. The former emerged victorious.

After the presidential election the fragmentation of Solidarity continued. With no common enemy to keep them united any more, various political and ideological orientations emerged from the movement. In 1991, after the 'contractual' Sejm had shortened its term of office, they entered an electoral campaign. The October 1991 elections produced a highly fragmented parliament, with about thirty parties represented in both chambers. This parliament in two years managed to generate three prime ministers, two governments, and its own early departure, but also a surprising continuity in economic and political reforms. The postcommunist Democratic Left Alliance, the second strongest faction in the Sejm, remained in opposition throughout the short tenure of this parliament.

In Hungary the reforms began within the communist party (Hungarian Socialist Workers' Party). At a party conference in May 1988, several reform-minded officials were elected to the Politburo. Some of them had been instrumental in setting up in 1987 a then semi-oppositionist group, the Hungarian Democratic Forum (HDF). The HDF, along with other dissident groupings (among them the Forum of Free Democrats and the Federation of Young Democrats) organised in March 1988 the Opposition Roundtable – an umbrella organisation, designed to represent the opposition in negotiations with the government. The negotiations lasted from June to September 1989, with the two major partners – the communist government and the opposition – being supplemented by communist-sponsored social organisations (trade unions, Popular Front) as a third party. Hence, the Hungarian discussions became known as the 'triangular table negotiations'.

The accord in the tripartite negotiations, providing among other issues for free elections early the following year, was reached in September 1989. In November, a national referendum decided the order of elections (legislative before presidential). Unlike elsewhere in Central and Eastern Europe, the Hungarian opposition entered the electoral process divided into several parties, but the same was true of the communists, split into a reform-socialist and a hardline faction. Eventually, in the spring 1990 elections, six parties cleared the threshold of 4 per cent: the Hungarian Democratic Forum, the Smallholders Party, the Christian Democrats (these three parties formed the ruling coalition), the Alliance of Free Democrats, the Federation of Young Democrats, and the Hungarian Socialist Party (reformed postcommunists). The parliament changed the mode of presidential election from a direct one to indirect (by parliament). Arpad Goncz of the Free Democrats was chosen as president.

While the Polish and Hungarian cases may be described as negotiated transitions in which a reformist wing of communist party played an active role, in the other Central and East European countries the ruling communists retreated under a rapidly growing pressure from below – as earlier chapters have demonstrated in more detail. In Czechoslovakia a series of mass demonstrations culminated in November 1989. That month, a group of veteran dissidents, led by Vaclav Havel, established in Prague a new organisation, the Civic Forum, which quickly became the only spokesgroup for all anti-regime forces. A parallel group in Slovakia adopted the name Public Against Violence. The communists agreed to negotiate with Civic

Forum, and, under constant pressure from below (especially a general strike on November 27), retreated step by step, until a coalition government under Marian Calfa was formed. Gustav Husak resigned as president and Havel was elected (unanimously by the still communist dominated Federal Assembly) to replace him. In the June 1990 elections Civic Forum and Public Against Violence mustered a majority in both chambers of the federal parliament, as well as in the national councils in the Czech Republic and Slovakia. Havel was re-elected president (for a two-year term). Soon after this victory the process of disintegration of Civic Forum and Public Against Violence began. In the course of only two years both organisations practically disappeared from public life. In the elections of June 1992 in the Czech Republic the Civic Democratic Party, a splinter group from Civic Forum, emerged as the major force, while in Slovakia a plurality of votes went to the Movement for a Democratic Slovakia – a nationalist-populist group. Their leaders, Vaclav Klaus and Vladimir Meciar respectively, were committed to separate both parts of the 74-year-old federation, which decision took effect on 1 January 1993.

In Bulgaria in November 1989 a group of more pragmatist communist leaders forced the resignation of Todor Zhivkov, one of the most autocratic and conservative communist rulers in Eastern Europe. This move prompted spontaneous anti-communist demonstrations in Sofia and the formation of a Union of Democratic Forces (UDF), which embraced several oppositionist and dissident groupings. In January 1990 this organisation entered roundtable talks with the government. After several setbacks, these talks led eventually to parliamentary elections in June 1990. The timing came as a compromise between the communists, who insisted on early elections, hoping to win and gain a renewed legitimacy, and the opposition, which preferred a later date, since it needed time to organise and gain momentum. In the elections the communists (now renamed the Bulgarian Socialist Party– BSP) mustered a majority, while the UDF finished second, and the Movement for Rights and Freedoms (MRF) (representing the interests of Turkish minority) came third. The UDF refused to join a coalition government with the BSP, but its leader Zhelyu Zhelev was elected interim president by the Grand National Assembly in August 1990 (his mandate was renewed by a popular vote in January 1992). A BSP-based government of Andrei Lukanov resigned in November 1990 under pressure from the opposition and protesters on the streets, and a caretaker government ruled until the new elections in October 1991. In these elections none of the parties gained a majority. A UDF minority government, supported by the MRF, was formed, but it collapsed in October 1992 after the MRF withdrew its support. A non-partisan government of Luben Berov survived until the autumn of 1994, when an early election gave a parliamentary majority to the postcommunist BSP. This outcome was, at least in part, due to the progressing disintegration of the UDF. The new government, led by Zhan Videnov, the young leader of the Socialists, abandoned the course of moderate reforms of its predecessors, and led the country into a deep economic crisis. In response, the mood of the electorate swung away from the postcommunists, and the candidate of the reunited opposition, Peter Stoyanov (the incumbent President Zhelev had lost to Stoyanov in opposition primaries), soundly defeated the Socialist candidate in the runoff of the November 1996 presidential election. Another early parliamentary election became necessary, and in April 1997 the Socialists lost, by a substantial margin, to the UDF.

The Bulgarian rhythm of transition was repeated, with some variations, in Albania. Even in this last bastion of genuine Stalinism in Central and Eastern Europe the pressure from the rapidly changing international environment could be felt, and its leader, Ramiz Alia, began in 1990 a process of very cautious reforms. This only encouraged the desperate population to protest. Further liberalisation by the regime prompted the emergence of the first oppositionist groupings. As in Bulgaria, the communists decided to have an early election, and legitimise their rule in the eyes of the international community and the Albanian population. The opposition threatened a boycott – and the elections were postponed from 10 February to 31 March 1991. None the less, the communists were victorious, by a 2 to 1 margin against the Democratic Party – a loosely organised, urban-based group. Unlike in Bulgaria, the opposition originally joined a grand coalition government with the communists, but left it in December 1991, demanding new elections. These were conducted in March 1992 and brought a reversal of fortune: the Democratic Party defeated the Socialist Party (renamed communists) by a 5 to 2 margin. The leader of the Democratic Party, Sali Berisha, was elected president by the People's Assembly in April 1992.

The course of events in Romania varied significantly from the patterns of developments elsewhere in East-Central Europe. There was no organised opposition, no reform-minded communist leaders, no roundtable talks; there was violence. The Communist Party vanished from the Romanian political scene after the December

1989 revolution, but the National Salvation Front (NSF), seemingly an *ad hoc* outcome of this revolt, in many ways substituted for a postcommunist party. Allegedly dominated by former communists, the NSF presented itself in 1990 as the only legitimate representation of all Romanians, and intimidated political opponents. It decisively won the May 1990 parliamentary elections, and its leader Ion Iliescu mustered 85 per cent of the popular vote for president. After two years of half-hearted reform policies, the ruling Democratic National Salvation Front (renamed after a split within the old NSF) gained a plurality of seats in the September 1992 parliamentary election, while Iliescu was re-elected in the runoff against Emil Constantinescu, the leader of a coalition of opposition forces – the Democratic Convention of Romania. The DCR finished a strong second in the elections to both chambers of the parliament. It had to wait another four years for its day: in the November 1996 election it mustered a plurality of votes and seats in both houses, while Constantinescu became president, after defeating Iliescu in the runoff.

Looking at the process of regime transition in Central and Eastern Europe from a comparative perspective one can observe that it passed through several distinct phases:

Phase zero: The communist regimes either resist pressure to reform from a more or less organised opposition, or rule practically uncontested.

Phase one: The communist regimes come under pressure from the opposition, the public, and/or the international environment to open up the process of negotiations. The opposition enters this process represented by an umbrella organisation, which covers groupings with various ideological and political orientations. The process of negotiations, usually called a round table, provides a mutual legitimisation for the opposition (recognised by the regime as a partner) and the institutions of the old regime, in particular the government and parliament. The round tables as such obviously exceeded the constitutional framework of a communist state; the state institutions make necessary provisions to legalise the outcome of the negotiations (including the adoption of a new electoral law and constitutional amendments). The institutional role of the communist party diminishes during this process (while its leaders still play a significant political role), and in most cases the 'leading role of the [communist] party' is dropped from the constitution. Developments in the former Soviet Union and Yugoslavia, unlike elsewhere in East-Central Europe, are in this phase marked not so much by the communist–

anticommunist cleavage, as by the conflict between the peripheral republics seeking sovereignty and the centre, desperately trying to salvage the federation's integrity.

Phase two: Both the regime and the opposition claim that they represent the interests of the people, but against each partner of the round-table negotiations a claim could be made that it represented nobody's but its own interests. These claims had to be weighed through the process of (more or less) contested elections. The elections provided also a broader legitimisation of the round-table accords, and, ultimately, led to the creation of indisputably legitimised institutions of political representation. Typically, the opposition entered the electoral process under the protective umbrella of one organisation, with only minor groupings running independently. Also the Communist Party usually participated in the elections as a united force, often under a changed name.

Phase three: Developments in this phase differ within the region. In the Northern Tier (Poland, Czechoslovakia, Hungary, Slovenia, Croatia, and the Baltic states) the elections bring about a landslide victory for the opposition. The defeat of the communists leads to a disintegration of this party and/or profound turnover in its leadership. But the victorious former opposition also disintegrates (Croatia is the only exception here), the umbrella organisations either lose their popular support or simply cease to exist, and the political scene becomes highly fragmented. This fragmentation was usually reflected in the outcome of the second set of general elections.

In the Southern Tier the postcommunist organisations win the first elections – the opposition is too weak and the population too intimidated to overcome the resistance of communists, entrenched in the state bureaucracy and mass media. But after the elections the opposition – still unified under a protective umbrella, and now a legitimate actor on the political scene – gains momentum and challenges the postcommunist governments. In Bulgaria and Albania this challenge leads, within about a year, to new elections, which tip the balance of power toward the opposition. In Romania, a united and better (compared with 1990) organised opposition still loses to the Democratic Front of National Salvation in the 1992 elections, only to win decisively in 1996. Developments in Ukraine, Moldova, and Macedonia differ, for specific reasons, from this pattern (as does the situation in Yugoslavia and the war-torn Bosnia).

Despite local variations, the process of political change in all the Central and East European countries occurred according to the same general pattern, from polarisation to fragmentation: a united opposition faced the old regime in a stand-off (at a round table and/or during elections) and remained united until the apparent defeat of the communists.

It is often stressed (O'Donnell, Schmitter and Whitehead, 1986) that the first free elections after a prolonged period of totalitarian or authoritarian rule play the role of 'founding elections': they lead to the establishment of a relatively stable configuration of actors on the political scene (although not necessarily a stable government). In the case of Central and Eastern Europe the definition of founding elections should be extended to encompass the first, the second, and sometimes also the third and perhaps further electoral acts. The first elections were, as a rule, a plebiscite against communism; not until after the defeat of the communists did the party system begin to shape in an unrestricted way.

Seats and Votes: The Politics of Electoral Reform

When in 1909 universal male suffrage was introduced in Sweden by a Conservative government, the same reform act substituted proportional representation for the existing winner-take-all system. The Conservatives, whose electoral base in the Swedish nobility, spread more or less evenly throughout the country, would suddenly become relatively narrow, wanted to assure for themselves at least a minimal level of representation in parliament (Pontusson, 1992, p. 433). Similar decisions were made at that time elsewhere in continental Europe, leaving Great Britain as the last European bastion of first-past-the-post elections and Westminster-type democracy. Many theorists believe that choosing the proportional representation (PR) voting system was a very unfortunate decision, since plurality voting (first-past-the-post in single-member constituencies) is conducive to two-party systems and stable, majoritarian governments, while PR, on the other hand, tends to generate multi-party systems and coalition or even minority governments, vulnerable to challenges and therefore unstable (Duverger, 1963 and 1986; Riker, 1986). This relationship between the type of voting system and political stability has been recently questioned (Lijphart, 1991), and the problem remains open to further inquiry. Central and Eastern Europe provides here several very interesting cases (for a summary overview, see Table 9.1).

TABLE 9.1 *Electoral systems in Central and Eastern Europe (as of 1 January 1998).[1]*

Country	Date of most recent election	Electoral system
Albania	June 1997	Mixed. Most deputies elected in single-member districts by majority vote (with runoff). A make-up distribution of seats from national list to achieve full proportionality (party list PR, 4% threshold), for the total of 155 seats.
Bosnia-Hercegovina	September 1996	Party list PR in two separate compartments: the Muslim-Croat Federation and the Bosnian Serb Republic.
Bulgaria	April 1997	Party list PR in districts, 4% threshold.
Croatia	October 1995	Mixed. 28 deputies elected by FPTP in single-member districts, 80 deputies by party list PR in single nationwide district, with 5% threshold.
Czech Republic	May–June 1996	Party list PR in districts, 5% threshold.
Estonia	March 1995	Mixed. A modified version of STV in districts. Compensation seats distributed by party list PR nationwide, 5% threshold.
Hungary	May 1994	Mixed. 176 seats distributed by majority-plurality vote (two rounds) in single-member districts, 152 by party list PR in multi-member districts (4% threshold, 58 compensation seats by party list PR nationwide (4% threshold).
Latvia	September–October 1995	Party list PR in districts, 5% threshold.
Lithuania	October–November 1996	Mixed. 71 deputies elected in single-member districts by majority vote (with runoff), 70 deputies by party list PR nationwide (4% threshold).
Macedonia	October–November 1994	Majority vote in single-member districts, with runoff.
Moldova	February 1994	Party list PR nationwide, 4% threshold.
Poland	September 1997	391 deputies elected by party list PR in districts (5% threshold), additional 69 seats distributed by party list PR nationwide (7% threshold).
Romania	November 1996	Party list PR in districts, 3% threshold.
Slovakia	September–October 1994	Party list PR in districts, 5% threshold.
Slovenia	November 1996	Party list PR in districts, modified to allow nationwide compensatory distribution of seats.
Ukraine	March–April 1994	Majority vote in single-member districts, with runoff.[2]
Yugoslavia	November 1996	Party list PR in districts.

[1] Electoral systems used in the most recent election to the main chamber of parliament. Abbreviations: PR = proportional representation, FPTP – first-past-the-post, STV = single transferable vote.
[2] For the 1998 election in Ukraine a mixed system was adopted.

The mechanisms of choosing electoral systems in Central and Eastern Europe were in many instances remarkably similar to those in Sweden eighty years earlier. The elections of 1989–97 may indeed be regarded as a case study in the introduction of universal suffrage. True, the people of the region did vote in communist times, and 99.9 per cent turnouts did not come exclusively from the stuffing of electoral boxes. But in reality these people were disfranchised: the act of voting was reduced to a ritual, with no real political meaning whatsoever. The communist masters had no reason to worry about the outcome of the voting – it had been known even before the elections began.

In 1989–90 this was no longer the case. Just like the Swedish Conservatives, the communists in power, still having the legislative process under their control, opted for solutions they perceived as advantageous. Interestingly, for the first election in a given country their typical choice was a plurality (or rather majority) vote. The communists were hoping to gain in this system of voting because of at least three factors: (1) they were better organised than the opposition; (2) their local bosses believed they could still intimidate voters, particularly in rural areas; (3) they had name recognition, while the leaders of opposition were in most cases practically unknown to the public. In some instances these calculations were correct; in others they proved fatal.

In the June 1989 elections in Poland, the communists, according to a very peculiar electoral law designed at the round table, were ensured 173 of the 460 seats in the Sejm, with an additional 126 allocated to their allies and 161 open to contest by anybody else. However, all 100 seats in the Senate were open to unrestricted contest, by majority vote in multi- (2 or 3) member constituencies, and 99 of them were won by Solidarity. The communists, who under a PR system would have won 25–30 seats in the Senate, were left empty-handed.

Unlike in Poland, in Bulgaria and Albania the communists profited from majority voting in the first contested elections (1990 and 1991, respectively). In Bulgaria, where a mixed system was used, the BSP fared better in the majority vote than in PR, and eventually won a majority of seats. In Albania, where all seats were allocated by majority vote, the victory of the communists was even more spectacular. In Ukraine, similarly, the postcommunists were able to assure their victory in a majoritarian vote.

For the 1990 elections in Hungary, a highly complicated mixed system was adopted – again a compromise between the communists (who insisted on single-member constituencies) and the opposition. The hopes of the postcommunists that they would profit from a majority vote proved overly optimistic: they won only one seat by this mode, while in the PR vote collected 10.9 per cent of the votes and 14 seats (plus an additional 18 after the make-up distribution on the national level). Similar was the fate of communists in the first multi-party elections in Croatia, Slovenia, and Macedonia, which used majoritarian systems. In Czechoslovakia the communists, wisely, did not object to the Civic Forum/Public Against Violence proposal to return in the June 1990 election to the traditional system of proportional representation (with a 5 per cent cut-off). They finished as the second strongest party. Romania and Moldova also adopted PR systems for their first and subsequent elections.

The transition to proportional representation systems in new Central and East European democracies was advanced further when Poland, Bulgaria, and Albania adopted such systems for their second parliamentary elections. This time the communists, so badly defeated in majority voting in Poland and losing popular support in Bulgaria and Albania, opted – like the Swedish Conservatives of 1909 – for a PR solution, and because of their strong representation in parliaments were able to secure the desired legislation. PR or mixed systems were adopted also in Croatia, Slovenia and (in September 1997) in Ukraine, leaving Macedonia as the only country in the region still using a fully majoritarian mode of elections.

While the umbrella organisations – although already crumbling, due to increasing factional struggle – survived until 1997 in Romania and Bulgaria, elsewhere in Central and Eastern Europe political fragmentation prevails. Is the PR-based electoral law to be blamed? As indicated above, when the electoral regulations were chosen, the effectively available options were very limited: from a certain point onwards the former communists were interested in adopting a PR system, and usually had enough control over the legislature to secure such a regulation. But perhaps more important, they were supported in this bid by many of their foes: new and renewed small parties, which could not afford the risks associated with a winner-takes-all system. Political fragmentation usually preceded adoption of a PR-based voting system, not vice versa. This does not mean that a well-designed electoral law would not have curtailed the number of parties represented in parliament (as in the 1993 election in Poland). But it could not prevent or even reduce political factionalism and fragmentation, because their major sources were outside the political and legislative process: in the peculiarities of social structure of a society undergoing rapid economic, social, and political change.

The political polarisation of the 1980s and early 1990s reflected sociological features of communist societies: petrified social structures, low levels of social mobility, and dichotomised visions of social order – vanguard versus masses, *nomenklatura* versus people, them versus us. The current fragmentation reflects the ongoing change of this order, the disintegration of old structures and the emergence of new ones. The group loyalties and group interests of the past dissolve (some of them die hard, as is true of the provincial *nomenklatura* or workers in the mammoth enterprises of socialist industry). What emerges to replace them is not yet new solid structures, but a state of *anomie* (normlessness), and a fragmented society. In the opinion of many, such a society is likely to become haunted by the spectres of the past.

The Politics of Democratic Consolidation

In his essay *Reflections on the Revolution in Europe*, Ralf Dahrendorf made the following prediction about the course of reforms in the region: 'I suspect that . . . in East Central Europe . . . the pendulum of normal politics will have to swing once in the liberal and once in the social direction before you feel that you have made it. The liberal direction . . . involves the jump start of economies . . . Opposition to this process is bound to arise, and it will be about the social cost of economic growth. At some point, in four or even eight years' time . . . other groups will take over. They may even be called Social Democrats' (Dahrendorf, 1990, pp. 71–2). In several countries of the region, the electoral pendulum swung in the social direction, often earlier than the four or eight years Dahrendorf had predicted. The victorious parties were called social democrats, socialists, or 'democratic left'. Without exception, they were reformed (more or less) communists. Elsewhere, however, the communists were not able to escape from the pit of electoral misfortunes, as they were defeated in the second or even third set of general elections. If Dahrendorf's prediction were to be used as a yardstick of successfully completed democratic transitions, the Czech Republic, Slovenia and Estonia would have to be viewed as less advanced on this road than Macedonia or Albania, while Lithuania and Poland would belong to the elite leadership of this race, since the electoral pendulum has twice swung there already:

from the liberal to the social, and back to the liberal end of the spectrum. One should doubt, however, whether Dahrendorf's analysis was meant to be used (or should be used) in such a mechanical fashion, and, certainly, when Dahrendorf mentioned Social Democrats he did not mean a party of the former communists. Also, one can question whether swings of popular support towards and from postcommunists occur really in the dimension defined by Dahrendorf as the liberal-social continuum. Still, the electoral resurgence of former communists constitutes one of the most fascinating aspects of democratic consolidation in East-Central Europe.

The former communists returned to power, after a defeat in the first (or second) free election, in five Central and East European countries: Lithuania, Poland, Hungary, Macedonia, and Albania. With some qualifications, Bulgaria may be added to this list. In five other countries – Croatia, the Czech Republic, Estonia, Latvia, and Slovenia – the former communists lost not only in the first, but also all subsequent general elections. Again, there is also one borderline case, that of Slovakia. Before we examine these two dominant patterns of voting sequences in East-Central Europe, we should, however, look briefly at the remaining, 'deviant' cases.

In the rump Yugoslavia and in Bosnia, the issue of the electoral fate of former communists is moot, because fully free and fair elections have yet to take place there. In Ukraine, where communists won the largest vote in the March 1998 parliamentary elections, patterns of electoral competition and voting behaviour resemble those of Russia and the other post-Soviet states more than those of East-Central Europe. In Moldova, a postcommunist resurgence of sorts did occur: President Mircea Snegur (who in 1991 ran unopposed) was defeated in his re-election bid in 1996 by Petru Lucinschi, the former first secretary of the Communist Party of Moldavia; and communists won the largest share of the vote in the March 1998 parliamentary elections. Both Snegur and Lucinschi, however, represented a very similar, centrist orientation in Moldovan politics. Finally, in Romania the postcommunist Democratic National Salvation Front and its leader Ion Iliescu lost power only in the third set of parliamentary and presidential elections in 1996.

If the six countries that have not (yet) returned the former communists to power have anything in common, it is that their experience with communism, although different from case to case, was particularly harsh, at least in their own perception. Estonia and Latvia (like Lithuania) were fully sovereign during the inter-war period, and the

Soviet system was imposed on them (in 1940–1 and again in 1945) from outside. Without any exaggeration, one can say that for half a century they were occupied by an alien force. Both countries (unlike Lithuania) face a serious problem with the sizeable ethnic Russian minority, perceived as a potential or even actual threat to their independence. Both Czechoslovak successor states experienced the rigid, orthodox, repressive neo-Stalinist regime of Gustav Husak in the 1970s and 1980s, that is, in the times when their neighbours in Hungary and Poland enjoyed, by and large, relative relaxation in the area of civil rights and freedoms. (Even during the period of martial law in 1981–3, Polish communism was less repressive than its Czechoslovak counterpart.) Finally, Slovenia and Croatia, although parts of the relatively westernised Yugoslavia, both underwent a steep economic decline in the 1980s, for which they have blamed the mismanagement of the federal government and its socialist policies of redistribution of national wealth from the haves (themselves) to the have-nots (other republics). Both republics, particularly Croatia, also suffered repression directed against various expressions of local (ethnic) nationalism.

This similarity, however, is too superficial to explain fully why in these six countries former communists were prevented from a success-ful comeback, while in Poland or Lithuania, which also suffered under the old regimes, such comebacks have been possible. Also, the patterns of voting behaviour and electoral politics differ within this group of six sufficiently to invite further explanations. In both Latvia and Estonia, after the first fully free elections (1992 and 1993, respectively), as well as after the next election (in 1995), highly fragmented parliaments were able to generate centrist or right-of-centre coalitions, and isolate the former communists. In Slovenia, the liberal policies of the right-of-centre government of Janez Drnovsek, endorsed and supported by the postcommunist President Kucan, secured the survival of this government after the 1996 legislative election (Kucan was successfully re-elected in December 1997). In Croatia, President Tudjman and his Croatian Democratic Union have clearly won all elections since independence, on a platform mixing nationalism, anti-communism, and authoritarianism. In the Czech Republic, the government of Prime Minister Vaclav Klaus during its first term (1992–6) enjoyed a comfortable majority in the House of Representatives, and skilfully managed to combine liberal, pro-market reforms (and rhetoric) with the protective policies of a welfare state (very low unemployment and low inflation). None the less, in the 1996 election, the electoral pendulum swung in the Czech Republic towards the social end, travelling only half-way. Klaus's liberal coalition stayed in power, but with only a minimal majority. The almost-successful challenge came from the Social Democrats, who – unlike other powerful leftist parties in the region – are not repainted communists. They are a historic party, which in 1948 was forcefully merged with the communists and was able to reclaim its identity only after 1989. The Czech Communists, still using this name, won parliamentary seats in both the 1992 and 1996 elections, but remained isolated on the political arena.

More complex than the above five is the case of Slovakia. After the 1992 election (conducted still within the constitutional framework of the now-defunct Czechoslovak federation) the Movement for a Democratic Slovakia (MDS) (a splinter group of Public Against Violence), led by Vladimir Meciar, formed a ruling coalition with the Slovak National Party (SNP). This government presided over the process of velvet divorce with the Czech Republic. The subsequent nationalistic and populist policies of Meciar's government, combined with his own authoritarian political style, alienated many deputies. In March 1994, a rainbow coalition of opposition parties and dissenters from the MDS overthrew Meciar's government. The new government, headed by Jozef Moravcik of the Democratic Union of Slovakia, enjoyed the support, in addition to this centrist party, of the Christian Democrats (right-of-centre), the Democratic Left Party (the reformed, pro-market wing of the former Communists), and several minor groupings. The September 1994 election brought Meciar and his MDS back to power, this time in coalition with the SNP and the Association of Slovakia Workers, a postcommunist group strongly opposed to market reforms. This government has been criticised by the opposition and international public opinion for its discriminatory policies towards ethnic minorities, in particular Hungarians. Hence, while postcommunist groups were junior partners in two post-transition Slovak governments, one cannot speak here about any communist electoral resurgence. On the other hand, Meciar's populist and anti-western policies brought him the electoral support of constituencies similar to those that elevated former communists to power in Poland or Hungary (see Kitschelt *et al.*, forthcoming).

Altogether, the six countries that have not yet experienced the full swing of the electoral pendulum to the left fall into three distinctive patterns:

(1) a successful transition without an economic shock therapy, which generated high growth rates, political pluralism, rule of law, political stability – conditions typically conducive to the pro-government and/or right-of-centre voting preferences of the electorate (the Czech Republic, Slovenia, to an extent also Estonia);

(2) the presence of the 'formidable foe factor' – specifically, a neighbouring superpower, represented locally by a numerous ethnic minority, often hostile to the very idea of independence and to the new governments, and associated with the communist past (Latvia and Estonia, with their Russian minorities);

(3) an authoritarian, populist, and nationalistic regime in a country that during the communist times was a weaker partner in a federal state (Slovakia, Croatia).

Those patterns merit further inquiry before they can be recognised as either necessary or sufficient conditions preventing former communists from scoring an electoral comeback. They are, however, conspicuously absent in the case of all six countries where such comebacks had become a reality before the end of 1997. The first is the case of Lithuania. Sajudis-supported candidates won there the March 1990 election, conducted before the formal end of Soviet rule. Only two and a half years later, the former communists (the Lithuanian Democratic Labour Party – LDLP) staged an impressive victory in the parliamentary election, followed in 1993 by the election of their leader, Algirdas Brazauskas, to the presidency. They obviously profited from the ill-conceived economic policies of the 1990–2 Sajudis government. In addition, Lithuania, unlike other Baltic republics, has no sizeable Russian minority (9 per cent, compared with more than 30 per cent in both Latvia and Estonia), and Lithuanian communists had been instrumental in promoting the independence cause. Four years later, in October–November 1996, the LDLP had to pay the same price for the same sins as its predecessor: it was voted out of power by an electorate dissatisfied with the slow improvement in standards of living.

In Poland, developments during the 1991–3 period mirrored the situation of the late 1980s: disintegration of the ruling camp and the effective use of an umbrella organisation by the challengers. Only this time the actors traded places: these were the former communists who, feeling overwhelmed by their foes, understood the advantages of organisational unity and discipline.

The September 1993 elections were called early, because the fragmented parliament (with no majority coalition of fewer than five parties possible) was unable to generate a viable ruling coalition. The election drastically reduced the number of parties in the Sejm (to only six), partly due to changes in the electoral law (5 per cent threshold nationwide, smaller districts, implementation of the d'Hondt seats allocation system) but chiefly to the continuing fragmentation of the political scene, particularly acute on the right and in the centre of the political spectrum. Hence, the parties of the left emerged victorious. Among them were the former communists, who – despite internal divisions – ran in this election as the Democratic Left Alliance (DLA), a coalition of the Social Democracy of the Republic of Poland (the successor of the Polish United Workers' or Communist Party), formerly pro-communist trade unions, and other organisations. They were joined in the ruling coalition by the Polish Peasant Party (PPP), the successor to the 1949–89 communist ally, the United Peasant Party. The once formidable Solidarity movement disintegrated completely, and of this camp only the Democratic Union and the Bloc in Support of Reforms (sponsored by President Walesa) managed to win seats in the Sejm. Further humiliation of the right came in 1995, when Lech Walesa, the legend of Solidarity, was defeated in his presidential re-election bid by the leader of the DLA and a former junior minister in the communist government in the 1980s, Aleksander Kwasniewski.

The DLA/PPP government, while arguably much more cautious in its approach to economic reforms than its predecessors, did not reverse the course of transition. During its tenure, the Polish economy began to capitalise on the effects of the shock therapy applied by the Mazowiecki/Balcerowicz government in 1990. The former communists did not hesitate to accept credit for economic growth, and many voters were apparently willing to share this point of view, as the DLA increased both its share of the vote (from 20.4 to 27.1 per cent) and the absolute number of votes (from 2.8 to 3.5 million) in the next, September 1997, election. However, the leaders of the right-of-centre parties had learnt their lesson the hard way, and opened again the Solidarity umbrella. The Electoral Action Solidarity, a coalition composed of five to six major and several minor parties of the right, and centred around the trade union Solidarity (chaired by Walesa's successor at this post, Marian Krzaklewski), fielded a joint slate of candidates, collected the votes that in 1993 had been dispersed and wasted, and emerged victorious. It gained enough seats to be able to form a majority coalition with the centrist Freedom Union (the fusion of the former Democratic Union and Liberal-Democratic Congress).

The most impressive of them all was the postcommunist victory in Hungary. In the May 1994 election, the Hungarian Socialist Party, led by the former foreign minister in the communist government of the late 1980s, Gyula Horn, won an outright majority in the parliament. Surprised by their spectacular success, and perhaps uncomfortable about assuming full control only four years after the fall of the communist system, they formed a coalition government with the liberal Alliance of Free Democrats. This government has been plagued by corruption scandals, and has been unable to curb inflation and unemployment. The next election is due in May 1998.

In Albania, the return of former communists to power came in circumstances much more dramatic than anywhere else. The 1992 election gave a solid parliamentary majority to the anti-communist Democratic Party. Its leader Sali Berisha was subsequently elected president by the People's Assembly. In 1994, he attempted to introduce a new constitution that would give substantial powers to the president, but the draft was rejected in a national referendum. Berisha's political style subsequently became increasingly authoritarian, alienating not only the opposition, but also many leaders of his own party. His government persecuted political opponents, often using against them their communist past (and often not without merit). In May–June 1996, the Democratic Party won the next election, in a landslide. The opposition, postcommunist as well as centrist and rightist, complained of widespread electoral fraud and other irregularities, boycotted the runoff round of the election, and refused to take the few seats it had won in the parliament. Independent international observers supported those charges. Berisha, chosen again by parliament as president, refused to bow to demands for a new, fair election. The impulse for new elections nevertheless came, when several pyramid investment schemes exhausted their growth potential and collapsed in late 1996. Since many Albanians had invested their life savings in those fraudulent enterprises, their bankruptcies caused massive popular unrest. People blamed the government for failing to regulate the investment market, and Berisha's Democratic Party for allegedly profiting from these schemes. The country was thrown into virtual chaos, with military and police giving up their arms to groups of civilians. Under pressure from foreign governments, Berisha agreed to dismiss the Democratic Party government, and appoint a caretaker one, charged with the preparation of new elections. The elections took place in June 1997, and brought a decisive victory for the Socialist Party (former communists). The Democratic Party lost amidst accusations of abuses of power and corruption.

Finally, Bulgaria may be considered a borderline case, as the former communists were not decisively beaten in a general election until April 1997. Still, they were in opposition (to a Union of Democratic Forces minority government) from 1991 to 1992, and later gave only qualified support to a non-partisan government. They recorded a major comeback in 1994, only to lose by a landslide in the 1997 election.

The six cases of successful resurgence by the former communists seem to confirm Dahrendorf's expectation of the electoral pendulum swinging from the liberal to the social end of the spectrum because of the social costs of economic growth. The hardships of the transition (which often reached the point of absolute pauperisation), whether caused by the ultimately successful 'shock therapy' (as in Poland), or by a 'shock without therapy' (as in Lithuania or Bulgaria), caused widespread popular dissatisfaction and gave a competitive advantage to political actors promising quick and easy solutions. The former communists were as eager as anyone else to make such promises. Having also the additional advantage of control over the assets of their predecessors (from material resources to connections in the media), they were able to mobilise electoral support sufficient to win, either as a single actor, or as a senior partner in a coalition. They could be prevented from scoring such a victory by the three patterns outlined above: a relatively smooth economic transition without a dramatic decline in standards of living (Slovenia, the Czech Republic), the presence of an external threat associated with the communist past (Latvia, Estonia), or an effective non-liberal alternative (the semi-authoritarian regimes in Croatia and Slovakia). But there were no quick and easy fixes for the ills of transition, and the victorious reformed communists were either forced to continue the reform policies of their predecessors (Poland, Hungary), or waste time and national resources (Bulgaria). The scrutiny of unfulfilled and fulfilled promises would come at the time of the next free and fair general elections, as in any democracy.

The 'Dahrendorf hypothesis' has been very widely accepted as the main explanation of the pendulum effect in Central European electoral politics (Holmes, 1997; Brown, 1994; Mason, 1996). However, its testing has to be limited to those cases for which a body of reliable empirical data on voting behaviour exists. Such data are rather scarce for the East and the South, but quite abundant for Central Europe: Poland, Hungary, and the Czech Republic (see Kitschelt *et al.*, forthcoming; Toka, 1997; Markowski and Toka, 1995). They seem to indicate that two major cleavages are particularly relevant for voting behaviour in postcommunist Europe: the socioeconomic cleavage between the supporters of a free-market/free-enterprise economy and those preferring welfare-oriented state interventionism, and a cultural cleavage between particularism and universalism. The latter may at specific times and places express itself as a conflict between the traditional and the modern, the confessional and the secular, or between exclusive nationalism and a more inclusive, pan-European orientation. But high levels of votability combined with the 'deviant' character of many election outcomes in the region suggest that stable cleavage patterns have yet to establish themselves, and that we should draw conclusions with some caution.

PART THREE

The Politics of the Policy Process

10

The Politics of Economic Transformation

GEORGE BLAZYCA

This chapter focuses on the economic dimension of transformation. Its starting point is a brief review of the economic model – the system of central planning – that shaped economic development in the region in the postwar period to the late 1980s. The intention is not to describe in detail how planning operated nor to dwell on the system's defects – many excellent works already do that – but rather to identify those features that have a clear bearing on what has happened to, and within, Central and East European economies since 1989. We then review some of the key aspects of economic development in the first phase of transformation in the early 1990s – the debate over economic 'shock therapy' versus 'gradualism', the impact of policy and circumstance on macroeconomic performance, the beginnings of a micro-level enterprise restructuring and adjustment to the new situation, the tangle of emerging group interests with its new patterns of winners and losers – each considered in turn. Finally, we ask what can be said about the success or otherwise of the variety of economic experiments launched throughout Central and Eastern Europe since the Berlin Wall fell in 1989.

The Decline of Central Planning

A System that had Exhausted its Modernising Capacity

By the late 1980s, if not before, it was clear that central planning was exhausted. The system was broken and could not be mended. It had shaped a set of national economies, encumbered by such great distortion and heavy inefficiency that they buckled and wilted. Uncompetitive in the international arena, increasingly unable to meet the everyday expectations of their citizens and poisonous in their effect on the environment, they stumbled along from one low-key crisis to another. Occasionally the temperature increased and a social or economic explosion would occur (the two were invariably linked) when even the communist authorities could not fail to notice that the trouble looked terminal. Throughout the region the so-called planned economy had steadily sapped the confidence and energy of the people. Profound social demoralisation was the inevitable accompaniment to years of economic irrationality. Then, when the morale of the leadership evaporated, as it did by, or during, 1989, the game was well and truly up. Deep social dissatisfaction combined with systemic and personal exhaustion and the economic model imploded.

Although the collapse was sudden the symptoms of decline had long been apparent, well documented and widely studied. Nevertheless the immediate events of 1989, the events that precipitated the final disintegration of the old system, were powerfully dramatic and replete with a European symbolism. When the Hungarian authorities began to dismantle the barbed-wire frontier along the 'iron curtain' in the summer of 1989 it was plain that the Berlin Wall, that stark monument to European division, no longer served any purpose. East German 'tourists' could now flow to the West regardless of the futile attempts of the old guard communists like Erich Honecker to cling to the past and keep people locked up in their place. A few weeks later the Czechoslovak leadership, still presided over by the aged Gustav Husak, and resistant to change to the last, also bowed to the inevitable. In Poland, uniquely in Central and Eastern Europe, but with a certain characteristic 'Polishness' of style, reforms were negotiated at a 'round table' of Communist and Solidarity activists. Of course, even at those March 1989 meetings the party's aim was still to cling to power. It was only when Solidarity swept the board in semi-free elections that summer that General Jaruzelski accepted that the era of the 'Polish People's Republic' – the PRL – was finished. Throughout East-Central Europe it was a remarkable time. Perhaps even more remarkably, everywhere except Romania (and tragically in Yugoslavia) the old system fell apart without immediate social convulsion and without great bloodshed.

Viewed from the vantage point of the late 1990s it may be difficult to believe that the old central planning system could once have been considered to be modernising and perhaps even civilising, a mechanism for economic development especially useful for the essentially 'backward' economies that had in most cases missed out on earlier European industrialisation. But with the passage of time the economic deficiencies of the system became clearer.

The *growth rate slowdown* was first noticed in the 1960s and it worried the planners and Communist leaderships sufficiently for them to launch a wide programme of economic reform and experimentation, mainly half-hearted and usually flawed attempts to get back on to the path to economic modernisation. The *inability of the system to break into the international market place*, notwithstanding its apparent modernity in terms of industrial development, steel and electricity production, and vast 'electro-engineering' sectors, was another signal of economic weakness. The *failure to meet the consumption aspirations* of its citizens was another telling sign. To be sure, the system did generate basic security – homes, jobs, education, access to health and other social welfare facilities. Yet its ability to sustain this 'social wage' also decayed with the passage of time. Moreover the people became increasingly persuaded that the 'historic contract' whereby political acquiescence was traded for basic material provision was more and more a raw deal.

Throughout the postwar period, as the Hungarian economist Laszlo Csaba has argued (Csaba, 1995), the system continued to lose whatever (little) adaptability it had. The global economy was changing fast, especially after the 'oil shocks' of the 1970s forced economic restructuring on Western economies. Yet with every shock and adjustment in the West the development gap with the East grew wider.

Opportunity Lost

The legacy of planning in Central and Eastern Europe lay in every case in economies with grossly 'overblown' industrial sectors. Fukuyama (1995, p. 225) has aptly referred to Soviet industrial development as 'Fordism on steroids'. Services, by contrast, were poorly developed. Where, in a typical developed capitalist economy of the late 1980s, one might expect to find services accounting for over 60 per cent of GDP and industry for around 33 per cent, for the typical planned economy the situation was diametrically reversed. In Poland, for example, in 1988 industry had a colossal 60 per cent of GDP and services only 26 per cent. These figures give some impression of the scale of the adjustment facing the former planned economies as they were forced, post-1989, to adapt to a more conventional and modern shape.

Yet there is a further dimension to the planning experience which also neatly and somewhat starkly summarises the overall cost of the experiment and the Polish case gives a particularly clear illustration of the problem. Many social scientists have been impressed by the structural similarities, in the early postwar years, of the economies of Poland and Spain. It is a comparison that the well-known Harvard economist, Jeffrey Sachs, returned to in the early 1990s to highlight the development opportunity lost by a Poland locked in the Soviet bloc for forty years (Sachs, 1993). In the early 1950s the two countries had similar populations (about 25 million), some similarity of economic structures (even then Poland produced more electricity and steel) and broadly equivalent level of income (GDP) per capita. Indeed in 1955 Polish income per head was slightly greater than Spain's ($750 and $500 respectively). However by 1988 Polish per capita income, at just below $1,900, was only one-quarter that of Spain's $7,700. After Franco's death, with the re-establishment of democracy, the Spanish economy was fairly quickly reintegrated into the mainstream of European development. An open and outward-looking trade and investment orientation helped ensure the conditions in the late 1980s for an acceleration in the growth rate. Of course the benefits of economic growth in Spain were not uniformly shared by the population and the economy remains plagued with the highest unemployment rates in the EU, well above 20 per cent in the early 1990s. Clearly, Poland will not want to replicate all aspects of Spanish experience, but there is no escaping the conclusion that Polish economic performance slipped disastrously behind its potential throughout the great planning experiment.

Another striking comparison in the same vein is that between the Czech Republic and Austria. Czechoslovakia was renowned even in the 1930s as a relatively well-developed industrial economy albeit with significant regional differentiation. In 1938 the country's per capita national income was 10 per cent greater than neighbouring Austria but by the late 1980s the situation had deteriorated to such an extent that Czechoslovak per capita income was reported to be 35 per cent *below* Austria's (Jeffries, 1993, p. 245). In the case of Russia, with the longest planning experience, it is estimated that income per head fell from a level equivalent to 90 per cent that of Spain in 1913 to 33 per cent of the Spanish level by 1994 (Martin Wolf, *Financial Times*, 2 July 1996).

Interest Groups and Planning Politics

The planning system was embedded in a political set-up with its own pervasive effect on the economy. Its main actors, the Communist Party and various special interest groups or lobbies, were pillars of the planned economy and, at the same time, major barriers to its effective reform. In some cases the side-effect of the reform experiments of the 1960s and 1970s was to create other pressure groups that would continue to exert a role even in the 1990s. In Hungary, to take perhaps the best-known example, the 'New Economic Mechanism' (NEM) of 1968 gave industrial managers a privileged economic role. In Poland, on the other hand, the events of August 1980, which saw the birth of the Solidarity movement, could hardly do other than elevate the influence of workers' organisations in enterprise level organisation. In Czechoslovakia the trauma of invasion by Warsaw Pact troops, ending the 'Prague spring' of 1968, led to a strengthening of the party and state apparatus. In Prague a return to planning orthodoxy and freeze on reform saw to it that no new interest groups of any significance emerged. When the planning system collapsed in 1989 and communist parties throughout the region vanished the state enterprise suddenly found itself in a control vacuum. It was however one that would soon be filled by various groups (mainly managers, sometimes trades unions) promoting particular and immediate interests. Some observers of industrial developments in Poland in 1990 identified the emergence of a 'Bermuda triangle', where managers, trades unions and workers' self-management committees captured state firms, steering them towards objectives such as preserving job security. But by the late 1990s in most Central and East European economies even state firms began to show interest in conventional practices like making profits.

Rebuilding the Economy: A Diversity of Experiences in the 1990s

The Macroeconomic Scene

While 1989 was a time of breathtaking and tumultuous political development it was, in the economy, simply another year of a long familiar steady decline. In most countries the wheels still turned (see Table 10.1) and production continued somehow to increase although growth rates were generally low. Exceptionally high growth rates in

TABLE 10.1   *A snapshot of Central and East European economies in 1989 and 1990*

	GDP (% change)		Inflation (% change)		Unemployment (% rate)	
	1989	1990	1989	1990	1989	1990
East Central Europe						
Czechoslovakia	1.4	−0.4	2.0	18.0	0.0	0.8
Hungary	0.7	−3.5	19.0	33.0	0.3	2.5
Poland	0.2	−11.6	640.0	249.0	0.1	6.1
Balkans and Southern Europe						
Bulgaria	0.5	−9.1	10	72.0	na	1.5
Romania	−5.8	−5.6	1	38.0	na	na
Slovenia	−1.8	−4.7	2,772.0	105.0	2.9	4.7
Croatia	−1.6	−8.6	na	136.0	na	na
Baltics and post-Soviet republics						
Ukraine	4.0	−3.0	na	na	0	0
Moldova	na	−2.4	na	na	na	na
Latvia	6.8	2.9	na	na	0	0
Lithuania	1.5	−5.0	na	na	na	na
Estonia	−1.1	−8.1	na	na	na	na

Note: Inflation is end-year, that is over the preceding 12 months rather than the average year-on-year; na – not available.
Source: EBRD.

Ukraine and Latvia, if taken at face value, showed that the planning model still appeared to have something to offer within the framework of the Soviet Union. But of course the broader picture emerging from the USSR at the time was that no matter what the highly suspect production figures reported the country was locked in an intractable economic crisis. In East-Central Europe growth was slower and the data credible: in Czechoslovakia GDP expanded by 1.4 per cent, in Hungary by 0.7 per cent, even in strike-ridden Poland GDP increased by 0.2 per cent in 1989. This was of course a distinctly unimpressive performance and given population growth there was little or no improvement in GDP per capita – a crude indicator of living standards. Alongside growth slippage inflationary pressures began to mount, or at least to become more open and visible. Among the major Central and East European economies Poland was plainly in the worst position: an unmistakable acceleration in prices growth in the second half of 1989 brought the end-year inflation rate to 640 per cent. Elsewhere the problem was yet to emerge as it did with a vengeance in the early 1990s in almost all the European economies of the former USSR (see appendix table 2).

The Polish economic situation was becoming extremely difficult and attracted much attention especially after the first Solidarity government came to power in September 1989. A complete breakdown of the economic mechanism in a small country like Slovenia with its 2 million people is bad enough but matters are even worse when a large European economy like the Polish, with a population of almost 40 million, and for long in an exceptionally sensitive 'geopolitical' situation, stares disaster in the face. But Poland had, as well as urgent economic problems, some unusual yet highly favourable political conditions. It was the first country in the region to establish a non-communist government, and that government commanded a generally loyal popular following. The Western love affair with Lech Walesa and Solidarity meant that there was a substantial commitment to ensuring that whatever economic experiment was tried simply *had* to work; there was too much at stake to allow the pioneer reformer to fail. This was the backdrop, in late 1989, to the Western effort to help the Solidarity government devise a strategy for economic transformation, the first strategy to map out a reasonably clear route from plan to market. The resulting reform strategy became widely known, after the Solidarity finance minister, as the 'Balcerowicz plan'. Although it outlined a variety of tasks for the future, including privatisation and economic restructuring, the Balcerowicz plan was essentially a programme for economic stabilisation. It focused squarely on the number one problem in Poland at that time – hyperinflation – and offered what became known as the 'shock therapy' or 'big bang' route to solving it.

'Shock' versus 'Gradualism'

Much ink has been spilled in a debate which polarised the issues facing postcommunist economies in terms of 'shock' versus 'gradualism'. To some extent the discussion continues, especially in relation to those economies, many of them formerly part of the Soviet Union, where hyperinflation in the later 1990s remained a critical barrier to economic development. But for the Visegrad economies (Hungary, Czech and Slovak Republics, Poland) the issue, by the mid-1990s, was no longer pressing and attention had mainly switched to less dramatic concerns such as 'corporate governance', the banking system and such like. The effort of the economics team around Leszek Balcerowicz, backed by support from leading international agencies like the IMF, and by the contribution of individual Western advisers, among whom Jeffrey Sachs became best known, did however help to crystallise an early 'transition orthodoxy'. This suggested that successful transition to the market hinged on a reform strategy based on three factors: economic stabilisation (also involving price liberalisation), privatisation and restructuring. If there was a dominant Western view, then, adding the need to be 'open' in international economic relationships, that was just about the size of it (see Blanchard *et al.*, 1991 and 1993). In the cases where economies had not lurched into an inflationary quagmire the policy effort could perhaps be more immediately directed to structural issues – privatisation, restructuring and how best to attract inward investment.

If the key actors on the stage in those early days had any clear economic vision for the future it tended to vary between an idealistic and perhaps naive faith in 'the market' to a modest enough attachment to aim to build market economies as they existed in Western Europe. Balcerowicz himself was very clear that in 1990 the time of searching for 'third ways' – understood as economic models lying somewhere between modern capitalism and 'actually existing socialism' – was over. However, with the passage of time views regarding 'the market' tended to become more sophisticated. Tempered by the lessons of real experience it became ever more plain that the economic vacuum following the collapse of planning would not *automatically* be filled by anything remotely resembling the well-ordered market mechanism of Western Europe. It gradually became more acceptable to suggest that the state had an important role to play in leading the way to 'the market', for example in shaping the legal and institutional infrastructure to support market transactions. If economists had generally and initially tended towards a too deterministic 'transition to the market' other social scientists (see the collection of essays brought together by Christopher Bryant and colleagues, 1994) began to argue that the process was better viewed as a more complex 'transformation' to a less clear destination.

If at the start of transformation it seemed that the room for economic policy manoeuvre was extremely limited it soon became apparent that this was so only if choices were viewed at the highest levels of abstraction such as that between 'market' (assumed to be good, in working order, modernising, efficient) versus 'plan' (known to be bad, clapped-out, fossilising, inefficient). In fact, even where galloping inflation was destroying the basis for the 'rational' economic calculation that market agents (firms, households, individuals) need to engage in, and shock therapy seemed the only solution, there was greater room for debate than first appeared. In Poland in the early months of 1990 that discussion opened up. At first, it was the preserve of the policy-makers and academics but it was not long before those on the receiving end of 'shock' – in the Polish case especially the already private farmers – began to complain. There should have been little surprise here: in Poland production and GDP nose-dived in those first weeks and months of 1990. The post-transformation shock led to an unprecedented and *unexpected* crash in output – GDP fell in 1990 by over 11 per cent – but nor was there any immediate bonus in inflation control. On the contrary, the average inflation rate accelerated from 251 per cent in 1989 to 586 per cent in 1990. Table 10.2 indicates the extent to which the Polish authorities were taken off guard by the economic response to the medicine applied.

The Polish experience fuelled debate over (a) whether shock therapy was appropriate and could work and (b) whether there might exist more appropriate policy mixes. In the early transformation period the critics drew attention to a number of potential weaknesses of shock therapy. Some argued that since these were not market economies they could not be expected to respond to traditional IMF-type stabilisation packages. Monopolistic state-owned industry, run by managers whose decision-making space was hugely enlarged after the collapse of planning, would behave in its own immediate interest. Others like the late Alec Nove focused on the crying need, if economic restructuring was to take place, for investment and argued that the

TABLE 10.2 *Polish shock therapy – official expectations versus actual outcomes*

	GDP (% change)		Inflation (% change)	
	1990	*1991*	*1990 (January)*	*1991 (first quarter)*
Assumptions	−3.5	+ 3.5	45.0	75.0
Actual	−11.4	−7.4	79.6	133.0

Source: Based on Gomulka (1995).

impoverishment of the population would destroy any hope of generating domestic savings. This, said Nove (1994), was the 'Achilles' heel' of the then conventional economic wisdom and a good reason for preferring gradualism to shock. Shock could easily destroy but could it create too? Balcerowicz and his colleagues in Poland, however, were firmly of the view that there was simply no other way. The Polish finance minister put the matter characteristically bluntly. Gradualism, where hyperinflation exists resembles, he said, 'putting out a fire slowly. This strategy is not just risky, it is hopeless'. Nevertheless the programme's critics believed that the policy mix was excessively restrictive (this view runs through the annual surveys of the European economy produced by the United Nations Economic Commission for Europe – UNECE) and offered too much to the anti-interventionist, anti-state sentiments current throughout Europe in 1990. In the Polish case for example it is sometimes argued that a less sharp zloty devaluation than was imposed in 1990 would have been helpful in moderating inflationary pressures: the huge 32 per cent overnight devaluation on December 31 1989 did much to stoke up prices growth in the months that followed. The interested reader can explore this debate further in an extensive and still expanding literature (see Bateman, 1997, ch. 7; Jeffries, 1993, ch. 17; Lavigne, 1995, ch. 7), but the point is that even in the, as it later turned out, successful case of Poland the room for policy choices was greater than may sometimes be assumed.

A year after Poland's 'big bang' the Czech authorities, led by Vaclav Klaus, another well-known economic liberal, also launched a programme of shock therapy – comprehensive prices and trade liberalisation combined with wages control. This contributed to a crash of 14 per cent in GDP in 1991 and, as in Poland, inflation at first accelerated before slowing in subsequent years (see appendix tables).

Immediate snapshots can however be deceptive and those of 1989–90 tell us little more than that postcommunist economies entered a period of great stress and turmoil. Over a medium-term perspective both Polish and Czech economic performance appeared to take off, although in the Czech case the lustre of an apparently dynamic performance was tarnished by a growing trade deficit and doubts among investors as to the depth of reform. This led, in 1997, to a run on the currency and the authorities were humbled into a devaluation of the koruna. It is worth adding that the performance of some economies which avoided shock therapy (Hungary is an example) also seemed not too bad. The Hungarian case is often characterised as one of 'muddling along', and 'muddle', provided it does not descend into chaos, may have something to commend it. If too ready acceptance of a 'model' (such as a blind commitment to 'the market') can be dangerous it is worth recalling that, in any case, the scope for utilisation of any shock therapy is constrained by political conditions. If there is no consensus in favour of such policy it is unlikely to be implemented and if implemented it is most unlikely to last or be effective. Balcerowicz (1995) in the Polish context has written about the 'extraordinary politics' that existed in the first months of 1990 when a government of neo-liberals could shelter under the protective 'parasol' of the workers' movement. It was a cosy relationship but one that would not last for long.

In summary, when viewed across key dimensions of macroeconomic performance – growth, inflation, trade and employment – the experience of Central and East European economies in the post-1989 period is immensely diverse. It is reflected in the GDP, inflation and unemployment data gathered in appendix tables 1, 2 and 3. Yet despite the variety of performance displayed some underlying patterns can be detected.

- Generally, the group of East-Central European countries, the Visegrad group, has the best performance in the region, with shortest recessions, lowest inflation and fastest economic growth. They were of course the most modern of the Comecon economies with the shortest experience of central planning, home to the most radical attempts to reform the planning system in the 1960s and 1970s, very often with fledgling private sectors and geographically well placed after 1989 to switch orbit from the USSR to the powerful German economy. In crude output terms Poland was the first country in the region to recover (in 1996) from the recession brought about by system collapse. Slovenia, the Czech and Slovak Republics, Slovenia and Hungary were not far behind.
- The Baltics and Southern Europe present an intermediate picture, while the European post-Soviet economies faced the greatest difficulties.
- It is worth noting too that no simple linear progression to recovery is evident. In some cases (unreformed Bulgaria and the highly reformed Czech Republic) economic conditions appeared to improve only for further shocks to occur later. The path to the market is evidently a stony one.

Fundamental Change in the Economic Mechanism – Behaviour in the Enterprise

An important but rather overlooked aspect of the early 1990s transition strategies, including shock therapy, was that they rested on several major 'unknowns'. One of the most important was that no one could be sure how economic actors in still state-dominated economies would react. The management of state firms was used to and adept at manipulating relationships with planners, other firms and political authorities. It was unclear country-by-country how it would react to financial pressures or to the new wave of liberalisation which had unleashed a gale of competition. Indeed, it was even unclear in many cases *who* was in charge of the firm. Which group or groups could make the critical decisions upon which the future of the enterprise depended? All that was certain was that the planning system had collapsed, that central authorities were generally weak and that the political-institutional structures of the past that had propped up the economy, such as the party, had disintegrated. This was the vacuum of the transition economy which the new authorities had to deal with.

Despite the unpromising conditions, significant headway was made, at least in the leading economies in the region, in laying the basis at micro level for a new economic mechanism. Perhaps most important of all, the authorities in many cases succeeded, where generations of previous economic reformers had failed, in persuading managers of state-owned firms that operations would have to be *self-financing*. They succeeded, in other words, in placing firms under the discipline of the long-elusive 'hard budget constraint' – firms could not spend more than they could earn, raise or borrow. Of course even among the fast-track performers there were exceptions in sectors like coal, steel and some others but those are areas where even in leading Western economies the budget constraint can be on the gentle side.

But the waters were still uncharted and the reefs numerous. One was timing. It was by no means clear at the outset how long it might take to persuade managers and others that they had better start to behave in more entrepreneurial style. Jeffrey Sachs describes the waiting, in the first weeks of Polish shock therapy, to see whether the farmers would respond to higher prices by bringing more produce to market, as 'gut-wrenching' (Sachs, 1993, p. 58). Among industrial enterprises there was a view, for a moment, that they could 'outsmart' and certainly 'outwait' the government by making little adjustment and falling back instead on a soft cushion of fast-growing inter-enterprise debt. One Polish writer described the atmosphere in the enterprise in early 1990 thus: 'Can't find sales – then limit production and send workers on holiday. Still trouble, substitute unpaid for paid leave . . . Then it's necessary to lose a few people. If the market still doesn't want our goods then instead of reducing prices or exporting we again cut production, let the next group of workers go, and so on. In this way the enterprise can die standing up so long as there is a solitary director in the plant to turn the lights off' (Blazyca and Rapacki, 1991, p. 2). Fortunately, in most cases in the leading economies in the region this slow death was avoided partly because even in state firms there *was* considerable adjustment and partly because a fast-growing private sector soon emerged.

Enterprise restructuring and adjustment has been much investi-gated and yet after seven years of transformation it remains hard to locate a uniform and definitive view among policy-makers and researchers on what precisely happened. One thorough review of the case-study evidence in the 1990–3 period across *state-owned firms* in Poland, Czech and Slovak Republics, Hungary and Romania concluded that in the bewildering array of experience 'there is little evidence of "deep restructuring". Most of what is commonly recorded as restructuring is shallow, such as the setting up of marketing departments or adjusting production lines' (Carlin *et al.*, 1995). There is also doubt in some cases as to whether *privatisation* in particular forms – and the styles are richly varied – has achieved much. One study of the Czech experience of privatisation which asked whether new owners tried to restructure their firms concluded that 'little of substance had been achieved' (Kenway and Klvacova, 1996). How-ever, World Bank researchers have come to the opposite view and suggest that the Czech Republic, thanks to its privatisation scheme, has a 'superior record' in enterprise restructuring (Claessens *et al.*, 1996). One explanation of these different conclusions is that they utilise different measures of adjustment and restructuring. Sometimes close examination of management styles, a search to see if managers behave with more entrepreneurial spirit, suggests that little has changed. On the other hand detailed investigations of firms' profit-ability can point to a better performance from which it is inferred that enterprises have restructured. For Poland a series of World Bank studies concluded even in the early 1990s that state firms often adapted remarkably well to new conditions.

The reason for the improvement is not hard to locate. First, it was impossible even for *nomenklatura* managers to ignore the fundamental change in political climate. Second, alongside this, enthusiasm for privatisation meant that even in state firms managers operated under a new threat *and* opportunity (for self-enrichment). Third, new economic policies tended to work well in countries like Poland, the Czech Republic and Hungary where a basic credibility in government policy existed.

What can we conclude in general terms as regards enterprise restructuring? Perhaps it is simply that yet again a genuine diversity of experience exists which is particularly sensitive to the way we try to measure it and is to some extent resistant to our attempts, at present, to codify it. But one way or another the vacuum left by the collapse of central planning was filled.

Privatisation

Privatisation as economic policy and an arena for political contest is, because of its importance, worth considering more thoroughly. The privatisation experience was also richly diverse across postcommunist economies and reflected greatly the pattern of group interests inherited from the old system. In most Central and East European countries the new political leaderships of the early 1990s were deeply committed to privatisation. The reasons for this were various and extended from politics to economics: from a political ambition to create on the basis of privatised enterprise a new middle class, to a desire to establish micro-level incentive mechanisms that would support 'rational' economic activity. The first postcommunist governments, at least in East-Central Europe, also wanted to transform their inherited state-dominated economies in the shortest time possible. They felt a compelling need to 'depoliticise' economic activity by disengaging the state from enterprise activity. But how to do it? One problem was that there was no ready guide to follow: the best-known West European approach (the UK's case-by-case public flotation of state businesses) was distinctly inappropriate to the scale of the task facing Central and Eastern Europe. The lack of any clear view on how to proceed combined with a doubtful political mandate as regards privatisation meant that the situation was ripe for exploitation by more or less well-organised special interest groups. This meant that privatisation often became highly politicised and excitedly contested.

The starting point looked, in 1989–90, deceptively straightforward: the state owned virtually all industry and sometimes much of agriculture and should therefore be able, if it wished, to dispose of assets swiftly. In practice it did not work out like this. The obstacles were many.

First, legal title was obscured by the potential challenge from former owners and their descendants. Second, although managers and workers could not claim ownership of state property, they could nevertheless effectively assert special privileges with respect to the enterprises they worked in. Third, pensioners had similar 'rights'. Fourth, local authorities could enter the fray, disputing with central authorities the legal title to land or other assets. Fifth, other groups of what might be called in the West 'stakeholders' (customers, suppliers) were not slow to demand some special privilege in the privatisation process. Sixth, even before any formal start to privatisation many existing managers found ways to hive off state assets into new private concerns that came into being in the interstices of the old planning system even before 1989. This laid the basis for what became known as 'spontaneous privatisation'. In Poland some writers observed the birth of a new social group – the '*kleptoklatura*' – where previously the managerial '*nomenklatura*' had stood.

If obscure legalities made privatisation difficult so too did the fact that in relatively poor economies, made immediately poorer by shock therapy (and even by its less shocking derivatives), it was not clear that anything very much could be sold off. Where were the savings that could be used to buy shares? This pointed to the need to attract foreign investors – fraught with political dangers – or simply to give away state assets. Despite the fact that free distribution was used in a number of countries economists frowned on it on the grounds that it would not raise a single zloty, koruna or forint of new investment and that it would make sensible 'corporate governance' (effective control over managers) virtually impossible to achieve.

It was clear that privatisation gave some economic actors a new stage to play on. And the outcomes across the region reflect closely the experience of reform in earlier decades. Frydman and Rapaczynski's attempt (1994) to give a systematic account of privatisation issues and processes remains one of the best. They draw attention to the importance of key 'insider' groups with a stake in privatisation. Those groups owed much of their existence to failed attempts to reform planned economies: in Hungary the New Economic Mechanism of 1968 had elevated the position of the managerial elite, and the

privatisation style, case-by-case selloff, offered much to that influential social group; in the Czech case the state had held rigidly to power
throughout the post-1968 period and, in the absence of significant
insider interest, could effectively drive the privatisation process,
ultimately perhaps in the favour of the still state-owned banks; in
Poland the workers' movement was impossible to ignore and this
ensured that worker–management buyout would figure as a prominent privatisation device while the privatisation process became
arguably the most highly politicised in the region.

A New Pattern of Winners and Losers

Shock therapy certainly contributed to the post-1989 crash in output
in the region. But the decline in production was also an inevitable
consequence of system shift. The collapse, in 1991, of Comecon
trading arrangements (Comecon was the Soviet bloc's attempt to
foster international economic integration, its answer to the EC)
further depressed demand as did the fact that Western economies
were about to move, unhappily and unluckily for Central and Eastern
Europe, into the downswing of the business cycle. It may be that the
proponents of shock therapy were too ready to ascribe much of the
output drop to the elimination of the 'unwanted production' of the
old system – the waste of 'pure socialist production' as Balcerowicz
has put it. But even this so-called 'waste production' gave people jobs,
incomes and a basic sense of security. In the period after 1990, as
output collapsed, so too did employment (although not to the same
extent implying that in some countries at least the old socialist 'over-
manning' problem persisted) and unemployment almost everywhere
exploded (see appendix table 3). The clear exception in East-Central
Europe was the Czech Republic where the jobless rate remained
enviably and spectacularly low. Of course it is noticeable too that the
unemployment rate remained low in those economies which were
previously part of the USSR. Nevertheless in Eastern Europe countries that had enjoyed forty years of full employment lurched suddenly in the early 1990s to despairingly high levels of joblessness even
if some allowance is given for job creation in the informal sector.

From the labour market a sense quickly emerges of a new pattern
of 'winners' and 'losers'. Transformation was a process of social and
political interaction that shaped emerging new group interests that
helped, sometimes through the ballot box, to modify economic policy
in the region. Even if the unemployed tend to be notoriously difficult

to organise as an interest group the 'near-unemployed' and those whose real incomes were falling knew where things stood. It was little surprise that in elections throughout Central and Eastern Europe in the early 1990s 'postcommunists' were frequently returned to power.

The policy choice, whether in the short term to prioritise inflation or unemployment reduction, would have different social outcomes. Permitting inflation to continue and risking its acceleration is undoubtedly a dangerous and costly policy course. It is well known that inflation hits hardest those whose incomes are fixed, those with no assets that can readily be index-linked to prices. Accelerating inflation will ultimately also destroy jobs, but taking tough action against inflation generates higher rates of unemployment – no joke for those who lose jobs. Assessing and then weighing the pattern of costs and benefits associated with transformation is clearly a critical matter for all concerned and one that merits greater study than it has so far received.

A key problem for the early reformers who inherited state power was that although they frequently had clear views on economic policy they lacked any significant political constituency on which to base support for their rather abstract ideas. In the classic case of Poland it has been remarked (by Bauman, 1994, p. 22) that Solidarity did not get in 1990 what it had bargained for but got instead much that it had not bargained for. In the negotiated settlement thrashed out at the round-table discussions of March 1989 the communist authorities yielded much to Solidarity's syndicalist, social-welfare and workers' management leanings. But by mid-1990, with a Solidarity government in power, the movement had reaped a harvest of wage cuts, unemployment and murkily spontaneous privatisation. Farmers' 'Rural Solidarity' did even worse since price liberalisation sent input costs soaring, the country's new trade 'openness' brought in a wave of imports and subsidies were virtually eliminated. Many Solidarity members must have asked in 1990–1 whether the price for the right to install Walesa in the presidential palace was not on the high side?

Outcomes

In the early 1990s the postcommunist economies went through an almost unimaginably severe economic crisis. The closest Western experience to the trauma of Central and Eastern Europe in the early 1990s lies sixty years ago in the Great Depression of the 1930s when the US economy lost over 30 per cent of its GDP between 1929 and 1933. The collapse of communism also saw GDP plummet, although the crash was by no means uniform. Measured in this way Poland and Slovenia suffered least and for the shortest period: GDP declined by around 18 per cent and recovery began in 1992. Some countries saw GDP fall by more than 60 per cent while in other cases (Ukraine) the recession had still to bottom out even in 1996. By the mid-1990s Poland was a singular success story in the sense of being the first and only country to restore output to the level of 1989.

The precise extent of the output shock is a matter over which there has been much debate. A persuasive view suggests that the decline in crude GDP overstates the damage done to living standards for at least two reasons: first, that the starting point (base GDPs of 1989) gives a misleading impression of the old system's useful productive capacity – it certainly produced, but few wanted the 'waste' product it turned out; second, liberalisation also generated much unrecorded or informal economic activity. These measurement issues are real and should not be dismissed as unimportant. There is also much that we simply do not know about the nature of the changes in social and economic system since 1989. Relatively little research has been conducted on patterns of income distribution although there is a widespread and surely justified belief that inequalities have sharply increased. It was to be expected that as market incentives became more important some sudden and dramatic shifts in income distribution would take place. The OECD (1996) has noted in Poland a shift which is beginning to reward better education with higher income. In many countries the traditionally privileged groups (miners, steel workers perhaps also farmers – the pattern varies from country to country) have lost significant ground. The new poor are usually easily found among the unskilled, the old and the unemployed.

Regional differentiation has also become sharper. Most transforming economies can point to booming cities but also to areas where unemployment remains persistently high and impervious to the economic policy medicine currently being applied. One of the testing features facing Central and East European economies over the years ahead will be the capacity of their political systems to cope with the inequalities that the market will inevitably generate.

The economies of the region have changed hugely over the 1990s but the pace of change has been uneven and it is still not easy to say what sort of system has emerged. In some – the Visegrad economies are usually pointed to – there are strong similarities to poorer Western economies where the state sector still plays an important role (perhaps Greece or southern Italy). Across Visegrad the share of the private sector was relatively high (60 per cent to 75 per cent of GDP, see Table 10.3) by the mid-1990s, but even so this was no 'normal' private sector. Laszlo Csaba (1995, p. 170) describes it as a 'more complicated form of bureaucratic ownership'; others have pointed to a movement from 'plan to clan', since in many cases ownership structures are not transparent, and institutions, like state-owned banks in the Czech Republic, may still have a strong influence. In some countries (Bulgaria and the post-Soviet states) serious efforts at economic transformation were yet to start and economies appeared to be steered by the state in a peculiar alliance with semi-autonomous enterprise-based groups. In some, like the Ukraine, matters were worse – the economy was still shrinking in 1996 with inflation at a rate that made sensible economic calculation almost impossible.

By the mid-1990s it was perhaps possible to begin to see more clearly some patterns in the progress made in economic transformation across the region. Figure 10.1 gives a snapshot in 1996 of success and failure in overcoming recession and restoring economic stability. Three broad country groups are evident:

- the cluster of countries in the bottom right-hand corner are those with most progress to show (Poland, Czech, Slovak and Slovenian Republics, Hungary);
- the Baltics form another fairly well-defined group, fast on the way to achieving stability but where recovery was by no means complete;
- and finally, a third cluster in the top of the chart formed by the laggards in the reform process (Bulgaria and the Ukraine).

Of course there is more to transformation than macroeconomic stabilisation. The market mechanism, if it is to work effectively, needs to be embedded in a complex set of legal and financial institutions and the transformation has shown how difficult it is to build such institutions. Table 10.3 locates countries according to progress in terms of this more subtle measure of transformation. Once again it is possible to cluster countries into different groups. As before, the Czech Republic, Hungary, Poland, Slovakia and Slovenia have made greatest progress in building a predominantly private economy and private market institutions. The Baltics form a second country cluster where much has been achieved. Those with least progress to report

TABLE 10.3   *Transformation progress*

	Private sector (% of GDP produced by private sector 1995)	Transition score (EBRD score in building new financial institutions)
Group 1		
East-Central Europe		
Czech Republic (Cz)	70	3
Hungary (H)	60	3
Poland (P)	60	3
Slovakia (Sk)	60	3
Group 2		
Balkans and Southern Europe		
Bulgaria (B)	45	2
Romania (R)	55	2
Slovenia (Sv)	45	3
Croatia (Cr)	45	2.5
Group 3		
Baltics and post-Soviet republics		
Ukraine (U)	35	2
Moldova (M)	30	2
Latvia (Lv)	60	2.5
Lithuania (Lh)	55	2.5
Estonia (E)	65	2.5

Note: The EBRD ranks countries according to a variety of transition indicators on a scale from 1 (least reformed) to 4* (most reformed). We have selected only those measuring progress in building new financial institutions on the grounds that they are probably the most testing of all the transition indicators used by the Bank. The score reported here is the average across two separate financial institutions indicators.
Source: EBRD.

were Moldova and the Ukraine, with Bulgaria and Romania in a somewhat uncomfortable intermediate situation.

The EBRD's chief economist, Nick Stern, has noted more than once that in the transformation some things were much easier to attend to than others. In almost all cases price and trade liberalisation was easy to introduce and happened quickly, but it has proved very much more difficult to create the legal and financial framework that in the West we take for granted. Thus, the great weaknesses in transformation by the mid-1990s were in areas such as banking and corporate governance. By and large those countries with greatest

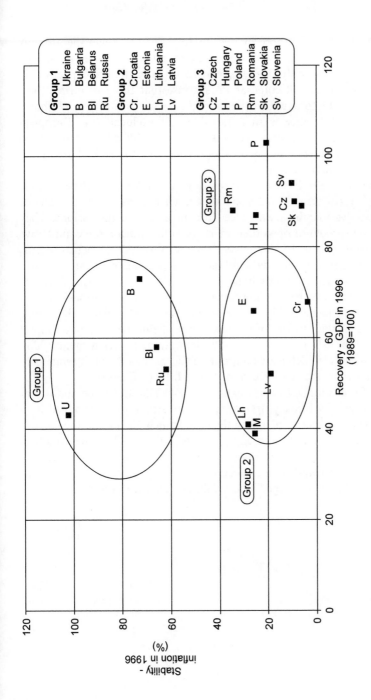

FIGURE 10.1 *Macroeconomic transformation: recovery and stability*

progress here were those invited, in July 1997, to begin the arduous process of negotiating a future EU membership. Out of ten applicants from the region only five were chosen to be in the first wave of EU enlargement. It will come as no surprise that those countries form essentially the 'progressive' country cluster we have identified above. The only difference is that Slovakia was excluded (the European Commission had doubts about the quality of Slovakian democracy) while Estonia was included, and singled out for special treatment among the Baltic group.

The process of EU enlargement looks set to dominate the economic and political scene in the years ahead. This opens a new chapter for prospective members who face difficult accession discussions. They will be expected to open their markets to the much more competitive enterprise of the EU and have no real prospect of benefiting, as previous new entrants did (Ireland, Portugal, Spain), from generous CAP or structural funds handouts. But this is no surprise. The EU itself appears to be heading towards significant 'gradations' of even its existing membership as the 'single currency' replaces the 'single market' as the emblem of the next stage of European integration. Of course, the EU in issuing its 1997 invitations to begin membership discussions also delineated a group of the 'excluded' and it remains to be seen what the significance of this will be to Europe.

As for economic transformation perhaps all that can be said is that after generally bleak years of forced industrialisation managed by a homogenous central planning the clearest new feature on the Central and East European landscape is sheer diversity. If some countries appear to be on track to rejoin 'mainstream' Europe and to get back on the path towards modernisation, a path they were forcibly diverted from half a century ago, others still face an uncertain future.

APPENDIX TABLE 10.1   *Central and East European economies: output*
performance in the first phase of transformation,
1990–95

	Output (real GDP % change)						
	1990	*1991*	*1992*	*1993*	*1994*	*1995*	*1995 (1990 = 100)*
Group 1							
East-Central Europe							
Czech Republic	0	−14	−6	−1	3	5	85
Hungary	−4	−12	−3	−1	3	2	86
Poland	−12	−7	3	4	5	7	99
Slovakia	−3	−15	−7	−4	5	7	84
Group 2							
Balkans and							
Southern Europe							
Bulgaria	−9	−12	−7	−2	2	3	76
Romania	−6	−13	−9	1	4	7	84
Slovenia	−5	−8	−5	1	5	4	91
Croatia	−9	−20	−10	−4	1	2	65
Group 3							
Baltics and post-							
Soviet republics							
Ukraine	−3	−9	−10	−14	−23	−12	46
Moldova	−2	−18	−29	−1	−31	−3	38
Latvia	3	−8	−35	−16	1	−2	51
Lithuania	−5	−13	−38	−24	1	3	40
Estonia	−8	−11	−14	−9	−3	3	64

Source: EBRD.

APPENDIX TABLE 10.2   *Central and East European economies: inflation performance in the first phase of transformation, 1990–95*

| | Inflation (% change year-end data) | | | | | |
	1990	1991	1992	1993	1994	1995
Group 1						
East-Central Europe						
Czech Republic	18	52	13	18	10	8
Hungary	33	32	22	21	21	28
Poland	249	60	44	38	29	22
Slovakia	18	58	9	25	12	7
Group 2						
Balkans and						
Southern Europe						
Bulgaria	73	339	79	64	122	33
Romania	38	223	199	296	62	28
Slovenia	105	247	93	23	18	9
Croatia	136	249	937	1,150	−3	4
Group 3						
Baltics and post-						
Soviet republics						
Ukraine	na	161	2,000	10,155	401	182
Moldova	na	151	2,198	837	116	24
Latvia	na	262	958	35	26	23
Lithuania	na	345	1,161	189	45	36
Estonia	na	304	954	36	42	29

Note: 1995 inflation is an EBRD estimate.
Source: EBRD.

APPENDIX TABLE 10.3 *Central and East European economies: unemployment in the first phase of transformation, 1990–95*

	Unemployment (% rate, end year)					
	1990	*1991*	*1992*	*1993*	*1994*	*1995*
Group 1						
East-Central Europe:						
Czech Republic	0.8	4.1	2.6	3.5	3.2	2.9
Hungary	2.5	8.0	12.7	12.6	10.9	10.4
Poland	6.1	11.8	13.6	15.7	16.0	14.9
Slovakia	1.5	11.8	10.3	14.4	14.8	13.1
Group 2						
Balkans and						
Southern Europe						
Bulgaria	1.5	11.5	15.6	16.4	12.8	10.5
Romania	na	3.0	8.1	10.2	11.0	8.9
Slovenia	4.7	8.2	11.6	14.4	14.4	13.8
Croatia	na	na	12.9	12.8	12.6	12.5
Group 3						
Baltics and post-						
Soviet republics						
Ukraine	0	0	0.3	0.4	0.4	0.6
Moldova	na	na	na	na	na	na
Latvia	0	0.1	2.1	5.3	6.5	6.0
Lithuania	na	0.3	1.0	2.5	4.2	6.6
Estonia	na	na	0.9	2.1	1.8	1.8

Note: 1995 unemployment is an EBRD estimate.
Source: EBRD.

11

The Politics of Social Change

TERRY COX

After the fall of the communist regimes in Central and Eastern Europe many of the new governments that came to power believed they would be able to build brand new institutions and introduce economic reforms that would quickly bring about Western-style capitalist forms of social organisation. If they could adopt the correct policies and implement them quickly, while the anti-communist consensus maintained its hold over public opinion, they thought they would be able to bring about radical social change without much political controversy or competition. The new governments therefore sought to introduce a variety of radical changes, including the transfer of state-owned productive assets to private hands, the creation of market-oriented firms geared to making profit rather than meeting plan targets, and a reduction in state subsidies on many goods and services. Their hope was that the new policies would bring about a more prosperous economy with a greater scope for initiative. This in turn would create a situation where most people would have a stake in the new market economy and would lend their support to it politically. Although there would be fewer jobs in uneconomical and hitherto subsidised state-owned enterprises, there would be more scope for people to become share owners in newly privatised industries, or to set up as entrepreneurs in new businesses, or to find employment in the new private companies.

In practice, however, rather than a smooth transition to capitalism, Central and Eastern Europe has experienced a more complex transformation process, the direction and end-point of which are still the subject of some debate. In part the complexity arises from the fact that economic transformation, as we saw in Chapter 10, has become the focus of broader political competition, involving a range of social groups beyond the state and political elites. Groups ranging from government bureaucrats and state enterprise managers to industrial workers and independent self-employed workers in the 'second economy' have all attempted to build on their existing positions under the old regime, and to use their existing rights of access to resources in order to defend or improve their position in the new market economy.

In each case, therefore, social transformation has been intensely political and has involved competition between groups over their property rights and access to employment and social welfare. In some countries such processes were beginning during the last years of communist rule in the 1980s while others only began to change after the fall of the communist regime. In virtually every country the reforms resulted in a rapid growth of small-scale private sector activity, especially in the service sector and retail trade, but different countries have followed quite different paths in the privatisation of formerly state-owned large and medium sized enterprises. While in all countries the centralised government control over production has been dismantled and a significant degree of ownership has been transferred from the state, a distinction must be made between the full transfer to private owners and the reconstitution of control by managers and state functionaries in the form of closed 'joint stock companies'. These outcomes reflect the different balance of forces in different countries between the various social groups with a stake in transformation process.

By the mid-1990s it was clear that the societies of Central and Eastern Europe were becoming increasingly different from each other. A leading group of the Czech Republic, Hungary, Poland, and Slovenia, perhaps along with Slovakia and the former Soviet Baltic republics, had moved further than their neighbours towards full privatisation and the creation of a market economy; a middle group including Bulgaria, Romania, Croatia and Ukraine had experienced more of a 'de-statisation' that had not led to full privatisation and a less complete transformation; while a third group, including the former Soviet republics of Belarus and Moldova as well as the former Yugoslavia, had moved least towards any significant changes. Different degrees of social transformation were associated with the emergence of different patterns of social inequalities and social problems. In turn, the extent of transformation and the character of social problems have been the subject of, and at the same time have helped to shape the politics of social change in different countries. The rest of this chapter will review the changing nature of social inequalities and social problems before discussing some of their political implications.

Aspects of the Social Inequality Under Communist Rule

Under communist rule political and economic power was distributed in a hierarchy of command. Elite positions in the ruling party and the state were reserved for a party-approved *nomenklatura* who held all the main policy-making and supervisory positions throughout society. The economy was administered through the structure of the party and state institutions by managers who were subordinate to government ministries. Beneath them various professionals and supervisors helped coordinate the activities of workers who were themselves differentiated by skill, status and income. While in theory power was exercised from the top down the hierarchy of command, in practice the system operated through unequal bargains between bureaucrats and managers up and down the different hierarchies of command and across the lines between different sectors of the economy. As a result any tendencies towards the polarisation of society into a ruling elite and a subordinated working class were complicated by the need for groups at different points in the chain of command to cooperate to secure resources and to ensure that their own work output targets were not set too high.

As a consequence of communist policies of industrialisation there emerged a range of new social groups with different levels of qualification, status and income. Over time, as the new structures were consolidated, upward social mobility slowed down and there was an increasing tendency for children to follow their parents into occupations of similar status (Lovenduski and Woodall, 1987, ch. 6). Although the official policy of the communist elites was eventually to eradicate inequalities between different social groups, and to some extent policies were implemented to limit the extent of income differences, nevertheless inequalities in income and standards of living persisted.

There were two main bases for social inequalities in the state-managed system. First, official income policies set different levels of pay for different sectors of the economy, and within them, for occupations requiring different levels of education and skill. In most industries there were marked differences between a core of skilled workers who tended to be male, and a periphery of unskilled workers, often containing a higher proportion of women. Secondly, there were inequalities in access to various goods and services which were not widely available for sale, but which were distributed through the workplace or on the basis of a person's professional or political position. For example free or subsidised catering, health care, child care and holidays were allocated to workers by managers or the trade unions in their workplace. Various professions and elite groups also had further access to scarce goods and services through special closed shops and restaurants.

Gradually, from the 1970s, and in some countries more than others, further bases for inequalities emerged as a result of decentralising market reforms. On the one hand, there was an expansion of various peripheral small-scale activities outside state control, especially in the provision of personal and consumer services by individuals and family groups. These both eased problems of supply for consumers and provided an extra source of income for those providing the services. In the 1980s, especially in Hungary, it became possible to set up small private businesses (Szelenyi, 1988). On the other hand, especially in Hungary and Poland in the 1980s, market-oriented economic reforms allowed managers in state enterprises and officials in the party and state bureaucracies to assume more independent forms of managerial authority and to assume *de facto* new ownership rights. Those most able to develop independent economic activity were those with skills and social capital in the form of contacts and networks of family and friends. Others, especially unskilled workers who had migrated away from their families' original home areas and whose current work did not provide effective support network, became increasingly impoverished as they depended only on their low state incomes (Szalai, 1996, pp. 72–5).

Social Inequality and Economic Transformation

Following the end of communist rule the new political leaders hoped to introduce economic reforms while avoiding any significant decrease in the standard of living and social security of the industrial working class or the majority of the population in general. In some cases, most notably in the Czech Republic, this involved an attempt to give the majority of the population a stake as owners of newly privatised property through a general voucher distribution scheme. In several other countries the privatisation reforms included either similar voucher-based schemes or schemes to transfer some of the shares of enterprises to their employees. In general, governments have been concerned, at the very least, to try and avoid alienating any substantial proportion of the population through the creation of high levels of poverty and unemployment.

In practice, however, economic transformation has resulted in a growth of inequality. Although it is difficult to measure changes in the distribution of income and wealth in Central and Eastern Europe, in general there is evidence of a growth in inequality of income distribution and a significant degree of redistribution of wealth. Inequalities in income distribution have resulted from a number of factors, including a growth of employment opportunities in the private sector where income differences are generally much greater than in the state sector and a general liberalisation affecting wages across the economy as a whole. Privatisation of the state sector and the growth of newly created private businesses have given rise to new opportunities for individuals to accumulate private wealth.

An often used way of measuring income distribution is the Gini coefficient which indicates the degree of income inequality between units (in this case households) on a scale ranging from the hypothetical extremes of 0, representing perfect equality, to 100, representing the complete monopolisation of all income by one household. This is shown for selected countries in Table 11.1. For a smaller selection of countries more detailed information is shown in Table 11.2 about the spread of income between different strata of the population.

According to these data, the countries of Central and Eastern Europe fall roughly into two different groups. On the one hand inequality in many countries of East-Central Europe (as well as the former Soviet republics of Latvia and Ukraine) registered lower figures more similar to some of the more egalitarian societies of Western Europe. While Slovakia registered only 19.5 in 1993 most countries in the region had figures ranging from 25 to 27, and Slovenia registered 28.2. On the other hand, a group mainly consisting of countries further to the east, including Bulgaria and some former Soviet republics, have experienced a dramatic growth of inequality since the 1980s to reach levels similar to those of some of the less equal Western industrial societies. In 1993, Estonia had a coefficient of 39.5 while Lithuania's figure was 33.6, and in 1992 Moldova's was 34.4. As shown in Table 11.1, the extent of the growth of inequality tended to be higher in the former Soviet republic of Estonia and in Bulgaria while the East-Central European countries

TABLE 11.1   *Changes in Gini coefficients for household income*

	1987–8	1993	Change from 1987–8
Bulgaria	23	34	+ 11
Czech Republic	19	27	+ 8
Estonia	23	39	+ 16
Hungary	21	23	+ 2
Latvia	na	27	–
Lithuania	na	34	–
Poland	25	30	+ 5
Slovakia	na	20	–
Slovenia	24	28	+ 4
Ukraine	na	26	–

Source: Adapted from World Bank (1996).

TABLE 11.2   *Income distribution 1993: selected countries*

	Lowest 10%	Lowest 20%	2nd quintile	3rd quintile	4th quintile	Top 20%	Top 10%
Bulgaria	3.3	8.3	13.0	17.0	22.3	39.3	24.7
Czech Republic	4.6	10.5	13.9	16.9	21.3	37.4	23.5
Estonia	2.4	6.6	10.7	15.1	21.4	46.3	31.3
Hungary	4.0	9.5	14.0	17.6	22.3	36.6	22.6
Poland	4.0	9.3	13.8	17.7	22.6	36.6	22.1
Slovenia	4.1	9.5	13.5	17.1	21.9	37.9	23.8

Source: As Table 11.1.

tended to experience less dramatic increases. The exception was the Czech Republic, but in this case the level of inequality has increased from a particularly low level in the 1980s. (For further discussion of the data, the difficulties in measuring it and an explanation of the method of calculating Gini coefficients, see Wyzan, 1996, pp. 24–5.)

The reasons for the emerging pattern of inequality across Central and Eastern Europe are complex. A major factor however is the degrees of success in different countries in developing a market economy. On the one hand, the relatively lower levels of inequality in the 'Visegrad' countries of East-Central Europe have been made possible by policies in those countries of maintaining high levels of spending on social security (Czech Republic and Hungary) and providing flat-rate unemployment benefits (Hungary and Poland). On the other hand, the lower levels in Ukraine may reflect an economy that has experienced only a more limited transformation from its form under state management and which still retains a pattern of income distribution formed under communist rule. In contrast to both of these patterns, the experience of Bulgaria and several of the former Soviet republics has been one of economic decline following the dismantling of many elements of the state-managed economy, but with little progress in establishing an effective new market economy (Wyzan, 1996, p. 26).

It is clear therefore that economic transformation has deepened social inequalities and divisions. However, there are a number of further questions concerning the character of the newly emerging patterns of inequality. In particular these concern both groups 'at the bottom' and the way they are vulnerable to poverty and unemployment, and groups 'at the top' who are accumulating greater power and wealth. Each of these issues will be discussed in turn.

Unemployment

Of all the social problems associated with the social transformation of the 1990s, unemployment has been one of the most shocking for the populations of Central and Eastern Europe. Under communist rule workers had been accustomed to policies of full employment and to management practices which kept them underemployed on enterprise payrolls rather than making them redundant. The general pattern in much of the region was for rates of unemployment to rise quite soon after the introduction of market transformation of the economy. As shown in Tables 11.3 and 11.4, there was a rise in unemployment in many countries, though at different rates in each. As can be seen in Table 11.3, the size of the employed workforce declined significantly in all countries in the region while Table 11.4 shows a lower parallel rise in those registering for unemployment. Of the two sets of figures, those showing the decline in employment probably reflect the situation in each country more accurately than the figures for registered unemployment. Those registered as looking for work were only a small part of the total unemployed: others who lost their jobs were obliged to take early retirement or register for a disability pension. In many countries the benefits for the registered unemployed were so low that there was little incentive for people to register.

TABLE 11.3   *Changes in employment, 1990–4*

	Labour force in 1994	% change 1990–4
Bulgaria	3,242,000	−25.7
Czech Republic	4,885,000	−9.6
Hungary	4,045,000	−26.1
Poland	14.475,000	−14.9
Romania	10,012,000	−8.5
Slovakia	2,110,000	−15.7
Slovenia	752,000	−20.5
Ukraine	23,025,000	−9.4

Source: Adapted from Szamuely (1996) p. 57.

TABLE 11.4   *Registered unemployed 1991–4*

	1991		1994	
	Numbers	% of labour force	Numbers	% of labour force
Bulgaria	419,000	11.5	488,000	12.8
Czech Rep.	222,000	4.1	167,000	3.2
Estonia	–	0.1	–	5.1
Hungary	406,000	7.4	520,000	10.4
Latvia	–	0.1	–	6.5
Lithuania	–	0.2	–	4.5
Poland	2,156,000	11.8	2,838,000	16.0
Romania	338,000	3.1	1,224,000	10.9
Slovakia	302,000	11.8	372,000	14.8
Slovenia	91,000	10.1	124,000	14.3
Ukraine	7,000	–	82,000	0.3

Source: Adapted from Szamuely (1996) p. 57; Wyzan (1997b) pp. 12–14.

Many who have lost their jobs have taken up casual work in the illegal or semi-legal 'shadow economies' that have mushroomed throughout most of the Central and East European countries. Typically jobs of this kind include the same range as formed part of the unofficial 'second economy' of the period under communist rule: gardening, building work, tailoring, personal services, trading and transport. In Poland, for example, it has been estimated that more than two million people were working in the shadow economy in 1995 and that it was the main source of income for more than 40 per cent of them. Of these, over 60 per cent were men and the majority were either young people under 24 years old or older people aged over sixty (Miroziewicz, 1996, pp. 26–7). The decline in employment was greater in Bulgaria, Hungary, Poland and Slovakia than elsewhere. While for the latter three countries this reflected the effects of the policies of liberalisation of the economy on market lines, in Bulgaria it reflected the failed attempt at similar policies in the early 1990s, followed by a general decline of the economy. On the other hand the smaller decreases in Romania and Ukraine probably reflected their relative lack of economic reform and industrial restructuring.

The explanation for lower rates of unemployment in the Czech Republic are more complex and the subject of much debate. Although the government under Vaclav Klaus implemented an extensive economic reform and liberalisation of the economy, including the mass voucher-privatisation scheme, in practice social policy has been governed by (largely unstated) support for maintaining a high rate of employment and softening the blows of economic transformation. One school of thought has argued that low levels of unemployment have been achieved because of the success of the Czech economic reform. This has enabled Czech industry to improve productivity, find new markets and thereby maintain or create jobs. At the same time the government has been able to maintain a social 'safety net' of unemployment benefits and job retraining while reducing the generosity of these schemes from the levels provided under communist rule. The other school of thought has argued that although some aspects of the Czech economy have been liberalised and the old system of state ownership has been dismantled, the state still controls a large share of the economy through its ownership of a dominant share of the large banks, which in turn dominate the main investment funds that hold most of the shares of companies privatised through voucher privatisation. This means that while the funds, as owners, should be proactive in the restructuring of companies, they also need to reflect the more cautious concerns of the state and banking interests in avoiding a disruption of economic performance. They therefore tend to maintain practices of hoarding more labour than would be necessary for the productivity of their companies (Munich and Sorm, 1996).

For the time being at least, in several of the countries that have undergone significant economic restructuring, the level of unemployment seems to have peaked and to be slowly falling. In Poland registered unemployment reached its peak of nearly 17 per cent in

July 1994 and had dropped back to 14.9 per cent by the end of 1995. However, the number of those officially in employment still continued to fall to a level slightly less than half the total of Poland's economically active population (Miroziewicz, 1996, p. 26). The percentage of registered unemployed reached its peak in Estonia in 1994 and by 1996 it had fallen to 4.1 per cent. In Lithuania it reached a peak of 7.3 per cent in 1995 and fell back to 6.2 per cent in 1996. However, in Latvia it was still rising in 1996 to a new level of 7.2 per cent (Wyzan, 1997b, pp. 12–14).

Within each country the growth of unemployment has generally been an uneven process with some regions and sections of the population affected more than others. For example, in Poland job losses were higher in south-east Poland than in Warsaw, in Hungary they were higher in the east of the country than in Budapest and the west, and in the Czech Republic they were higher in northern Bohemia than in Prague. In the Prague metropolitan area in 1995 the unemployment rate was a negligible 0.3 per cent and there were eight vacancies per each person unemployed. Many of the new jobs in the private sector are in very small firms in the service industries, often family businesses employing fewer than five employees, and these too tend to be concentrated in certain metropolitan areas rather than spread broadly within each country.

In terms of the social profile of the unemployed, the burden has fallen most heavily on women, young people and those with lower levels of education. In many countries women have been the first to be made redundant as firms have restructured their workforces. In the Czech Republic the proportion of women in the unemployed has risen from 50 per cent to 60 per cent in the last few years. In Poland, even though women are more likely than men to take up retraining opportunities they are still less successful than men in finding new jobs afterwards. In Hungary, less-skilled, lower-educated workers and gypsies have been affected particularly (Miroziewicz, 1996, p. 27; Munich and Sorm, 1996, pp. 23–4).

Poverty

The incidence of poverty rose significantly in most parts of Central and Eastern Europe after the end of communist rule so that in most countries a majority have experienced increased poverty. According to Deacon, the region's living standards dropped in real terms by up to one-third in the early 1990s (1993, p. 227). As shown in Table 11.5, for those at the bottom end of the scale of income distribution this meant that larger numbers of people fell below the officially designated poverty line.

There are a number of different reasons for the fall in living standards and rise of poverty. As well as loss of income through unemployment, the growth of the market economy has also led to price inflation. In the early 1990s many people, especially pensioners and those employed by the state, suffered a decline in real wages ranging from less than 10 per cent per year in Hungary to 70 per cent in Ukraine. If workers did not have skills which could be easily employed in the new private sector, or if they lived in areas where there were few opportunities to enter the private sector, they were particularly vulnerable to inflation. Furthermore, in addition to the falling real value of their money income, they saw a decline in the level of social services provided by the state or their formerly state-owned places of employment. Throughout the region, enterprises had to meet new profit criteria by closing crèches, clinics, subsidised canteens and other fringe benefits.

A further factor affecting poverty has been the decline in minimum wage levels following the introduction of strict incomes policies as part of the move to greater market regulation of the economy. As Standing and Vaughan-Whitehead have noted, while the minimum wage had helped to provide 'a barrier to severe poverty' for lower-paid families in the state-managed economy, in the new market-oriented economy it became 'the means by which their impoverishment was

TABLE 11.5 *Percentage of the population below the poverty line, 1987–8 and 1993*

	1987–8	1993
Bulgaria	2	33
Czech Republic	0	1
Estonia	–	23
Hungary	1	2
Poland	6	12
Slovenia	0	1

Source: Adapted from World Bank (1996).

intensified'. In most countries in the region, with the partial exception of Poland, the Czech Republic and Slovakia, the minimum wage has fallen to levels well below either the average wage or the minimum subsistence level. Moreover, the declining level of minimum wages has had implications not only for the lowest-paid workers, but in many countries for a wider range of workers whose wage rates are set in relation to the official minimum wage. Other social welfare benefits are also often set with reference to the minimum wage (Standing and Vaughan-Whitehead, 1995, pp. 1, 16, 22–30).

Those sections of society with the highest incidence of poverty include single-parent households, the unemployed, the elderly and those with low levels of education or qualifications. As Julia Szalai (1996) has noted, to a significant extent these groups had experienced increasing impoverishment under communist rule and developments during the 1990s have tended to exacerbate this trend. Two main processes have been at work, one economic and the other political. First, as a result of the economic transformation, wage workers who depended only on their wage from the state became increasingly impoverished. This was especially the case for those who had given up their rural roots and moved to single industry towns as part of the 'socialist' industrialisation process, and who had lost or never had effective support networks based on family or work colleagues. Lacking the skills and contacts necessary to take up opportunities in the new private sector, they have now come to depend increasingly on their low state incomes at the same time as the level of social service provision has been cut back.

Second, the situation of the poor has been undermined further as a result of their lack of representation in the new forms of pressure group politics that have emerged as a result of democratisation. In Hungary, according to Szalai, despite the rhetoric of marketisation the state has continued to be a major source of resources and it is the focus of attention of pressure groups representing a wide range of business and worker interests. In this situation the poor are further disadvantaged by their lack of effective pressure group representation. While the provision of various state subsidies and social services has declined, they have tended to be the first to be eliminated from the competition for the redistribution of state property, and since they have no property they benefit neither from the tax relief that others enjoy on their property nor from the increased credit worthiness that property ownership bestows:

The poor are victims of this tacit new compromise that is gradually taking shape . . . In contrast with the majority it is they who depend in practice only on incomes derived from official sources for their livelihood – hence the appearance that they are being supported by the public purse. The uniformity of their sources then creates the false impression that it is they who are using up the thin trickle of dwindling state resources. The majority are in agreement on reducing state expenditure on support of the poor (Szalai, 1996, p. 77).

A New Middle Class?

While the immediate consequence of economic transformation for the majority in Central and Eastern Europe has been a decline in their living standards, for a minority of people it has provided new lucrative opportunities. As a result a small group of very wealthy people has emerged. While some have made their millions from their entrepreneurial skills in newly formed businesses, others have been able to transform their control of former state property into newly privatised firms. Also, a further group have taken advantage of the new situation to transform illegal earnings into new legal forms of wealth. Little is known in detail about the size of these groups in each country or the extent of their wealth.

In addition two other new groups have emerged as beneficiaries of the transformation process. On the one hand there are the moderately wealthy managers and professionals who are earning high salaries in the market economy and enjoying middle-class lifestyles and standards of living in the new consumer-oriented society. On the other hand there are the new 'political class' of politicians and policymakers, some of them former communists, others who were former dissidents, and many who have only entered politics since the fall of communism. As well as the very wealthy, there is probably also widespread share-ownership among these managers, professionals and political leaders.

Although it is widely recognised that the market economy has brought about the emergence of these groups, there is much less agreement about how to characterise them sociologically. According to the neo-liberal ideology of the postcommunist reformers, marketisation and privatisation are bringing into being a 'new middle class' which is seen as distinct from the new political leaders, who are usually described as the new (upper) 'political class'. However, for the new neo-liberal political leaders it is essential that a larger middle class emerges in order to play the roles of both the agents and the main support group for the new capitalist economy:

> It is said that the new middle class is being born in pain, lacking local capital and strong traditions and in an atmosphere of growing social resistance to liberal reforms. The conclusion is that its birth has to be protected and expedited – and this has to be achieved, somewhat paradoxically for neo-liberal theory, by the state, through its promotion of liberalisation and privatisation. The new middle class will result from privatisation and restitution of property as a 'category of new owners and new entrepreneurs'. (Mokrzycki, 1995, pp. 218, 225)

According to neo-liberal theory the middle class will be formed from elements of three existing social groups: small-scale private entrepreneurs, former members of the communist *nomenklatura* and the intelligentsia. An alternative view, however, sees the coalescence of these different groups into a new middle class as problematic. First, there is the question of whether the resources and social connections of small 'second economy entrepreneurs', *nomenklatura* and the intelligentsia can be converted into the basis for developing modern capitalist businesses (Stark, 1990). They may instead only adapt their activities as a defensive move which, once achieved, enables them to make use of their former expertise and contacts to continue to manage their affairs according to a modified version of the old criteria, rather than according to new profit-oriented principles.

Second, there is the question of whether business groups and those holding political power will remain distinct or whether they will merge into a new ruling class. Furthermore, what would be the basis of the power of such a new class? Different views have been put forward. On the one hand, if their power derives from their ownership of capital they should be seen as a new ruling capitalist class (Staniszkis, 1991a; Rona-Tas, 1994); on the other hand, if their power derives from their expertise as managers or intellectuals they may form the basis of a new 'managerial ruling class'. For example, in the case of Hungary and more widely in Eastern Europe, Ivan Szelenyi (1995) has argued that the current transformation process has allowed for the emergence of 'cultural capital', and especially the expertise possessed by the managers, as the main basis for exercising power in both political and economic spheres. For Szelenyi it is managers rather than owners who are the real controllers of the newly emerging privately owned capital throughout the region.

It is still too soon to come to any final conclusions about the class character of the new dominant groups in Central and East European societies and the subject is still under debate. However, in either case, it seems clear that the gap is widening between such groups, whatever their precise social character, and those lower down the social scale in terms of income, wealth or influence.

Political Responses

The social problems associated with economic transformation have created serious political dilemmas for governments throughout the region. In each country the goal of implementing effective economic reforms has had to be weighed against the problems of increasing inequalities, unemployment and poverty and the popular discontent such problems could provoke. In the early 1990s opinion polls revealed high levels of support for the transition to the market in most countries. For example, in 1991 the Eurobarometer surveys showed highly positive balances between the numbers of favourable and unfavourable responses to the market economy in nearly all Central and East European countries, ranging from positive balances of 55 per cent in Lithuania and 52 per cent in Hungary to 32 per cent in Estonia and 29 per cent in Slovakia. By 1994, however, public belief in the benefits of a market economy had begun to decline, for example to 20 per cent in Hungary, only 9 per cent in Lithuania, and an equal balance between positive and negative responses in Slovakia. Of the countries surveyed, only Romania bucked the trend by showing a negative balance in 1991 and a highly positive balance by 1994. Between 1991 and 1994 there was an average decline of 22 per cent in public belief in a market economy in the region overall (Eurobarometer, 1994).

Governments in different countries have reacted in different ways in confronting this dilemma, both in terms of the mix of policies they have adopted and in the degree to which they have allowed open political debate on economic reform. A useful means of categorising the different ways in which governments reacted has been offered by Charles Gati who has suggested that three different groups of Central and East European countries can be identified: the 'leaders', the 'laggards' and the 'losers' (1996, pp. 11–12).

The 'losers', in which he includes the former Soviet republics of the Transcaucasus and Central Asia, dismantled elements of the Soviet system of centralised economic management but maintained a combination of authoritarian politics and a lack of movement towards economic reform. The ruling elites resisted both political and economic liberalisation for fear of causing further social disruption and provoking political unrest.

Meanwhile the 'laggards', such as Bulgaria, Romania, Ukraine and Croatia, pursued limited economic reforms while maintaining the form of a democratic politics, but not its full content. For example a formally free press was subjected to various restrictions in practice and the government's rule was legitimated 'in seemingly fair but manipulated elections'. Governments kept significant sections of the economy under their control and sought to limit popular discontent by maintaining state subsidies on some areas of consumption. Nevertheless, such governments have found it increasingly difficult to sustain the political 'balancing act' that such policies require, and in some countries declining living standards and a growing discontent at the lack of political direction of the country have provoked growing signs of unrest. For example, in late 1996 and early 1997 there were massive street demonstrations in both Serbia and Bulgaria, leading in the latter to the fall of the Socialist-led government and its replacement by a more radical reformist administration. In some countries there has been a popular reaction against the cautious policies of 'laggard' governments and recent general elections have brought more radical reforming governments to power in Bulgaria and Romania.

The third group, the 'leaders', includes the Czech Republic, Hungary, Poland and Slovenia, possibly along with the former Soviet Baltic states of Estonia, Lithuania and Latvia. These countries both pursued more radical economic reform and introduced a largely free press and a fully functioning parliamentary democracy. After electing liberal reformers or national conservatives in their first free elections, some of these countries, for example Hungary, Lithuania and Poland, subsequently returned reform communists, while in the Czech Republic the liberal conservatives have stayed in power but there has been increased electoral support for social democrats. While such shifts to the centre-left did not signal any abandonment of policies supporting privatisation and the market economy, they did represent a move towards policies combining economic reform with a greater explicit concern for its social costs. However, as Gati has noted, it has proved very difficult in practice to combine such conflicting aims:

> The popular appeal of such a neo-egalitarian course is beyond dispute. In theory it combines the dynamism of free enterprise with efforts to ease the pain of change for pensioners, teachers, state employees, and everyone on fixed incomes. In practice however, poor countries in particular cannot afford to pay the high cost of social support structures. . . . As for the incipient protectionist impulse, it can only produce stagnation because of the lack of sufficient domestic resources, including capital, for investment. (Gati, 1996, p. 10)

The move towards a more socially directed policy agenda brings the concerns of political elites into conflict with the interests of the new owners of capital for a further extension of economic reform and a deepening of the transformation process. Governments therefore are faced with very difficult balancing acts to perform. On the one hand, they need to secure their future re-election by maintaining their credibility with their electorates, who are suffering continuing cuts in their real incomes, access to services and employment. Furthermore, in order to fulfil their foreign policy aims of achieving membership of the EU and NATO, they need to maintain their commitments to freedom of expression and open parliamentary democracy. On the other hand, in the eyes of liberal reformers and business interests, the process of transformation of the economy cannot be delayed. While a significant amount of the ownership of capital has been formally transferred to private interests the state still plays a dominant role in economic management, and questions of corporate governance of companies, of how private owners can intervene in the management of production to ensure profitability, still remain to be resolved. The requirements of EU membership also require further liberalisation of the economies of Central and East European candidates for member-ship. Although the economic policy agenda creates pressures for austerity measures and cuts in the provision of social services, governments will be afraid to fully implement these for fear of losing electoral support.

These dilemmas may lead to different reactions in different coun-tries. 'Laggard' governments have sought to delay economic reform, maintain authoritarian constraints on democratic institutions, and in some cases to mobilise support around nationalist sentiments or by blaming outsiders. On the other hand, the semi-authoritarian option will be more problematic for many other governments in the region, although they may be under challenge from oppositions favouring such agendas (see, e.g., Sylwestrowicz, 1995 on Poland). These include not only the 'leaders' in the transformation process, who are pressing to be in the first wave of EU expansion towards Central and Eastern Europe, but also countries such as Bulgaria and Romania which have belatedly opted for more radical reforms.

For the countries of the region, the likely choices of policy direction would seem to lie between retrenchment leading to probable stagnation, a new authoritarianism supporting a push for further restructuring, or a difficult holding operation, probably by governments with social democratic tendencies, offering further but slower restructuring 'with a human face'. In each case, social change, and the social problems arising from economic restructuring are likely to continue to exert a significant influence on politics throughout the region.

12

The Politics of Gender in Central and Eastern Europe

CHRIS CORRIN

Since the breakdown of communist rule in the countries of Central and Eastern Europe sweeping changes in political, economic and social life have taken place. This chapter considers the gendered aspects of such change in order to assess how women's situations have been altered and how women are effecting change. Gender differences are often imperfectly understood and left unexplained, or they are exaggerated and described in perjorative terms which stress the ways in which women fail to be equal to men. In what follows I shall consider varying conceptions and conditions of political participation by women in Central and Eastern Europe, and how different situations have highlighted shifts in focus regarding the integration and autonomy of women's groups.

There are clearly many differences amongst women in terms of ethnicity, class, dis/ability, wealth, age, sexuality and opportunities. It is necessary to be clear which women are being considered and at which levels of political participation and activism. Equally, after the Cold War 'Sovietisation' of the region post-1948, the definitions of politics and of what the Hungarian writer Konrad (1984) has called 'anti-politics' – of social movements and civil society – were developing and changing over time.

Women have never been a single 'category', in Central and Eastern Europe or elsewhere. There are basic differences between them in terms of economic activity, ethnicity, household patterns, sexuality and lifestyles which means they are differently located with regard to state structures. Yet the party/state systems in the various countries under consideration did produce policies based on a specific collective identity – 'women'. In this context, it is apparent that women suffer inequalities on the basis of their ability to give birth and on this basis are assigned gender characteristics that are socially and often officially constructed. Many of the expectations imposed on women result in their direct and indirect oppression *as women* in terms of childbearing and caring, and as women workers.

The massive upheavals of 1989 opened the gates for great changes in this part of the world. In the most general terms, all the former 'state socialist' countries, including Romania, Bulgaria and later Albania, rejected the rigid systems of Communist Party control. Yet, with the disintegration of the centralised systems of the past, much change has been at once chaotic, violent and contradictory in its social impact. Many women are experiencing quite devastating social, personal and political changes. Throughout Central and Eastern Europe these changes are often contradictory and happening at differing paces. The aftermath of war in Bosnia, Croatia and Serbia has made the situation oppressive for many women in these countries in a variety of ways.

Gendered Inequalities

The political inequalities experienced by women are symptomatic of inequalities in economic, social and domestic life. In the twentieth century women in many countries have been mobilised into the workforces as a result of war or labour shortage, and in the western world have generally been expelled again during peacetime and recession. The inclusion of the majority of women of working age into paid public work in the Central and Eastern European countries was a major feature of 'state socialism' following World War II. Different ideas regarding what emancipation or liberation for women could include can be seen to arise from these vastly different working situations for women all across Europe. Family patterns have been altered by changes in reproductive technologies as well as by alterations in divorce laws and employment opportunities. In the Central and Eastern European countries controls on women's reproductive health, in the form of abortion laws and lack of contraceptives and sex education, drastically controlled women's choices regarding fertility. Since the establishment of Soviet-type systems in these countries several important changes in women's situations took place against a background of increased access to education, the mass entry of women into public paid work with guarantees of full employment, public childcare and other (gendered) welfare benefits.

Rather than recapitulating other accounts of women's life experiences and analyses of their situations (see Corrin, 1992; Funk and Mueller, 1993; Rueschemeyer, 1994; Corrin, 1994; Renne, 1997), I briefly note some significant points regarding women's situations in Central and Eastern Europe under communist rule. Firstly it is apparent that under such circumstances women's rights and duties were fused and confused, leaving women bearing heavy burdens. The right to work which many Western women and women's groups struggled for was in fact a duty to work in the 'other half' of Europe, with laws of parasitism punishing those (including single mothers) who did not work. This is not to say that many women did not gain some fulfilment from public, paid work but to point up the lack of *choice* that was available. Women had a high rate of paid employment and in some industries successful performance was due primarily to the presence of skilled female workforces. In the early 1980s, for example, women in these centrally planned economies constituted on average 45–50 per cent of the labour force and a large proportion of these were concentrated in industrial employment. Whilst women could be found in most occupations, they were generally employed at the lower-middle levels and were not well represented among the higher management ranks (Corrin, 1992). Findings from a recent three-country study are significant in the context of women's coping mechanisms in times of change, when these employment patterns have become disrupted (Corrin *et al.*, 1996).

Work in many forms, paid or unpaid, valued or undervalued, is a central feature in women's lives, and tensions between paid work and domestic work, including housework, childcare and responsibility for creating homes, have long been apparent in many societies. When changes were first being discussed in Central and Eastern Europe in 1989–90 some analysts suggested that women might now be happy to 'return to the home' and be full-time housewives. That this choice had not been open to women in these countries for over 40 years meant that some women might well have wished to choose this option. Yet in chaotic economic situations few women have the choice to give up their wages, so that for the majority of women unemployment has created a whole new set of problems of household management on less money with increasing food, fuel and rent costs. The two-income model had become a necessity in these countries and with rising inflation and the removal of subsidies from goods and services which had previously kept prices low, many families are having difficulty managing on their combined incomes. Where one or both partners become unemployed, great hardship and deprivation is apparent.

Whilst arguing that 'At a global level, and over time, the integration of women into economic and political life – and feminist activism – has radically altered definitions of gender, leading to a decline of the patriarchal ideology which associated women exclusively with family and reproduction', Valentine Moghadam also points out that 'In both the Third World and the former state socialist societies, restructuring has had dubious developmental consequences and adverse effects on women's roles and status' (Moghadam, 1992, p. 22). Initial information gathered by the United Nations Industrial Development Organisation (UNIDO) indicates that women's employment patterns prior to the transition period made them more liable than men to layoffs and redundancy as part of the restructuring processes.

There are various explanations for this, including the character of occupations in which women workers were the first to feel the impact of plant closures and employment cutbacks. For example, in Poland, light industries and textiles, branches employing mostly women, were hard hit by economic changes. Not only have women lost their jobs but they are having difficulty finding alternative work. Moghadam notes: 'the expansion of an informal labour market and informal services sector . . . This will not necessarily be to women's advantage' (Moghadam, 1992, pp. 20–1). Older women are amongst the worst affected because even though they may be eligible for retraining, their age becomes a barrier. Other factors including traditional attitudes to women's unpaid work within the home and in caring for children and older family members, which affect women's opportunities for paid employment.

As can be seen from Table 12.1, of the four countries noted, Hungary remains the only one in which women have consistently accounted for less than 50 per cent of those unemployed. The figures for Slovakia have remained steady over the five-year period whilst those for Poland and the Czech Republic have risen steadily.

Sometimes as mothers, or as women of a certain age, these women are considered 'too expensive' to employ and/or retrain. Some of the social protection legislation for mothers was still in place until 1993–4 so that women were still entitled to reasonable maternity leave and to some days off if their children were ill. The changing patterns of such legislation have altered in different ways over time in the countries in Central and Eastern Europe, with the main emphasis being placed on reducing maternity costs to the enterprise and to the state. Polish maternity benefits have remained more stable than others, perhaps given the pervasive influence of the pro-natalist ideology of Catholicism. So-called 'protective legislation' in certain areas (such as women not being able to drive buses) could however be seen as blatant sex discrimination in other contexts, certainly within the terms of European Union Equal Opportunities legislation. It can be seen from Table 12.2 that many employers do indeed have a preference for employing men rather than women.

Arguments for cutbacks were often posed in terms of cost-cutting exercises – 'either the nursery or creche closes or a certain number of staff would be made redundant'. Opting for closure of childcare facilities automatically meant that a percentage of the female labour force would be redundant, as no alternative care was available for their children. It is now very expensive to place children within private childcare centres in these countries, so the private nurseries that are opening are in practice open only to the select few women who can afford to use them. Situations in which women are forced into unemployment with fewer opportunities to gain alternative employment whilst struggling to make ends meet will take time, courage and stamina to resolve satisfactorily.

TABLE 12.1   *Number of registered unemployed by sex, and share of women in registered unemployment, 1989–94 (thousands and percentages)*

	End year	Total	Men	Women	Share of women* (%)
Czech Republic	1989	0.3	–	–	–
	1990	39.4	19.4	20.0	50.9
	1994 October	160.5	63.4	97.1	60.5
Hungary	1989	28.5	16.7	11.8	41.4
	1990	79.5	48.1	31.4	39.5
	1994 June	556.5	319.5	237.0	42.6
Poland	1990	1126.1	552.4	573.7	50.9
	1994 June	2933.0	1383.8	1549.2	52.8
Slovakia	1989	0.3			
	1990	37.6	18.8	18.8	50.0
	1994 October	359.9	181.8	178.1	49.5

*   Calculated from unrounded figures.
Source: Data communicated to the ILO by government services of countries concerned; and national statistical publications.

TABLE 12.2   *Managers' gender preferences for recruitment by occupation (percentages)*

Occupation	Czech Republic			Hungary			Slovakia		
	Men more suitable	*Women more suitable*	*Equally suitable*	*Men more suitable*	*Women more suitable*	*Equally suitable*	*Men more suitable*	*Women more suitable*	*Equally suitable*
Managerial and administrative	35.8	2.1	62.1	27.7	2.8	69.6	45.6	3.1	51.2
Supervisors	–	–	–	56.7	11.0	32.3	–	–	–
Professional and technical	58.3	2.2	39.5	3.1	27.2	69.7	47.2	5.0	47.8
Clerical	–	–	–	0.4	76.4	23.2	–	–	–
General service and organisation	39.7	8.7	51.5	–	–	–	43.3	12.1	44.6
Skilled operatives	42.6	15.2	42.2	52.8	17.7	29.5	35.4	13.9	50.6
Semi-skilled operatives	19.7	27.9	52.4	16.9	40.2	42.9	22.4	25.7	52.0
Unskilled operatives	19.7	24.8	55.5	50.4	11.8	37.8	22.7	18.0	59.3
Maintenance and repair	93.5	0	6.5	92.1	0.4	7.5	93.0	0.6	6.3
Service work	–	–	–	35.8	9.1	55.1	–	–	–

Source: Derived from ILO Labour Force Surveys, 1993.

Older women, particularly those on fixed incomes such as pensioners, are being hit very hard by the economic reforms. Rents, fuel and food are all becoming increasingly expensive, but pensions have not risen to cover these increases. That older people paid into pension schemes all of their working lives does not now guarantee even a minimum on which to survive. Many social policy issues involving health care, education, housing and benefits are overdue for consideration by policy-makers, and social problems arising from poverty, homelessness, unemployment and ill-health are increasing throughout many Central and East European countries. The hopelessness felt by many Albanians wishing to accumulate savings via pyramid schemes quickly developed into violent clashes against the government forces during 1997. Questions regarding the legitimation of state power naturally arise when economic chaos of this kind prevails.

Rights and Duties: Production and Reproduction

Concentration on heavy industrial development under state socialism meant that consumer needs for domestic chores such as clothes washing, house cleaning and cooking were virtually ignored. Minimal restructuring of family units with little regard for the importance of women's unpaid work underpinned 'socialist' development. Official women's organisations took care that women need not be involved in their own negotiations with party/state officials and often in their own trades unions. This had later implications for women's views regarding 'liberation' and for official attitudes towards feminist ideas and activities. With the survival and reinforcement of traditional gender values and attitudes of male superiority in many spheres, women's rights were projected and 'protected' by state policy-making and structures. The legacy of this traditionalism of attitudes in general towards the family and gender roles is an apparent reality that women have to deal with in these countries today. 'Rights' to abortion were often the only means of fertility control for many women, with some severe consequences for women's health and well-being. In the 'personalised dictatorships' such as that of Ceausescu in Romania and of Hoxha in Albania, women's fertility was controlled by making abortion illegal and in Romania the 'five children' rule compounded this situation.

Childcare services were very necessary if all women were to be in paid employment. Despite the availability of state care for many children during working hours, women were still responsible for most of the work in the household. This often meant extra work such as queuing for food and cleaning and caring for children and elderly relatives at home. State benefits and services were introduced to ease women's situation, yet there were contradictions. As women (rather than men) often had to take time off when children were ill, they were viewed as less reliable workers. This often meant that they were not offered training programmes or promotions under the same conditions as their male colleagues. Yet as the *Women and Democratisation* study shows, women were expected to be mothers and were seen as less than adult if they did not have children:

> During the Communist regimes it was clear that there was a double-model of citizenship within which it was important for women to be mothers. By having children women were supported by the Communist regime. Single women did not really qualify on

the same terms as full citizens. There was an informal points system whereby women collected points for children . . . The 'motherhood' archetype was prolonged by the Communist regime, especially with the revival of archetypal femininity in the 1950s, in a way that industrially developed societies in the West had broken with (Corrin *et al.* 1996, p. 7).

Links with enforced benefits from the state reinforced continuing pro-natalist policies. As Irene Dolling points out (in Lewis, 1992), state forces became official 'protectors' of women, allowing them certain rights – which could be withdrawn. The lack of educational campaigns aimed at breaking down conservative 'sex roles' and giving positive encouragement for women to organise for themselves meant that women's situations seemed to be largely determined within power relationships outside their control. Several authors, such as Siklova (1996) and Szalai (1994), have pointed out that men were equally oppressed by prohibitions on organisation. These two factors taken together have affected women's situations in various concrete ways since 1990 and are in evidence within debates about the establishment and development of women's campaigns and initiatives.

It is important to note here that early attempts at assessing women's situations in the changed conditions of this region through a 'balance sheet' of gains and losses have little value after almost a decade of change. This approach is problematic for two reasons. Firstly the entire framework of the old times was different, and those apparent 'advantages' that women had were deeply embedded into the oppressive logic of party-based control over their entire lives. Secondly, many elements of the structure of daily life changed in the 1990s so that such an evaluation of gains and losses would require the construction of a new framework. One element in this new framework would be the expansion of what is considered as constituting 'the political'. This would enable the political participation of women at local levels and outside formal political mechanisms to be assessed.

Up to the 1960s, with the resurgence of feminist thought and activism, Western political science had very little to say about women. Crucial here are definitions of politics. In Western political thought, traditionalist views initially implied a distinctive 'public' political arena, and despite changes over time and an expansion of the 'public' arena, traditional views still tend to hold that an apolitical private sphere exists. This private sphere centres on family life which still defines and limits most women's wider socio-political role. Feminist analyses (see, for instance, Pateman, 1988; Philips, 1991) have broken down public/private distinctions in recognising politics as concerned with the working out of power relations so that politics is not separated from social life as a whole. Family politics and women's reproductive health, in this context, become key areas of study. The questioning of public/private distinctions by Western feminist claims that the 'personal is political' can be viewed as in some ways analogous to the 'anti-politics' arguments of Central and Eastern Europe about politics as a moral choice. The opening up of traditional views of 'the political' shows a shift in traditional notions of politics. From a feminist perspective this shift meant that family and sexual identities were located as sites of power relations. Such analyses have not arisen in a social vacuum but as a response to changing social and political circumstances and opportunities.

In both Western feminist and Eastern oppositionist circles conceptions of politics were not simply framed in terms of electoral battles or state power. How people lived became central to politics – recognising the political character of our engagements at various interpersonal, community and familial levels. Different conceptions of the public/private distinction were being explored during the 1980s within the discussions regarding 'anti-politics' under state socialism and state/civil society relations and divisions (see Corrin, 1993). It is sufficient to note here that discussions focusing on women's rights and interests within the Central and Eastern European countries during the early 1990s did not incorporate Western feminist conceptions of public/private distinctions without taking account of apparent differences in context (see Gal, 1996, p. 75).

Transitional Debates

The new terms of discourse in Central and East European countries make use of neoclassical economics and liberal and conservative political thought. There is an apparent resistance to the ideology of socialism and the consequences of such thought in social policy. Two aspects of significance are apparent for current issues of women's interests affecting attitudes towards politics and policies made in the name of 'women'. Firstly, as Jirina Vrabkova notes regarding women's political participation in Czechoslovakia:

Forty years of communist patriarchal rule and its hypocritical proclamations on women's artificial emancipation, motivated by the need to employ the cheapest labour force, have caused their reluctance and aversion to politics, both national and international alike. (Vrabkova in Renne, 1997, p. 72)

Secondly, critics of current policy are viewed as tainted by the past, as has been pointed out in the Polish context:

One who dares to criticise the neoliberal economic philosophy of Friedrich Hayek and Milton Friedman is against the free market and is a supporter of communism. 'Socialist' as well as 'feminist' is a discrediting label. (Nowakowska in Renne, 1997, p. 26)

This confusion of assertions concerning 'then' and 'now' can often be utilised in defence of poor policy-making and an unwillingness to work through complex arguments. When some women experience declining living standards this can be blamed on the excesses of the 'communist past' and then expressed in terms of the necessity for 'reform', which is not gender neutral.

For those women throughout Central and Eastern Europe who wish to use feminist analysis to help to understand their and other women's situations, the resistance against this means of social enquiry is doubled when the active content is noted. That is, feminism, like Marxism, involves a *praxis* which links theory with experience and explanation with attempts at developing change in various realms. In assessing women's changing situations interesting questions can be posed in terms of whether certain Western problems are being reproduced and in what areas changes are accentuating differences. One arena of debate in which these questions are being posed is that of women's activism and feminist analysis all across Europe. Many women within Central and East European countries have resisted what they perceive to be the imposition of 'Western feminist' values and prescriptions (Siklova, 1996; Smejkalova, 1996; Nemenyi, 1996).

Evidence has shown that fewer women than men in Central and East European countries had been active in the formal areas of party involvement or within the underground opposition before 1989, although of course some women were involved in both of these areas (Siklova, 1990). Often women's leadership in certain groups was kept hidden or unrecognised. Prior to 1989 national political participation was 'expected' but often very narrowly controlled. Given the tight party control of organisations few independent thinkers were able to emerge, except for those involved in oppositional groupings. The possibility of organising even a mother and toddler's group was generally denied, as officially 'the party' catered for all needs. The women's councils in existence within these countries were generally viewed as 'arms of the party' and as such very few women took notice of their activities outside the workplace, where some basic safeguards for women were maintained. Since 1989–90, the 'opening up' of politics within these societies could have meant that some real opportunities for change opened for some women.

The lack of strong women's organisations in defensive or proactive campaigns in the immediate aftermath of the first elections of 1990–1 meant that many women who needed to defend their jobs, childcare services and benefits were not well placed to do so. Nor were many women in a position to articulate their interests and needs. Yet from the early days women's groups and organisations throughout the region have been formed and those that became established are actively attempting to make interventions in various aspects of social and political change. Some such involvement as with housing committees, parent–teacher associations, health groups and peace and environmental movements had been developing in countries such as Poland and Hungary over the last ten to fifteen years, and in others they have been active since 1989. Women, also, are generally very active in the non-governmental organisational sector (NGOs). In the *Women and Democratisation* study it is noted that 'the high numbers of women participating in NGOs (rather than parties) was very apparent. Women did not regard such involvement in community and/or non-governmental work in such negative terms as public political involvement on the part of women' (Corrin *et al.*, 1996, p. 6). It is in this area, of extending notions of 'the political', that women's participation can be most fully appreciated.

In the area of formal political participation, one obvious feature of the changeover of power from the communist parties in Central and Eastern Europe has been the decline in the number of women at various levels of government. As has been noted, in the former regimes 'women' were often included on a quota basis and some women presumably joined 'the party' for the same careerist reasons as men (Szalai, 1991). Following the free elections in most countries of the region the numbers of women standing for office and becoming elected as MPs fell quite markedly, as Table 12.3 shows. By 1994–6

TABLE 12.3 *Percentages of women holding seats in parliaments, 1988–96*

	1988	*1991–94*	*1996*[*]
Albania	28.8	3.6	12.1
Bulgaria	21.0	8.5	13.3
Czechoslovakia/Czech Rep.	29.5	8.7	15.0/**
GDR/Germany	32.2	20.4	26.2/19.1
Hungary	20.9	7.0	11.4
Poland	20.2	13.5	13.0/13.0
Romania	34.4	3.6	7.0/2.1
Slovakia	–	–	14.7
Slovenia	–	–	7.8

* Percentages for Single or Lower Chambers are given in addition to 2nd Chamber/Senate where applicable.
** Not available.
Source: Adapted from Inter-Parliamentary Union (1997).

these percentages were beginning to rise again in most countries, with the biggest increase apparent in Germany. The two most dramatic drops in female representation were in two countries with the cruellest forms of dictatorship and the lowest standards of living – Romania and Albania. This may suggest that women in these two countries were more concerned than ever with everyday struggles for survival. In the 1996 elections the figures rose for both countries; however, the outbreak of violence in Albania in 1997 suggests that democratic gains are very vulnerable there and survival strategies are still very much a priority.

In comparative perspective the numbers of women involved at the parliamentary level of politics equalled or were above certain Western democracies such as in the lower chambers in the United Kingdom (1992 9.5) and France (1995 6.4) yet they fall far short of participation rates in Sweden (in 1994, 40.4) and Denmark (in the same year, 33) (IPU, 1997). It is apparent that in many parts of Central and Eastern Europe women are very active within political life in party offices, writing social policy documents, working in the trade unions and labour offices. Such women are vital activists within various 'civil society' contexts, as are those women who are involved in making 'everyday' decisions in their homes, at their children's schools, on hospital committees and in the local housing committees. Since 1990 more of these women's activities are becoming 'visible' to social researchers yet remain absent from much analysis. As Joanna Regulska has recently noted:

> As women's political activities are concentrated predominantly at the local level, outside of formal politics, the general lack of attention to the local scale – both in national debates and theoretical analysis – reinforced the structural rejection of women's contributions and shows how political change under transition is exclusionary. (Regulska, 1998, p. 2)

Social Change and Women's Organisation

In some contexts, such as that in Albania and Romania, the struggle for survival has been primary since 1990, with little available food, heat, or in some cases light. In Albania today the fear of chaos is apparent. The new democratic forces across the region had different beginnings and certainly where dictatorship was strong these societies are now restructuring from very disadvantaged positions. It is often women from so-called minority groups – such as Romas, minority ethnic women within larger national groups, and lesbians – who suffer most as they tend to be poorer, are less protected by social policy measures, and have less access to resources such as health care, education, and of course, jobs. As noted, many women in Central and Eastern Europe are also reeling under the impact of constitutional or legislative changes, such as in the abortion law, which have radically affected their lives.

Figures were often quoted about the so-called 'demographic crises' that structured the debate on women's childbearing and fertility. The needs of the state were often cited in this context as if it were a 'natural' expectation that women should control their childbearing only in certain ways and for particular reasons. Family ideology regarded the nuclear family model as the basic social unit and as a key source of social and economic stability. In this situation women's 'double burden' was very necessary to the smooth functioning of these systems. In Hungary and Poland arguments concerning the 'dying out' of the nation have resulted in women's preferences being given a very low priority. Awarded 'paper rights' to abortion (generally no safe, cheap alternatives were available) under the state-socialist regimes, women in several countries including Poland, Croatia, Slovakia and Hungary were having these 'rights' challenged or taken away from them by their newly formed postcommunist governments (Corrin, 1992).

Through local, national and international networking, however, women's groups and campaigns throughout Central and Eastern Europe were able to develop their bases and build up their skills and resources. Following a pan-European women's meeting of the Helsinki Citizens' Assembly (HCA) on Women and Reproductive Health, some of the groups gained funding from The Global Fund for Women and the Hungarian Feminist Group were able to undertake a media campaign with their funding. This first weekend conference held in Liblice, Czechoslovakia in December 1991 concentrated on women's reproductive health in Central and Eastern Europe. More than 60 women participated from at least thirteen different countries, including Albania, Bulgaria, Czechoslovakia, Hungary, Serbia and Slovenia. The workshops highlighted how decisions concerning women's reproductive rights were being made in changing political contexts and considered the options that were open to feminists to challenge some of these developments.

Hopes for more space for women to be heard and to participate in different ways in their societies have none the less been difficult to realise in most countries in the region. The point has been well made that 'What is now in place is another, perhaps softer, form of dictatorship. There is no democracy. Men still make the decisions' (Castle-Kanerova, 1992, p. 117). The coalition of church and state forces in some countries is an additional factor that seeks to constrain women's choices. In others the reality of war has been such that women's bodies have become the battleground in battles over territorial power (Corrin, 1996). Arguments have been proposed that the paternal state oppression of women is being replaced by the oppression of the market. Certainly, the very much increased availability of pornography and sexual advertising is harmful to women's interests as is the, sometimes fatal, trafficking in women.

It can be seen that women's active participation is attempting to effect change and this is apparent in the large variety of women's groups that have been forming over the last seven years, be they at the level of the Women's Studies Centres in Warsaw, Budapest and Sofia, or the various groups helping women abused by war and refugee women in Croatia, Bosnia and Serbia. The work of such groups was noted internationally when the International Women in Black awarded their 1994 Peace Price to the Centre for Women War Victims in Zagreb, the Zagreb Women's Lobby, Women in Black Belgrade and Medica Zenica (Boric in Corrin, 1996). There has, in parallel, been a growth in international conferences to which many women throughout the region have travelled. This is a change from the past when only 'official women' were allowed to represent different women's interests abroad.

In terms of women's resistance to male violence, research is being carried out at local and national levels by women's groups and organisations. In Poland the work of the Women's Committee of NGOs has highlighted the plight of many Polish women forced into prostitution. There is also a lack of information about the women (often from the former Soviet Union) who work in Polish sex clubs. The registration of prostitutes by police in Poland was ended in 1989 so that there are no official data on which to base any judgement as to the scale of the problem. It is in this context that the state interest is juxtaposed to that of social interests in certain women's situations:

> These spheres of social life seem to be beyond the state's scope of interest. Only women's and feminist organisation recognise prostitution and trafficking in women as a problem and have undertaken activities aimed at forcing the Polish government to comply with the United Nations' provisions counteracting violence against women. (Polish Committee of NGOs, 1995, p. 53)

As these are problems that women face all across Europe and elsewhere, responses to global criminality and resistance to women's oppression require the work of international feminists. In this context, networking takes on added significance.

Much has been written on women's self-organisation and feminist international links in this connection, from early anthologies on global sisterhood (Morgan, 1984) to recent collections about women building upon and challenging various conceptions of sisterhood (Renne, 1997; Ang-Lygate, Corrin and Henry, 1997). Lack of space limits full consideration here, so an example of work within the Women's Commission of the Helsinki Citizens' Assembly (HCA) is considered. This work over the 1990s has largely been coalition building, involving individual women and women's groups and networks from many countries across the continent. Some of those concerned had never met in a voluntary grouping of women, some had not encountered feminist ideas, some had not met women from 'Western' or 'Eastern' countries, yet all were able to discuss shared experiences and discover new ways of working together. At the first meeting and at the follow-up in Bratislava in March 1992, it was apparent that one of the primary sites of oppression for women was the violence they experienced at many different levels within their societies.

Another workshop on Issues of Violence Against Women in 1993 included women from Albania, Belgrade, Bosnia and Hercegovina, Bulgaria, Croatia, the Czech Republic, Hungary, Poland, Russia, and the Transcaucasus. The extent of the commonalities discovered over the course of the weekend was striking, both in East–West and in East–East comparisons. Many differences were also apparent at this time for those women from Central and Eastern European countries where their rapidly changing situations with the dismantling of older systems of government, rapid marketisation, the spread of pornography and increasing prostitution were being experienced in very telescoped and chaotic situations. Much discussion centred on approaching the 'authorities' – the police, legal structures and officials – and it was recognised that in many countries women do so with varying amounts of fear and suspicion. The most marked differences were in relation to the official recognition of male sexual violence as a crime. As Delino Fico noted in her report on Albania:

> How much protection do Albanian women ask of the State? Very little. Women are not educated to actively resist violence. No one has gone so far as to denounce violence officially. Unfortunately people do not even report cases of rape because they are afraid of revenge from gangsters, and feel better keeping it a secret, away from the eyes of others . . . There is no office or special centre to deal with reporting cases of violence or to provide counselling or protection. (HCA, 1993, p. 19)

Certainly the dire economic problems within Albania exacerbated this already grave situation for women. In comparing Bulgarian laws on violence against women with those of the Declaration on the Elimination of Violence against Women adopted at the United National Human Rights Conference in Vienna in 1993, Velina Todorova (a member of the Bulgarian Women Jurists' Association) noted that

> Bulgarian legislation cautiously approaches the identification and punishment of acts of violence, such as rape in the family. No legal protection is provided for battering, psychological violence, etc. On

the other hand, effective protection is made difficult by the court procedures envisaged in the Penal Code. A victim must lodge a complaint in cases where she has suffered moderate or light bodily injury. Yet complaints are often withdrawn at a later stage of the court proceedings because of pressure from the husband. Further violence ensues. (ibid., p. 39)

The increasing sexual harassment at work and trafficking in women are not touched upon in Bulgarian law and Velina Todorova also stresses that 'our country bears the consequences of an economic crisis and political instability which will inevitably compete with women's problems in attracting the attention of the public and legislative organs' (ibid., p. 40). Our discussion focused on ways in which we could establish women's agendas as part of national policy-making. Communication between women's groups on the local level into a national arena was considered important as were ways of networking internationally. It is clear from the work of Bily Kruh (White Circle of Safety) in the Czech Republic, NaNE (Women working with Women against Violence) in Hungary and the Rape Crisis Centre in St Petersburg that the need for research and education in the area of male violence is extensive in many societies across 'Europe' in which public political discussion of gendered power relations has long been absent (Corrin, 1996).

Conclusion

Attempts at 'equalising' women's situations with those of men during the state socialist period in these countries was largely structured by constitutional legislation and certain social policies concerning work opportunities. This involved women's entry into the national economy but not their relative withdrawal from the domestic economy. Women's rights to work were stressed alongside their duties as mothers. Experience has confirmed that structural changes must be accompanied by some form of cultural revolution aimed at changing attitudes, in order to eliminate gendered power imbalances and open up domestic opportunities and responsibilities. That caring for children can be a pleasure denied to men has not been actively considered in terms of extending and exploring notions of masculinity and femininity.

On issues to do with establishing political agendas which reflect and voice women's concerns, ensuring the safety of refugees, creating safe reproductive health conditions, resisting male violence against women and improving certain social, political and economic situations, women across all of Europe are working in many different ways, locally, nationally and internationally, for positive changes in the lives of women, children and men.

Many questions of this kind remain unanswered within the Central and Eastern Europe countries. Whilst certain groups such as entrepreneurs and some professionals have been able to create new opportunities in the new market conditions, others on fixed incomes, vulnerable groups such as older women, Roma women and women managing household budgets on dwindling resources are suffering greatly in these transitional times. The legacy of 'security' from former times means that poverty and long-term unemployment have direct negative psychological implications for many people. Meanwhile, some powerful groups are considering attempts at organising their societies along ethnic or religious lines, which could lead to great upheaval and even more dangers for vulnerable groups. Despite a more participatory social and political situation in some countries the reality of nationalism, racism and war has radically affected people's lives. In such situations the ability and willingness of different groups of women to organise towards progressive change become vitally important as a source of resistance to nationalist violence, and in establishing other ways of living and working together in our societies.

PART FOUR

Central and Eastern Europe and the Wider World

13

Patterns of International Politics

ADRIAN HYDE-PRICE

Mars, the god of war, has cast a long and terrible shadow over the lands between Russia and Germany. For centuries, these borderlands have been ravaged by marauding armies as contending empires have clashed in an incessant struggle for power and territory. All too often in Central and Eastern Europe, violence has been the midwife of history. When, after centuries of rule by multinational empires, the peoples of this region gained their sovereignty and independence at the end of the Great War, they did so through force of arms and internecine conflict. As the titanic struggle of the European great powers reached its bloody denouement in 1918, a wave of smaller – but no less terrible – wars gripped Central and Eastern Europe. 'The war of the giants has ended', wrote Winston Churchill, 'the wars of the pygmies begin' (quoted in Davies, 1996, p. 926).

During the cold war, Central and Eastern Europe was dominated by just one giant – the USSR. The Soviet Union used its military and political hegemony to suppress conflicts between the smaller states under its sway. With the end of the cold war between the superpower giants, some have feared that wars between the 'pygmies' might once again shatter the fragile peace of the region. A number of influential neo-realists have indeed suggested that the end of cold war bipolarity will mean an increasingly intense and brutal struggle for power between competing states in an anarchical multipolar system, 'with the possibility of war always in the background' (Mearsheimer, 1995, p. 9; see also Waltz, 1993). Yet with the partial exception of the former Yugoslavia and parts of the former Soviet Union, the end of the cold war has not been followed by a recurrence of wars between the pygmies, nor have the great powers resumed their traditional

Realpolitik machinations in Central and Eastern Europe; differences of interest and clashes of identity persist, but the recourse to armed force is less prevalent than in the past.

The aim of this chapter is to analyse the evolving nature of international politics in Central and Eastern Europe, and to reflect upon the implications of the changing patterns of cooperation and conflict in this region. It begins by considering the changing geopolitics of the region. It then assesses the significance of new regional forms of multilateral cooperation and international organisation in areas such as East-Central Europe, the Baltic and the Black Sea. This is followed by an evaluation of the significance for the international politics of the region of the idea of the 'return to Europe' – a notion which has provided the *Leitmotiv* of domestic and foreign policy reform in most of the new democracies in Central and Eastern Europe. Given that many of the hopes and expectations of the new democracies are focused on the European Union, the prospects and implications of the eastern enlargement of the EU will be briefly assessed. This in turns leads on to a consideration of the changing security agenda in the region, along with a critical assessment of the issue of NATO's eastern enlargement. The chapter concludes by reflecting on the evolving nature of international politics in the lands between Germany and Russia.

The Changing Geopolitics of Central and Eastern Europe

Napoleon Bonaparte once asserted that 'the policy of a state lies in its geography'. Few would endorse such sweeping epistemological claims today. None the less, whilst geography alone does not determine the fate of nations, it does provide an important context within which diplomatic exchanges and strategic calculations are made. A consideration of 'geopolitics' (as the study of the interaction between geographical space and politics has become known) can therefore help shed light on the development of international politics in Central and Eastern Europe.

In many ways, geography has not been kind to the peoples of this region. Whilst the mountains and rivers of the Balkans have provided defendable frontiers for empires and dynasties through the centuries, the North European plain offers few natural barriers to invasion. Indeed, the name of one of the region's largest states – Poland – is derived from the ancient Slavic word 'pole', meaning 'field'. The only significant Alpine-type fold mountains in Central Europe are the Carpathians, which sweep southwards through Slovakia and parts of northern Hungary into Romania. However, they have historically provided little protection from invading armies from either east or west. Given the absence of major mountain ranges or waterways, the North European plain has historically provided an avenue for invading armies, either from east to west (as with the waves of invading Asiatic nomads in the early history of the continent), or from west to east (the prime examples being Charles XII of Sweden, Napoleon and Hitler).

Central and Eastern Europe's spatial location and physical topology have given it a distinctive geopolitical function. Historically the region has constituted a 'crush zone' between Christian Europe and the Eurasian heartland – in other words, a 'large, strategically located region that is occupied by a number of conflicting states and is caught between the conflicting interests of the adjoining great powers' (Cohen, 1973, p. 85). Located on the cultural faultlines between Europe and Asia, this vast swathe of territory to the east of the Elbe and the Danube rivers has historically been perceived as the borderlands of European civilisation. In the time of the Roman Empire, the Rhine and Danube rivers provided defendable natural borders, whilst the lands to the east acted as a kind of buffer zone. With the emergence of medieval Christendom, the kingdoms of Poland, Hungary and Bohemia acquired a distinctive role as the bulwark of European civilisation against perceived threats from Asia and the East. This perception has deeply marked the peoples of the region. As the then Polish prime minister, Tadeusz Mazowiecki, said in January 1990, 'The idea of being the "ramparts of civilisation" and, by the same token, of Europe, has remained alive in Poland throughout three centuries' (Rotfeld and Stützle, 1991, p. 131).

Traditionally, therefore, the peoples of this region have not enjoyed a very propitious geopolitical location. Yet with the end of the 'short twentieth century', their geopolitical role may be changing (O'Loughlin and Wusten, 1993). As new patterns of global economic, political and societal exchange reshape the international system, Central and Eastern Europe's historical role as a 'crush zone' appears to be receding. The end of the cold war has revealed the extent to which deeper processes of globalisation and complex interdependence have been steadily transforming the structural dynamics of the global system in the late twentieth century. In this new context, Central and Eastern Europe's geopolitical role has begun to change. The region is already beginning to function as a 'gateway region' within the international system. Saul Cohen, a contemporary theorist of geopolitics, has defined gateway regions as those which stimulate socio-economic and political interaction; act as a link in an increasingly interdependent world; and 'facilitate the boundaries of accommodation'. Cohen argues that Central and Eastern Europe is increasingly acting as a gateway region, 'fully open to economic forces from East and West'. He also suggests that '[a] gateway region has "hinges" – key states that take the lead as economic and social mediators in opening up the region in both directions' (Cohen, 1994, pp. 38–46).

As regards Central and Eastern Europe, there may well be not one but several hinges: the Visegrad countries will provide as a hinge between Germany and Eastern Europe; the Baltic states are already functioning as hinge between the Scandinavian countries and Russia; and Slovenia may increasingly provide a hinge between the Danubian lands of *Mitteleuropa* and the Balkans. The lands between Germany and Russia have long been the cultural, economic and political crossroads between east and west, Europe and Asia. The influences of Byzantium, Ottoman Turkey, Orthodox Christianity, Latin Christendom, western Asia and Nordic-German culture have all competed and fused in this regional European 'melting pot'. It is therefore not too fanciful to suggest that in an increasingly interdependent, globalising international system, Central and Eastern Europe will increasingly come to function as a gateway region facilitating 'the transfer of economic innovation from west to east and, ultimately, the reverse' (Cohen, 1994, p. 46).

The Pluralisation of Central and Eastern Europe

During the cold war years, Soviet hegemony imposed a superficial uniformity on much of Central and Eastern Europe. Soviet control was based on two institutions – the Warsaw Pact and the Council for Mutual Economic Assistance (CMEA). Whilst formally these were multilateral organisations, in reality Moscow exerted its influence through a series of bilateral relations with individual national communist elites in the Warsaw Pact countries. When this proved inadequate, Moscow had the ultimate sanction of military intervention. The effect of this was to suppress indigenous regional or sub-regional conflicts (for example, between Hungarians and Romanians, or Poles and Lithuanians) in the interests of Soviet-imposed unity in the face of the perceived 'Western imperialist threat'. The Soviet system thus epitomised what has been termed superpower 'overlay' on the cold war European security 'complex' (Buzan 1991, p. 220). In other words, indigenous security dynamics in this regional security complex were subordinated to the larger security concerns of the overlaying power – the USSR.

The end of the cold war has both removed superpower 'overlay' from Europe and led to the disintegration of the Soviet 'inner empire'. The result of these twin developments has been profound and far-reaching. Central and Eastern Europe has emerged as a much more heterogeneous and diverse region within the global system, with new international actors, more volatile relationships and complex patterns of regional cooperation and conflict. In this fluid and somewhat unstable international environment, the potential for a downward spiral of misperception, misinformation and mistrust is considerable – particularly in the Balkans and the former Soviet Union (Dawisha and Parrott 1994, p. 195).

Four key developments have generated this new, more pluralist pattern of international politics in Central and Eastern Europe. The first is the lack of effective international structures for multilateral cooperation and integration. The disintegration of the USSR, combined with the break-up of the Warsaw Pact and the CMEA, has created a host of new states but a dearth of multilateral structures. In this situation, the institutions and structures of international society remain relatively weak and underdeveloped in the region. Consequently inter-state relations are still considerably swayed by *Realpolitik* calculations and the search for a stable regional balance of power. In the Balkans and much of Eastern Europe, it has been argued, 'a traditional anarchic state system' continues to function in which 'the issue of force is still on the agenda in relations between states' (Miall, 1993, p. 22). This contrasts sharply with Western Europe, where the existence of robust institutions for multilateral cooperation and integration, combined with stable democracies and a high degree of societal interdependence, has created a zone of stable peace in which the balance of power no longer functions (Cooper, 1996).

The second key development is the emergence of an independent and sovereign Ukraine. This constitutes 'the most significant geostrategic development in Europe since the end of the Second World War' (Allison, 1993, p. 36). With a population of over 51 million, rich agricultural land, significant industrial potential and substantial military assets, Ukraine is almost bound to be a major power in the region. Its geostrategic location is also significant in that it stands at the heart of the traditional 'borderlands' between Russia and Latin Christendom (Garnett, 1997). Ukraine's ability to sustain its independence and carve out a distinctive foreign policy role for itself in the shadow of its large and intimidating Slavic neighbour constitutes one of the key strategic questions facing Central and Eastern Europe as a whole (Bukkvoll 1997). Since his accession to power in July 1994, Ukrainian President Leonid Kuchma has pursued a dual policy of cultivating a 'special partnership' with Russia, whilst simultaneously fostering closer links with Europe and the West (Sherr, 1996). Given that for the Ukraine the road to Europe lies through Poland, Ukraine has also sought to cultivate a 'strategic partnership' with Warsaw (Brzezinski, 1993).

The third important development is that with the break-up of the USSR, Czechoslovakia and Yugoslavia, Central and Eastern Europe is a much more pluralist and heterogenous region. There are now many more states in the borderlands between Russia and Germany than ever before. This gives the governments of Central and Eastern Europe greater scope for diplomatic and political manoeuvring. It also reduces the geopolitical saliency of the 'giants' in the region. For the Visegrad countries of East-Central Europe this means that they no longer share a border with Russia – with the partial exception of Poland, which borders on Kaliningrad, a thin strip of territory cut off from the rest of the Russian Federation by Lithuania and Belarus. Russia itself is now back in the borders it had roughly three centuries ago, before the 1654 Treaty of Union between Russia and Ukraine. This geopolitical diversity has important strategic and political consequences: as one analyst has noted, 'the multipolarisation of the continent, with Germany and Russia as the dominant powers in the East, and with an unprecedented number of smaller independent states, makes possible a wide variety of potential alliances' (Mueller, 1995, p. 38).

The fourth distinctive feature of the international politics of Central and Eastern Europe is the prevalence of national minorities and arbitrarily drawn borders. Across the region, there are a series of potential controversies over minority rights and unresolved *irredenta*. In former Yugoslavia and Moldova, this has led to armed conflict. Elsewhere it has generated inter-communal tension, political controversy and diplomatic wrangling – notably in the Baltic states, and in those countries with significant Magyar minorities such as Slovakia, Romania and Serbia (Ludanyi, 1996). Since 1989, issues of nationalism and ethnicity have assumed a growing importance on the international agenda (Gärtner, 1997; Walker, 1993). At the same time, questions of minority rights are increasingly regarded as a matter of international concern, rather than simply being a domestic political issue.

Regional Cooperation: East-Central Europe, the Baltic and the Black Sea

The political pluralisation of the lands between Germany and Russia has created a more complex web of international relations in the region. In this more polycentric international system, traditional patterns of regional cooperation and conflict have re-emerged in a number of areas. In the Balkans and the Caucasus, deep-seated historical animosities have combined with more contemporary resentments to ignite bitter conflicts. Elsewhere in Central and Eastern Europe, however, historical patterns of regional cooperation have re-emerged. While drawing their inspiration from historical precedents, these represent an attempt to heal the East–West divide and develop new forms of cooperation and integration. This is most clearly apparent in three areas: East-Central Europe, the Baltic Sea region and around the Black Sea.

In East-Central Europe, Poland, the Czech Republic, Hungary and Slovakia have since 1990 developed multilateral forms of cooperation designed to facilitate their joint return to Europe (Hyde-Price, 1996). The leaders of what were originally three East-Central European countries – Poland, Hungary and Czechoslovakia – first met in Bratislava in April 1990 to exchange views on the 'new European order'. In February 1991, they met again in Visegrad and agreed a 'Declaration of Cooperation on the Road to European Integration'. This did not create any organisational structures, nor did it involve a new military alliance. Rather, it sought to develop more limited forms of multilateral cooperation, ministerial consultation and policy harmonisation. Whilst the Visegrad forum has enjoyed only limited successes in these areas, it has facilitated practical economic cooperation through the creation of the Central European Free Trade Association (CEFTA). The aim of the CEFTA agreement, which was signed in December 1992, was to gradually remove barriers to trade in order to create a free trade zone of 65 million people. By creating a more liberal trading regime, CEFTA, which now includes Slovenia and Romania, has provided a major fillip to economic growth in the region (Balicka 1996). One indication of its success is that Bulgaria, Ukraine, Lithuania and Latvia have all applied to join, while Russia is keen to develop closer cooperation with CEFTA.

The second important area of multilateral cooperation in Central and Eastern Europe is in the Baltic Sea region. There have been a number of initiatives to develop regional cooperation in this area, many of them harking back to the medieval Hanseatic League. The most important multilateral initiative in the Baltic since the end of the cold war has been the creation of the Council of Baltic Sea States (CBSS). This is of particular interest because it brings together the wealthy and social-democratic countries of Scandinavia (Sweden, Norway, Finland and Denmark); Germany, the pivotal power in *Mitteleuropa*; Poland, the key country in East-Central Europe and a prospective member of both NATO and the EU; the three Baltic states (Lithuania, Latvia and Estonia); and Russia, Eastern Europe's regional great power. The CBSS was created in March 1992, and has two primary concerns: environmental protection, and the expansion of trade around the Baltic. More recently, the countries of the Baltic have become concerned about transnational crime, and have looked to the CBSS as a forum within which to coordinate crime-prevention policy and cross-border police cooperation (Huldt and Johannessen, 1997).

The Black Sea Economic Cooperation (BSEC) is the third significant regional grouping in Central and Eastern Europe. Founded in June 1992, it brings together eleven countries: Turkey, Romania, Bulgaria, Greece and Albania, along with six Soviet successor states, Russia, Ukraine, Georgia, Moldova, Azerbaijan and Armenia. The BSEC is a nascent trading group which seeks to lay the political foundations for functional economic cooperation in a region with a potential market of 400 million. The prime mover in the BSEC is Turkey. Turkey aspires to become the entrepot for energy and raw material exports from the former Soviet republics to the west. It also hopes to develop a strategic relationship with Russia, and to demonstrate its value to the EU by providing leadership along the southern periphery of the European continent (Sperling and Kirchner, 1997, pp. 139–40). However, given the deep-seated historical animosities in this conflict-prone area, and the fragile domestic political situation in many of the states in this region, developing regional cooperation will not be easy. 'Like the terminal moraine of a glacier,' Neal Ascherson has written, 'the Black Sea shore is a place where the detrius of human migrations and invasions has been deposited for more than four thousand years'. It is therefore a region deeply scarred by 'the mysteries of nationalism and identity, with all their shameless games with shadows and mirrors and their enormous creative power' (Ascherson, 1995, p. 10).

The end of the cold war has thus generated a variety of forms of regional cooperation. In addition to the Visegrad group, the CBSS and the BSEC, there is Alpe-Adria, the Central European Initiative and the Euroregions – organisations which seek primarily to stimulate cross-border cooperation between local authorities and economic enterprises. Such regional structures – which have been dubbed the 'Cinderellas of European security' (Bailes, 1997) – are significant in four respects. First, they are a manifestation of the process of regional differentiation and integration which has become evident throughout Europe since the fall of the Berlin Wall. With the end of cold war bipolarity, new patterns of regional cooperation have emerged, often drawing sustenance from historical precedents, and building on a shared sense of regional identity. Second, they reflect the multi-dimensionality of the integration process in Europe. Whilst the EU has long been at the forefront of European integration, the integration process itself has generated wider forms of cooperation and multilateralism. These have involved a variety of mechanisms for intergovernmental consultation, policy harmonisation and functional cooperation, often at a local and regional level. Third, participation in regional organisations provides the new postcommunist democracies with valuable experience of multilateral cooperation. By experiencing the potential benefits of mutual compromise and consensus, participation in regional bodies constitutes a 'necessary transitional step towards full membership of the European Union' (Weclawowicz, 1996, p. 12). Finally, they are a prime example of what have been called 'international regimes', that is 'sets of explicit or implicit principles, norms, rules and decision-making procedures around which actor expectations converge' (Krasner, 1983). Whilst these regimes do not involve any significant pooling of sovereignty, they do change the context within which states act and define their interests. They can help build consensus and identify areas of common interest between states, and also facilitate a process of socialisation for elite groups. In this way, they contribute to the consolidation of an international society of states in the region – a theme to which we will return at the end of this chapter.

'Returning to Europe': The International Dimension

One of the key factors in determining the post-cold war pattern of international politics in Central and Eastern Europe is the expressed desire of many of the new democracies in the region to 'return to Europe'. Although this concept remains somewhat amorphous and loosely defined, it has a number of important policy implications.

To begin with, it demonstrates the magnetic attraction of the West European societal 'model'. The democratic revolutions of 1989 were largely inspired by the West European example of liberal-democratic government, welfare societies, social market economies and multi-lateral cooperation. This model has provided the template for the political and economic reforms which have been transforming the region since 1989. While the end result of the reform process is likely to be the emergence of *sui generis* forms of political and economic organisation rather than simple replicas of West European models (Kaldor and Vejvoda, 1997, p. 80), the West still has enormous political and normative influence over developments in the region. This 'soft power' gives Western governments and multilateral organisations a significant degree of leverage over the international politics of Central and Eastern Europe.

Secondly, the commitment to 'rejoin Europe' reflects a changing conception of identity in the region. Given their desire to be seen as 'European', many of the new postcommunist democracies have defined their national identity in terms compatible with what they regard as 'European' norms and values. As Batt (1996) makes clear in her analysis of Slovak–Hungarian relations, the precise meaning and content of these 'European norms' is widely contested. None the less, they are generally considered to include a commitment to democracy and human rights, liberalism, tolerance of national minorities, the peaceful resolution of disputes and a willingness to reach compromise and consensus – all of which have been codified in the documents and declarations of the OSCE (the Organisation for Security and Co-operation in Europe, formerly the CSCE), and in the conventions and protocols of the Council of Europe.

This changed conception of national identity, combined with the political influence of Western governments and organisations, has had a significant impact on the international politics of the region. Above all, it has helped strengthen a commitment to the peaceful resolution of international disputes, along with respect for human rights, democratic government and the rule of law. This can be seen from two examples. The first is Hungarian–Slovak disputes over minority rights and the Danube dams. These two issues have soured bilateral relations since the end of the cold war, and have on occasions threatened to generate violent forms of conflict. However, given the desire of both states to join the EU and develop closer relations with the West in general, they have striven to resolve their disputes through legal and peaceful channels (Reisch, 1996, p. 459; Samson, 1997). A similar commitment to the peaceful resolution of conflicts has been evident in the Baltic states, where problems of national minorities (of Russians in Latvia and Estonia, and Poles in Lithuania) have threatened to destabilise regional peace and security. However, these tensions have been successfully managed, and to a large extent defused, by the constructive intervention of the Scandinavian countries, the EU, the Council of Europe and the OSCE's High Commissioner for National Minorities.

Thirdly, the notion of returning to Europe expresses a desire to join Western organisations and multilateral institutions. One of the defining features of late-twentieth-century European politics is the existence of a dense network of international organisations, which has facilitated the emergence of novel forms of multilateral cooperation and multilevel governance (Ruggie, 1993; Young, 1994). For the new democracies in Central and Eastern Europe, 'returning to Europe' entails joining this dense institutional matrix. All of them have sought membership of organisations like the Council of Europe, and have striven to develop closer links with the EU (through 'Europe Agreements'), with NATO (through the Euro-Atlantic Partnership Council, formerly the North Atlantic Cooperation Council, and the Partnership for Peace scheme) and with the OECD. However, the key prize remains membership of the EU. Membership of the European Union is widely regarded as symbolising their return to the European community of nations. It would constitute the consummation of their foreign and domestic policy reforms since 1989, and is seen as providing the only reliable guarantee of democratic consolidation, economic wellbeing and national security.

Widening the membership of the European Union to the East is a process which will have a series of profound and far-reaching implications: for the new members themselves; for the policies and decision-making processes of the EU; and for the wider constitution of European order. For the new democracies in the East, membership of the EU will involve a significant pooling of sovereignty and a further penetration of their societies by West European ideas, values and economic interests. Having only recently recovered their autonomy and independence, this may generate some political disquiet. As regards the EU, Eastern enlargement will necessitate major changes to institutions and decision-making processes designed originally for a community of six. It will also require major changes to the EU's two largest budgetary policies: the Common Agricultural Policy (CAP) and the Structural Funds. The consequence of this may well be the emergence of a significantly different EU based on novel forms of flexibility and differentiated integration (Hyde-Price, 1996, pp. 197–205).

In terms of European order, the original EEC (and its forerunner, the European Coal and Steel Community) was designed as a peace project to make war structurally impossible between former enemies. It was also geographically limited to the West European lands of the former Romano-German Carolingian kingdom (Krasuski, 1994, p. 82). An enlarged Union of up to twenty-six members function will not only be based on very different principles of integration and multilateral cooperation, it will also play a different political and security role in a Europe no longer divided into East and West. This will have significant consequences for the future constitution of European order, and introduces a new element of fluidity and uncertainty into European politics.

This brings us to one final reflection on the notion of the 'return to Europe' – its long-term implications for Europe as a whole. One of the most misleading but pervasive illusions generated by the end of the cold war was that the 'return to Europe' of the new postcommunist democracies would simply entail the 'Westernisation' of Central and Eastern Europe. It is now clear that this is not going to be the case. Not only are *sui generis* forms of political and economic organisation emerging in Central and Eastern Europe, but the Eastern enlargement of Western organisations like the EU and NATO will inevitably lead to far-reaching changes in these organisations. An enlarged EU of up to twenty-six members will clearly be significantly different from the EU of today. As regards NATO, enlargement of the Alliance will provide a catalyst for far-reaching reforms of its structure, strategy and doctrines, whilst at the same time making it even harder to reach consensus in a larger and more geostrategically diverse alliance. The return to Europe of the postcommunist democracies will therefore transform the purpose and functioning of the multilateral organisations which have provided the institutional foundations for postwar European order. As EU Commissioner Hans van den Broek has observed, 'Enlargement to the east is in the very first place a political issue relating to security and stability on our continent' (*The Guardian*, 5 November 1994).

Security in Central and Eastern Europe

The search for security has been a perennial concern of the peoples of this geopolitically exposed region. In the past, there have been two primary sources of insecurity in the region: the *Realpolitik* machinations of the regional 'giants', Russia and Germany; and the ethnonational conflicts which have bedevilled Central and Eastern Europe. Security policy has focused on the prevention of regional inter-state conflict, and has tended to be defined in predominantly military terms.

With the end of the cold war and the removal of superpower 'overlay' from the European security system, the countries of Central and Eastern Europe have been given the opportunity of framing anew their national security and defence policies. They are doing so in the context of a fundamentally changed international environment. To begin with, Europe itself has changed. Whereas in the past – notably in the inter-war years – regional security was determined by the wider balance of power in Europe as a whole, in the late twentieth century a new environment has emerged. A pluralistic security community has developed in Western Europe and the transatlantic area in which war, and the threat of war, no longer plays a role in relations between states. This reflects the consolidation of stable democracies in Western Europe, the existence of robust forms of institutionalised multilateral cooperation and a myriad of ties of economic and societal interdependence (Hyde-Price, 1991, pp. 116–19). The search for security in Central and Eastern Europe – which remains a primordial concern of the states in the region – thus takes place in a very different external environment from that of the nineteenth or early twentieth centuries.

At the same time, the character of the regional giants has changed. Germany is now a stable democracy anchored in a network of multilateral institutions, and no longer constitutes a security threat to Central and Eastern Europe. Whilst Germany undoubtedly exerts a powerful economic and political influence in the lands to its east, its role is that of a benign hegemon (Katzenstein, 1997).

Developments in Russia are more ambiguous and far less encouraging (Baranovsky, 1997). On the one hand, Russian troops have been withdrawn from Central and most of Eastern Europe, and Moscow is party to a series of important arms control agreements. Russia has also cooperated with the West on the UN Security Council, signed the Partnership for Peace agreement, and worked alongside NATO in Bosnia. More importantly for the future, Russia has embarked on the rocky road of democratisation, and has committed itself to respect human rights and the rule of law. On the other hand, Russia today is the 'sick man of Europe': its economy is in dire straits, it is politically unstable, its military is disgruntled and its national identity is uncertain and contested. The Russian foreign policy elite also remains wedded to old-fashioned *Realpolitik* conceptions. These less benign developments have created considerable unease in the postcommunist countries on Russia's western border.

A new security agenda has thus emerged in Central and Eastern Europe. One key issue is whether Russia will seek to build a cooperative relationship with its western neighbours, or whether it will seek to carve out for itself a sphere of interest in Central and Eastern Europe. The litmus tests will be Russian policy towards Ukraine, the Baltic Republics and East-Central Europe (Blackwill and Karaganov, 1994; Shearman, 1995). Yet while Russia's future constitutes the biggest unknown factor facing European security today, the contemporary regional security agenda is less focused on the behaviour of the regional giants than in the past. Instead, it is more concerned with internal issues, many of which are non-military in character. These include ethno-national conflict; large-scale economically motivated migration; a reversion to authoritarianism in one of more of the new democracies; transnational criminal organisations; drug-smuggling; economic collapse; and environmental degradation.

In the heady and optimistic days which followed the fall of the Berlin Wall, many of the new democratic elites in Central and Eastern Europe hoped that the old bloc alliances could be replaced by a collective security system based on an institutionalised and strengthened Conference on Security and Cooperation in Europe. The more ambitious schemes for a CSCE-based collective security system were, however, quietly discarded given opposition from most NATO countries, and the failure of the CSCE to respond adequately to either Soviet repression against Lithuania in January 1991 or the slide towards war in Yugoslavia. None the less, a broad pan-European consensus has coalesced around the institutionalisation of the CSCE and its transformation into a framework for a more cooperative system of European security. At the Paris CSCE Summit in November 1990, the decision was taken to transform the CSCE from a means of peacefully managing the East–West conflict into the institutional basis of a post-cold war cooperative security system. This summit adopted the Paris Charter for a New Europe which marked the formal end of the cold war and codified the new pan-European consensus on human rights, democratic government and market economics.

The newly institutionalised CSCE was further developed and refined at summit meetings in Helsinki (1992), Budapest (1994) and Lisbon (1996). Today the Organisation for Security and Cooperation in Europe – as the CSCE has been called since the end of 1994 – fulfils five valuable functions in Europe's post-cold war cooperative security system. First, it provides a forum for promoting and codifying common standards, values and norms of behaviour, particularly in the area of human rights and the peaceful resolution of conflicts; second, it offers a series of mechanisms for the continuous monitoring of human rights, both for individuals and for national minorities; thirdly, it acts as a forum for promoting military transparency, arms controls and confidence- and security-building measures; fourth, it provides a framework for pan-European multilateral diplomacy across a comprehensive range of issues; and finally, it is developing instruments for preventive diplomacy, conflict avoidance and crisis management.

With the failure of proposals for a CSCE-based pan-European collective security system, other ideas were put forward. Among them were calls for regional security cooperation in Central and Eastern Europe (Cottey, 1995, pp. 17–19). The idea underlying such proposals was that a union of the small and medium-sized states in the region would increase their collective weight in the international system and provide more effective resistance to the hegemonic ambitions of the regional giants – specifically Russia. In any such arrangement, Ukraine – given its size and location – would be the central pillar (Bleiere, 1995, p. 83). Several ideas for such a regional security grouping have been floated. Former Polish president Lech Walesa has spoken of the creation of a 'NATO-2'; former Belarus president

Shushkevich has proposed the creation of a 'belt of neutral states' in Central and Eastern Europe; the Lithuanian and Ukrainian presidents have jointly suggested the creation of a Baltic to Black Sea security zone; former Ukrainian president Leonid Kravchuk has proposed the creation of a 'Central and East European Space of Stability and Security'; and Belarus has called for the creation of a nuclear-weapon-free zone in Central and Eastern Europe (Prawitz, 1997). None of these plans has come to anything: the countries of the region remain too divided to consider giving robust mutual security commitments; the East-Central European countries have been unwilling to do anything that would detract from their return to Europe; and the Russians have made known their hostility to any such regional grouping from which they are excluded.

Consequently, since about 1993–4, the security debate in the region has focused almost exclusively on the issue of NATO enlargement. The Visegrad countries were the first to seek NATO security guarantees and membership, but now there are eleven declared and accepted candidates for membership of the Alliance. NATO's initial response to this courting was cool. At first the Alliance simply offered multilateral consultation through the North Atlantic Cooperation Council (NACC). As pressure for enlargement mounted, NATO proposed the Partnership for Peace (PfP) scheme, which offered functional military cooperation and political dialogue between NATO and individual partner countries, but no prospect of membership.

By late 1994, however, NATO enlargement was firmly on the agenda. The Alliance's change of heart was largely brought about by a shift in US policy. For a variety of domestic political reasons, the Clinton administration has decided to make the issue of NATO enlargement a test of its 'leadership' in Europe (Rudolf, 1996). The Germans, who want to see their eastern borders stabilised, have enthusiastically endorsed this, as has the UK government, given its concern to preserve an active US role in Europe. The Alliance formally signalled its willingness to enlarge with the publication in September 1995 of the *NATO Study on Enlargement*. Subsequently, at the historic July 1997 NATO summit in Madrid, the decision to accept three new members (Poland, Hungary and the Czech Republic) in 1999 was taken.

In order to assuage some of Russia's legitimate security concerns and prevent a serious deterioration in relations with Moscow, NATO has taken a number of significant steps. First, it has declared that no nuclear weapons or foreign troops will be deployed on the territory of the new NATO members. Second, it has signalled a willingness to renegotiate the Conventional Forces in Europe (CFE) Treaty, particularly as regards troop levels in the 'flanking' zones. Third, a Russia–NATO Founding Act was signed in May 1997 creating the Joint Permanent Council, a forum for regular consultations and discussions between Moscow and the Sixteen. This first met in September 1997, and is designed to provide a means for Russia to be included in substantive discussions on European security developments without giving Moscow a right to veto NATO operations or policies. Finally, a Europe-Atlantic Partnership Council was created to provide a pan-European multilateral forum for discussions on security matters. The EAPC, which brings together the 16 NATO members and 26 partner countries, met for the first time at Heads of State and Government level in July 1997.

NATO's Eastern enlargement is the most controversial and divisive decision taken in the post-cold war era, and will have profound implications for security and international relations in Central and Eastern Europe. Its advocates argue that enlargement is not directed against anyone, but is rather designed to project stability and peaceful cooperation into the former communist East. Madeleine Albright, the US Secretary of State, has argued that 'the new NATO can do for Europe's east what the old NATO did for Europe's west: vanquish old hatreds, promote integration, create a secure environment for prosperity, and deter violence in the region where two world wars, and the cold war began' (Albright, 1997, p. 22). Not to expand NATO, it is argued, would leave NATO increasingly irrelevant to the changed geostrategic situation in Europe, and lead to disappointment and frustration in those new democracies seeking to 'rejoin Europe' (Asmus, Kugler and Larrabee, 1995).

Critics of NATO's Eastern enlargement argue that it is a policy which is, at best, an irrelevance, and at worst, a mistake (Brown, 1995; Ruggie, 1996). To begin with, they argue, NATO membership does not address the most pressing security concerns of the new democracies. As a military alliance designed for collective territorial defence, NATO is not particularly relevant to the current security challenges of the East Central Europeans – which include large-scale migration, economic dislocation, political unrest, nationalist agitation, and so on. Second, the sad irony is that enlargement may well produce the very insecurity it is designed to avert. It may well lead to a Russian military build-up in Kaliningrad and the Kola peninsula; to renewed Russian pressure on Ukraine and the Baltic Republics; to more intense Russian pressures for security integration within the CIS; and to 'the worst nightmare of the post-Cold War era: Weimar Russia' (Mandelbaum 1996a, p. 62). Finally, enlargement will not achieve its stated goals. The official NATO study on enlargement argues that it is a policy designed to 'reinforce the tendency towards integration and cooperation in Europe', in order to overcome the division of the continent. Yet, a selective opening up of the Alliance to the East-Central Europeans will create new lines of division in Central and Eastern Europe, and exacerbate the security dilemmas facing those states excluded from NATO membership. Thus expanding NATO – a collective defence alliance – may well undermine cooperative security in Europe as a whole, and generate renewed divisions in Central and Eastern Europe.

Whatever its merits or demerits, NATO is now committed to opening up to a first wave of new members in 1999. Alternative policies, such as concentrating on EU expansion ahead of NATO expansion (Hyde-Price, 1996, p. 252), or trying to develop a Nordic-style alignment balance (see Mueller, 1995, pp. 57–63, and Sherr, 1996, p. 55), have been ignored in the push for early NATO enlargement (the exception here being the three Baltic Republics, particularly Estonia, which has been offered EU membership but not NATO membership). If the enlargement process were now to be derailed for any reason, the consequences would be severe: it would shatter the confidence of the East-Central Europeans in the West and cast doubt on the value of 'returning to Europe'; it would undermine the US commitment to European security; and it would encourage hardliners in Moscow to believe that bellicose posturing and geopolitical calculations can be effective.

None the less, whilst NATO enlargement has now become a *fait accompli*, it is important to bear in mind that NATO can at best only make a partial contribution to security in Central and Eastern Europe. The contemporary security agenda is primarily concerned with non-military issues, with which NATO is ill-equipped to deal. Security in the region depends first and foremost on democratic consolidation, successful economic reform and managing ethno-national diversity. The organisations best suited to addressing these needs are the EU, the Council of Europe and the OSCE – not NATO. Building a durable peace order in Europe will be a difficult and long-term process involving both the consolidation of a pan-European cooperative security system (involving Russia and other CIS states), and the gradual eastwards expansion of the transatlantic security system (based on institutionalised cooperation between stable democracies). In policy terms, this means finding a solution to the dilemma of integrating the East-Central Europeans into NATO and the EU, while maintaining a cooperative relationship with Russia. The key task facing the future of European security is therefore to find new ways to involve Russia and its neighbours in Central and Eastern Europe in a network of regional and pan-European structures of multilateral cooperation, consultation and integration.

The Antinomies of Central and Eastern Europe

The demise of cold war bipolarity, the collapse of the Warsaw Pact and the disintegration of the USSR has transformed the states system in Central and Eastern Europe. As we have seen, this postcommunist states system is characterised by a high degree of heterogeneity, diversity and fluidity. New states and a wide array of transnational actors have emerged, along with changing bilateral relationships and complex patterns of regional cooperation and conflict. In parts of the Balkans and the Caucasus, this has created an anarchical system characterised by a Hobbesian 'war of all against all'. Yet the international politics of Central and Eastern Europe as a whole cannot be characterised in these 'realist' terms. The region has not simply reverted to past patterns of conflict and rivalry, with the traditional *Realpolitik* machinations of the regional great powers and the Machiavellian intrigues of the small and medium-sized states.

The reality is that the international politics of Central and Eastern Europe exhibit elements of both cooperation and conflict, fragmentation and integration, continuity and change. The contradictory pressures acting on Central and Eastern Europe can be symbolised in terms of two cities: Sarajevo and Maastricht. These represent the forces of fragmentation and division on the one hand, and those of integration and cooperation on the other (Schori, 1994). It is these antinomies which make the study of this region so intriguing and so intellectually exciting from the international relations perspective. Whilst nationalist sentiments and traditional patterns of cooperation and conflict have re-emerged in Central and Eastern Europe, they have done so in the context of a continent being inextricably transformed by complex interdependence, economic globalisation, democratisation and institutional integration. Deep-rooted historical animosities have resurfaced in parts of the Balkans and the Caucasus, but elsewhere in Central and Eastern Europe new forms of regional cooperation have emerged, often drawing their inspiration from historical precedents.

The effect of the European integration process, democratisation and regional cooperation in Central and Eastern Europe has been to facilitate the emergence of a society of states in the region. According to Hedley Bull, a *'society of states* (or international society) exists when a group of states, conscious of certain common interests and common values, form a society in the sense that they conceive themselves to be bound by a common set of rules in their relations with one another, and share in the working of common institutions' (1977, p. 13). The institutions and practices of international society are most developed in central Europe, where the 'idea of Europe' is strongest (Kumar 1992). This reflects both the magnetic pull of the European integration process, and the cultural links within the old *Mitteleuropäische* lands of the Habsburg Empire.

Yet the consolidation of international society in Central and Eastern Europe is threatened by the potentially divisive impact of the enlargement of western institutions on the region. Enlarging NATO and the EU eastwards risks drawing new lines of inclusion and exclusion (Wallace, 1997, p. 102). There are disturbing signs that a growing part of the political class in the West has become increasingly sceptical about the prospects for pan-European cooperation, and is thinking primarily in terms of pushing the boundaries of the 'West' further to the east. This is most clearly evident in proposals for the eastern expansion of NATO. One writer has suggested that

> Statesmen, who once enthusiastically anticipated the unity of Europe, are looking away from the seige of Sarajevo, wishing perhaps that it were happening on some other continent. Alienation is in part a matter of economic disparity, the wealth of Western Europe facing the poverty of Eastern Europe, but such disparity is inevitably clothed in the complex windings of cultural prejudice. The iron curtain is gone, and yet the shadow persists. (Wolff, 1994, p. 3)

Larry Wolff goes on to argue that the shadow persists because of the enduring power of the *idea* of Eastern Europe, an idea which is much older than the cold war and which can be traced back to the Enlightenment. This idea of Eastern Europe rests on the 'paradox of simultaneous inclusion and exclusion, Europe but not Europe' , and is defined by the twin formulas 'between Europe and Asia, between civilisation and barbarism' . He suggests that 'the rubric of Eastern Europe may still be invoked to perpetuate the exclusion of the rest, to preserve the distinction that nourishes our own identity'. He thus concludes that 'in the Europe of the 1990s Eastern Europe will continue to occupy an ambiguous space between inclusion and exclusion, both in economic affairs and in cultural recognition' (1994, pp. 7–15). If a new politics of exclusion does come to dominate Western thinking, then the prospects of developing a Europe 'whole and free' will fade, and Europeans will continue to live in the shadow of an iron curtain.

It has been said that Central and Eastern Europe has always been either a forgotten region in international relations, or a region of central importance (Bialer, 1989, p. 432). With the end of the cold war, Central and Eastern Europe has lost its former geostrategic significance. The danger now is that the region may be largely forgotten as the West Europeans concentrate on ambitious plans for economic, monetary and political union, and the USA pursues its economic and strategic interests in the Pacific. Yet the future evolution of domestic and foreign policies in Central and Eastern Europe is of decisive importance for the future of European order in the twenty-first century. The opening up of the iron curtain has created new patterns of pan-European interaction and changed the geographical scope of the European integration process. The future of West European security and prosperity has thus become increasingly bound up with the outcome of the reform process in Central and Eastern Europe. In this sense, therefore, 'Eastern Europe today is a hinge of history, including ours' (Simons, 1993, p. 260).

14

Prospects for Democracy in Postcommunist Europe*

RICHARD ROSE

Democracy is only one among many answers that can be given to the question: Where are postcommunist countries going? The establishment of a stable democracy is not the only possible outcome. Nazi Germany, Fascist Italy, Vichy France and Franco Spain refute generalisations about the democratic basis of Western civilisation. In the latest 'third wave' of global democratisation, at least ten countries of Latin America have experienced significant declines in freedom since 1987, against six registering improvements (Huntington, 1996; Diamond, 1996). The movement toward democracy in Africa is by fits and starts, with missteps too (Bratton and de Walle, 1997). The statement that 'all' countries are becoming democratic or, for that matter, undemocratic, can be disproved by a single example.

Global theories of democratisation are appealing because they are clear, but clarity can be purchased by reducing democracy to a single simple attribute – holding elections. Elections are a necessary condition of democratisation, but they are not sufficient. The conduct of elections must be free and also fair. Not only should there be

* The New Democracies Barometer survey is conducted by the Paul Lazarsfeld Society, Vienna, with grants from the Austrian Ministry for Science and Research and the Austrian National Bank. The New Russia Barometer is conducted by the Centre for the Study of Public Policy, University of Strathclyde. Parts of this chapter appeared in a different form in *Journal of Democracy*, vol. 8, no. 3 (July 1997).

institutions in civil society independent of the state, but they should also be free to organise political parties that compete in opposition to existing holders of power. Elected representatives must also have the authority to hold governors accountable for their actions, and to defeat legislation, withhold funds, or force the government of the day to resign. A fundamental condition of democracy is the rule of law, for if the government acts outside the law, then constitutional guarantees and courts are meaningless, as was shown by the practice of government in communist regimes.

Because there are four criteria to complete democratisation – elections, accountability, civil society and the rule of law – it is possible for a country to make substantial progress on one front while lagging on another. For example, every postcommunist government has held elections, and every postcommunist country of Central and Eastern Europe has held free and fair elections. However, independent institutions of civil society, especially political parties, have not had time to recover from their brutal elimination by the communist party-state. Corruption, encouraged by a non-market command economy in which connections and favours were more important than price, has flourished with the rapid privatisation of state assets, thus undermining the rule of law. In its 1997 ratings of corruption around the world, Transparency International classified Russia as more corrupt than India or Pakistan, and the Czech Republic and Hungary were both in the bottom half of countries in its international league table.

The definition of democracy is today important for understanding what Europe is and is not. At the start of the twentieth century, Europe was a league of undemocratic multi-national empires. Central and Eastern Europe was controlled by the German, the Habsburg, the Russian and the Ottoman emperors. The end of World War I marked the end of empire; Central and Eastern Europe turned into a set of undemocratic nation-states. The end of World War II marked the disappearance of Central Europe; the continent split between a democratic Western (or North Atlantic) Europe and a communist Eastern bloc. The division was ideological, not geographical. Barbed wire and Soviet-trained guards ready to shoot on sight defined its perimeter. The fall of the Berlin Wall in 1989 brought about the return of Central Europe. But democracy has remained as the dividing line between countries that are part of Europe, and countries that are not, with the Council of Europe monitoring standards (see Rose, 1996a, especially chs 1 and 14). While many non-European countries are, or are becoming democratic, a country that ceases to be democratic is now outside the pale of the idea of Europe.

In postcommunist countries the totalitarian past is dead. Monuments to freedom are the empty plinths that formerly had statues of Marx, Lenin and Stalin. In front of the Lubyanka in Moscow, where once stood a statue of the founder of the KGB, even the plinth has been removed! Bits and pieces of the Berlin Wall are being sold from market stalls by the Brandenburg Gate in Berlin. Souvenir stalls in postcommunist capitals selling Red Army gear are another sign that the power of the commanders of the command economy has been broken. Atrocities in Bosnia are the exception rather than the rule. The great waves of genocidal killing occurred between Stalin's collectivisation of agriculture and purge of his enemies in the 1930s, Hitler's war on the Jews and then on neighbouring countries, and the settlement of many scores in Central and Eastern Europe during and immediately after World War II. The postcommunist world has not seen the emergence of an ideology that its proponents believe is worth killing for. The dominant ideology among ex-*nomenklatura* apparatchiks today is summed up in the old motto: Enrich yourself.

However, the freest postcommunist countries cannot yet be described as established democracies, for it takes time to demonstrate stability. None has held free elections for as long as a decade – and many have unresolved problems. For example, Estonia and Latvia have not finally settled the political rights of a large number of resident Russians who at present face substantial difficulties in becoming citizens. In Slovakia, the pressures that Premier Vladimir Meciar exerts on his opponents give grounds for anxiety about opposition rights. The *mafia* brazenly challenges the rule of law in Russia, and elsewhere too.

What about the future? Since there are more than two dozen postcommunist countries, examples can be found of movement in many directions. The Czech Republic, Hungary and Poland are already integrated in OECD, an organisation that requires members to adhere to principles of democracy as well as the market economy. Ten Central and East European countries now have associate status with the European Union, the first step toward membership, and the Czech Republic, Hungary and Poland have been offered membership in NATO (the North Atlantic Treaty Organisation). However, Central Asian Republics of the former Soviet Union are establishing rule by a strong man, a reminder that democracy is not the only possible outcome of the collapse of communist authority.

Free, Partly Free and Unfree Successor States

All communist countries share a common curse, the legacy of totalitarianism. Totalitarian regimes aggressively sought to destroy the institutional foundations of democracy, including civil society and the rule of law. Socialist legality was not the same as the rule of law; communist front organisations, even if described as trade unions or writers' guilds, were not independent institutions. Unfree elections did not make the government accountable to the mass of the population but rubber-stamped nominations approved by the party. Totalitarian regimes could not achieve their ideals fully – though the East German 'Stasi' recruitment of adults to spy on their spouses and children to spy on their parents showed that life could imitate George Orwell's novels.

Latterly, communist regimes became post-totalitarian, relaxing their efforts to mobilise the bodies, hearts and minds of their population. Liberalisation went furthest in Hungary. Small groups of intellectuals could meet in coffee houses and be interviewed by Western journalists, but if they sought to organise a mass movement this could be deemed a crime against the state. Elections in the Soviet Union produced totalitarian results up to a few years before the collapse; in 1984 there was a 99.99 per cent turnout and 99.95 per cent of the votes were cast for the official slate of candidates. Outward compliance was sufficient to satisfy rulers; the cynical slogan of Hungary's Janos Kadar was, 'They who are not against us are with us'. Elemer Hankiss (1990, p. 7) called this the achievement of 'ironical freedom', that is, '*living outside the system in which they lived* [his emphasis], the freedom of not identifying themselves with the system'. Eminently untrustworthy institutions left a legacy of 'negative social capital', the opposite of what is required to make democracy work (Mishler and Rose, 1997).

The collapse of repressive institutions greatly increases individual freedom from the state, but it does not create the 'bourgeois' institutions that made a peaceful transition from oligarchy to democracy possible in England or Scandinavia. The rule of law and institutions of civil society made it possible for Parliament to hold the Crown accountable as early as the seventeenth century in England; granting everyone the right to vote was the last step in the process of democratisation. By contrast, communist regimes used universal suffrage to coerce a show of popular support from many unwilling subjects, destroyed the rule of law and institutions of civil society, and made governors accountable to the party not the people. When free elections were introduced in 1990 the absence of institutions of civil society resulted in a 'floating' party system. In the absence of independent organisations of civil society, politicians had to create parties from scratch, and voters often found it easier to identify a party they would never vote for than a party that they trusted (Rose, 1995a).

The totalitarian legacy in postcommunist countries is much less favourable for establishing democracy than the legacy of authoritarianism in Mediterranean Europe and Latin America (Linz and Stepan, 1996a). Authoritarian regimes did not suppress all institutions of civil society. Political opponents had their civil rights restricted, but all institutions of society are not harrowed by an ideologically committed and coercive totalitarian party-state. Some dictators maintained their position by balancing competing interests and institutions against each other. In Spain General Franco encouraged plans for a peaceful transition after his death, in which the interests of democrats as well as the old regime were taken into account, The spectacular failure of Mikhail Gorbachev's attempts to restructure the Soviet Union shows the difficulties of reforming a party-state founded with a totalitarian vocation.

The abrupt collapse of the Warsaw Pact, Comecon and the Communist Party of the Soviet Union forced countries to choose a new regime. There is no common pattern in their response. While all have held elections, some have been neither free nor fair. The most comprehensive evaluation is the Freedom House index of civil and political liberties, essential elements for democracy (Table 14.1). Ten countries are classified as free, and six – the Czech Republic, Estonia, Hungary, Lithuania, Poland and Slovenia – are credited with being just as free as France, Germany or Spain. In each of these countries there remain big problems and debates about what government ought to do. This is not a sign of failure but of success in achieving an open society in which political issues can be freely discussed, and people can mobilise government measures without fear of losing their job or being thrown in jail. It is often forgotten that many established democracies also face difficulties: Britain has a continuing conflict with terrorist organisations in Northern Ireland and France has a significant racist anti-immigrant vote. The median postcommunist country is partly free. This is a big step forward in a country such as Albania or Romania, where the right to protest publicly against the conduct of the old regime was unheard of a decade ago.

TABLE 14.1 *Free, partly free and unfree postcommunist countries, 1997 (ratings, Freedom House scale)*

Free	Partly free	Not free
1.5	*3.0*	
Czech Republic	Bulgaria	
Estonia		
Hungary	*3.5*	*5.5*
Lithuania	Macedonia	Azerbaijan
Poland	Moldova	Kazakhstan
Slovenia	Russia	
	Ukraine	
2.0	*4.0*	*6.0*
Latvia	Albania	Belarus
	Croatia	Yugoslavia (Serbia and
2.5	Georgia	Montenegro)
Bulgaria	Kyrgyzia	
Mongolia		*6.5*
Slovakia	*4.5*	Uzbekistan
	Armenia	
		7.0
	5.0	Tajikistan
	Bosnia-Herz'ia	Turkmenistan

Source: Freedom House, New York, 1997 ratings. Three communist countries, China, Cuba and Vietnam, are each rated 7, the lowest of the 'not free' categories.

It is wrong to describe unfree countries as having failed to become democracies, when democratisation is not the intent of their leaders. In Turkmenistan, the new powerholders are succeeding in establishing an unfree and undemocratic regime. In 1992 Saparmurad Niyazov was elected as Turkmenbashi unopposed with 99.5 per cent of the vote. Two years later 99.99 per cent of votes were reported as endorsing a referendum proposal to prolong his term until 2002. Similarly, Azerbaijan, Kazakhstan, Tajikistan and Uzbekistan are in the hands of leaders pushing their countries along the path of dictatorship.

The main fault-line between democratic and non-democratic postcommunist regimes is within the former Soviet Union. The countries that are most clearly democratic – Estonia, Lithuania and Latvia – were not properly Soviet; they were forcibly integrated into the USSR as a consequence of the 1939 pact between Stalin and Hitler. The 'partly free' category appears unstable. Notwithstanding many political and economic difficulties, Russia and Ukraine have avoided becoming completely undemocratic, while in Belarus, President Lukashenka has had some success in establishing a dictatorship. Tajikistan and Turkmenistan are the equals of Burma, Iraq and the Sudan in their denial of freedom. Another fault-line runs through the former Yugoslavia, separating Slovenia from Serbia. In this chapter, the term Central and Eastern Europe will be used to refer to seven countries: the Czech Republic, Slovakia, Hungary, Poland, Slovenia, Bulgaria and Romania; comparisons will also be drawn with Russia, to the east of the countries with which this book is directly concerned.

Patterns of Change

Europe today is divided between stable democracies and countries where governments are more or less trying to become established democracies. It is much easier for a country to catch up in politics. Since established democracies are not changing, catching up with their political standards 'only' requires postcommunist countries to show that they too have institutionalised its critical elements. Such totalitarian institutions as censorship and shoot-to-kill border police can be dismantled quickly. However, in economics, there is a need to create the institutions of a market economy, such as banks, laws of property and a private sector in which firms can make profits or go bankrupt.

Notwithstanding the turmoil of transformation and the inter-war prevalence of authoritarian or fascist parties in Central and Eastern Europe, since 1990 anti-democratic parties have won relatively few votes. Right-wing extremist parties create anxieties by contesting elections, but the result usually reveals their weaknesses. For example, even though Hungarians were experiencing a major economic recession and nostalgia for 'goulash Socialism', in the 1994 election the radical right-wing party of Istvan Csurka won less than 2 per cent of the popular vote. In the Czech Republic, a xenophobic Republican party won only 8 per cent of the vote in 1996. In Romania, extreme nationalist parties win about the same share of the vote as George Wallace took in the American presidential election in 1968 and Jean-Marie Le Pen won in the 1995 French presidential election.

A second hallmark of democracy is that if dissatisfied electors vote against the government of the day, the incumbents will surrender office if defeated at an election. In Western Europe it often took decades for newly created democratic regimes to experience such a swing of the pendulum. In Germany, the Social Democrats did not supplant the Christian Democrats as the government until 20 years after the founding of the Federal Republic. In the Fifth French Republic, Socialists required 23 years before they took the presidency from right-wing politicians. In Central and Eastern Europe, almost every country has experienced a change of governing party at least once, and some have done so more often.

Changes of government include ex-communists winning office by popular election. In Poland a former communist defeated Lech Walesa's bid for the presidency in 1995. Hungary now has a prime minister who supported the Communist Party in its repressive days. If one believes that all communists were committed Marxist-Leninists, this is cause for alarm. But that is not the case. Ex-communists can easily become anti-communists; Boris Yeltsin is a spectacular example of the dissident communist. The patronage power of the Communist Party made it attractive to people who were seeking non-ideological payoffs. The good news is that many successful ex-communist politicians have not changed; 'once an opportunist, always an opportunist'. In a regime with competing parties, ex-communists are as ready to adopt new policies as are American presidential hopefuls running in the New Hampshire primary (Rose, 1996b).

A democratic political culture is often cited as a third criterion for democracy; however, there is disagreement and confusion about the significance of culture (for a good review, see Fleron, 1996). Some theorists argue that a democratic culture is a consequence of establishing democratic institutions, while others say it is a prerequisite for achieving a stable democracy. If the latter is the case, it could take generations before democracy is secure, insofar as persons socialised under an authoritarian or totalitarian regime would persist in undemocratic ways even after democratic institutions are introduced.

The normal practice in studying political culture is to identify ideal attributes of democracy, and then formulate questions assessing the extent to which a representative cross-section of a country's population endorse democratic ideals. The leading theorist of democratic ideals is Robert Dahl (1971, p. 8). His criteria for democracy are so demanding that, as he recognises, 'No large system in the real world is fully democratised.' Public opinion surveys in the United States and Western Europe confirm his judgement: no mass public anywhere fully endorses the multiplicity of values in the liberal democratic creed. In the extreme case, figures can be produced indicating that Russia is equal to the United States in democratic values, because the minority rejecting some democratic precepts is similar in both countries (Gibson, 1993, table 14.2).

Leading European theorists of democracy tend to be realists, following in the footsteps of Joseph Schumpeter (1952, ch. 22). He defined democracy as teams of elites competing for votes to win office. This does not require that every elector believe in democracy or that every politician believe in anything: it simply requires governors to be periodically accountable to the electorate in free elections. As an economist, Schumpeter appealed to self-interest rather than idealism: party leaders were viewed as opportunistic entrepreneurs, producing policies that the public wanted to buy. Voters only had to choose between voting for or against the government of the day or abstaining. Winston Churchill, no theorist but a lifelong defender of democracy, offered the ultimate in realism, defending democracy as the lesser evil. In a House of Commons speech two years after the end of World War II, Churchill (1947, col. 206) called democracy 'the worst form of government, except all those other forms that have been tried from time to time'.

The realist approach is very apt for analysing how people in postcommunist societies evaluate governance, for everyone has lived under at least two different regimes, 'real existing socialism' with unfree elections and Leninist institutions, and 'real existing democracy', with many of the faults that Churchill imagined and then some. Older people have lived under two forms of totalitarianism – Nazi and Stalinist – and national forms of undemocratic rule too. Given such a life history, everyone is qualified by experience to make a choice between regimes. Even if a new democracy is far from ideal, people may still prefer it as the lesser evil.

The Churchill hypothesis can be tested empirically by asking people to evaluate both old and new regimes on a 'heaven/ hell' scale; the name reflects the fact that the scale goes from plus 100 to minus 100. Asking people to rate both regimes on the same scale avoids jumping to the false conclusion that just because democracy is less than ideal it will be rejected. The scale also enables people to show a preference for democracy as a lesser evil. Contemporary American and British politicians employ a similar logic when they use negative campaign tactics to make their opponents look bad and promote their party as the lesser evil.

The 'heaven/hell' scale is consistently used in the representative nationwide Barometer surveys of public opinion in postcommunist societies conducted by the Paul Lazarsfeld Society, Vienna and the Centre for the Study of Public Policy (CSPP), University of Strathclyde, Glasgow. The Lazarsfeld Society's New Democracies Barometer (NDB) started in autumn 1991, and the parallel New Russia Barometer of the CSPP in January 1992. We thus have comparable data about public opinion in Central and East European countries, where new political institutions appear most consistent with democracy, and in Russia, where institutions are rated as only partly free. Equally important, we have trend data showing how much or how little change is occurring within and between countries.

When NDB surveys ask people in Central and Eastern Europe (CEE) to evaluate their old regime, the majority give it a negative rating. In autumn 1991, across seven countries – the Czech Republic, Slovakia, Hungary, Poland, Slovenia, Bulgaria and Romania – only 35 per cent were favourable about the former communist regime (Figure 14.1). The passage of time has not made the communist regime appear more attractive. After four years of experiencing all the problems of a new regime, a majority remained negative about the old regime. While there is a division of opinion within every country about the old regime, more people see it as an absolute hell rather than as heaven. In the fourth NDB survey, 20 per cent of Romanians placed the Ceausescu regime at minus 100 and in Poland 18 per cent similarly rated the communist regime at the very bottom. In six of the seven CEE countries, a majority has consistently been negative about the old regime. Only in Hungary, the most liberal of the old systems, is there a majority positive in evaluating the communist regime.

The new system of government is consistently endorsed by a majority of people in Central and Eastern Europe. In the first NDB survey an average of 59 per cent were positive about their new system. Since then, governments in every country have been defeated in free elections, and in Czechoslovakia the state itself has broken up. However, rejection of a particular party or politician is consistent with Schumpeter's definition of democracy as a means of allowing people to turn one party out of office and place another in power while the regime remains intact. Subsequent NDB surveys confirm that Central and East Europeans approve a system that allows them to vote the government out of office if they are dissatisfied. By the fourth NDB survey, the proportion endorsing their new regime had risen to almost two-thirds, and was up in five of the seven Central and

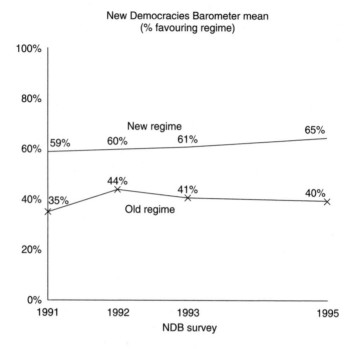

FIGURE 14.1   *Evaluating old and new regimes in Central and Eastern Europe*

Source: Mean for nationwide representative sample surveys in the Czech Republic, Slovakia, Hungary, Poland, Slovenia, Bulgaria and Romania, organised by the Paul Lazarsfeld Society, Vienna. Average based on approximately 7,000 interviews in each year; for full details, see Rose and Haerpfer (1996).

East European countries. In the Czech Republic, 77 per cent are now positive about their new regime, and 76 per cent in Poland. In every country except Hungary, a majority has consistently been in favour of the new regime.

Russia is different. The Gorbachev reforms were not about introducing democracy but about introducing pluralism into a one-party state with a totalitarian vocation. The Russian Federation emerged by accident from the wreckage of the Soviet Union in December 1991 and there has been no agreement among political elites about how it ought to be governed. In the first New Russia Barometer survey, conducted in January 1992, only one Russian in seven was positive about the new regime, while half were positive about the pre-*perestroika* regime (Figure 14.2). Events since – the parliament's vote of no confidence in the president and the president's shelling of parliament in 1993; the war in Chechnya; and wholesale corruption – have made the new Russian regime unpopular. Immediately after the July 1996 presidential election, Russian endorsement of the new regime reached a 'high' of 38 per cent, far below the three-fifths of Russians who gave a positive rating to the old communist regime.

Russian attitudes toward their old and new regimes are almost a mirror image of opinion in Central and Eastern Europe (for similar data on Belarus and Ukraine, see Rose and Haerpfer, 1996, pp. 84ff).

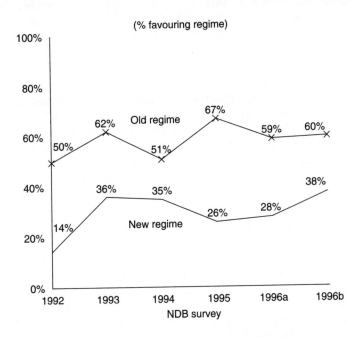

FIGURE 14.2 *Russians evaluate old and new regimes*

Source: New Russia Barometer surveys organised by the Centre for the Study of Public Policy, University of Strathclyde, Glasgow. The 1996a survey was by the All-Union Centre for the Study of Public Opinion in January, immediately after the Duma election, and the 1996b survey in late July, immediately after the presidential ballot. Nationwide representative samples of about 2,000 respondents each. For full details, see Rose and Tikhomirov, 1995 and 1996.

In Russia, a majority are positive about the old communist regime and negative about the present, while in Central and Eastern Europe the opposite is the case. The readiness of Russians to be positive about the Soviet Union does not mean that Russians reject democracy. Like people in every other postcommunist country, Russians welcome big gains in the first freedom, freedom from the state (Rose, 1995a).

Dissatisfaction with the new regime, equally, does not necessarily imply support for a return to an undemocratic system of rule. This becomes clear when we look at the divisions of opinion that exist within every postcommunist country about old and new regimes. In each country, the population divides into four groups according to whether they give a positive or negative rating to the former communist regime and to their fledgling democracy. In the 1995 NDB survey, the distribution across seven countries of Central and Eastern Europe was:

- *Democrats* (disapprove communist regime, approve new regime: 41 per cent). This large group is most supportive of political change. Their average rating of the old regime on the heaven/hell scale is minus 57; their rating of the new regime is plus 44.
- *Sceptics* (disapprove both regimes: 20 per cent). Churchill was a sceptic rather than an idealistic proponent of liberal democracy; a fifth of Central and East Europeans share his view. They are negative about both past and present political regimes. On average, the communist regime is viewed as worse, minus 45 on the heaven/hell scale, 13 points lower than the mean rating for the current regime.
- *Compliant* (approve both communist and new regimes: 23 per cent). Given a history of pressures to bow to those in power, it is hardly surprising that some people endorse both old and new regimes. The mean rating on the heaven/hell scale is almost identical for the communist regime (plus 47) and the current regime (plus 44).
- *Reactionaries* (approve communist regime, dislike new: 16 per cent). This is the mirror image of democrats. The mean rating given the communist regime on the heaven/hell scale is plus 58; that for the new regime is minus 45.

In addition to differences within every country, there are also substantial differences between countries. In the Czech Republic and Poland, more than half are unambiguous democrats, endorsing the new regime and rejecting the old. In Romania and Slovenia, the

TABLE 14.2   *How individuals compare old and new regimes (% in category)*

	Democrats	Sceptics	Compliant	Reactionary
Czech Republic	61	15	16	8
Poland	58	16	18	8
Romania	44	28	16	11
Slovenia	41	23	26	11
Bulgaria	31	10	34	24
Slovakia	30	18	31	22
Hungary	22	21	27	29
NDB mean	41	20	24	15
Russia	20	20	18	42

Source: As in Figure 14.1. Central and Eastern Europe figures are for the New Democracies Barometer (NDB) IV (1995); Russia for NRB VI (1996).

democrats are the largest single group; in Bulgaria and Slovakia those positive about both the old and new regime are the largest single group; and Hungarians divide almost equally into four different groups. In Russia, by contrast, in every New Russia Barometer survey since 1992 reactionaries have been most numerous, at least two-fifths of the population. Those preferring the new regime to the old have increased but after Yeltsin's election victory in 1996 they were still only a fifth of the population.

While reactionaries unambiguously favouring a communist regime are very much a minority, the median Central or East European is not a democrat but a sceptic, giving both the old communist regime and the new democracy a negative rating. Altogether, 43 per cent are sitting on the fence in their evaluations, being passively compliant or sceptical. In the course of time, they could come off on either side. Thus, we must view democratisation as a process, rather than something that was achieved by a single event such as the collapse of the Soviet empire. It also raises questions about the potential support for undemocratic alternatives.

What About Undemocratic Alternatives?

The optimistic scenario is that while postcommunist regimes have not yet become established democracies, they soon will catch up with the other countries of Europe. After all, Spain and Portugal were admitted to the European Union little more than a decade after the downfall of their dictatorships, and the Republic of Italy was a founder member of NATO, even though a half dozen years earlier Fascist Italy had been on the Axis side. The pessimistic scenario is that the past will catch up, and countries will revert to an undemocratic regime similar to that before the Soviet Army arrived, or devise a new form of undemocratic rule.

In every political system, and especially postcommunist regimes, there is a political potential among elites to supply an undemocratic alternative – if the demand is there. However, the demand for undemocratic rule is low. To test demand, the NDB surveys follow the logic of the Churchill hypothesis and ask people about historically meaningful alternatives to democratic governance.

In every Central and East European country, a majority consistently rejects each undemocratic alternative. On average, only 6 per cent say that they would welcome the army ruling, only 16 per cent want a communist regime back, and less than a quarter endorse rule by a strong man without parliament and elections, or military rule (Table 14.3). The biggest demand for change is found in Poland, but even there only one in three say they would prefer a strong leader to parliamentary government. In Slovakia, where Vladimir Meciar has attributes of a 'strong man' ruler, fewer than one in five would welcome a strong man suspending parliament and free elections. On average, two-thirds of Central and East Europeans reject all three undemocratic alternatives, and in the Czech Republic as many as four-fifths do so (for more details, see Rose and Mishler, 1996a).

Even though Russians show a high level of dissatisfaction with their current regime, a majority appear to accept Churchill's logic. Seven out of eight Russians do not want the Army to rule, hardly surprising in view of the disastrous showing of the Russian Army in Afghanistan and Chechnya. Two-thirds do not want a strong leader unchecked by parliament and election; and two-thirds do not want a return to the communist regime. While Russians are more likely to endorse an undemocratic regime than people in Central and Eastern Europe, the largest group reject all three undemocratic alternatives.

Catching Up or Divergence?

Postcommunist countries have not responded in the same way to the collapse of the old regime. There is a fundamental difference in

TABLE 14.3   *Undemocratic alternatives rejected*

	(% endorsing each alternative)			
	Army	*Communist regime*	*Strong leader*	*Reject all*
Czech Republic	3	10	14	80
Slovakia	1	19	19	71
Hungary	2	20	21	69
Slovenia	4	12	29	65
Poland	4	8	33	63
Romania	12	12	29	61
Bulgaria	15	29	23	55
CEE mean	6	16	23	67
Russia	12	35	32	45

Question: Our present system of government is not the only one that this country has had. Some people say that we would be better off if the country was governed differently. What do you think?
Source: New Democracies Barometer IV; New Russia Barometer VI.

direction between Central and East European countries moving toward membership in the European Union and Central Asian states establishing regimes that, like most member states of the United Nations, are only partly free and without a democratic system of governance. However, given divisions within each country. there is also scope for change as public opinion evolves.

One theory is that mass publics divide into leaders and laggards, with some people quicker to endorse the new regime than others. If this is the case, the development of overwhelming mass support for democracy is only a matter of time, as sceptics come round to endorsing the new regime, and reactionaries, who tend to be older, die off. But if such changes do not occur, the result will be polarisation between reactionaries preferring the old regime and democrats supporting the new regime. Polarisation would make every election a contest between those for and against the new regime. This was the pattern in France during the Fourth Republic, before it was overthrown in 1958 by General de Gaulle.

To measure future expectations, Barometer surveys ask people to rate their country's system of governing 'in five years' time'. Given all that has happened in the past five years, the question is an ink-blot, allowing people to express whatever fears or hopes they may have. In Central and Eastern Europe, the majority positive about the regime in future is even bigger than for the present. In the 1991 NDB survey, 82 per cent were positive about the regime in five years. Notwithstanding grounds for disillusionment, in the fourth NDB survey 79 per cent were positive.

Within each Central and East European country, there is a division between leaders and laggards on the road to democracy. In the 1995 NDB round, 63 per cent were in the vanguard, already positive about the new regime and also positive about the future. An additional sixth were laggards, negative today but expecting to be positive in five years. One in five were pessimists, negative about the current regime and also about the situation in five years' time. The pessimists subdivide into sceptics congenitally negative about government and frustrated authoritarians who would like to see a change of regime but do not think it will happen soon.

Russian expectations are different. Only 38 per cent of Russians are optimists, already positive about the new regime and positive about the future; 23 per cent are laggards, expecting governance to improve in five years. The biggest Russian group, 39 per cent, are pessimists, dissatisfied with the current regime and with how they expect to be governed at the millennium.

Any statement about the future based on current evidence should carry the caution: these figures are subject to change. But what might cause change to occur? A military takeover, a scenario long familiar in Latin America and in Eastern Europe between the wars, is hardly relevant in postcommunist countries. There is no popular demand for it, communist parties were good at asserting civilian control over the military, and Warsaw Pact forces were trained to fight the next world war and to stay out of national politics. Demoralised soldiers are more likely to desert than seize the government.

The European Union and its member states are actively encouraging the integration of Central and East European countries in a democratic Europe. Four EU countries – Germany, Sweden, Finland and Austria – have borders with ex-communist countries, and Vienna is closer to seven postcommunist countries than it is to some other parts of Austria. Because the European Union is an open membership organisation, Central and East European countries cannot be refused membership if they want to join and can meet the economic and political criteria of membership. The political task is not so difficult as it appears, for the majority of the 15 EU member states have only become established as democracies after World War II. In 1997 the European Union commenced negotiating membership in with five countries: the Czech Republic, Estonia, Hungary, Poland and Slovenia. It also confirmed that Bulgaria, Latvia, Lithuania, Romania and Slovakia were considered potential candidates for membership.

There are major obstacles to economic integration across Europe. To join the Single Europe Market, postcommunist countries must develop institutions of a market economy that work, for example, commercial banks that can promptly and routinely transfer payments from one country to another, central banks that keep inflation down and customs guards that respect the rule of law. In addition, Brussels must also make big changes to accommodate additional members, such as abandoning the requirement of unanimity for most decisions and reducing the enormous sums spent in inefficient agricultural subsidies.

The covert Marxism of neoclassical economists assumes that if people are not guaranteed employment as in communist times, they will reject regimes that give them freedom. Leonid Brezhnev shared this assumption; his attempt to established a secure but undemocratic regime on the foundations of 'welfare state authoritarianism' failed (see Cook, 1993). The above shows this assumption is false, for Central and East Europeans were ready to support new political institutions when their economies were rapidly contracting in the early 1990s. The majority of people will pay a price in material discomfort to get rid of the political discomforts caused by commissars. People tend to accept the basic precept of the dismal science of economics, namely, costs come before benefits.

The greater the credence given to economic determinism of political values, the greater the reason to be optimistic about the political future in Central and Eastern Europe. In every country there was a wholesale contraction of the official economy in the early 1990s. To some extent, official statistics exaggerate the degree of contraction, for products in the old non-market economy were often overvalued and official statistics do not cover 'unofficial' activity in the second economies that have flourished in the new political and economic climate (cf. Rose, 1993). Yet the radical shift from a command to a market economy has been a major shock.

While real, the shock of transformation is temporary; the countries of Central and Eastern Europe have now passed their economic turning points (Figure 14.3; and see Chapter 10). By 1997 Poland

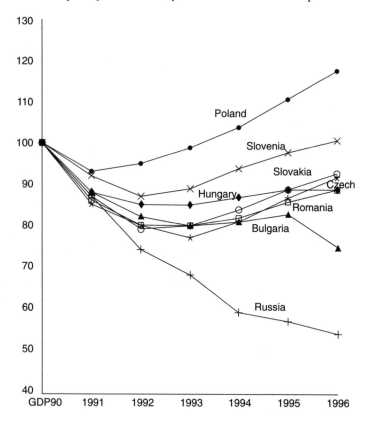

FIGURE 14.3   *Cumulative change in the economy, 1990–6*

Source: Adapted from European Bank for Reconstruction and Development (EBRD), *Transition Report 1997*.

and Slovenia had an official economy that was more prosperous than before transformation. Four more countries were showing strong signs of sustained recovery; Bulgaria has been the only laggard in recovering. The rate of growth in most economies is now higher than in Western Europe. Since accelerated growth is normal when a country is recovering from a major recession, inflation rates have fallen dramatically, and in some cases are within the range of OECD countries. In so far as sceptics and reactionaries have withheld support for the new regime because it has been associated with economic contraction, their views should change as the economy recovers and achieves higher levels of prosperity and efficiency than in the era of the non-market command economy.

In economics as in politics, Russia is different. According to official statistics, the Russian economy in 1996 had scarcely half the national product of 1990, and the cumulative rate of inflation was several thousand per cent. While the 'turnaround' of the official Russian economy has been heralded more than once (e.g. Layard and Parker, 1996), the scale of transformation is undoubtedly much greater than in Central and Eastern Europe – and the losses due to mismanagement of transformation are far greater too. The New Russia Barometer registers dissatisfaction with economic as well as political regime change. Some of the dissatisfaction comes from Russians committed to democratisation. However, there is no consensus among opponents of the old regime or among supporters of the new regime about how to improve conditions in Russia – or whether they can be improved.

Political and economic changes in Central and Eastern Europe are increasing its integration with the democratic state system of Europe. The European Union's placement of Central and East European countries into two groups – those ready to commence integration in the EU and those that have still to demonstrate stronger commitment to democracy and the market – is a realistic distinction (see Table 14.1 and Figure 14.3).

Collectively, the course of postcommunist countries today shows *asymmetric divergence*. While Central and East European countries are moving toward integration in a state system with similar boundaries but much more democracy than Europe before World War II, Russia and other successor states of the Soviet Union appear to be 'broken back' democracies; they cannot lift the burdens of transformation yet their citizens do not want to sacrifice the freedoms they have gained for an undemocratic regime. By going nowhere, Soviet successor states run the risk of falling further behind Central and East European countries that are ready to return to Europe after more than two generations of being locked in to a one-party system that aggressively rejected both the market and democracy.

Further Reading

It might be best to begin with one of several useful histories of nationalism and of the peoples of Central and Eastern Europe, such as Seton-Watson (1977) or Fernandez-Armesto (1994). On more recent developments, see, for instance, Okey (1986), Held (1992), Swain and Swain (1993), Crampton (1997), and Bideleux and Jeffries (1997). Schopflin (1993) covers politics since 1945, as do Rothschild (1993) and Lewis (1994). On the transition from communist rule, Brown (1991) and Stokes (1993) are particularly useful. White (1991) provides a detailed reference guide to the period of transition; a briefer account is available in East and Pontin (1997). Ash (1990) is a more impressionistic journalist's study, emphasising developments in Poland, Czechoslovakia and Hungary; Stokes (1996) provides a number of key documents in a convenient form. Dahrendorf (1990) is a thoughtful essay on the changes and the meaning of 'Europe' in this connection; see also Rose (1996a).

Several general studies of early postcommunism are available, among them Holmes (1997), Crawford (1996) and Henderson and Robinson (1997). Studies of individual countries in the late communist and early postcommunist period are more numerous. On the former Czechoslovakia, see Wolchik (1991) and Leff (1996); on the transition from communist rule, see more particularly Wheaton and Kavan (1992) and Bradley (1992). On Poland, see, for instance, Kaminski (1991), Staniszkis (1991b), Sanford (1992), Staar (1993), and Millard (1994). On Hungary, see Swain (1992), Cox and Furlong (1995), and a magisterial study of the 'negotiated revolution' by Tokes (1996). Horvath and Szakolczai (1992) and Bozoki and Korosenyi (1992) provide an additional 'insider' perspective. On the former Yugoslavia, see Glenny (1992), Magas (1993), Denitch (1994) and Dyker and Vejvoda (1996); and on Romania, Rady (1992) and Gallagher (1995). The evolution of communist rule and its eventual demise in the German Democratic Republic is considered in Fulbrook (1995) and Maier (1997).

Accounts of the late Soviet period and the emergence of the independent post-Soviet states include Hosking (1991) and White (1994). Nationalities issues more particularly are considered in Hajda and Beissinger (1990), Smith (1996) and Bremmer and Taras (1993, 1997). The background to developments in the Baltics can be found in Taagepera and Misiunas (1983); the early independence period is covered in Smith (1994) and a comprehensive but more journalistic account of the late Soviet and early post-Soviet years can be found in Lieven (1994). The best overview of the drive for independence in Ukraine is Kuzio and Wilson (1992); Motyl (1993), though less detailed, is highly accessible and covers much of the same material. Wilson (1997) contains an excellent analysis of recent developments in Ukrainian politics, and Kuzio (1997) provides a wealth of information. For a review of Soviet and post-Soviet developments in Moldova, see King (1995); on Belarus, Fedor (1995) and Marples (1996) are helpful.

There is a further substantial literature on particular themes. The framing of new constitutions is considered in Howard (1993); the texts are conveniently reprinted in Raina (1995) and International Institute for Democracy (1995, 1996) and current developments are analysed in the *East European Constitutional Review* (back issues available on-line at www.law.uchicago.edu/Publications/CSCEE/EECR). On leadership, see Taras (1997) on the presidencies and Baylis (1996) on prime ministers; elite change more generally is considered in Higley *et al.* (1996). On parliaments, see Olson and Norton (1996). Reports on current election-related developments in Central and Eastern Europe may be found in the RFE-RL Newsline, published daily by Radio Free Europe/Radio Liberty, available on-line at www.rferl.org/newsline. Election results are published in *Elections Today*, a quarterly newsletter of the International Foundation for Electoral Systems (current and back issues are available on-line at www.ifes.org) as well as, in abbreviated form, in the Election Watch section of the *Journal of Democracy* (also available on-line at www.muse.jhu.edu/journal/journal_of_democracy/election watch). Several other journals give particular attention to elections in Central and Eastern Europe, including *Electoral Studies, Parliamentary Affairs*, and *Political Data Yearbook* (an annual special issue of the *European Journal of Political Research*). The Wissenschaftszentrum Berlin has launched (in English) a book series on Founding Elections in Eastern Europe under the general editorship of Hans-Dieter Klingemann and Charles L. Taylor. The first volume in the series, on Hungary, appeared as Toka (1995); see also Gabal (1996) on Czechoslovakia and Karasimeonov (1997) on Bulgaria. On political parties, see particularly Lewis (1996) and the journal *Party Politics*.

On changing values and the wider comparative politics of the region, see Miller *et al.* (1998) and Rose, Mishler and Haerpfer (1998).

On economic change, a comprehensive guide is available in Jeffries (1996) and also in Turnock (1997). On privatisation and economic change, see more particularly Frydman *et al.* (1993, 1994), Estrin (1994), and Gros and Steinherr (1995). Current developments may most easily be followed through a number of internet sites, including those of the European Bank for Reconstruction and Development in London, which was established following the collapse of communism as a development agency operating on commercial principles whose main task is to stimulate investment throughout the former European Comecon region. The Bank's web site is at www.ebrd.com; its reports, especially the annual *Transition Report*, provide much useful background date and analysis. The EBRD also produces a Working Papers series and is cosponsor of the journal *Economics of Transition*. The World Bank, on which the EBRD was modelled, is also engaged in supporting the transformation of East European economies. The Bank publishes a Newsletter, *Transition*, focusing on such issues; it can be read at the Bank's web site (www.worldbank.org/). The United Nations Economic Commission for Europe also provides useful statistical and other background information on the Central and East European economies. The annual *Economic Survey of Europe* is particularly useful. The UNECE web site is at www.unece.org/. For more immediate business and economic developments the Central European Business Daily is useful and can be consulted at www.cebd.com.

On policy issues with particular reference to gender see Funk and Mueller (1993), Rueschemeyer (1994), Corrin (1996) and Renne (1997). There are useful discussions of social questions in the former Czechoslovakia in Wolchik (1991), in Poland in Weclawowicz (1996), and in Bulgaria in Zloch-Christy (1996). Social and organisational aspects of economic transformation are discussed in Grabher and Stark (1997) and in Kovacs (1994). Questions of political culture and citizenship are dealt with in Bruszt, Simon and Barnes (forthcoming), while questions of national identity are dealt with in Kurti and Langman (1997). There are penetrating studies of 'winners' and 'losers' in Stark (1990, 1992, and 1996).

On the international politics of the region, see Cottey (1995) and Hyde-Price (1996). Russia's contemporary role in European affairs is given particular consideration in Baranovsky (1997). On Ukraine's foreign and security policy dilemmas, see Bukkvoll (1997) and

Garnett (1997). Judy Batt's thoughtful analysis of 'the new Slovakia' (1996) raises issues of much greater relevance to the international politics of this region. On the concept of international security more generally see Hedley Bull's classic account (1977). Detailed studies of a changing public opinion are available from several sources, particularly from the *Central and Eastern Eurobarometer* (Brussels, annual, since 1991) and the New Democracies Barometer produced by the Centre for the Study of Public Policy at the University of Strathclyde (for a listing and abstracts see the Centre's web site at www.strath.ac.uk/Departments/CSPP/). On wider processes of democratisation, see, for instance, Linz and Stepan (1996a), Mandelbaum (1996b), Ekiert (1996) von Beyme (1996) and a four-volume work edited by Dawisha and Parrott (1997).

In a rapidly changing situation, developments and changing theoretical perspectives must be followed through the scholarly and more popular literature. There are several periodicals that deal specifically with Central and Eastern Europe, among them *Communist and Post-Communist Studies*, *East European Politics and Societies*, *East European Quarterly*, *Europe-Asia Studies* (formerly *Soviet Studies*), the *Journal of Communist Studies and Transition Politics*, *Problems of Post-Communism*, *Slavic Review*, and *Transition*. Daily access to developments in the region is available from a variety of on-line services, particularly those of the Open Media Research Institute (www.rferl.org/newsline).

Bibliography

Agh, Attila (ed.) (1994) *The Emergence of East Central European Parliaments: The First Steps*. Budapest: Institute of Democracy Studies.

Agh, Attila (1995) 'Partial consolidation of the East-Central European parties', *Party Politics*, vol. 1, no. 4 (October).

Agh, Attila (1996) 'Democratic Parliamentarianism in Hungary: The First Parliament (1990–94) and the Entry of the Second Parliament' in Olson and Norton (1996).

Agh, Attila and Sandor Kurtan (eds) (1996) *Democratization and Europeanization in Hungary: the First Parliament 1990–1994*. Budapest: Hungarian Centre for Democracy Studies.

Albright, M. (1997) 'Why bigger is better', *The Economist*, 15 February, pp. 21–3.

Allison, Roy (1993) *Military Forces in the Soviet Successor States*, Adelphi Paper 280. London: Brasseys for the IISS.

Almond, Gabriel and G. Bingham Powell (eds) (1983) *Comparative Politics Today*. Boston, MA: Little, Brown.

Amsden, Alice H. *et al.* (1995) *The Market Meets its Match*. Cambridge, MA: Harvard University Press.

Ang-Lygate, M., Chris Corrin and Milsom Henry (eds) (1997) *Desperately Seeking Sisterhood: Still Challenging and Building*. London: Taylor & Francis.

Arel, D. and V. Khmelko (1996) 'The Russian factor and territorial polarization in Ukraine', *The Harriman Review*, vol. 9, nos 1–2 (March).

Arriagada, G. (1992) 'Reflections on recent elections in Latin America and Eastern and Central Europe', in L. Garber and E. Bjornlund (eds) *The New Democratic Frontier*. Washington, DC: National Democratic Institute for International Affairs.

Ascherson, Neil (1995) *Black Sea*. London: Jonathan Cape.

Ash, Timothy Garton (1990) *We The People: The Revolution of 1989*. Harmondsworth: Penguin.

Asmus, R., R. Kugler and S. Larrabee (1995) 'NATO expansion: the next steps', *Survival*, vol. 37, no. 1, pp. 7–33.

Augarde, T. (1991) *The Oxford Dictionary of Modern Quotations*. Oxford and New York: Oxford University Press.

Bach, S. (1996) 'From Soviet to Parliament in Ukraine: the Verkhovna Rada during 1992–94', in Olson and Norton (1996), pp. 213–43.

Bailes, Alyson (1997) 'Subregional organizations: the Cinderella of European security', *NATO Review*, vol. 45, no. 2, (March), pp. 27–31.

Balcerowicz, Leszek (1993) *Eastern Europe: Economic, Social and Political Dynamics. A Lecture*. London: School of Slavonic and East European Studies.

Balcerowicz, Leszek (1995) 'Understanding postcommunist transitions', *Journal of Democracy*, vol. 5, no. 4 (October).

Balicka, M. (1996) 'CEFTA lepsza niz RWPG. Koks za Piwo', *Polityka*, no. 44 (2061).

Baranovsky, V. (ed.) (1997) *Russia and European Security*. Oxford: Oxford University Press for SIPRI.

Bateman, Milford (ed.) (1997) *Business Cultures in Central & Eastern Europe*. Oxford: Butterworth-Heinemann.

Batt, Judy (1993) *Czecho-Slovakia in Transition: From Federation to Separation*, Discussion Paper no. 46. London: Royal Institute of International Affairs.

Batt, Judy (1996) *The New Slovakia. National Identity, Political Integration and the Return to Europe*, Chatham House Discussion Paper 65. London: RIIA.

Bauman, Zygmunt (1994) 'After the patronage state: a model in search of class interests', in Bryant and Mokrzycki (1994).

Baylis, Thomas A. (1996) 'Presidents versus prime ministers: shaping executive authority in Eastern Europe', *World Politics*, vol. 48, no. 3 (April), pp. 297–323.

Beyme, Klaus von (ed.) (1996) *The Transition to Democracy in Eastern Europe*. London: Macmillan.

Bialer, Seweryn (1989) 'Perestroika and the future of the Cold War', in Griffiths (1989).

Bibo, Istvan (1991) 'The distress of the East European small states', translated in *Democracy, Revolution, Self-Determination: Selected Writings*, edited by K. Nagy. Boulder, CO: Social Science Monographs, pp. 13–86.

Bideleux, Robert and Ian Jeffries (1997) *A History of Eastern Europe: Crisis and Change*. London: Routledge.

Bielasiak, Jack (1997) 'Substance and process in the development of party systems in East Central Europe', in *Communist and Post-Communist Studies*, vol. 30, no. 1 (March), pp. 23–44.

Blackwill, R., and S. Karaganov (eds) (1994) *Damage Limitation or Crisis? Russia and the Outside World*, CSIA Studies in International Security No. 5. London: Brassey's.

Blanchard, Olivier *et al.* (1991) *Reform in Eastern Europe*. Cambridge, MA: MIT Press.

Blanchard, Olivier *et al.* (1993) *Post-Communist Reform: Pain and Progress*. Cambridge, MA: MIT Press.

Blanning, T. C. W. (1994) *Joseph II*. Harlow: Longman.

Blazyca, George and Ryszard Rapacki (eds) (1991) *Poland into the 1990s: Economy and Society in Transition*. London: Pinter.

Bleiere, D. (1995) 'Ukraine's integration with Central and Eastern Europe: the potential for regional cooperation', in Jonson (1995), pp. 81–9.

Borger, Julian (1996) 'Serbia's conjugal despots', *The Guardian*, 3 December.

Borger, Julian (1997) 'Wartime ally denounces Milosevic', *The Guardian*, 31 January.

Boric, R. (1996) 'Croatia: three years after', in Corrin (1996a), pp. 133–52.

Bozoki, Andras and Andras Korosenyi (eds) (1992) *Post-Communist Transition: Emerging Pluralism in Hungary*. London: Pinter.

Bradley, J. F. N. (1992) *Czechoslovakia's Velvet Revolution: A Political Analysis*. Boulder, CO: East European Monographs.

Bratton, Michael and Nicolas van de Walle (1997) *Democratic Experiments in Africa*. New York: Cambridge University Press.

Bremmer, Ian and Ray Taras (eds) (1993) *Nations and Politics in the Soviet Successor States*. Cambridge: Cambridge University Press.

Bremmer, Ian and Ray Taras (eds) (1997) *New States, New Politics: Building the Post-Soviet Nations*. Cambridge: Cambridge University Press.

Brokl, Lubomir and Zdenka Mansfeldova (1995) 'Members of Parliament as Political Elites', Conference paper, Warsaw, mimeo.

Brown, J. F. (1991) *Surge to Freedom. The End of Communist Rule in Eastern Europe*. Durham, NC: Duke University Press.

Brown, J. F. (1994) *Hopes and Shadows: Eastern Europe after Communism*. Durham, NC: Duke University Press.

Brown, M. (1995) 'The flawed logic of NATO expansion', *Survival*, vol. 37, no. 1, pp. 34–52.

Bruszt, Laszlo, Janos Simon and Samuel Barnes (eds) (forthcoming) *The Postcommunist Citizen*. Budapest: Central European University Press.

Bryant, Christopher G. A. and Edmund Mokrzycki (eds.) (1994) *The New Great Transformation? Change and Continuity in East-Central Europe*. London: Routledge.

Bryant, Christopher and Edmund Mokrzycki (eds) (1995) *Democracy, Civil Society and Pluralism*. Warsaw: IFiS.

Brzezinski, I. (1993) 'Polish–Ukrainian relations: Europe's neglected strategic axis', *Survival*, vol. 35, no. 3 (Autumn), pp. 26–37.

Buckley, Mary (1989) *Women and Ideology in the Soviet Union*. Hemel Hempstead: Harvester.

Building Democracy: OMRI National Survey 1995 (1996). Armonk, NY: Sharpe.

Bukkvoll, T. (1997) *Ukraine and European Security*. London: Pinter.

Bull, Hedley (1977) *The Anarchical Society. A Study of Order in World Politics*. London: Macmillan.

Buzan, Barry (1991) *People, States and Fear. An Agenda for International Security Studies in the Post Cold War Era*, 2nd edn. Hemel Hempstead: Wheatsheaf.

Carey, Henry F. (1995) 'Irregularities or rigging: the 1992 Romanian parliamentary elections', *East European Quarterly*, vol. 29, no. 1, pp. 43–66.

Carlin, Wendy *et al.* (1995) 'Enterprise restructuring in early transition: the case study evidence', *Economics of Transition*, vol. 3.

Castle-Kanerova, Mita (1992) 'The culture of strong women in the making?', in Corrin (1992a), pp. 97–124.

Churchill, Winston (1947) House of Commons *Hansard*, 11 November, col. 206.

Claessens, Stijn *et al.* (1996) 'Ownership and Corporate Governance: Evidence from the Czech Republic', mimeo.

Cohen, Lenard J. (1995) *Broken Bonds*, 2nd edn. Boulder, CO: Westview.

Cohen, S. (1973) *Geography and Politics in a World Divided*, 2nd ed. Oxford: Oxford University Press.

Cohen, S. (1994) 'Geopolitics in the new world era: a new perspective on an old discipline', in G. Demko and W. Wood (eds), *Reordering the World:*

Geopolitical Perspectives on the 21st Century. Boulder, CO: Westview, pp. 49–70.

Cook, Linda J. (1993) *The Soviet Social Contract and Why It Failed.* Cambridge, MA: Harvard University Press.

Cooper, R. (1996) *The Post-Modern State and the New World Order.* London: Demos.

Corrin, Chris (ed.) (1992) *Superwomen and the Double Burden: Women's Experience of Change in East-Central Europe and the Former Soviet Union.* London: Scarlet Press.

Corrin, Chris (1993) 'Is liberalization damaging Albanian women's health?', *Focus on Gender: Perspectives on Women and Development.* Oxford: Oxfam.

Corrin, Chris (1994) *Magyar Women: Hungarian Women's Lives 1960s–1990s.* Basingstoke: Macmillan.

Corrin, Chris (ed.) (1996) *Women in a Violent World: Feminist Analyses and Resistance across Europe.* Edinburgh: Edinburgh University Press.

Corrin, Chris *et al.* (1996) 'Women and democratization', unpublished research report, ESRC R000234258.

Cottey, Andrew (1995) *East-Central Europe after the Cold War. Poland, the Czech Republic, Slovakia and Hungary in Search of Security.* London: Macmillan.

Council of Europe (1994) *International Workshop on the Problems of Equality in the Current Period of Transition in the Countries of Central and East Europe.* Netherlands: Council of Europe Press.

Cowen Karp, R. (ed.) (1993) *Central and Eastern Europe: The Challenge of Transition.* Oxford: Oxford University Press for SIPRI.

Cox, Terry and Andry Furlong (eds) (1995) *Hungary: The Politics of Transition.* London: Cass.

Crampton, Richard J. (1997) *Eastern Europe in the Twentieth Century – and After,* 2nd edn. London: Routledge.

Crampton, Richard and Ben Crampton (1996) *Atlas of Eastern Europe in the Twentieth Century.* London: Routledge.

Crawford, Keith (1996) *East European Politics Today.* Manchester and New York: Manchester University Press.

Crowther, W. (1997) 'Moldova: caught between nation and empire', in Ian Bremmer and Ray Taras (eds), *New States, New Politics: Building the Post-Soviet Nations.* Cambridge: Cambridge University Press, pp. 316–49.

Crowther, W. and S. D. Roper (1996) 'A comparative analysis of institutional development in the Romanian and Moldovan legislatures', in Olson and Norton (1996), pp. 133–60.

Csaba, Laszlo (1995) *The Capitalist Revolution in Eastern Europe: A Contribution to the Economic Theory of Systemic Change.* Aldershot, Hants: Edward Elgar.

Dahl, Robert A. (1971) *Polyarchy: Participation and Opposition.* New Haven: Yale University Press.

Dahrendorf, Ralf (1990) *Reflections on the Revolution in Europe.* New York: Random House.

Davies, Norman (1996) *Europe: A History.* Oxford: Oxford University Press.

Dawisha, Karen and Philip Hanson (eds) (1981) *Soviet-East European Dilemmas: Coercion, Competition and Consent.* London: Heinemann for the RIIA.

Dawisha, Karen and Bruce Parrott (eds) (1994) *The New States of Eurasia. The Politics of Upheaval.* Cambridge: Cambridge University Press.

Dawisha, Karen and Bruce Parrott (eds) (1997) *Authoritarianism and Democratization in Postcommunist Societies*, 4 vols. Cambridge: Cambridge University Press.

Deacon, Bob (1993) 'Social change, social problems and social policy', in White, Batt and Lewis (1993), pp. 225–39

Denitch, Bogdan (1994) *Ethnic Nationalism: The Tragic Death of Yugoslavia.* Minneapolis and London: University of Minnesota Press.

Diamond, Larry (1996) 'Is the third wave over?', *Journal of Democracy*, vol. 7, no. 3, pp. 20–37.

Dolling, Irene (1992) 'Between hope and hopelessness: women in the GDR after the turningpoint', in Lewis (1992), pp. 128–33.

Domazet, Borna (1996) 'Surviving in Croatia', *Transition*, vol. 2, no. 20.

Druker, J. (1997) 'Is there a skeleton in your closet ?', *Transition*, vol. 4, no. 5.

Duverger, Maurice (1963) *Political Parties.* New York: Wiley.

Duverger, Maurice (1986) 'Duverger's law: forty years later', in Bernard Grofman and Arend Lijphart (eds), *Electoral Laws and Their Political Consequences.* New York: Agathon Press.

Dyker, David and Ivan Vejvoda (eds) (1996) *Yugoslavia and After: A Study in Fragmentation.* London: Longman.

East, Roger and Jolyon Pontin (1997) *Revolution and Change in Central and Eastern Europe*, 2nd edn. London: Pinter.

EBRD (1995) *Transition Report 1995.* London: EBRD.

EBRD (1996) *Transition Report update.* London: EBRD.

EBRD (1997) *Transition Report 1997.* London: EBRD.

Ekiert, Gregorcz (1996) *The State Against Society: Political Crises and Their Aftermath in Eastern Europe.* Princeton, NJ: Princeton University Press.

Elster, Jon (1993) 'Constitution-making in Eastern Europe: rebuilding the boat in the open sea', *Public Administration*, vol. 71 (Spring/Summer).

Estrin, Saul (ed.) (1994) *Privatization in Central and Eastern Europe.* London: Longman.

Eurobarometer Survey (1994) Brussels: European Commission.

Evans, Geoff and Stephen Whitefield (1995) 'Economic ideology and political success: communist successor parties in the Czech Republic, Slovakia and Hungary compared', *Party Politics.* vol. 1, no. 4 (October).

Fedor, Helen (ed.) (1995) *Belarus and Moldova: Country Studies.* Washington, DC: Federal Research Division, Library of Congress.

Fernandez-Armesto, Felipe (ed.) (1994) *The Times Guide to the Peoples of Europe.* London: Times Books.

Fisher, S. (1996) 'Backtracking on the road to democratic reform', in Pridham and Lewis (1996).

Fleron, Frederic J. (1996) 'Post-Soviet political culture in Russia: an assessment of recent empirical investigations', *Europe-Asia Studies*, vol. 48, no. 2, pp. 225–60.

Frydman, Roman and Andrzej Rapaczynski (1994) *Privatization in Eastern Europe: Is the State Withering Away?*. London: Central European University Press.

Frydman, Roman *et al.* (1993) *The Privatization Process in Central Europe*. London: Central European University Press.

Frydman, Roman, K. Murphy and A. Rapczynski (1996) 'Capitalism with a comrade's face', *Transition*, vol. 2, no. 2.

Fukuyama, Francis (1995) *Trust: The Social Virtues and the Creation of Prosperity*. London: Hamish Hamilton.

Fulbrook, Mary (1995) *Anatomy of a Dictatorship. Inside the GDR 1949–1989*. Oxford: Oxford University Press.

Funk, Nanette and Magda Mueller (eds) (1993) *Gender Politics and Post-Communism*. New York: Routledge.

Gabal, Ivan (ed.) (1996) *The 1990 Election to the Czechoslovakian Federal Assembly: Analyses, Documents and Data*. Berlin: Sigma.

Gal, S. (1996) 'Feminism and civil society', in *Replika*, special issue, Colonization or partnership? Eastern Europe and Western social sciences. Budapest: University of Economic Sciences, pp. 75–81.

Gallagher, Tom (1995) *Romania after Ceausescu*. Edinburgh: Edinburgh University Press.

Gallagher, Tom (1996) 'Nationalism and post-communist politics: the Party of Romanian National Unity, 1990–96', in Lavinia Stan (ed.), *Romania in Transition*. Aldershot, Hants: Dartmouth.

Garnett, J. (1997) *Keystone in the Arch. Ukraine in the Emerging Security Environment of Central and Eastern Europe*. Washington, DC: Carnegie Endowment for International Peace.

Gärtner, Heinz (1997) 'States without nations: state, nation and security in Central Europe', *International Politics*, vol. 34, no. 1 (March), pp. 7–32.

Gati, Charles (1996) 'The mirage of democracy', *Transition*, vol. 2, no. 6.

Gebethner, Stanislaw (1995) 'System Wyborczy: Deformacja czy reprezentacja?' in Stanislaw Gebethner (ed.), *Wybory Parlamentarne 1991 i 1993* Warsaw: Wydawnictwo Sejmowe, pp. 9–48.

Gebethner, Stanislaw (1996) 'Parliamentary and electoral parties in Poland', in Lewis (1996).

Gibson, James L. (1993) 'Perceived political freedom in the Soviet Union', *Journal of Politics*, vol. 55, no. 4, pp. 936–74.

Girnius, S. (1997) 'The political pendulum swings back in Lithuania', *Transition*, vol. 3, no. 2 (7 February), pp. 20–1.

Glenny, Misha (1992) *The Fall of Yugoslavia*. Harmondsworth: Penguin.

Gomez, Victor (1996) 'Czech nouveaux riches find pleasure – and pitfalls – in celebrating status', *Transition*, vol. 2, no. 20.

Gomulka, Stanislaw (1995) 'The IMF-supported programs of Poland and Russia 1990–1994: principles, errors and results', *Journal of Comparative Economics*, vol. 20.

Grabher, Gernot and David Stark (1997) *Restructuring Networks in Post-Socialism: Legacies, Linkages, and Locations*. Oxford: Oxford University Press.

Griffiths, E. (ed.) (1989) *Central and Eastern Europe: The Opening Curtain?*. Boulder, CO: Westview.

Gros, Daniel and Alfred Steinherr (1995) *Winds of Change in Central and Eastern Europe: The Economics of Transition*. Harlow: Longman.

Hajda, Lubomyr and Mark Beissinger (eds) (1990) *The Nationalities Factor in Soviet Politics and Society*. Boulder, CO: Westview.

Hankiss, Elemer (1990) *East European Alternatives*. Oxford: Clarendon Press.

Havel, Vaclav (1993) 'The postcommunist nightmare', *New York Review of Books*, 27 May, p. 9.

Havel, Vaclav *et al.* (1985) *The Power of the Powerless*. Armonk, NY: Sharpe.

Held, Joseph (ed.) (1992) *The Columbia History of Eastern Europe in the Twentieth Century*. New York: Columbia University Press.

Helsinki Citizens' Assembly (HCA) (1992) *Reproductive Rights in East and Central Europe*. Prague, HCA Publications 3.

Helsinki Citizens' Assembly (HCA) (1993) *Violence Against Women in Central and Eastern Europe*. Prague, HCA Publications 8.

Henderson, Karen and Neil Robinson (1997) *Post-Communist Politics. An Introduction*. Hemel Hempstead: Prentice-Hall.

Hibbing, John R. and Samuel C. Patterson (1994) 'Public trust in the new parliaments of Central and Eastern Europe', *Political Studies*, vol. 42, no. 4, pp. 570–92.

Higley, John, Judith Kullberg and Jan Pakulski (1996) 'The persistence of postcommunist elites', *Journal of Democracy*, vol. 7, no. 2 (April), pp. 133–47.

Holden, Gerald (ed.) (1988) *The Warsaw Pact: Soviet Security and Bloc Politics*. Oxford: Blackwell.

Holmes, Leslie (1997) *Post-Communism: An Introduction*. Durham, NC: Duke University Press.

Horvath, Agnes and Arpad Szakolczai (1992) *The Dissolution of Communist Power: The Case of Hungary*. London and New York: Routledge.

Hosking, Geoffrey (1991) *The Awakening of the Soviet Union*, 2nd edn. Cambridge, MA: Harvard University Press.

Howard, A. Dick (ed.) (1993) *Constitution Making in Eastern Europe*. Washington, DC: Woodrow Wilson Center Press.

Huldt, Bo, and Johannessen, Ulrika (eds) (1997) *1st Annual Stockholm Conference on Baltic Sea Security and Cooperation*. Stockholm: Utrikespolitiska Institutet.

Huntington, Samuel P. (1996) *The Clash of Civilizations and the Remaking of World Order*. New York: Simon & Schuster.

Hyde-Price, Adrian (1991) *European Security Beyond the Cold War: Four Scenarios for the Year 2010*. London: Sage.

Hyde-Price, Adrian (1996) *The International Politics of East Central Europe*. Manchester: Manchester University Press.

International Institute for Democracy (1995; 2nd edn. 1996) *The Rebirth of Democracy: 12 Constitutions of Central and Eastern Europe*. Strasbourg: Council of Europe.

International Organization for Migration (1995) *Trafficking and Prostitution: The Growing Exploitation of Migrant Women from Central and Eastern Europe*. Budapest: Migration Information Programme.

Inter-Parliamentary Union (IPU) (1997) *Men and Women in Politics: Democracy Still in the Making*. Reports and Documents No. 28, Geneva: IPU.

Ishiyama, John T. (1995) 'Communist parties in transition: structures, leaders, and processes of democratization in Eastern Europe', *Comparative Politics*, vol. 27, no. 1.

Jackiewicz, Irena (1994) 'The Polish Parliamentarians Under Post-Communism: The Antinomy of Representation' in Agh (1994), pp. 252–69.

Jasiewicz, Krzysztof (1993) 'Polish politics on the eve of the 1993 elections: toward fragmentation or pluralism?', *Communist and Post-Communist Studies*, vol. 26, no. 4.

Jeffries, Ian (1993) *Socialist Economies and the Transition to the Market: A Guide*. London: Routledge.

Jeffries, Ian (1996) *A Guide to Economies in Transition*. London: Routledge.

Jonson, L. (ed.) (1995) *Ukraine and Integration in the East. Economic, Military and Military–Industrial Relations*. Stockholm: Utrikespolitiska Institutet.

Kaldor, Mary and Ivan Vejvoda (1997) 'Democratization in central and eastern European countries', *International Affairs*, vol. 73, no. 1 (January), pp. 59–82.

Kaminski, Bartlomiej (1991) *The Collapse of State Socialism: The Case of Poland*. Princeton, NJ: Princeton University Press.

Karasimeonov, Georgi (1995) 'Parliamentary elections of 1994 and the development of the Bulgarian party system', *Party Politics*, vol. 1, no. 4 (December).

Karasimeonov, Georgi (1996) 'The Legislature in Post-Communist Bulgaria' in Olson and Norton (1996).

Karasimeonov, Georgi (ed.) (1997) *The 1990 Election to the Bulgarian Grand National Assembly and the 1991 Election to the Bulgarian Grand National Assembly: Analyses, Documents and Data*. Berlin: Sigma.

Kask, P. (1996) 'Institutional development of the parliament in Estonia', in Olson and Norton (1996), pp. 193–212.

Katzenstein, P. (ed.) (1997) *Tamed Power: Germany in Europe*. Cornell: Cornell University Press.

Keane, John (1988) *Civil Society and the State*. London: Verso.

Kenway, Peter and Eva Klvacova (1996) 'The web of cross-ownership among Czech financial intermediaries: an assessment', *Europe-Asia Studies*, vol. 48, no. 5 (July), pp. 797–809.

Kettle, S. (1996a) 'Slovakia's one-man band', *Transition*, vol. 2, no. 17.

Kettle, S. (1996b) 'An "economic miracle" plagued by social complacency', in Pridham and Lewis (1996).

Khodyreva, N. (1996) 'Sexism and sexual abuse in Russia', in Corrin (1996), pp. 27–40.

King, Charles (1995) *Post-Soviet Moldova: A Borderland in Transition*. London: Royal Institute of International Affairs.

Kitschelt, H. *et al.* (forthcoming) *Post-Communist Party Systems*.

Kommers, Donald P. and W.J. Thompson (1995) 'Fundamentals in the liberal constitutional tradition', in Joachim J. Hesse and Nevil Johnson (eds), *Constitutional Policy and Change in Europe*. Oxford: Oxford University Press.

Konrad, Georgy (1984) *Anti-Politics: An Essay*. London: Quartet.
Kopecky, Petr (1995), 'Developing party organizations in East Central Europe', *Party Politics*, vol. 1, no. 4 (October).
Kornai, Janos (1980) *Economics of Shortage*. Amsterdam: North-Holland.
Kovacs, Janos (ed.) (1994) *Transition to Capitalism? The Communist Legacy in Eastern Europe*. New Brunswick, NJ: Transaction.
Krasner, Stephen D. (1983) *International Regimes*. Ithaca, NY: Cornell University Press.
Krasuski, J. (1994) 'Polnische Bedenken zur europäischen Integration', *WeltTrends*, no. 2 (March), pp. 82–96.
Kumar, Krishan (1992) 'The 1989 revolutions and the idea of Europe', *Political Studies*, vol. 40, pp. 439–61.
Kurti, Laszlo and Juliet Langman (eds) (1997) *Beyond Borders; Remaking Cultural Identities in the New East and Central Europe*. Boulder, CO: Westview.
Kuzio, Taras (1997) *Ukraine under Kuchma: Political reform, economic transformation and security policy in independent Ukraine*. London: Macmillan.
Kuzio, Taras and Andrew Wilson (1992) *Ukraine: Perestroika to Independence*. London: Macmillan.
Lane, David (1995) 'Political elites under Gorbachev and Yeltsin in the early period of transition: a reputational and analytical study', in Timothy J. Colton and Robert C. Tucker (eds), *Patterns in Post-Soviet Leadership*. Boulder, CO: Westview.
Lasswell, Harold D. (1986) 'Democratic leadership', in Barbara Kellerman (ed.), *Political Leadership*. Pittsburgh, PA: University of Pittsburgh Press.
Latawski, Paul (ed.) (1995) *Contemporary Nationalism in East Central Europe*. London: Macmillan.
Lavigne, Marie (1995) *The Economics of Transition: From Socialist Economy to Market Economy*. Basingstoke: Macmillan.
Layard, Richard and John S. Parker (1996) *The Coming Russian Boom*. New York: The Free Press.
Leff, Carol K. (1996) *The Czech and Slovak Republics: Nation Versus State*. Boulder, CO: Westview.
Lewis, Paul G. (1990) 'Non-competitive elections and regime change: Poland 1989', *Parliamentary Affairs*, vol. 40, no. 1 (January).
Lewis, Paul G. (ed.) (1992) *Democracy and Civil Society in Eastern Europe*. London: Macmillan.
Lewis, Paul G. (1994) *Central Europe Since 1945*. London: Longman.
Lewis, Paul G. (ed.) (1996) *Party Structure and Organization in East-Central Europe*. Cheltenham: Edward Elgar.
Lewis, Paul G. (1998) 'Party funding in post-communist East-Central Europe', in Peter Burnell and Alan Ware (eds), *Funding Democratization*. Manchester: Manchester University Press.
Lewis, Paul G. and Radzislawa Gortat (1995) 'Models of party development and questions of state dependence in Poland', *Party Politics*, vol. 1, no. 4 (October).
Liebich, André (1997) 'The communists reincarnated: their return in Russia and Eastern Europe', *World Affairs*, vol. 1, no. 1 (January–March).

Lieven, Anatol (1994) *The Baltic Revolution: Estonia, Latvia, Lithuania and the Path to Independence*, 2nd edn. New Haven and London: Yale University Press.

Lijphart, Arend (1991) 'Constitutional choices for new democracies', *Journal of Democracy*, vol. 2, no. 3.

Linz, Juan J. and Albert Stepan (1996a) *Problems of Democratic Transition and Consolidation*. Baltimore, MD: Johns Hopkins University Press.

Linz, Juan J. and Albert Stepan (1996b) 'Toward consolidated democracies', *Journal of Democracy*, vol. 7, no. 2 (April), pp. 14–33.

Loewenberg, Gerhard (1994) 'The New Political Leadership of Central Europe: The Example of the New Hungarian National Assembly' in Remington (1994).

Lomax, Bill (1996) 'The structure and organization of Hungary's political parties', in Lewis (1996).

Lovenduski, Joni and Jean Woodall (1987) *Politics and Society in Eastern Europe*. London: Macmillan.

Ludanyi, A. (ed.) (1996) 'Hungary and the Hungarian minorities', special issue of *Nationalities Papers*, vol. 24, no. 3.

Magas, Branka (1993) *The Destruction of Yugoslavia*. London: Verso.

Mahr, Alison and John Nagle (1995) 'Resurrection of the successor parties and democratization in East-Central Europe', *Communist and Post-Communist Studies*, vol. 28, no. 4.

Maier, Charles S. (1997) *Dissolution: The Crisis of Communism and the End of East Germany*. Princeton, NJ: Princeton University Press.

Malova, D. (1995) Slovakia, in *1995 Political Data Yearbook*, special issue of *European Journal of Political Research*, vol. 28, nos 3/4.

Malova, Darina and Danica Sivalkova (1996) 'The National Council of the Slovak Republic Between Democratic Transition and National State-Building' in Olson and Norton, (1996).

Mandelbaum, Michael (1996a) *The Dawn of Peace in Europe*. New York: Twentieth Century Fund.

Mandelbaum, Michael (ed.) (1996b) *Post-Commumism: Four Perspectives*. New York: Council on Foreign Relations.

Markowski, R. and Gabor Toka (1993) 'Left turn in Poland and Hungary five years after the collapse of communism', *Sisyphus. Sociological Studies*, vol. 9, no. 1.

Marples, David (1996) *Belarus: From Soviet Rule to Nuclear Catastrophe*. London: Macmillan.

Mason, David (1993) 'Poland', in White, Batt and Lewis (1993), pp. 36–50.

Mason, David (1996) *Revolution and Transition in East-Central Europe*, 2nd edn. Boulder, CO: Westview.

McGregor, James (1994) 'The Presidency in East Central Europe', *RFE/RL Research Report*, vol. 3, no. 2 (January).

Mearsheimer, John J. (1990) 'Back to the future: instability in Europe after the cold war', *International Security*, vol. 15, no. 1, pp. 5–56.

Mearsheimer, John (1995) 'The false promise of international institutions', *International Security*, vol. 19, no. 3 (Winter), pp. 5–49.

Meseznikov, Grigorij (1995) 'The parliamentary elections 1994: a confirmation of the split of the party system in Slovakia', in S. Szomolanyi and

G. Meselnikov (eds), *Slovakia: Parliamentary Elections 1994: Causes–Consequences–Prospects*. Bratislava: Slovak Political Science Association and Friedrich Ebert Foundation.

Meseznikov, Grigorij (1997) 'Domestic political developments and the political scene in the Slovak Republic', in Martin Butora and Peter Huncik (eds), *Global Report on Slovakia. Comprehensive Analyses from 1995 and Trends from 1996*. Bratislava: Sandor Marai Foundation.

Miall, Hugh (1993) *Shaping the New Europe*. London: Pinter.

Millard, Frances (1994) *The Anatomy of the New Poland: Post-Communist Politics in Its First Phase*. Aldershot, Hants: Elgar.

Miller, B. and K. Kagan (1997) 'The great powers and regional conflicts: Eastern Europe and the Balkans from the post-Napoleonic era to the post-cold war era', *International Studies Quarterly*, vol. 41, no. 1 (March), pp. 51–86.

Miller, William L., Stephen White and Paul Heywood (1998) *Values and Political Change in Postcommunist Europe*. London: Macmillan.

Milton, Andrew K.(1996) 'News media reform in Eastern Europe: a cross-national comparison', in O'Neil (1996).

Miroziewicz, Dagmar (1996) 'Polish economic reform marred by high unemployment', *Transition*, vol. 2, no. 13.

Mishler, William and Richard Rose (1997) 'Trust, distrust and skepticism: popular evaluations of civil and political institutions in post-communist societies', *Journal of Politics*, vol. 59, no. 2, pp. 418–51.

Moghadam, Valentine M. (ed.) (1992) *Privatization and Democratization in Central and Eastern Europe and the Soviet Union: The Gender Dimension*. Helsinki: World Institute for Development Research of the United Nations University.

Moghadam, Valentine M. (ed.) (1993) *Democratic Reform and the Position of Women in Transitional Economies*. Oxford: Clarendon Press.

Mokrzycki, Edmund (1995) 'A new middle class?', in Bryant and Mokrzycki (1995).

Morgan, Robin (ed.) (1984) *Sisterhood is Global: The International Women's Movement Anthology*. Harmondsworth: Penguin.

Motyl, Alexander (ed.) (1992) *The Post-Soviet Nations: Perspectives on the Demise of the USSR*. New York: Columbia University Press.

Motyl, Alexander (1993) *Dilemmas of Independence: Ukraine After Totalitarianism*. New York: Council on Foreign Relations.

Mueller, K. (1995) 'Patterns of alliance: alignment balancing and stability in Eastern Europe', *Security Studies*, vol. 5, no. 1 (Autumn), pp. 38–76.

Munich, Daniel and Vit Sorm (1996) 'The Czech Republic as a low-unemployment oasis', *Transition*, vol. 2, no. 13.

Nastase, Adrian (1992) 'A new security order in Europe', *Symposium of the Assembly of the Western European Union*. Paris: Assembly of the WEU.

Nemenyi, M. (1996) 'The social construction of women's roles in Hungary', *Replika,* special issue, pp. 83–9.

Norgaard, Ole, L. Johannsen and A. Pedersen (1994) 'The Baltic Republics: Estonia, Latvia, and Lithuania', in Bogdan Szajkowski (ed.), *Political Parties of Eastern Europe, Russia, and the Successor States*. Harlow: Longman, pp. 47–65.

Norton, Philip and David M. Olson (1996) 'Parliaments in Adolescence', in Olson and Norton (1996).

Nove, Alec (1994) 'A gap in transition models? A comment on Gomulka', *Europe-Asia Studies*, vol. 46, no. 5.

O'Donnell, Guillermo (1996) 'Illusions about consolidation', *Journal of Democracy*, vol. 7, no. 2.

O'Donnell, Guillermo, Philippe C. Schmitter and Lawrence Whitehead (eds) (1986) *Transitions From Authoritarian Rule: Tentative Conclusions about Uncertain Democracies*. Baltimore: Johns Hopkins University Press.

O'Loughlin, John and Herman van der Wusten (eds) (1993) *The New Political Geography of Eastern Europe*. London and New York: Belhaven Press.

O'Neil, Patrick H. (ed.) (1996) 'Post-Communism and the Media in Eastern Europe', special issue of *The Journal of Communist Studies and Transition Politics*, vol. 12, no. 4 (December).

OECD Economic Surveys (1996) *Poland 1997*. Paris: OECD.

Offe, Claus (1991) 'Capitalism by democratic design? Democratic theory facing the triple transition in East Central Europe', *Social Research*, vol. 58, no. 4 (Winter).

Okey, Robin (1986) *Eastern Europe 1740–1985: Feudalism to Communism*, 2nd edn. London: Hutchinson.

Olson, David M. (1993a) 'Political Parties and Party Systems in Regime Transformation: Inner Transition in the New Democracies of Central Europe', *American Review of Politics*, no. 14 (Winter), pp. 619–58.

Olson, David M. (1993b) 'Dissolution of the State: Political Parties and the 1992 Election in Czechoslovakia', *Communist and Post-Communist Studies*, vol. 26, no. 3 (September), pp. 301–14.

Olson, David M. (1994) 'The Sundered State: Federalism and Parliament in Czechoslovakia' in Remington (1994), pp. 97–124.

Olson, David M. (1997a) 'The Paradoxes of Institutional Development: The New Democratic Parliaments of Central Europe', *International Political Science Review*, vol. 18, no. 4 (October).

Olson, David and Philip Norton (eds) (1996) *The New Parliaments of Central and Eastern Europe*. London: Cass.

Olson, David M., van der Meer, M. Simon, and I. Jackiewicz (1998) 'Committees in the Post-Communist Polish Sejm: Structure, activity and Members', *Journal of Legislative Studies* (forthcoming).

Olson, David M., Jindriska Syllova and Jana Reschova (1993) 'Prvni volebni obdobi demokratickeho parlamentu v CSFR: Federalni shromazdeni 1990–92: komparacni pohled', *Pravnik*, vol. 132, no. 2, pp. 125–41.

Orenstein, Mitchell (1996) 'The failures of neo-liberal social policy in Central Europe', *Transition*, vol. 2, no. 13.

Pateman, Carole (1988) *The Sexual Contract*. Cambridge: Polity.

Patzelt, Werner (1994) 'Legislators of New Parliaments: The Case of East Germany' in Agh (1994).

Pearson, Raymond (1991) 'The historical background to Soviet federalism', in A. McAuley (ed.), *Soviet Federalism, Nationalism and Economic Decentralisation*. Leicester: Leicester University Press, pp. 13–24.

Pearson, Raymond (1994) *The Longman Companion to European Nationalism 1789–1920*. London: Longman.

Peterson, V. Spike and A. Sisson Runyan (1993) *Global Gender Issues*. Boulder, CO: Westview.

Phillips, Anne (1991) *Engendering Democracy*. London: Polity.

Polish Committee of NGOs (1995) *The Situation of Women in Poland: The Report of the NGOs Committee*. Warsaw: Polish Committee of NGOs.

Pontusson, J. (1992) 'Sweden', in Mark Kesselman and Joel Krieger (eds), *European Politics in Transition*. Lexington, MA: D. C. Heath & Co.

Powers, D. V. and J. H. Cox (1997) 'Echos from the past: the relationship between satisfaction with economic reforms and voting behaviour in Poland', *American Political Science Review*, vol. 91, no. 3.

Prawitz, J. (1997) 'A nuclear-weapon-free zone in Central and Eastern Europe', *Programme for Promoting Nuclear Non-Proliferation Issue Review*, no. 10 (February).

Preuss, Ulrich K. (1995) 'Patterns of constitutional evolution and change in Eastern Europe', in Joachim J. Hesse and Nevil Johnson (eds), *Constitutional Policy and Change in Europe*. Oxford: Oxford University Press.

Pridham, Geoffrey, Eric Herring and George Sanford (eds) (1994) *Building Democracy? The International Dimension of Democratisation in Eastern Europe*. London: Leicester University Press.

Pridham, Geoffrey and Paul G. Lewis (eds) (1996) *Stabilizing Fragile Democracies: Comparing New Party Systems in Southern and Eastern Europe*. London: Routledge.

Przeworski, Adam (1991) *Democracy and the Market*. Cambridge: Cambridge University Press.

Rady, Martyn (1992) *Romania in Turmoil: A Contemporary History*. London: Tauris.

Raina, Peter (ed.) (1995) *The Constitutions of New Democracies in Europe*. Cambridge: Merlin.

Regulska, J. (1998) 'The political and its meaning for women: transitional politics in Poland', in J. Pickles and A. Smith (eds) *Theorizing Transition: The Political Economy of Change in Central and Eastern Europe*. New York: Routledge.

Reisch, A. (1996) 'Hungarian foreign policy and the Magyar minorities: new foreign policy priorities', *Nationalities Papers*, vol. 24, no. 3, pp. 447–65.

Remington, Thomas F. (ed.) (1994) *Parliaments in Transition*. Boulder, CO: Westview.

Renne, Tanya (ed.) (1997) *Ana's Land: Sisterhood in Eastern Europe*. Boulder, CO: Westview.

Reschova, Jana (1992) 'Nova politika s novymi ludmi: Federalne zhormazdenie v roku 1990', *Sociologicky Casopis*, vol. 28, no. 2 (Duben), pp. 222–36.

Rigby, T. H. and Ferenc Feher (eds) (1982) *Political Legitimation in Communist States*. New York: St Martins Press.

Riker, W. H. (1986) 'Duverger's law revisited', in Bernard Grofman and Arend Lijphart (eds), *Electoral Laws and Their Political Consequences*. New York: Agathon Press.

Rona-Tas, Akos (1994) 'The first shall be last? Entrepreneurship and the communist cadres in the transition from socialism', *American Journal of Sociology*, vol. 100, no. 1.

Rose, Richard (1993) 'Contradictions between micro and macro-economic goals in post-communist societies', *Europe-Asia Studies*, vol. 45, no. 3, pp. 419–44.

Rose, Richard (1995a) 'Mobilizing demobilized voters in post-communist societies', *Party Politics*, vol. 1, no. 4 (October), pp. 549–63.

Rose, Richard (1995b) 'Freedom as a fundamental value', *International Social Science Journal*, no. 145, pp. 457–71.

Rose, Richard (1996a) *What Is Europe? A Dynamic Perspective*. New York and London: Longman.

Rose, Richard (1996b) 'Ex-communists in post-communist societies', *Political Quarterly*, vol. 67, no. 1, pp. 14–25.

Rose, Richard and Christian Haerpfer (1996) *Change and Stability in the New Democracies Barometer: A Trend Analysis*. Glasgow: University of Strathclyde, Studies in Public Policy No. 270.

Rose, Richard and William Maley (1994) *Nationalities in the Baltic States: A Survey Study*. Glasgow: University of Strathclyde, Studies in Public Policy No. 222.

Rose, Richard and William Mishler (1996a) 'Testing the Churchill hypothesis: support for democracy and its alternatives', *Journal of Public Policy*, vol. 16, no. 1, pp. 29–58.

Rose, Richard and William Mishler (1996b) 'Representation and leadership in post-communist political systems', *Journal of Communist Studies and Transition Politics*, vol. 12, no. 2 (June), pp. 224–46.

Rose, Richard, William Mishler and Christian Haerpfer (1998) *Democracy and Its Alternatives: Understanding Postcommunist Societies*. Baltimore, MD: Johns Hopkins University Press.

Rose, Richard and Evgeny Tikhomirov (1995) *Trends in the New Russia Barometer*. Glasgow: Centre for the Study of Public Policy, University of Strathclyde, Studies in Public Policy no. 256; and *Supplement* (1996).

Rotfeld, Adam D. and Walther Stützle (eds) (1991) *Germany and Europe in Transition*. Oxford: Oxford University Press for SIPRI.

Rothschild, Joseph (1993) *Return to Diversity: A Political History of Eastern Europe since World War II*, 2nd edn. New York: Oxford University Press.

Rudolf, P. (1996) 'The future of the United States as a European power: the case of NATO enlargement', *European Security*, vol. 5, no. 2 (Summer), pp. 175–95.

Rueschemeyer, Marilyn (ed.) (1994) *Women in the Politics of Postcommunist Eastern Europe*. Armonk, NY: Sharpe.

Ruggie, John G. (ed.) (1993) *Multilateralism Matters. The Theory and Praxis of an Institutional Form*. New York: Columbia University Press.

Ruggie, John G. (1996) 'Consolidating the European pillar: the key to NATO's future', *The Washington Quarterly*, vol. 20, no. 1, pp. 109–24.

Rupnik, Jacques (1990) 'Central Europe or Mitteleuropa?', *Daedalus*, vol. 119, no. 1 (Winter), pp. 249–78.

Rychard, Andrzej (1992) 'Politics and society after the breakthrough: the sources and threats to political legitimacy in post-communist Poland', in George Sanford (ed.), *Democratization in Poland, 1988–90*. London: Macmillan.

Sachs, Jeffrey (1993) *Poland's Jump to the Market Economy*. Cambridge, MA: MIT Press.

Samson, I. (1997) *Die Slowakei zwischen Annäherung an Moskau und Streben nach Westintegration*. Köln: Berichte des Bundesinstituts für Ostwissenschaftliche und Internationale Studien, no. 2.

Sanford, George (ed.) (1992) *Democratization in Poland 1988–90: Polish Voices*. London: Macmillan.

Schmidt, Fabian (1996) 'Albania: election fraud sparks protest', *Transition*, vol. 2, no. 13 (28 June).

Schopflin, George (1993) *Politics in Eastern Europe, 1945–1992*. Oxford: Blackwell.

Schori, P. (1994) *Mellan Maastricht och Sarajevo. Samtal om Europa*. Stockholm: Tidens Förlag.

Schroeder, Gertrude (1990) 'Nationalities and the Soviet economy', in Lubomyr Hajda and Mark Beissinger (eds), *The Nationalities Factor in Soviet Politics and Society*. Boulder, CO: Westview, pp. 43–71.

Schumpeter, Joseph A. (1952) *Capitalism, Socialism and Democracy*. London: George Allen & Unwin.

Seton-Watson, Hugh (1977) *Nations and States: An Enquiry into the Origins of Nations and the Politics of Nationalism*. London: Methuen.

Shearman, Peter (ed.) (1995) *Russian Foreign Policy Since 1990*. Boulder, CO: Westview.

Sherr, James (1996) *Ukraine, Russia, Europe*. Sandhurst: Royal Military Academy, Conflict Studies Research Centre.

Shugart, Matthew S. (1996) 'Executive-Legislative Relations in Post-Communist Europe', *Transition*, vol. 2, no. 25 (December 13), pp. 6–11.

Siemienska, Renata (1991) 'Dialogue: Polish Women and Polish Politics Since World War II', *Journal of Women's History*, vol. 3, no. 1 (Spring), pp. 108–25.

Siklova, J. (1990) 'Women and democracy in Czechoslovakia', interview by Ruth Rosen, *Peace and Democracy News*, Fall.

Siklova, J. (1996) 'Different region, different women: why feminism isn't successful in the Czech Republic', *Replika*, special issue, pp. 91–5.

Simon, Maurice D. (1996) 'Institutional Development of Poland's Post-Communist Sejm: A Comparative Analysis', in Olson and Norton (1996).

Simons, Thomas W. (1993) *Eastern Europe in the Postwar World*, 2nd edn. London: Macmillan.

Smejkalova, J. (1996) 'On the road: smuggling feminism across the post-iron curtain', *Replika*, special issue, pp. 97–102.

Smith, Graham (ed.) (1994) *The Baltic States: The National Self-Determination of Estonia, Latvia and Lithuania*. London: Macmillan.

Smith, Graham (ed.) (1996) *The Nationalities Question in the Post-Soviet States*, 2nd edn. London and New York: Longman.

Somogyvari, Istvan (1996) 'The Operation of the Standing Orders' in Agh and Kurtan (1996).

Sperling, James and Emil Kirchner (1997) *Recasting the European Order. Security Architectures and Economic Cooperation*. Manchester: Manchester University Press.

Staar, Richard F. (ed.) (1993) *The Transition to Democracy in Poland*. New York: St Martins.

Standing, Guy and Daniel Vaughan-Whitehead (eds) (1995) *Minimum Wages in Central and Eastern Europe: From Protection to Destitution*. London: Central European University Press.

Staniszkis, Jadwiga (1991a) ' "Political capitalism" in Poland', *East European Politics and Societies*, vol. 5, no. 1.

Staniszkis, Jadwiga (1991b) *The Dynamics of the Breakthrough in Eastern Europe: The Polish Experience*. Berkeley: University of California Press.

Stark, David (1990) 'Privatisation in Hungary: from plan to market or from plan to clan?', *East European Politics and Societies*, vol. 4, no. 3.

Stark, David (1992) 'Path dependence and privatisation strategies in East Central Europe', *East European Politics and Societies*, vol. 6, no. 1.

Stark, David (1996) 'Recombinant property in East European capitalism', *American Journal of Sociology*, vol. 101, no. 4.

Steele, Jonathan (1995) in *The Guardian*, 8 September.

Stern, Nicholas (1997) 'The transition in Eastern Europe and the former Soviet Union: some strategic lessons from the experience of 25 countries over six years', *Working Paper* no. 18 (April).

Stokes, Gale (1993) *The Walls Came Tumbling Down: The Collapse of Communism in Eastern Europe*. New York: Oxford University Press.

Stokes, Gale (ed.) (1996) *From Stalinism to Pluralism: A Documentary History of Eastern Europe since 1945*, 2nd edn. New York: Oxford University Press.

Swain, Geoffrey and Nigel Swain (1993) *Eastern Europe since 1945*. London: Macmillan.

Swain, Nigel (1992) *Hungary: The Rise and Fall of Feasible Socialism*. London: Verso.

Swain, Nigel (1993) 'Hungary', in White, Batt and Lewis (1993), pp. 66–82.

Sylwestrowicz, Jan (1995) 'Capitalist restoration in Poland: a balance sheet', *Labour Focus on Eastern Europe*, no. 52.

Szalai, Erzsebet (1994) 'Political and social conflicts arising from the transformation of property relations in Hungary', in Cox and Furlong (1995).

Szalai, Julia (1991) 'Some aspects of the changing situation of women in Hungary', *Signs*, vol. 17, no. 1 (Autumn).

Szalai, Julia (1994) 'Women and democratization: some notes on recent changes in Hungary', unpublished paper, Budapest.

Szalai, Julia (1996) 'Why the poor are poor', *The Hungarian Quarterly*, vol. 37, no. 144.

Szamuely, Laszlo (1996) 'The social costs of transformation in Central and Eastern Europe', *The Hungarian Quarterly*, vol. 37, no. 144.

Szarvas, Laszlo (1995) 'Personnel and Structural Changes in the First Hungarian Parliament' in Agh and Kurtan (1996).

Szayna, T. S. (1997) 'The extreme-right political movements in post-communist Central Europe', in P. H. Merkl and L. Weinberg (eds), *The Revival of Right-Wing Extremism in the Nineties*. London: Cass.

Szelenyi, Ivan (1988) *Socialist Entrepreneurs: Embourgeoisement in Rural Hungary*. Cambridge: Polity.

Szelenyi, Ivan (1995) 'The rise of managerialism: the "new class" after the fall of communism', *Collegium Budapest Study Papers*, no. 16.

Taagepera, Rein and Romuald Misiunas (1983) *The Baltic States: Years of Dependence 1940–80*. London: Hurst.

Taht, J. B. (1996) 'Estonia: scandals mar success story', in *The OMRI Annual Survey of Eastern Europe and the Former Soviet Union: Building Democracy*. New York: M. E. Sharpe, pp. 71–55.

Taras, Raymond (1995) *Consolidating Democracy in Poland*. Boulder, CO: Westview.

Taras, Raymond (ed.) (1997) *Postcommunist Presidents*. Cambridge: Cambridge University Press.

Toka, Gabor (ed.) (1995) *The 1990 Election to the Hungarian National Assembly*. Berlin: Edition Sigma.

Toka, Gabor (1997) 'Political parties in East Central Europe', in L. Diamond, M. F. Plattner, Yun-han Chu and Hung-mao Tien (eds), *Consolidating the Third Wave Democracies*. Baltimore, MD: Johns Hopkins University Press.

Tokes, Rudolf (1996) *Hungary's Negotiated Revolution*. Cambridge: Cambridge University Press.

Traynor, Ian (1995) in *The Guardian*, 1 December.

Tucker, Robert C. (1981) *Politics as Leadership*. Columbia, MO: University of Missouri Press.

Turnock, David (1997) *The East European Economy in Context: communism and transition*. London: Routledge.

Tworzecki, Hubert (1996) *Parties and Politics in Post-1989 Poland*. Boulder, CO: Westview.

UNECE (1996) *Economic Survey of Europe in 1995–1996*. Geneva: United Nations.

US Department of State (1997) 'Moldova country report on human rights practices for 1996', Washington, DC: Bureau of Democracy, Human Rights, and Labor.

Walker, J. (1993) 'Regional organizations and ethnic conflict', in Cowen Karp (1993), pp. 45–68.

Wallace, W. (1997) 'On the move – destination unknown', *The World Today* (April), pp. 99–102.

Waller, Michael (1993) *The End of the Communist Power Monopoly*. Manchester: Manchester University Press.

Waller, Michael (1995) 'Adaptation of the former communist parties of East-Central Europe', *Party Politics*, vol. 1, no. 4 (October).

Waltz, Kenneth (1993) 'The emerging structure of international politics', *International Security*, vol. 18, no. 2 (Fall), pp. 44–79.

Weber, Max (1921) 'Politik als Beruf' in Hans Gerth and C. Wright Wills (eds), *From Max Weber: Essays in Sociology*, London: Routledge and Kegan Paul, pp. 77–128.

Weclawowicz, Gregory (1996) *Contemporary Poland: Space and Society*. London: UCL Press.

Wesolowski, Wlodzimierz and Jacek Wasilewski (eds) (1992) *Poczatki Parlamentarnej Elity*, Warsaw: Institute of Philosophy and Sociology, PAN.

Wheaton, Bernard and Zdenek Kavan (1992) *The Velvet Revolution. Czechoslovakia 1988–1991*. Boulder, CO: Westview.

White, Stephen (ed.) (1991) *Handbook of Reconstruction in Eastern Europe and the Soviet Union*. London: Longman.

White, Stephen (1994) *After Gorbachev*, revised 4th edn. Cambridge: Cambridge University Press.

White, Stephen, Judy Batt and Paul G. Lewis (eds) (1993) *Developments in East European Politics*. London: Macmillan.

Wightman, Gordon (1993) 'The Czech and Slovak Republics', in White, Batt and Lewis (1993).

Wightman, Gordon (1995a) 'The 1994 Slovak parliamentary elections', *The Journal of Communist Studies and Transition Politics*, vol. 11, no. 4 (December), pp. 384–92.

Wightman, Gordon (ed.) (1995b) *Party Formation in East-Central Europe*. Aldershot: Edward Elgar.

Wightman, Gordon and Sona Szomolanyi (1995) 'Parties and society in Slovakia', *Party Politics*, vol. 1, no. 4 (October).

Wilson, Andrew (1997) *Ukrainian Nationalism in the 1990s: A Minority Faith*. Cambridge: Cambridge University Press.

Wolchik, Sharon (1991) *Czechoslovakia in Transition: Politics, Economics and Society*. London: Pinter.

Wolf, Martin (1996) 'Way out of the wasteland', *Financial Times*, 2 July.

Wolff, Larry (1994) *Inventing Eastern Europe. The Map of Civilisation in the Minds of the Enlightenment*. Stanford: Stanford University Press.

World Bank (1996) *World Development Report 1996: From Plan to Market*. New York: Oxford University Press.

Wyman, Matthew, Stephen White, William M. Miller and Paul Heywood (1995) 'The place of "party" in post-communist Europe', *Party Politics*, vol. 1, no. 4 (October), pp. 549–64.

Wyzan, Michael (1996) 'Increased inequality, poverty accompany economic transition', *Transition*, vol. 2, no. 20.

Wyzan, Michael (1997a) 'The making of middle classes', *Transition*, vol. 3, no. 5.

Wyzan, Michael (1997b) 'Economies show solid performance despite many obstacles', *Transition*, vol. 3, no. 6.

Young, Oran (1994) *International Governance. Protecting the Environment in a Stateless Society*. Ithaca, NY: Cornell University Press.

Zajc, Drago (1996a) 'Functions and Powers of the Committees in the New Parliaments: Comparison Between the East Central and West Central European Countries'. Paper presented to an international conference on the Changing Roles of Parliamentary Committees (June), pp. 20–2.

Zajc, Drago (1996b) 'From Systematic Change to Consolidation: The Slovenian Parliament in the Process of Transition'. Paper presented to an international conference on the New Democratic Parliaments: The First Steps (June), pp. 24–5.

Zaslavsky, Victor (1992) 'Nationalism and democratic transition in post-communist societies', *Daedalus*, vol. 121, no. 2 (Spring), pp. 97–122.

Zemko, Milan (1995) 'Political Parties and the Election System in Slovakia', in Sona Szomolanyi and Grigorij Meseznikov (eds), *Slovakia Parliamentary Elections 1994*. Bratislava: Slovak Political Science Association, pp. 40–55.

Zloch-Christy, Iliana (ed.) (1996) *Bulgaria in a Time of Change: Economic and Political Dimensions*. Aldershot, Hants: Avebury.

Index